The Paleo Chocolate Lovers' COOKBOOK

80 **GLUTEN-FREE** Treats for Breakfast & Dessert

written and photographed by

KELLY V. BROZYNA

author of www.TheSpunkyCoconut.com

First Published in 2013 by Victory Belt Publishing Inc.

ISBN 13: 978-1-936608-12-6

Printed in the U.S.A.

RRD 0113

All text © Kelly V. Brozyna, with the exception of "Science, History, and Ethics" by Andrew Brozyna.
All photos © Kelly V. Brozyna, with the exception of: iStockPhoto, p. 12 and 23; Shutterstock, p. 14, 214; The Library of Congress, Reproduction Number: LC-USZ62-98874, p.17; Bibliothèque Nationale de France, p. 18; and Found Image Press, p. 20.
Cover design, interior design, and illustrations by Andrew Brozyna.

Contents

Foreword

I'm a big fan of Kelly's. I love her recipes, especially her chocolate recipes, so I am beyond delighted that she has written *The Paleo Chocolate Lovers' Cookbook*—her fourth book in four years.

I spent an entire summer with Kelly's last book, *Dairy-Free Ice Cream*, and I consider it the definitive tome on making ice cream according to the principles of Paleo. Kelly's ice creams consist of coconut milk, hemp seed, and natural sweeteners, although you would not guess this by tasting them. They taste just like the real thing.

Some may wish to argue that ice cream is not Paleo—that it is not a food cavemen ate. Yes! You are correct. Still, I eat ice cream and enjoy Kelly's superfood version of this all American dessert, a treat that we all long for on a hot summer's day.

While I adore Kelly's book *Dairy-Free Ice Cream*, I love her new one, *The Paleo Chocolate Lovers' Cookbook*, even more.

You'll find that trying to decide which of the recipes in this incredible book are your favorites is quite a challenge—I myself love them all. And you will too, whether you're making the Chocolate Pie with Raw Graham Cracker Crust, Mocha Fudge treats, Mint Chocolate Brownies, or Salted Caramel Bacon Bark.

In our house we eat very clean, very real food. Yet we enjoy the occasional treat, every now and then. And my husband and children are freaks when it comes to chocolate. So this book is perfect for us. My family gets breakfasts, breads, entrees (such as Spicy Chocolate Massamam) and desserts that taste amazing, and I get to know that I am fixing them food that is far more nutritious than the average American fare.

Congratulations Kelly on an outstanding collection of recipes! Your readers (including myself) are very lucky. I am thrilled with your new book.

Best of luck and looking forward to more cookbooks from you!

Elana Amsterdam
elanaspantry.com
Author of *Paleo Cooking from Elana's Pantry*

With Gratitude and Love

There are so many people who helped in the creation of this cookbook.

To my husband, you are my best friend, my talented business partner, and the dearest father. I can't get enough of you. Thank you so much for this awesome book cover, the interior design, and all the research and writing you did. I couldn't have done it without you. I love you.

To my husband's mom, Patti, I really can't thank you enough for all the lovely props you sent me. From baskets and plates to unique silverware and serving pieces, you made the book so beautiful with the treasures you found.

To Elana, my dear friend and prop-shopping buddy, I am so grateful for your friendship. I can't thank you enough.

To my daughters, thank you so much for being such an inspiration to me. Every day, I am in awe of the people you are.

To Michele and Erich, thank you so much for creating this book with me and for all your support. I couldn't imagine working with anyone else. You guys rock.

To Pinterest (yes, Pinterest), for giving me so many amazing ideas for recipes and food photography. I don't know how I would have accomplished this book otherwise.

To the fair trade and Rainforest Alliance chocolate makers, thank you so much for making sure that people are ethically treated and for such delicious chocolate.

This book is dedicated to my readers. Thank you so much for all your love and support.

Introduction

Over the years, my family has gravitated toward the Paleo diet. The concept of eating the types of foods that our ancestors ate is a good one and my family and I feel better than ever eating this way.

But cavemen didn't eat cupcakes or ice cream. So, in that case, I guess we aren't really Paleo, and I'm okay with that. To me, following a Paleo lifestyle isn't about being extreme or trendy. It's about being healthy and feeling great. I have celiac disease, while my daughter Ashley is allergic to gluten. Eating grains affects her behavior terribly. Going from gluten-free to grain-free took our wellbeing from pretty good to awesome. That's what it's all about.

I really struggled over this introduction. Then, a wise friend told me just to write from my heart. But my heart is heavy when it comes to our diet and why we eat this way, like I know it is for a lot of you. Our reasons were serious. Ashley suffered brain damage and developed autism from vaccines when she was a baby. I know a lot of my readers hate it when I say that. Vaccine safety is a controversial issue, and I, for one, can't stand being at the center of a controversy—it gives me a major stomachache. But the truth is that vaccines, like all drugs, have serious risks.

I wish I could say that Ashley's brain damage and autism were the result of some other common prescription. It would be so much easier for me if the cause were medications, which people understand have dangerous side effects. People wouldn't get mad at me, question me, or argue with me. What I can say is that Ashley has come incredibly far thanks to her Paleo diet and biomedical treatments. Her early doctors and therapists said that she would never talk, never walk, and possibly never feed herself. I am so grateful that she can do all those things. She probably won't be able to move out on her own, but there is no one else (other than my husband) with whom I would rather spend the rest of my life.

I created *The Paleo Chocolate Lovers' Cookbook* so that we could still enjoy all our favorite chocolate treats, but make them with ingredients that don't make us sick.

You won't find any grains, legumes, or dairy here. You will find nutrient-dense recipes that are high in protein and good fats. That doesn't mean you should eat these treats every day! The point of this book is that when we treat ourselves, we don't have to break from our Paleo diet.

By using stevia, an herb that scores a zero on the glycemic index, I'm able to keep the total amount of honey or coconut sugar very low as compared to the sugar content of conventional recipes. Coconut oil, coconut milk, and nut and seed flours are high in protein and good fat. When you eat these treats, you feel more satisfied than you would if you ate a carb-centric dessert.

As with the Paleo emphasis on ethically treated meat, it's important to buy chocolate from fair trade or Rainforest Alliance sources, where human beings are treated ethically and workers aren't child slaves. Where your chocolate comes from is as important as where your meat and produce come from. See page 22 for more information.

I created a limited color palette for my photography in *The Paleo Chocolate Lovers' Cookbook*. I chose shades of black and white, brown, and turquoise. My family and friends helped by giving me dishes and silverware that have a nice aged quality. Finding fabrics and boards in my color palette was the most fun part for me. And the food is so beautiful all by itself.

For those of us with celiac disease, autism, or other autoimmune disorders, cheating on our diet isn't an option. But even if I could cheat once in a while, I wouldn't want to. I would rather stick to my healthy way of eating when I have a chocolate treat. And none of my typical-eating guests have ever been anything less than thrilled with my Paleo chocolate recipes.

Happy Paleo chocolate-eating!

♥, Kelly

Cacao
BEANS

Getting Started

If you're new to the Paleo lifestyle you may not be familiar with all the ingredients used in this book. Below is a description of each, including some notable nutrition facts, and where they can be found.

INGREDIENTS

A. Full-fat coconut milk. Made from pressed coconut meat and water, coconut milk contains a good amount of fat (see coconut oil below for more information about the fat in coconut), as well as protein and iron. I use Natural Value coconut milk (cans), and Aroy-D 100% coconut cream (cartons), because both are gum-free and BPA-free. They can be found at health food stores and on Amazon.com, but they cost less at Asian grocery stores.

B. Coconut Cream. I get coconut cream from Natural Value full-fat coconut milk (cans), and Aroy-D 100% coconut cream (cartons). See page 108 for how to make coconut cream.

C. Coconut oil. At about 7 grams per tablespoon, coconut oil has the most lauric acid of any component of the coconut. A medium-chain saturated fat, coconut oil should not be confused with other sources of saturated fat, which are unhealthy. The medium chain fat in coconut oil is easy to digest and is converted to energy rather than stored as fat in the body. Coconut oil actually increases your metabolism while protecting against bacteria and viruses. I prefer Tropical Traditions coconut oil.

D. Coconut flour. Approximately 20% protein and 50% fiber (more fiber than any other flour), it also contains 5% iron. Does it seem expensive? Don't worry—a little goes a long way, and most of my recipes call for about half of a cup. I use Tropical Traditions coconut flour.

E. Coconut Butter/Cream Concentrate. Made from fresh or dried coconut meat, this butter/concentrate is mostly fat, but also contains protein, fiber, vitamins, and minerals. It can be purchased raw from fresh coconut meat or not raw from dried coconut. You can also make coconut butter yourself. My friend, Lexie, (LexiesKitchen.com) has a great tutorial on her site for making it. I buy Artisana (coconut butter) or Tropical Traditions (cream concentrate).

F. Shredded unsweetened coconut. I use Tropical Traditions.

A.

B.

C.

D.

E.

F.

G.

H.

I.

J.

K.

L.

M.

A. Raw honey. I use Mudhava. Another good one is Clark's.

B. Nut/seed butters. I use organic SunButter (sunflower seed butter), Artisana Raw Almond Butter, Artisana Macadamia Butter with Cashews, and Artisana Cashew Butter. You can make all these yourself in a food processor fitted with an S blade. If you make them yourself, don't add anything to the nuts/seeds. Just process, scrape the sides, and process again until you have butter. It will take about twenty minutes. Always store nut/seed butters in the refrigerator because they will become rancid otherwise.

C. Soft Medjool dates. I buy them in health food stores and from iHerb.com.

D. Arrowroot flour/starch. I buy it at health food stores and from iHerb.com.

E. Golden flax seeds. I buy them at health food stores and from iHerb.com.

F. Chia seeds. I usually use white chia seeds from a health food store or from iHerb.com. To make chia meal, grind the seeds in a coffee grinder or mini blender.

G. Nut flour. I buy Bob's Red Mill and Honeyville almond flours, and I make my own walnut, hazelnut, and macadamia nut flours in the food processor fitted with an S blade.

H. Soft vanilla beans. I buy Starwest Botanicals organic vanilla beans on Amazon.com. After scraping out the seeds, you can save vanilla pods in an airtight container and use them to infuse hot chocolate.

I. Organic fair trade cocoa powder. Raw cacao powder is made without roasting the cacao beans. I buy both powders from iHerb.com.

J. Coconut sugar. This sweetener comes from the sap of the flowering branch of the coconut tree. Once the flowering branch is tapped, the sap flows for twenty years, making it extremely sustainable. The sugar is created by boiling the sap for a short period until the liquid evaporates and crystals form. Coconut sugar is low on the glycemic index and is rich in vitamins and minerals, as opposed to refined sugars which have been depleted of nutritional value. I buy it at health food stores and from iHerb.com.

K. Liquid vanilla stevia. Stevia is an herb that you can grow yourself and eat the leaves! It scores a zero on the glycemic index, and its sweetness is extremely concentrated. There is no equal substitution. I much prefer NuNaturals and NOW Foods brands, which I buy at health food stores or on iHerb.com.

L. Chocolate bars. For homemade dark and white chocolate bar recipes, see pages 164 and 166. For store-bought, see page 9.

M. Organic raw cacao butter. I buy the Tisano brand on Amazon.com.

TECHNIQUES & TROUBLESHOOTING

OVEN TEMPERATURE

If your baked goods come out burned or undercooked, there are two possible explanations:

Your oven is lying to you. (That was supposed to be funny, but it's actually true.) For one thing, when the oven beeps to tell you that it has reached the desired temperature, it most likely hasn't. It may be as much as 50°F below temperature when it beeps. Even when your oven has been heating for 30 minutes or more, it may be completely off the projected temperature. My last oven ran hot, and my new one runs cool. The easiest way to ensure that your oven is at the correct temperature is to buy an oven thermometer. They cost about $20.

VOLUME & WEIGHT

Using volume (cups) is not as accurate as using weight (ounces and grams). For example, I might measure a cup of nut flour that weighs 100 grams, while the cup I measured the week before weighed closer to 120 grams. Strange, but true. This is probably due to moisture (or lack thereof) and pressure (how firmly you pack your cups). The bottom line is that weight is much more precise than volume. All you have to do is buy an inexpensive kitchen scale ($25 and up), or you can use a scale meant for mail like I do (less than $20).

NO CHOCOLATE CHIPS?

You may notice that I don't use store-bought chocolate chips in a single recipe here. There is a very good reason for this. Store-bought chocolate chips contain way more sugar than store-bought dark chocolate bars. To compare:

A 1/4 cup of dairy-free mini chocolate chips contains about 28 grams of sugar.

A heaping 1/4 cup of chopped store-bought 85% chocolate contains about 6 grams of sugar.

That's more than 4 times the sugar in store-bought chips! So, take the extra minute to chop your own "chips" or use cacao nibs for completely sugar-free chocolate chips. Just note that not everyone enjoys cacao nibs, especially kids.

HOW TO MELT COCONUT BUTTER / CREAM CONCENTRATE

Note: The coconut butter/cream concentrate should be in a glass jar.

1) Loosen the lid of the jar. Place the jar in a small heavy-bottomed pot, and fill the pot with enough water to cover most of the butter/cream in the jar.

2) Remove the jar of butter/cream from the pot, and bring the water to a boil.

3) Turn off the heat, and put the jar of butter/cream in the hot water. Leave it to soften for about 20 minutes.

4) Take the jar out of the pot, and stir the butter/cream with a butter knife.

HOW TO MELT COCONUT OIL

Note: If you buy coconut oil in bulk like I do, transfer some to a large glass Mason jar with a lid for daily use.

1) Place the glass jar in a small heavy-bottomed pot, and fill the pot with enough water to cover about half the oil in the jar. (If the water level is higher than the oil level, the jar will tip over.)

2) Remove the jar of oil from the pot, and heat the water. (It needs to be hot, but it doesn't need to boil.)

3) Turn off the heat, and put the jar back in the water. The oil will liquefy very quickly.

EQUIPMENT

BLENDER

If you're already a reader of my blog (www. TheSpunkyCoconut.com) then you know that I'm obsessed with my Blendtec. If you're meeting me for the first time, let me just say… that I'm obsessed with my Blendtec. It's more powerful, shorter (it fits on the counter under the upper cabinets), and easier to clean than a Vitamix. Plus, it has a BPA-free carafe and a model with a four-inch blade. I use mine at least twice a day. Honestly! Not just for the recipes in this book, but for soup, green smoothies, nut milks, and more. If you don't want to make such an expensive investment, though, another blender can be used.

MINI BLENDER

Mini blenders are really useful little guys. In this book, I use my Magic Bullet for making candy, cream sauces and cheese dressings, powdered coconut sugar, and ground spices. However, a coffee grinder or food processor will also work for these jobs.

FOOD PROCESSOR

A food processor is important for grinding your own nut flours and often can be used in place of a blender. I also use it to shred zucchini (for zucchini bread) and cauliflower (for Cauli-Rice), and to purée fudge, cheesecake, and more.

ICE CREAM MACHINE

Although it doesn't add as much air as a commercial machine, your home ice cream maker does add air and volume. For more dairy-free ice cream flavors (and an excuse to use your ice cream machine

more often), check out my cookbook, *Dairy-Free Ice Cream*.

SMALL SCOOP WITH LEVER

I use a 3/4-ounce (size 40) scoop with a lever in several recipes. It's faster than hand-rolling, and creates uniform cookies and candies.

TRUFFLE MOLD

To make truffles easily and quickly I use a mold, which has the added benefit of creating uniformly-round candies. Inexpensive molds can be found at craft stores. If you want to make a large quantity for a party or as gifts, I recommend the 63-Cavity Medium Round Truffle Mold by Truffly Made, which I purchased from Amazon.com.

STORE-BOUGHT CHOCOLATE TASTE TEST

One of the first recipes I developed for this book was my own Dark Chocolate Bar (page 164). I also use store-bought chocolate, so here are my reviews of a variety of brands. My comparison includes only chocolate bars that have an 80% or higher cocoa solid content, are dairy-free, and are fair trade or Rainforest Alliance certified (page 22). Since I'm celiac and my daughter is allergic to gluten, I narrowed it down even further to exclude bars that are made on equipment shared with gluten. If gluten is not a concern for you, there are some yummy bars that meet my other criteria, but not this one. They include Chocolove, Newman's Own, and Theo, to name just three. Perhaps these bars will be made on dedicated gluten-free equipment in the future, so keep checking those labels. I know I will.

TASTE TEST SUMMARY:

Alter Eco 85%: Tasted great and was very creamy.

Dagoba 87%: Was our least favorite in taste and creaminess.

Endangered Species 88%: Tasted great and was somewhat creamy.

Equal Exchange 80%: Tasted great and was very creamy.

Green & Black 85%: Tasted great and was very creamy.

All five bars had about the same amount of sugar per serving. There are two servings (or 10 to 14 grams of sugar) in each bar. At the time this book was published, the following brands did not contain soy lecithin: Alter Eco, Equal Exchange, and Green & Black.

Cacao NIBS

Science, History and Ethics

by ANDREW BROZYNA

I have a keen interest in food science and history, and I'm a great lover of chocolate. So, when Kelly told me about her idea for this book I was surprised to realize that I didn't know where chocolate comes from. I heard that it was made from some kind of bean in the tropics, but that was the extent of my limited knowledge. After much fascinating research, I'm happy to share a few facts about the plant, its long history, and how it's made into a delicious treat.

CACAO BOTANY

The chocolate tree, *Theobroma cacao*, is native to the Amazon River Basin, perhaps originating along the eastern range of the Andes Mountains. A persnickety plant, cacao thrives only in a narrow band along the Equator. Fruit-producing trees must be cultivated in areas with constant moisture at no higher elevation than about nine hundred eighty-five feet (three hundred meters), and the temperature cannot dip below 60°F (16°C). The tree itself is fragile, and it's easily damaged by high winds or intense sun. These plants do best when growing in the shade of taller trees. Very particular indeed!

The chocolate we love so much is made from seeds that grow in fruit pods. Curiously, these pods sprout directly from the tree's trunk and the sides of its older branches. The fruit of our more familiar trees (apples, oranges, olives, plums, etc.) grow on the ends of branches, but in the tropics, trunk-borne fruit is actually common among shade-growing plants. A single cacao tree might produce a few thousand flowers during the year, but only 1%-5% are pollinated by midges and develop into fruit.

The fruit pod has somewhat of an elongated lemon shape with ridges along its length. The pod color starts out as green and ripens to a variety of possible shades of green, yellow, red, orange, purple, or brown. The pods can grow to eight inches long (twenty centimeters), and each contains twenty to forty seeds within sweet white pulp. As with coffee, the seeds of *Theobroma cacao* are usually called "beans," but neither plants are legumes. The flavor of chocolate depends greatly on where the cacao was grown and the plant's particular variety.

Historically, cacao trees have been categorized into three main groups: *criollo*, *forastero*, and *trinitario*. Within each of these general groupings are many cacao varieties exhibiting a wide

range of traits. A genetic study published in 2008 separated cacao plants more precisely. This more scientific classification does away with the three vague groups, and it assigns each variety to one of ten genetic clusters. Botanists currently follow the genetic method, while farmers, chocolate makers, and chocolate connoisseurs continue to use the old terms.

CRIOLLO

You might say that *criollo* is the most gourmet of the three cacao groups. It's the most difficult to grow, and it has the lowest yield. Its chocolate is thought to be the very highest quality, however. Originally cultivated in Central America, *criollo* trees supply only about 5% of the world's cacao production. Ripe *criollo* pods tend to be long and narrow, and they contain the fewest seeds (twenty

to thirty). Because of its rarity and expense, *criollo* chocolate is usually mixed with another variety.

FORASTERO

A typical chocolate bar is made from cacao beans of the *forastero* subspecies. A native South American crop, it accounts for roughly 80% of the world's cacao. *Forastero* is a hardier plant: It is more resistant to disease, and produces the most pods with the most seeds (thirty to forty). Ripe pods tend to have a more rounded shape.

TRINITARIO

The *criollo* and *forastero* varieties can be mated to produce fertile hybrid plants. The first hybridization took place in the eighteenth century to create the *trinitario* tree. In 1727, a disease (or perhaps a hurricane) destroyed many of the Spanish *criollo* plantations on the island of Trinidad. To replace the losses, *forastero* trees were brought from Venezuela, and these cross-pollinated with the surviving *criollo* trees. The hybrid *trinitario* beans have much of the superior *criollo* flavor, while the tree itself enjoys the more robust health of the *forastero* plant. The ripe pods, typically red-orange in color, contain thirty to forty seeds.

Mokaya chocolate vessel, 1900-1500 BC.

ANCIENT HISTORY

In 1502, Christopher Columbus was on his fourth and final voyage to the Americas. He was sailing off the coast of what is now Honduras when his four ships encountered a great Mayan trading canoe. His crew commandeered the vessel and took its cargo. Among the high-value goods they found was a great quantity of seeds. This was the Europeans' first encounter with cacao, a treat that had been enjoyed in the New World for thousands of years.

Early Classical Mayan glyph for "cacao."

The people who migrated to Central and South America began to develop agriculture about 8,500 years ago. Hunter-gatherers and early farmers were probably drawn to cacao for the sweet pulp inside the pods. The earliest direct evidence of the consumption of chocolate comes from almost 4,000 years ago. On the Pacific coast of southern Mexico, archaeologists have found pottery that still contains chemical residue that is unique to chocolate. This early chocolate was produced by the Mokaya, who were among the first ceramic-using people in Central America. Scholars of linguistics corroborate this discovery, determining that the word "*cacao*" originates from the same time and place.

A similar ancient find comes from an Olmec site on Mexico's Gulf Coast. The ceramic chocolate vessel there was dated at 1650 to 1500 BC. Chocolate-related finds in the form of Mesoamerican

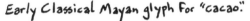

Preclassical Mayan chocolate vessel.

Cacao tree from pre-Columbian Aztec book.

sculptures, inscriptions, and paintings become more common in subsequent years.

The cultivation and consumption of chocolate was adopted by a succession of civilizations—the Izapan, Olmec, Maya, Zapotecs, Mixtecs, Toltecs, and Aztecs. Held sacred in these cultures, chocolate was reserved for only the elite of society. The royalty, nobility, warriors, and high-status merchants drank chocolate as a ceremonial beverage. The many varied recipes called for a mixture of ground cacao, water, and flavorings of chili, vanilla, and other herbs and spices. Aerating the liquid to build a hefty foam was a crucial step, and the Mayans and Aztecs are known to have taken their drink cold.

The Spanish conquerors were initially unimpressed with chocolate, complaining that the drink was too bitter. It only became a welcome addition to their diet after it was sweetened with cane sugar and their familiar Old World spices like cinnamon and black pepper. In the sixteenth and seventeenth centuries, hot chocolate appeared as a fashionable novelty drink in the courts of Europe. Due to its high cost, it remained a privilege of the elite until the early nineteenth century.

Modern chocolate production began in 1828, when a Dutch chemist patented a hydraulic press to remove the cocoa butter from the seeds. The cacao butter extracted by this new process was added to the age-old ground cacao paste, allowing for a more fluid mixture that could be molded into the first chocolate bars. Chocolate could be produced efficiently on a large scale, at last making the treat affordable to the general public. By the end of the nineteenth century, numerous chocolate companies were operating in Britain, Europe, and the United States.

CACAO FARMING

Today, cacao is cultivated around the world in Mexico, South America, Africa, Asia, and the Pacific Islands. Roughly two-thirds of the world's cacao is grown on small farms, while large plantations can be found in countries like Brazil and Malaysia.

On most farms, the cacao trees are shaded by taller crops such as bananas, coconuts, and mangoes. Some growers clear forest undergrowth and plant the cacao under existing trees. Wild cacao trees can grow to 50 feet (15 meters), but on farms, they are pruned to be no taller than half that height. This pruning enables the pods to be removed by hand or with long-bladed poles.

Pods can be harvested two or three times a year. Ripe pods are split by hand, and the seeds are piled on the ground or in wooden boxes and covered to ferment for three to six days. Fermentation prevents the seeds from sprouting, helps remove the surrounding pulp, and begins the

flavor development. Fermentation also destroys the seeds' phytic acid (a substance that inhibits our absorption of minerals). The seeds are then raked out to dry in the sun for a couple of weeks. At the end of this process, the seeds have lost almost half of their weight and are ready to sell. Brokers purchase the seeds and then sell them to the world's chocolate companies.

Previous page: A cacao farm in Ecuador, 1907.

Above: A grinding macine at a French chocolate factory, 1936. Photo courtesy of Bibliothèque Nationale de France.

CHOCOLATE PRODUCTION

At the factory, the first step in the chocolate-making process is to sort the incoming cacao beans. A machine removes foreign objects such as bits of rope, sticks, stones, etc. Sometimes, the odd knife or hat is found among the beans.

To develop their flavor, the cacao beans are roasted in large ovens at temperatures ranging from 210° F to 290° F (100° C to 145° C). The roasting time varies depending on the type of cacao and the desired finished chocolate. Higher-quality beans, such as *criollo* or *trinitaro*, require less roasting than *forastero*. The hot beans are then quickly cooled.

After roasting and cooling, a winnowing machine cracks and removes the outer shell of the beans. The discarded shells have various uses such as animal feed, garden mulch, or as a source of theobromine for the medical industry.

The cacao nibs, which are the inner part of the bean, are crushed and ground to a fluid paste called, "chocolate liquor." Although chocolate liquor is not actually alcoholic, the nibs do carry notes of alcohol-like flavor. The friction of the grinding process produces heat that melts the cacao fats. At room temperature, the substance solidifies and is then called "cacao block," "cacao paste," "cocoa mass," or "cocoa solids." This pure chocolate can be sold as a confectioners' product. The chocolate liquor remaining at the factory has two different options for further processing.

OPTION 1: COCOA POWDER AND COCOA BUTTER

Following the century-old Dutch process, chocolate liquor is pressurized in a great hydraulic press. The cacao butter passes through screens, leaving a solid cake behind. Depending on the cacao type, a whole bean contains 46% to 61% cacao butter (55% on average). After pressing, the cocoa cake is left with only 10% to 24% cacao butter. The cake is crushed to create cocoa powder, which is also called "baking cocoa." The powder is called "Dutch cocoa" when it is treated with alkali to make it mix well with liquids. The separated cacao butter is sold to the cosmetic industry, used to make white chocolate, or added to other chocolate products.

OPTION 2: CHOCOLATE

The chocolate liquor is ready to mix with other ingredients such as sugar, vanilla, or milk powder. The concoction is mixed into a dough and passed through rollers to reduce the size of its solid particles. It is then poured into a conche machine that uses paddles like a giant mixer. Additional cacao butter, cheap vegetable oil, or soy lecithin is added. The agitation of the conching process and the heat of friction blends the mass into a smooth consistency. This conching process can range from hours to days until the desired texture and flavor have been reached.

The still-liquid chocolate is then piped into a tempering machine. Tempering is a delicate heating process that places the crystals of the cacao butter in an even and stable arrangement. The tempered chocolate is poured into molds and quickly cools to a smooth and shiny solid.

The percentage printed on chocolate packaging refers to the amount of cocoa solids a bar contains. For example, a bar of Alter Eco 85% Dark Blackout Organic Chocolate is mostly pure cacao, with the remaining 15% made up of cacao butter and sugar. Conversely, a bar of Hershey's Milk Chocolate contains about 11% cacao, which means 89% of what you are eating is sugar, cacao butter, lactose, milk fat, soy lecithin, polyglycerol polyricinoleate, and artificial flavors.

HEALTH BENEFITS

Cacao has supported the well-being of chocolate lovers for thousands of years. The archaeological remains of ancient Mayan rulers show that they were in better health and lived far longer than the commoners who went without chocolate. Today, the native Kunas

French advertising cards showing a cocoa bean sorting machine and roaster (above),
and a conche machine and "Dutch" press (below), 1915.

people who live on islands off the coast of Panama drink chocolate with almost every meal and enjoy greater cardiovascular health than their countrymen who moved to the mainland and gave up their traditional drink. In these examples, we can't definitively attribute chocolate to their good health, however. The elite Mayans had better access to food in general, and the island and mainland Kunas have different diets. Still, it's apparent that drinking massive amounts of chocolate did these people no harm.

Hundreds of chemical compounds are found naturally in cacao, making it difficult for food scientists to define the exact health effects of chocolate. The most studied components of chocolate are its alkaloids and flavonoids. Alkaloids are compounds occurring in 10% of the world's plants. Two found in cacao are theobromine and caffeine, making up 2% of its weight. Considered a mood-enhancer, theobromine releases relaxing endorphins when consumed and lowers blood pressure. It is thought to energize the body like caffeine but is non-addictive. Dark chocolate holds ten times more theobromine than caffeine. Eating an entire 3-ounce bar of dark chocolate provides about the same amount of stimulation as drinking a cup of regular coffee.

Flavonoids are antioxidants found in plants and are beneficial to the human body. They fight cell-damaging free radicals, support the immune system, reduce inflammation, lower blood pressure, and reduce levels of bad cholesterol. Cacao contains more beneficial antioxidants than any other widely consumed food. It contains two to three times the amount found in green tea, topping other antioxidant-rich foods like blueberries, cranberries, pomegranates, acai, and red wine.

Cacao is also very high in magnesium, and it contains impressive amounts of other essential minerals such as calcium, iron, manganese, potassium, and zinc. Cacao beans do contain phytic acid, which inhibits our absorption of minerals. However, much of these troublesome phytates are destroyed when the cacao is fermented at the farm, roasted at the chocolate factory, and baked in your oven.

MYTHS

Contrary to popular belief, chocolate is not known to cause acne. Dr. Kanade Shinkai, a dermatologist at the University of California, San Francisco School of Medicine, was quoted in an April 23, 2013 article in the Huffington Post: "Although there's a lot of talk about chocolate and other foods playing a role in acne, there's very little evidence to show they do." Occasional studies attempt to link chocolate consumption to acne, but the chocolate tested contains only 30% cacao or less. This means that the "chocolate" bars are more sugar, milk, and vegetable oil than actual chocolate.

Some might be wary of the fat found in cacao butter, but there is no need to fear for your heart or weight. Cacao beans do contain saturated fat, but it consists mostly of stearic and oleic acids. Studies show that these fats do not raise blood cholesterol levels. Cacao also contains monosaturated fat, but this is the same desirable "good fat" found in avocados and olive oil. Much of the cacao butter is not absorbed by the body at all.

Chocolate has been considered an aphrodisiac since the Spanish conquered the Aztecs. There are no scientific findings to suggest this theory is true, either. The salacious reputation comes from

European cultural views of chocolate as an indulgent and exotic food.

ORGANIC AND FAIR TRADE

The tropical climate necessary for cacao trees is also home to a multitude of pests. On vast plantations, cacao trees grow alone or paired with just one or two other crops. The lack of biodiversity leaves the cacao more susceptible to fungi, insects, and rodents. The response of conventional cacao farmers is to treat their trees with a frightening amount of pesticides. Of all crops, cotton is the only one that receives a greater volume of pesticides than cacao. Conventional growers also rely heavily on chemical fertilizers.

Conventionally grown cacao beans are fumigated before exportation and again when they arrive at ports around the world. Methyl bromide has long been the preferred poison used to kill hitchhiking insects on this crop. This substance is highly toxic, is carcinogenic, and depletes the earth's ozone layer. An international treaty was signed to phase out the production of methyl bromide, but an exception allows for its continued use in pest control. Phosphine, another poisonous gas, is a common substitute. Organic shipments of cacao are treated in a safe, albeit more time-consuming, way. Organic cacao is hermetically sealed, causing the insects to suffocate over a period of weeks.

The US and European governments have set maximum levels for chemical residues in chocolate, but buying organic avoids eating those poisons altogether. Happily, organically grown cacao is also beneficial to the environment. The typical small organic cacao farm is nestled in the existing forest. The healthy ecosystem of plants, animals, and microbes combats pests and disease and fertilizes the soil naturally. Preserving the land as forest absorbs carbon dioxide from the atmosphere, slows global warming, and provides habitat for wildlife

Buying a bar of certified Fair Trade chocolate ensures that the workers on that cacao farm were treated fairly and paid a livable wage. Shockingly, much cacao is harvested by child laborers working under hazardous conditions. Thousands of these young children are kept on cacao farms as slaves. This dreadful practice is centered on West Africa, the largest cacao-producing region. The major chocolate companies that buy unethically sourced cacao have been slow to effect change, and African governments have been equally reluctant.

Chocolate lovers can take action by supporting only those companies that produce chocolate that is certified organic and Fair Trade or Rainforest Alliance Certified.

FURTHER READING

Bell, C. H. "Report for link Project AFM87 - Modified atmospheres at raised temperature, an alternative to methyl bromide as a means of ensuring clean, pest-free, hygienic standards in food commodities"
This scientific report discusses the chocolate industry's options for cacao pest control. The PDF can be found on the website for the Federation of Cocoa Commerce: www. cocoafederation.com/issues/fumigation/

Coe, Sophie D., and Michael D. Coe. *The True History of Chocolate*. 2nd ed. London: Thames & Hudson, 2003.
A scholarly, yet approachable history of chocolate.

Dreiss, Meredith L., and Sharon Greenhill. *Chocolate: Pathway to the Gods*. Tucson: University of Arizona, 2008.
This informative book includes many beautiful color photos, and it comes with a documentary film DVD.

Jayne-Stanes, Sara. *Chocolate: The Definitive Guide*. London: Grub Street, 2005.
This British cookbook includes a good deal of history, facts, and figures about chocolate.

Terry G. Powis, W. Jeffrey Hurst, et al. "Oldest Chocolate in the New World" in Antiquity, Vol. 81, Issue 314, December 2007 viewed online at http://antiquity.ac.uk/projgall/powis/
This archaeology paper details the oldest evidence of the existence of chocolate.

Presilla, Maricel E. *The New Taste of Chocolate: A Cultural and Natural History of Cacao with Recipes*. Berkeley: Ten Speed, 2009.
This beautifully illustrated book discusses the history of chocolate and its cultural role.

A cacao pod split to show its interior. In South America the seeds surrounded by their white pulp are together called, "cacao en *baba*".

Breakfast

CHOCOLATE SWIRL CHEESE DANISH CAKE 26

BANANA-WALNUT CHOCOLATE CHIP MUFFINS 28

PALEO BAKING POWDER 28
EGG-FREE

CHOCOLATE-STUFFED FRENCH TOAST 30

CHOCOLATE-GLAZED CAKE DOUGHNUTS 32

CHOCOLATE BANANA PANCAKES 34

CHOCOLATE CHUNK BUTTERMILK MUFFINS 36

CHOCOLATE ZUCCHINI BREAD 38

CHOCOLATE GRANOLA 40
EGG-FREE

RASPBERRY CHOCOLATE CHUNK WALNUT BISCUITS 42

HAZELNUT PANCAKES WITH CHOCOLATE SYRUP 44

VANILLA CREPE CAKE WITH CHOCOLATE CREAM 46

This recipe is very near and dear to my heart. It takes me back in time because I grew up eating all sorts of cheese Danish and kringles. Instead of chocolate, you can also make this recipe with warmed fruit spread like Bionaturae or St. Dalfour, both of which are free of added sugar.

CHOCOLATE SWIRL CHEESE DANISH CAKE

CREAM CHEESE INGREDIENTS

1 cup (136 g) raw cashew pieces

1/2 cup unsweetened almond milk

1/4 cup melted coconut oil

2 tablespoons honey

2 teaspoons vanilla extract

1 egg white

1/8 teaspoon sea salt

DRY CAKE INGREDIENTS

2 cups (224 g) almond flour

1/4 cup (34 g) arrowroot flour

1 teaspoon baking powder

1/2 teaspoon baking soda

WET CAKE INGREDIENTS

1/4 cup melted coconut oil

1/4 cup honey

1 egg

1 teaspoon vanilla extract

1/8 teaspoon liquid vanilla stevia

CHOCOLATE SWIRL INGREDIENTS

3 ounces dark chocolate

1/3 cup canned full-fat coconut milk

1) Preheat your oven to 325°F.

2) Grease an 11" x 8" or 8" x 8" baking dish. Set the dish aside.

3) In a blender, purée the cream cheese ingredients—cashews, almond milk, coconut oil, honey, vanilla extract, egg white, and salt—until completely smooth. Transfer the purée to a dish, and set it aside.

4) In a mixing bowl, whisk together the dry cake ingredients—almond flour, arrowroot flour, baking powder, and baking soda.

5) In separate mixing bowl, use an immersion blender or a whisk to combine the wet cake ingredients—coconut oil, honey, egg, vanilla extract, and liquid vanilla stevia.

6) Add the dry cake ingredients to the wet cake ingredients and mix with an electric mixer until just combined. (Be careful not to accidentally add the dry ingredients to the cream cheese.)

7) Transfer the batter to the greased baking dish, and spread it evenly with wet hands or a flexible silicone spatula.

8) In a double boiler, heat the dark chocolate until just barely melted. Remove it from the heat, and set it aside.

9) Spread the cream cheese evenly over the cake, and drizzle the thick melted chocolate over the cream cheese.

10) Use a knife in a figure-8 motion to swirl the chocolate and cream cheese.

11) Bake the cake for about 25 minutes. Let cool on the counter, and then refrigerate to set.

Makes at least 6 servings.

I love banana bread and banana muffins, especially when chocolate and walnuts are involved!

BANANA-WALNUT CHOCOLATE CHIP MUFFINS

DRY INGREDIENTS

1/2 cup (67 g) coconut flour, sifted

1/3 cup (51 g) coconut sugar

1/4 cup (21 g) chia seed meal

1 teaspoon ground cinnamon

1/2 teaspoon baking soda

1/2 teaspoon baking powder

1/4 teaspoon sea salt

WET INGREDIENTS

1 cup mashed bananas

3 eggs

1/4 cup canned full-fat coconut milk

1/4 teaspoon liquid vanilla stevia

FOLD INS

1 & 1/2 ounces dark chocolate, chopped, or 1 ounce cacao nibs

1/2 cup walnut pieces

1) Preheat your oven to 350°F.

2) In a mixing bowl, whisk together the dry ingredients—coconut flour, coconut sugar, chia seed meal, cinnamon, baking soda, baking powder, and salt.

3) In a separate mixing bowl, use an electric mixer to combine the wet ingredients—bananas, eggs, coconut milk, and liquid vanilla stevia.

4) Add the dry ingredients to the wet ingredients, and combine them with an electric mixer.

5) Fold in the chocolate and walnuts.

6) Pack the mixture into a large (1/3 cup) ice cream scoop, and level it off. Use the lever to transfer the batter into muffin tins lined with paper cups, creating nice rounded tops. Add 1 scoop to each paper cup. *Note: If the tops are flat going into the oven, they will be flat coming out as well.*

7) Bake the muffins for about 27 minutes or until a toothpick inserted into the center comes out clean.

Makes about 9 muffins.

Store-bought baking powder contains corn. You can quickly make your own grain-free baking powder to use in all of my recipes.

PALEO BAKING POWDER

2 tablespoons baking soda

1/4 cup cream of tartar

1/4 cup arrowroot powder

1) In a small glass container with a lid, add the baking soda, cream of tartar, and arrowroot powder.

2) Screw the lid on tightly and vigorously shake the container to blend the baking powder.

3) I store mine in the refrigerator.

Makes over 1/2 cup.

When I was young, there was this café that my mom and I visited once in a while. My favorite dish there was stuffed French toast. The bread was so thick—crispy on the outside, soft on the inside, and filled with fruit. I was in awe of the way it tasted, so it thrills me to have my own variation now.

CHOCOLATE-STUFFED FRENCH TOAST

1 pan of Mock Cornbread (p. 112)

1/4 teaspoon liquid vanilla stevia

2 ounces store-bought dark chocolate, cut into 1" squares

6 eggs

1 cup canned full-fat coconut milk

1/8 teaspoon sea salt

Coconut oil for frying

1) Make the Mock Cornbread, but add 1/4 teaspoon liquid vanilla stevia to the recipe with the wet ingredients.

2) When the bread is completely cool, trim the crust from the sides and bottom.

3) Preheat your oven to 300°F.

4) Cut the bread into 4 squares. Then cut each square on the diagonal so that you have 8 triangles that are about 1 & 1/4" thick.

5) Line a baking sheet with unbleached parchment paper, and bake the cut bread for 15 minutes.

6) Flip the bread pieces over, and bake them for another 15 minutes. (Baking dries the bread so that it will absorb the egg mixture.)

7) When the bread is done, remove it from the oven to cool, and turn off the oven.

8) When the bread is cool, use a serrated knife to make an incision in the longest side of each triangle. Move the knife from left to right inside the incision to create a pocket for the chocolate.

9) Stuff 2 squares of dark chocolate into each pocket. Repeat until all the bread has been stuffed.

10) In a 9" x 13" or 3-quart baking dish, thoroughly combine the eggs, coconut milk, and salt with a fork.

11) Place the stuffed bread in the egg mixture, and soak each side for a few minutes.

12) Preheat a 12" heavy-bottomed skillet over about medium heat. Fry the stuffed French toast in coconut oil until nicely browned on each side.

Makes 8 servings.

My husband and I were obsessed with doughnuts in our previous (junk food) life, and this was always his favorite flavor.

CHOCOLATE-GLAZED CAKE DOUGHNUTS

WET INGREDIENTS

5 eggs

1/2 cup applesauce with no added sugar

1/2 cup honey

1/4 cup melted coconut oil

1 tablespoon vanilla extract

3/4 teaspoon liquid vanilla stevia

DRY INGREDIENTS

1 cup (112 g) almond flour

1/2 cup (46 g) cocoa powder

1/4 cup (34 g) arrowroot flour

1/4 cup (34 g) coconut flour

1 teaspoon baking soda

1/2 teaspoon sea salt

GLAZE

6 ounces homemade dark chocolate (p. 164)

1) Preheat your oven to 350°F, and grease the doughnut pans.

2) In a blender, purée the wet ingredients—eggs, applesauce, honey, coconut oil, vanilla extract, and liquid vanilla stevia—until smooth.

3) Add the dry ingredients—almond flour, cocoa powder, arrowroot flour, coconut flour, baking soda, and salt—to the blender and purée until smooth.

4) Let the batter rest for about 15 minutes or until thickened.

5) Transfer the batter to a large plastic food storage bag. Cut about 1/2" off a corner of the bag, and pipe the doughnuts into the pans.

6) Bake for about 12 minutes or until a toothpick inserted comes out clean.

7) Let the cooked doughnuts cool in the pans for a few minutes. Run a spoon around the edges to loosen them, and carefully remove the doughnuts. Let them cool completely on wire racks.

8) In a double boiler, melt the dark chocolate, then remove it from the heat. Stir occasionally until the melted chocolate is at room temperature, about 5 minutes.

9) Put the melted chocolate in a 2-cup bowl that is about 4" wide.

10) Dip the doughnuts in the chocolate, and return them to the racks to dry.

11) Store the doughnuts in a glass container with a lid. They also freeze well.

Makes 18 doughnuts.

If you've never had fried bananas, I hope you will try them. If you follow my directions and tips, they're easy to make, and they taste crazy good. You may even forget all about the pancakes.

CHOCOLATE BANANA PANCAKES

PANCAKE INGREDIENTS

4 large eggs

1/2 cup full-fat coconut milk

1/4 cup banana (about half a banana)

1/4 cup raw almond butter

1/4 cup (34 g) coconut flour

1/4 cup (23 g) cocoa powder

1 teaspoon vanilla extract

1/4 teaspoon sea salt

1/4 teaspoon liquid vanilla stevia

2 tablespoons melted coconut oil, plus more for the skillet

FRIED BANANAS

1 banana per person

Coconut oil for frying

PANCAKE DIRECTIONS

1) In a blender, purée all of the pancake ingredients until smooth , adding the melted coconut oil last.

2) Warm a 12" skillet over medium-low heat for a few minutes.

3) Add 1 tablespoon melted coconut oil to the skillet, and spoon the batter into the pan, using 2 tablespoons of batter per pancake. In a 12" pan, you can fit 4 pancakes at a time.

4) Using the back of a spoon, spread out the batter to make each pancake about 3 & 1/2" wide. Any larger and they will be difficult to flip.

5) Flip the pancakes when they're slightly browned on one side, and repeat until you have used all the batter.

FRIED BANANAS DIRECTIONS

1) To make the fried bananas, slice each banana in rounds, about 1/2" thick.

2) In a skillet, heat 1/4" of coconut oil over medium heat.

3) After the oil has heated for a few minutes, add the bananas to the skillet, flat side down. Use tongs, and place the bananas all the way into the oil to prevent splattering. The trick is not to disturb the bananas. Once you put them in the oil, don't touch them again for about 3 minutes. *Note: You may need more or less time, depending on the temperature of the pan and the oil.*

4) When the bananas are nicely browned, flip them. If your tongs become sticky, flipping the bananas will become difficult, so keep the tongs clean.

5) Don't disturb the bananas while they fry on the other side. After about 3 minutes, they should be browned on both sides and ready to top the pancakes.

Makes about 14 pancakes.

A great trick to giving dairy-free recipes a hint of buttermilk flavor is to add a tablespoon of apple cider vinegar. I've added it here in these heavenly muffins, and I often add it to my classic pancake recipe as well.

CHOCOLATE CHUNK BUTTERMILK MUFFINS

DRY INGREDIENTS

2 cups (224 g) almond flour

1/2 cup (68 g) coconut flour, sifted

1/2 cup (48 g) white chia seed meal

1 teaspoon baking soda

1 teaspoon baking powder

1/2 teaspoon sea salt

WET INGREDIENTS

4 eggs

1 cup canned full-fat coconut milk

1/4 cup honey

1 tablespoon apple cider vinegar

20 drops liquid vanilla stevia

1/4 cup melted coconut oil

FOLD IN

3 ounces dark chocolate, roughly chopped, or 2 ounces cacao nibs

1) Preheat your oven to 325°F.

2) In a mixing bowl, whisk together the dry ingredients—almond flour, coconut flour, white chia seed meal, baking soda, baking powder, and salt.

3) In a separate mixing bowl, use an electric mixer to combine the wet ingredients—eggs, coconut milk, honey, apple cider vinegar, and liquid vanilla stevia. Add the melted coconut oil last while the mixer is running.

4) Add the dry ingredients to the wet ingredients, and combine them with an electric mixer.

5) Fold the chocolate into the batter.

6) Pack the mixture into a large (1/3 cup) ice cream scoop, and level it off. Use the lever to transfer the batter into muffin tins lined with paper cups, creating nice rounded tops. Add 1 scoop to each paper cup. *Note: If the tops are flat going into the oven, they will be flat coming out as well.*

7) Bake the muffins for about 25 minutes or until a toothpick inserted into the center comes out clean. Let them cool on wire racks. (They will continue cooking after coming out of the oven.)

Makes 14 muffins.

I think that "chocolate zucchini bread" is kind of a joke. It doesn't taste like zucchini, and it's more of a cake than a bread. But putting the words "zucchini bread" in there will make you think that it's healthy. And my version is as healthy as chocolate zucchini bread gets. The real reason to eat this treat, though, is that it's super yummy.

CHOCOLATE ZUCCHINI BREAD

WET INGREDIENTS

1 & 1/2 cups packed shredded zucchini

5 large eggs, brought to room temperature in a bowl of warm water (cold eggs will harden the coconut oil)

1/4 cup melted coconut oil

1/2 teaspoon liquid vanilla stevia

DRY INGREDIENTS

1/2 cup (78 g) coconut sugar

1/2 cup (68 g) coconut flour, sifted

1/2 cup (46 g) cocoa powder

1 teaspoon baking soda

1/4 teaspoon sea salt

1) Preheat your oven to 350°F.

2) To shred the zucchini, peel it, and chop it into 1" pieces. Shred it in a food processor fitted with an S blade. Measure 1 & 1/2 packed cups. *Note: Don't use your spiralizer for this step, or your bread will look like it's full of worms. (Yes, I did that once.)*

3) In a mixing bowl, combine the wet ingredients—zucchini, eggs, coconut oil, and liquid vanilla stevia.

4) In a separate mixing bowl, whisk together the dry ingredients—coconut sugar, coconut flour, cocoa powder, baking soda, and salt.

5) Combine the dry and wet ingredients with an electric mixer.

6) Line a loaf pan with a piece of unbleached parchment paper so that the paper goes down one long side, across the bottom, and back up the other long side. Grease the ends of the pan with coconut oil.

7) Use a flexible silicone spatula to transfer the batter to the prepared pan, and bake the bread for about 52 minutes.

8) Let the bread cool in the pan for 5 minutes. Then loosen the ends with a knife and remove the loaf to cool on a wire rack. Cover and store it on the counter.

Makes 6 servings.

I'm wild about the convenience of this granola. It's magic to wake up in the morning, add a few handfuls of this granola to our bowls, and be done with breakfast preparation.

CHOCOLATE GRANOLA

2 cups whole almonds

1 cup hazelnuts

1 cup macadamia nuts

1 cup applesauce with no added
  sugar

1/2 teaspoon liquid vanilla
  stevia

1/2 teaspoon sea salt

1/4 cup chia seed meal

1 cup shredded unsweetened
  coconut

1/2 cup (46 g) cocoa powder*

1/2 cup (80 g) coconut sugar

*If you are using a dehydrator this
 is a good opportunity to replace the
 cocoa powder with raw cacao powder.

1) Place the almonds, hazelnuts, and macadamia nuts in a bowl. Add enough water to the bowl to cover the nuts plus 3". Soak them overnight or for about 8 hours.

2) Strain the nuts, and discard the soaking water. Rinse them in fresh water, and strain them again.

3) In a food processor with an S blade, roughly chop the nuts in 3 batches.

4) In a very large mixing bowl, combine the applesauce, liquid vanilla stevia, salt, and chia seed meal.

5) Add the chopped nuts, coconut, cocoa powder or raw cacao powder, and coconut sugar to the bowl, and combine well.

6) Dehydrate the granola on lined trays at 120°F until crunchy (about 24 hours), or bake it in the oven at the lowest possible heat setting (about 160°F) until crunchy (about 10 hours).

7) Store the granola in the refrigerator in a glass container with a lid.

Makes 2 quarts.

You can make these biscuits with all almond flour, but trust me, they're way better if you take the extra minute to grind some walnuts into meal. The walnuts add an amazing flavor.

RASPBERRY CHOCOLATE CHUNK WALNUT BISCUITS

DRY INGREDIENTS

2 cups (213 g) walnut flour (from walnuts finely ground in a food processor)

1 & 3/4 cups (198 g) almond flour

1/4 cup (34 g) coconut flour, sifted

2 tablespoons flax meal

1/4 teaspoon sea salt

1/4 teaspoon baking soda

1/4 teaspoon baking powder

WET INGREDIENTS

1/2 cup canned full-fat coconut milk

1/4 cup honey

1 egg

1 teaspoon vanilla extract

1/4 teaspoon liquid vanilla stevia

FOLD INS

6 ounces (about 1 cup) fresh raspberries

2 ounces dark chocolate (homemade or store-bought), chopped, divided

*Note: If you use homemade chocolate, the chunks should be cold from the refrigerator when you press them into the biscuits.

1) Preheat your oven to 350°F.

2) In a mixing bowl, whisk together the dry ingredients—walnut flour, almond flour, coconut flour, flax meal, salt, baking soda, and baking powder.

3) In a separate mixing bowl, whisk together the wet ingredients—coconut milk, honey, egg, vanilla extract, and liquid vanilla stevia.

4) Add the dry ingredients to the wet ingredients, and mix with an electric mixer until the ingredients are just combined.

5) Using a flexible silicone spatula, fold the raspberries and half of the chopped chocolate into the batter.

6) On a baking sheet lined with unbleached parchment paper, use a large (1/3 cup) ice cream scoop with a lever to shape the batter into round piles.

7) Using wet hands, flatten each biscuit until it is about 3" wide. Once flattened, the biscuits should be approximately 2" apart on the baking sheet.

8) Press the other half of the chopped chocolate into the tops of the biscuits so that you can see them after they bake. The chocolate chunks should be level with the tops of the biscuits, or the chocolate will run down the sides.

9) Bake the biscuits for about 24 minutes or until a toothpick inserted into the center comes out clean, and let them cool on wire racks.

Makes about 12 biscuits.

With two weeks to go before this book was due to the publisher, I thought that I was finished with the recipes and photographs. Then one morning, with pancakes on my mind, I saw that I had some leftover hazelnut flour in the refrigerator, and the idea for this recipe came to me. The pancakes were such a hit that we had to include them in the book!

HAZELNUT PANCAKES WITH CHOCOLATE SYRUP

PANCAKE INGREDIENTS

Heaping 1/2 cup (68 g) hazelnut flour

5 eggs

1 cup unsweetened almond milk

1/2 cup (68 g) coconut flour

1/4 cup (34 g) arrowroot flour

2 tablespoons coconut sugar

2 tablespoons melted coconut oil

1/4 teaspoon baking soda

1/4 teaspoon sea salt

1/8 teaspoon liquid vanilla stevia

TOPPING

Crushed hazelnuts

CHOCOLATE SYRUP INGREDIENTS

1 cup canned full-fat coconut milk (this will not work with almond milk or lite coconut milk)

1 teaspoon honey

20 drops liquid vanilla stevia, or more to taste

3 ounces store-bought dark chocolate, chopped

PANCAKE DIRECTIONS

1) In a food processor with an S blade, grind hazelnuts to make the flour, or use store-bought flour.

2) In a blender, purée all of the pancake ingredients until smooth , adding the melted coconut oil last.

3) In a 12" skillet preheated on medium-low heat, add 1 tablespoon coconut oil.

4) Pour 4 small pancakes into the pan at a time. Use the back of a spoon to spread the batter, making each pancake about 3 & 1/2" wide.

5) When the bottoms of the pancakes are lightly browned, flip them over, and cook them until they are lightly browned on the second side.

6) Top the pancakes with crushed hazelnuts and Chocolate Syrup (see below).

CHOCOLATE SYRUP DIRECTIONS

1) In a saucepan, bring the coconut milk, honey, and liquid vanilla stevia to a boil, watching it carefully so that it doesn't boil over. Reduce the heat, and simmer for about 2 minutes.

2) Place the chocolate in a bowl, and pour the hot coconut milk over it. Let it sit for 2 minutes.

3) Stir the chocolate and milk. Transfer the mixture to a blender, and purée it to fully combine the ingredients.

4) Let the syrup cool to thicken.

Makes about 15 pancakes and 1 & 1/3 cups syrup.

I put this crepe cake in the breakfast chapter because it isn't very sweet. It makes a great breakfast treat, especially on holidays or for brunch with friends. To add a little more sweetness, serve it with warm blackberry spread. I prefer Bionaturae Wild Blackberry Fruit Spread because it's free of added sugar.

VANILLA CREPE CAKE WITH CHOCOLATE CREAM

CREPE INGREDIENTS

1 cup egg whites (leftover from Vanilla & Chocolate Bread Pudding, p. 112)*

2 whole eggs

3/4 cup canned full-fat coconut milk

1/3 cup (50 g) coconut flour

1/4 cup (34 g) arrowroot flour

1 teaspoon vanilla extract

1/8 teaspoon liquid vanilla stevia

1/8 teaspoon sea salt

1 tablespoon melted coconut oil, plus more for the skillet

*Egg whites are used in coconut flour crepes so that the crepes don't taste like omelettes.

CHOCOLATE CREAM FILLING

2 cups coconut cream**

1/2 cup (about 8) soft, pitted Medjool dates

1/4 cup water

2 teaspoons vanilla extract

1/4 cup (23 g) raw cacao powder

2 tablespoons coconut flour, sifted

Fresh blackberries

**To get coconut cream, refrigerate canned full-fat coconut milk overnight to get it to separate. Open the can, and remove the cream on top. You can also make homemade fresh coconut cream (page 108). Note: Coconut butter/cream concentrate will not work for whipped cream.

CREPE DIRECTIONS

1) In a blender, purée all of the crepe ingredients until smooth , adding the melted coconut oil last.

2) Heat an 8" stainless steel skillet over medium-low heat.

3) When the skillet has heated for 1-2 minutes, add 1/2 teaspoon melted coconut oil, and swirl it around.

4) Measure 1/4 cup of the batter, and pour it into the skillet.

5) Lift the skillet and swirl the batter outward, making the crepe slightly larger.

6) Flip the crepe when it's ready, and cook it for only a few seconds on the other side.

7) Repeat the process for the rest of the crepes, adding 1/2 teaspoon melted coconut oil to the skillet before each new crepe.

8) Let the crepes cool completely before assembling with the Chocolate Cream Filling (see below).

CHOCOLATE CREAM FILLING DIRECTIONS

1) In a blender, purée the coconut cream, dates, water, and vanilla extract until smooth. The mixture will separate, but that's okay.

2) Transfer the mixture to a saucepan, and bring it to a simmer to re-emulsify.

3) Add the raw cacao powder, and whisk until incorporated.

4) Pour the mixture into a mixing bowl, and let it come to room temperature, stirring frequently to prevent a skin from forming.

5) Refrigerate the mixture until cold.

6) Add the sifted coconut flour, and whip the mixture with an electric mixer for 1 minute.

7) Let the chocolate cream come to room temperature before assembling the cake.

TO ASSEMBLE

1) Layer the cooled crepes with the filling, using a very thin layer of filling between crepes.

2) Top the cake with a very thin layer of filling and fresh blackberries.

3) Serve the cake in thin slices laid on their sides.

4) Store on the counter, covered, or refrigerate.

Makes 12 or more servings.

Cakes

CHOCOLATE CLAFOUTIS 50

GERMAN CHOCOLATE CAKE 52

CHOCOLATE CUPCAKES WITH COOKIE DOUGH FROSTING 54

CHOCOLATE CHIP MERINGUE CAKE 56

MINI ROSE WATER POUND CAKES WITH WHITE CHOCOLATE 58

MACADAMIA BROWNIES 60
EGG-FREE

LAVA CAKES 62
EGG-FREE

ICE CREAM CONE CUPCAKES WITH CHOCOLATE FROSTING 64

FUNNEL CAKES WITH CACAO POWDER 66

MINT CHOCOLATE BROWNIES 68
EGG-FREE

CHERRY CHOCOLATE ROULADE 70

BUNDT CAKE WITH GANACHE 72

GANACHE 72
EGG-FREE

CHOCOLATE CREPE CAKE WITH COCONUT CREAM 74

BLACK FOREST CUPCAKES 76

The idea to make a clafoutis came from my friend Aran Goyoaga's book, Small Plates & Sweet Treats. The recipe itself was inspired by Jamie Oliver's chocolate version.

CHOCOLATE CLAFOUTIS

2 tablespoons melted coconut oil for the skillet

WET INGREDIENTS

1 cup canned full-fat coconut milk

1/2 cup (about 8) soft, pitted Medjool dates

1/4 cup melted coconut oil

3 egg yolks

3 whole eggs

3 ounces dark chocolate, melted over a double boiler

1/8 teaspoon liquid vanilla stevia

DRY INGREDIENTS

1 cup (112 g) almond flour

1/4 cup (23 g) cocoa powder

1/4 cup (34 g) coconut flour

1/4 cup (39 g) coconut sugar

1/2 teaspoon sea salt

TOPPING

Thinly sliced fresh strawberries

1) Preheat your oven to 350°F.

2) In a 12" cast iron skillet, add 2 tablespoons melted coconut oil, and set it aside.

3) In a blender, purée the wet ingredients—coconut milk, dates, coconut oil, egg yolks, whole eggs, melted chocolate, and liquid vanilla stevia.

4) Add the dry ingredients—almond flour, cocoa powder, coconut flour, coconut sugar, and salt—to the wet ingredients in the blender, and purée again.

5) Transfer the mixture to the prepared skillet.

6) Top with the sliced strawberries.

7) Bake for about 30 minutes or until a toothpick inserted into the center comes out clean, and serve warm.

Makes about 8 servings.

This big, beautiful cake makes a delicious dessert for parties and special occasions. It's best enjoyed the day it's made. The frosting will be much firmer the next day.

GERMAN CHOCOLATE CAKE

DRY INGREDIENTS

1 & 1/2 cups (130 g) cocoa powder

2/3 cup (100 g) coconut flour, sifted

2/3 cup (55 g) chia seed meal

1 teaspoon baking soda

1 teaspoon baking powder

1/2 teaspoon sea salt

WET INGREDIENTS

10 eggs

2 cups applesauce with no added sugar

1/2 cup honey

2 tablespoons vanilla extract

1 teaspoon liquid vanilla stevia

1/2 cup melted coconut oil

COCONUT PECAN FROSTING INGREDIENTS

1 cup + 2 tablespoons shredded unsweetened coconut

1 & 1/2 cups water

1/2 cup coconut sugar

1 tablespoon vanilla extract

1/8 teaspoon liquid vanilla stevia

1/2 teaspoon coconut extract (I use Flavorganics) (optional)

1 & 3/4 cups (16 ounces of the Artisana brand) melted coconut butter/cream concentrate

1 & 1/2 cups chopped pecans

Tip: Save your parchment paper circles, and use them again next time.

CAKE DIRECTIONS

1) Preheat your oven to 325°F.

2) Line the bottoms of three 9" x 1 & 1/2" round cake pans with unbleached parchment paper. Set them aside.

3) In a mixing bowl, whisk together the dry ingredients—cocoa powder, coconut flour, chia seed meal, baking soda, baking powder, and salt.

4) In a separate mixing bowl, use an electric mixer to combine the wet ingredients—eggs, applesauce, honey, vanilla extract, and liquid vanilla stevia, adding the coconut oil last.

5) Add the dry ingredients to the wet ingredients, and combine them with the electric mixer.

6) Divide the batter evenly among the 3 prepared cake pans, and bake for about 22 minutes or until a toothpick inserted into the center comes out clean.

7) Let the cakes cool in the pans for about 15 minutes.

8) Run a knife around the edges to loosen the cakes, and carefully remove them to cool completely on wire racks before frosting.

COCONUT PECAN FROSTING DIRECTIONS

1) Preheat your oven to 350°F.

2) Toast the shredded coconut for 5-10 minutes, stirring it once and keeping a close eye on it to make sure that it doesn't burn. Set it aside.

3) In a small saucepan on low heat, simmer the water and coconut sugar until the sugar is just dissolved.

4) Transfer the dissolved coconut sugar to a mixing bowl, and add the vanilla extract, liquid vanilla stevia, and coconut extract (if using). Stir to combine.

5) Add the melted coconut butter/cream concentrate, pecans, and 1 cup of the toasted shredded coconut. Stir to combine.

TO ASSEMBLE

1) Let the frosting set for about half an hour. If it sits longer or becomes too stiff, place it in a bowl over a pot of barely simmering water for a few minutes to soften it.

2) Lay one of the cakes on a cake plate, and spread a third of the frosting on top of the cake.

3) Add another cake, and spread another third of the frosting on top.

4) Add the last cake, and spread the remaining frosting on top.

5) Garnish the cake with the remaining 2 tablespoons toasted shredded coconut and extra pecan pieces.

6) Serve the cake in thin slices laid on their sides.

7) Cover and store the cake on the counter. Do not refrigerate.

Makes 12 to 16 servings.

The idea for this recipe came from some cookie dough frostings that I saw on Pinterest. Who doesn't love cookie dough?

CHOCOLATE CUPCAKES WITH COOKIE DOUGH FROSTING

DRY INGREDIENTS

3/4 cups (62 g) cocoa powder

1/3 cup (50 g) coconut flour, sifted

1/3 cup (29 g) chia seed meal

1/2 teaspoon baking soda

1/2 teaspoon baking powder

1/4 teaspoon sea salt

WET INGREDIENTS

5 eggs

1 cup applesauce with no added sugar

1/4 cup honey

1 tablespoon vanilla extract

1/2 teaspoon liquid vanilla stevia

1/4 cup melted coconut oil

COOKIE DOUGH FROSTING INGREDIENTS

1 cup palm shortening

1/2 cup honey

2 teaspoons vanilla extract

1/4 cup (34 g) coconut flour, sifted

1/4 cup (34 g) almond flour

1/4 teaspoon sea salt

Liquid vanilla stevia to taste

Yellow India Tree natural food coloring (optional)

Finely chopped dark chocolate for sprinkling on top

CUPCAKE DIRECTIONS

1) Preheat your oven to 325°F.

2) In a mixing bowl, whisk the dry ingredients—cocoa powder, coconut flour, chia seed meal, baking soda, baking powder, and salt.

3) In a separate mixing bowl, use an electric mixer to combine the wet ingredients—eggs, applesauce, honey, vanilla extract, and liquid vanilla stevia, adding the melted coconut oil last.

4) Add the dry ingredients to the wet ingredients, and combine them with the electric mixer.

5) Place 12 unbleached paper liners in a muffin tin and fill liners three-quarters full with the batter.

6) Bake the cupcakes for about 28 minutes or until a toothpick inserted into the center comes out clean. Let them cool completely before frosting.

COOKIE DOUGH FROSTING DIRECTIONS

1) Mix together the palm shortening, honey, vanilla extract, coconut flour, almond flour, salt, liquid vanilla stevia, and food coloring (if using). *Note: Add more almond flour to make the frosting even more like cookie dough. Just note that you may need to spread the frosting in this case, as it will be more difficult to pipe.*

2) Pipe the frosting onto the cupcakes. I use a #1M Open Star Tip for piping. The frosting (as directed, without extra flour) tastes even better the day after it's made. The flours absorb some of the moisture, making it slightly thicker.

3) Sprinkle the chopped chocolate on top.

Makes 12 frosted cupcakes.

This cake happened by accident while I was trying to develop some airy baked doughnuts. After a few tests, I had this batter and realized that it would make a delicate cake. So I put the batter in my 7" springform pan (which you may notice I'm a bit obsessed with), and everyone loved the result.

CHOCOLATE CHIP MERINGUE CAKE

4 large eggs, separated

1/4 teaspoon cream of tartar

1 teaspoon vanilla extract

1/8 teaspoon liquid vanilla stevia

1/4 cup honey

1/4 cup unsweetened almond milk

Pinch of sea salt

1/4 cup (34 g) coconut flour, sifted

FOLD IN

3 ounces dark chocolate, chopped

1) Preheat your oven to 350°F.

2) Line the bottom of a 7" springform pan with unbleached parchment paper, and lightly grease the sides.

3) In a small mixing bowl, use an electric mixer to whip the egg whites, cream of tartar, vanilla extract, and liquid vanilla stevia to form stiff peaks. In order to achieve stiff peaks, make sure that the bowl and beaters are completely clean and free of oil. Set aside.

4) In a separate bowl, use the electric mixer to beat the egg yolks and honey for 3 minutes until they are very pale.

5) Add the almond milk and salt to the egg yolk mixture, and beat for a few seconds.

6) Add the sifted coconut flour to the egg yolk mixture, and beat for a few seconds until the ingredients are just combined.

7) Quickly pour the coconut flour batter into the stiffened egg whites, and use a flexible silicone spatula to fold the batter into the whites. It's important to do so right away because the coconut flour will immediately begin to absorb the liquids and thicken the batter, making it hard to fold in.

8) Gently fold the chopped chocolate into the batter.

9) Transfer the batter to the prepared springform pan, and bake for about 25 minutes or until the middle is just set but still slightly jiggly.

10) As soon as you take the cake out of the oven, run a knife around the outside to loosen it, but let it cool completely in the pan.

11) This cake is very airy and delicate, which makes it tricky to slice. I suggest using a long serrated knife heated in a tall glass of hot water and dried before each slice.

12) Store the cake at room temperature, or refrigerate it.

Makes 6 servings.

When I first began dreaming up chocolate recipes for this book, I decided that I had to do something with white chocolate and rose water. These mini cakes are the perfect pairing of the two ingredients. If the combination doesn't appeal to you, simply substitute coconut milk as directed.

MINI ROSE WATER POUND CAKES WITH WHITE CHOCOLATE

ROSE CREAM INGREDIENTS

1/4 cup canned full-fat coconut milk

1/4 cup rose water (or an additional 1/4 cup coconut milk if you want vanilla pound cakes)

1/2 cup honey

1/2 cup cashew pieces

1 tablespoon lemon juice

DRY CAKE INGREDIENTS

2/3 cup (95 g) coconut flour, sifted

1/4 cup (35 g) arrowroot flour

1 teaspoon baking soda

WET CAKE INGREDIENTS

4 eggs

1/3 cup canned full-fat coconut milk

1 tablespoon vanilla extract

1/2 teaspoon liquid vanilla stevia

1/4 cup melted coconut oil

TOPPING:

4 & 1/2 ounces homemade white chocolate (p. 166)

1) Preheat your oven to 325°F.

2) In a blender, purée the rose cream ingredients—coconut milk, rose water, honey, cashews, and lemon juice—until smooth. Set aside.

3) In a mixing bowl, combine the dry cake ingredients—coconut flour, arrowroot flour, and baking soda.

4) In a separate mixing bowl, use an electric mixer to combine the rose cream and the wet cake ingredients—eggs, coconut milk, vanilla extract, and liquid vanilla stevia, adding the melted coconut oil last while the mixer is running.

5) Add the dry ingredients to the wet ingredients, and combine with the electric mixer.

6) Fill 5 lightly greased mini cake pans three-quarters full with the batter.

7) Place the cakes on a baking sheet, and bake for about 32 minutes or until a toothpick inserted into the center comes out clean.

8) Let the cakes cool in their pans for 5 minutes, carefully remove them, and let them finish cooling on wire racks.

TO ASSEMBLE

1) Put the cakes in the freezer for about 15 minutes. (The cool surface will help the white chocolate stick as it runs down the sides.)

2) In a double boiler, melt the white chocolate. When the white chocolate is just melted, remove it from the heat.

3) Let the white chocolate cool to room temperature for about 5 minutes, whisking occasionally.

4) Remove the cakes from the freezer, and slowly pour the white chocolate over them.

5) Serve the cakes warm or at room temperature.

6) Cover and store the cakes on the counter overnight, or refrigerate them for longer storage. They taste best the day after they're made.

Makes 5 mini cakes.

I wanted to put chocolate and macadamia nuts in more than one recipe because I adore the combination. If you don't fancy macadamia nuts, however, you can substitute almond butter.

MACADAMIA BROWNIES

DRY INGREDIENTS

1/4 cup (34 g) coconut flour, sifted

1/4 cup (23 g) cocoa powder

2 tablespoons flax meal

1 teaspoon baking powder

1/2 teaspoon baking soda

WET INGREDIENTS

1 cup macadamia and cashew butter (I use an 8-ounce jar of Artisana Macadamia Butter with Cashews)

1/2 cup canned full-fat coconut milk

1/4 cup honey

1 tablespoon vanilla extract

1/4 teaspoon liquid vanilla stevia

TOPPING

Handful of chopped macadamia nuts (optional)

1) Preheat your oven to 325°F.

2) Grease an 8" x 8" baking dish, and set it aside.

3) In a mixing bowl, whisk together the dry ingredients—coconut flour, cocoa powder, flax meal, baking powder, and baking soda.

4) In a separate mixing bowl, use an electric mixer to combine the wet ingredients—macadamia and cashew butter, coconut milk, honey, vanilla extract, and liquid vanilla stevia.

5) Add the dry ingredients to the wet ingredients, and combine with the electric mixer.

6) Transfer the batter to the prepared dish, and spread it evenly.

7) Sprinkle the chopped macadamia nuts (if using) over the top.

8) Bake for about 30 minutes or until a toothpick inserted into the center comes out clean.

9) The brownies will hold together best when refrigerated. I like to slice them into quarters, and then cut each quarter on the diagonal for a triangle shape.

Makes 8 brownies.

Lava cake, molten chocolate cake, pudding cake—whatever you call it, you can't have a chocolate lover's cookbook without one.

LAVA CAKES

DRY INGREDIENTS

1 & 1/2 cups (168 g) almond flour

1/4 cup (34 g) coconut sugar

2 tablespoons (17 g) arrowroot flour

1/2 teaspoon baking soda

1/2 teaspoon baking powder

WET INGREDIENTS

3 ounces dark chocolate, melted over a double boiler

1/4 cup applesauce with no added sugar

2 tablespoons melted coconut oil

2 teaspoons vanilla extract

1/8 teaspoon liquid vanilla stevia

ADD IN

1 ounce dark chocolate, cut into large pieces*

*Homemade chocolate works better here. Store-bought chocolate will harden faster, so if you use it, serve the cakes right away!

1) Preheat your oven 400°F.

2) In a mixing bowl, whisk together the dry ingredients—almond flour, coconut sugar, arrowroot flour, baking soda, and baking powder.

3) In a separate mixing bowl, use an electric mixer to combine the wet ingredients—melted chocolate, applesauce, coconut oil, vanilla extract, and liquid vanilla stevia.

4) Add the dry ingredients to the wet ingredients, and combine with the electric mixer.

5) Grease 4 small (1/3 cup) ramekins, and divide the batter evenly among them. The batter will be quite thick and look almost like cookie dough.

6) Press the chocolate chunks partially into the batter in the middle of each ramekin.

7) Place the ramekins on a baking sheet, and bake for about 18 minutes or until a toothpick inserted into the cake comes out clean.

8) Let cool for only a few minutes before serving. The chocolate centers will solidify as the cakes cool.

Makes 4 small cakes.

My oldest daughter is forever asking me to bake cupcakes in ice cream cones. When I saw a cupcake pan in the shape of ice cream cones, I had to get it for her. Of course, if you prefer, you can make these as regular cupcakes. "What are those pretty red sprinkles?" you ask. They're simply ground freeze-dried strawberries. They look beautiful and taste great, too!

ICE CREAM CONE CUPCAKES
WITH CHOCOLATE FROSTING

CUPCAKE INGREDIENTS

Bundt Cake recipe (p. 72)

CHOCOLATE FROSTING INGREDIENTS

1 cup palm shortening

1/2 cup honey

2 teaspoons vanilla extract

1/4 cup (34 g) coconut flour, sifted

1/4 cup (23 g) raw cacao powder, sifted

1/8 teaspoon sea salt

Liquid vanilla stevia to taste

ADD ON

Freeze-dried strawberries, ground

CUPCAKE DIRECTIONS

1) Preheat your oven to 325°F.

2) Using the Bundt Cake recipe, make the cake batter.

3) Grease the ice cream cone cupcake pan lightly, and fill each cone three-quarters full with the batter.

4) Bake the cupcakes for about 18 minutes or until a toothpick inserted into the center comes out clean.

5) Let the cupcakes cool in the pan for 15 minutes, and carefully transfer them to a wire rack to cool completely before frosting.

CHOCOLATE FROSTING DIRECTIONS

1) Mix together all the ingredients—palm shortening, honey, vanilla extract, coconut flour, raw cacao powder, salt, and stevia.

2) Pipe the frosting onto the cooled cupcakes. I use a #1M Open Star Tip for piping. Sprinkle with ground, freeze-dried strawberries.

Makes 6 frosted cupcakes.

I admit that there isn't much chocolate in this recipe, but I love the idea of topping a healthier version of a funnel cake with raw cacao powder rather than powdered white sugar.

FUNNEL CAKES WITH CACAO POWDER

EQUIPMENT

1 tall, heavy-bottomed pan, about 9" wide x 4" deep

1 small splatter screen/guard (small enough to fit inside the pot when the handle is bent at a 90-degree angle)*

Candy thermometer

Enough coconut oil to fill the pot to about 2" high**

1 cup measuring cup

Stainless steel spatula

Small sieve

*If the screen has plastic inside the steel handle, use a hammer to break the plastic and remove it. Otherwise, the plastic will melt into the frying oil. You can find small splatter screens/guards at hardware stores and on Amazon.com.

**I don't know if these funnel cakes would work fried in a different kind of oil.

INGREDIENTS

1 & 1/4 cups (146 g) almond flour

1 cup unsweetened almond milk

5 eggs

1/4 cup (34 g) coconut flour

1/4 cup (34 g) arrowroot flour

2 tablespoons honey

1/4 teaspoon sea salt

1/4 teaspoon baking soda

1/4 teaspoon liquid vanilla stevia

2 tablespoons melted coconut oil

1) In a blender, purée all of the ingredients, adding the melted coconut oil last, just before blending. Set the batter aside.

2) Fill the pot to about 2" high with the coconut oil, and turn the heat to medium.

3) Bend the handle of the splatter screen/guard so that it makes a right angle, and place it into the oil. (See diagram.)

4) Place the candy thermometer in the oil.

5) Fill the measuring cup half full, or three-quarters full for a fatter fried dough. Make sure that the measuring cup is dry before adding the batter. If water makes contact with the oil, it will splatter, and someone could get burned.

6) When the thermometer reaches 325°F, put on oven mitts, and take out the thermometer. Slowly pour the batter into the oil in a spiral motion.

7) If the screen floats, use your mitted hands to press it down by the handle.

8) Count 5-10 seconds, and lift the screen handle to remove the funnel cake. Let the excess oil run back into the pot.

9) Put the screen on a plate, and use the stainless steel spatula to scrape the funnel cake off.

10) Use the sieve to sprinkle the top of the funnel cake with raw cacao powder, and serve it hot.

11) Scrape the crumbs off the screen, and put the screen back into the pot.

12) Put the thermometer back in the pot, and when it reaches 325°F again, make another funnel cake.

13) Save any leftover batter in a glass jar in the refrigerator, and let it warm on the counter for an hour before use. You can speed up this process by putting the jar in a bowl of hot water. To reheat leftover funnel cakes, preheat your oven to 375°F. Put the leftovers on a baking sheet, and bake them for about 5 minutes or until hot.

Makes about 5 funnel cakes.

I was sitting in my favorite coffee shop one day while writing this book when I saw a low-fat cooking magazine on the coffee table. On the cover was a photo of mint chocolate brownies, and they looked so good! I didn't flip to the recipe because I figured it included all kinds of ingredients that I would never use, but I couldn't wait to get home and make my own version.

MINT CHOCOLATE BROWNIES

DRY INGREDIENTS

1/4 cup (34 g) coconut flour, sifted

1/4 cup (23 g) cocoa powder

2 tablespoons flax meal

1 teaspoon baking powder

1/2 teaspoon baking soda

WET INGREDIENTS

1 cup almond butter

1/2 cup canned full-fat coconut milk

1/4 cup honey

1 tablespoon vanilla extract

1/4 teaspoon liquid vanilla stevia

TOPPING

Handful of chopped macadamia nuts (optional)

MINT FROSTING INGREDIENTS

1 cup melted coconut butter/ cream concentrate

1/4 cup water

2 tablespoons honey

1 teaspoon vanilla extract

1/4 teaspoon alcohol-free peppermint extract (you may need less if you use extract that is not alcohol-free)

1/4 teaspoon yellow India Tree natural food coloring (optional)

3/4 teaspoon blue India Tree natural food coloring (optional)

GANACHE (PAGE 72)

BROWNIE DIRECTIONS

1) Preheat your oven to 325°F.

2) Grease an 8" x 8" baking dish, and set it aside.

3) In a mixing bowl, whisk together the dry ingredients—coconut flour, cocoa powder, flax meal, baking powder, and baking soda.

4) In a separate mixing bowl, use an electric mixer to combine the wet ingredients—almond butter, coconut milk, honey, vanilla extract, and liquid vanilla stevia.

5) Add the dry ingredients to the wet ingredients, and combine with the electric mixer.

6) Transfer the batter to the prepared dish, and spread it evenly.

7) Sprinkle chopped macadamia nuts (if using) over the top.

8) Bake for about 30 minutes or until a toothpick inserted into the center comes out clean.

9) Let the brownies cool completely before adding the frosting and Ganache.

MINT FROSTING DIRECTIONS

1) Mix together all the ingredients—coconut butter/cream concentrate, water, honey, vanilla extract, peppermint extract, and food colorings (if using).

2) Spread the frosting evenly over the cooled brownies.

3) Pour the Ganache over the mint frosting on the brownies, and spread it evenly.

4) Let the frosted brownies sit for a few hours, allowing the frosting and Ganache to set.

5) Store the brownies, covered, on the counter; the frosting and Ganache would harden in the refrigerator.

Note: If you use India Tree food colorings in this frosting, the color will look awful at first. Don't worry; after the frosting sets for a few hours, it will look like it does in the photo.

This cake may look complicated, but it's actually very simple. It's fantastic with cherries when they are in season, but don't let that stop you from making it at other times of the year. Substitute strawberry extract in the frosting and top it with fresh strawberries, or omit the extract to make plain frosting and top it with your favorite compote.

CHERRY CHOCOLATE ROULADE

CAKE INGREDIENTS

1 tablespoon honey

4 eggs, separated

20 drops liquid vanilla stevia

Pinch of sea salt

1/2 cup (46 g) cocoa powder, sifted

CHERRY FROSTING INGREDIENTS

1 cup palm shortening

1/2 cup honey

1/4 cup (34 g) coconut flour, sifted

1/4 cup (34 g) almond flour

1/4 teaspoon almond or amaretto extract (I use Olive Nation brand)

1/8 teaspoon sea salt

Liquid vanilla stevia to taste

Cherries for garnish

CAKE DIRECTIONS

1) Preheat your oven to 425°F.

2) Lightly grease unbleached parchment paper with coconut oil, and flour the greased paper with cocoa powder, shaking off the excess. Place the prepared paper on a baking sheet, and set it aside.

3) Set out 2 medium-sized mixing bowls. Place the honey and egg yolks in one bowl and the egg whites, liquid vanilla stevia, and salt in the other.

4) Use an electric mixer to beat the egg whites until stiff peaks form. (It's important to beat the egg whites first.) Set them aside.

5) Beat the egg yolks and honey for 3 minutes until they are very pale.

6) Use a flexible silicone spatula to transfer the yolk mixture to the bowl with the stiff egg whites.

7) Add the sifted cocoa powder, and gently fold the yolks and cocoa into the whites. A little bit of the air will be lost, but that's okay.

8) Transfer the batter to the prepared paper. Use the spatula to spread the batter into a 9" x 12" rectangle.

9) Bake the cake for about 6 minutes. It will crack slightly.

10) Use the paper to lift the cake onto a cooling rack, keeping the paper between the cake and the rack. Cover the cake with a lightly damp kitchen towel, and let it cool completely before adding the frosting.

CHERRY FROSTING DIRECTIONS

1) In a mixing bowl, use an electric mixer to combine the palm shortening, honey, coconut flour, almond flour, almond or amaretto extract, salt, and liquid vanilla stevia.

2) Use a flexible silicone spatula to spread just over half of the frosting onto the cooled cake. *Note: If you use too much frosting, the cake will squat like a flat tire. If you use too little frosting, the cake will break too much when you roll it.*

3) Use the paper to help you lift the cake by the short end, and begin rolling fairly tightly. The cake may crack a bit when you begin rolling, but the cracks won't be visible after you've finished.

4) Transfer the rolled cake to the serving tray, seam side down, and trim the ends slightly. Spoon the remaining frosting onto the top of the rolled cake, and garnish it with cherries.

5) Cover the roulade, and store it at room temperature.

Makes 6 servings.

Ten years ago (when I ate a very different diet), I learned that you could add sour cream to a store-bought cake mix for added moisture and a richer, denser cake. I re-created this concept by making a cream with cashews, honey, coconut milk, and lemon juice. Although it is dairy-free, it achieves the same terrific effect.

BUNDT CAKE WITH GANACHE

CREAM INGREDIENTS

1/2 cup canned full-fat coconut milk

1/2 cup honey

1/2 cup cashew pieces

1 tablespoon lemon juice

CAKE DRY INGREDIENTS

1/4 cup (35 g) arrowroot flour + 2 tablespoons for the pan

2/3 cup (95 g) coconut flour, sifted

1 teaspoon baking soda

CAKE WET INGREDIENTS

4 eggs

1/3 cup canned full-fat coconut milk

1 tablespoon vanilla extract

1/2 teaspoon liquid vanilla stevia

1/4 cup melted coconut oil

1) Preheat your oven to 325°F.

2) Grease a Bundt pan. *Note: I use a ceramic Bundt pan that I bought on eBay because I avoid nonstick coatings whenever possible. If your Bundt pan isn't ceramic, your baking time may differ.*

3) Sift 2 tablespoons arrowroot flour into the greased Bundt pan. Tap the pan to coat evenly, and shake out the excess. Set the pan aside.

4) In a blender, purée the cream ingredients—coconut milk, honey, cashew pieces, and lemon juice—until smooth. Set the cream aside.

5) In a mixing bowl, whisk together the dry cake ingredients—arrowroot flour, coconut flour, and baking soda.

6) In a separate bowl, use an electric mixer to combine the cream with the wet cake ingredients—eggs, coconut milk, vanilla extract, and liquid vanilla stevia, adding the melted coconut oil last while the mixer is running.

7) Add the dry ingredients to the wet ingredients, and combine with the electric mixer.

8) Transfer the batter to the prepared pan, and spread it evenly. The top won't be smooth, but it will even out in the oven.

9) Bake the cake for about 40 minutes or until a toothpick inserted comes out clean.

10) Let the cake cool in the pan for 15 minutes, and go around all the edges (especially the center) with a butter knife to make sure that they are loose.

11) Place a small wire cooling rack over the top of the pan, and carefully flip the cake over onto the rack. Remove the pan, and let the cake cool completely before adding the Ganache.

Makes 10 servings.

GANACHE

GANACHE INGREDIENTS

2/3 cup canned full-fat coconut milk (this will not work with almond milk or lite coconut milk)

3 ounces store-bought dark chocolate, chopped

GANACHE DIRECTIONS

1) In a small saucepan, heat the coconut milk until it begins to simmer.

2) Place the chopped chocolate in a bowl, pour the hot coconut milk over it, and let it sit for 1-2 minutes.

3) Whisk as the heat of the coconut milk melts the chocolate, and continue whisking until the milk and chocolate are well combined.

Note: The hotter the Ganache, the runnier it will be.

I love the look of this cake almost as much as my friends and family love the taste of it.

CHOCOLATE CREPE CAKE WITH COCONUT CREAM

CREPE INGREDIENTS

1 cup egg whites* (leftover from Vanilla & Chocolate Bread Pudding, p. 112)

2 whole eggs

3/4 cup canned full-fat coconut milk

1/4 cup (34 g) coconut flour

1/4 cup (23 g) cocoa powder

2 tablespoons (17 g) arrowroot flour

1 teaspoon vanilla extract

1/8 teaspoon liquid vanilla stevia

1/8 teaspoon sea salt

1 tablespoon melted coconut oil + more for cooking

*Egg whites are used in coconut flour crepes so that the crepes don't taste like omelettes.

COCONUT CREAM FILLING

1 & 1/2 cups coconut butter/ cream concentrate, melted

1/2 cup honey

1/4 cup + 2 tablespoons water

1 tablespoon vanilla extract

1/8 teaspoon liquid vanilla stevia

TOPPINGS

Fresh raspberries

Fresh mint leaves for garnish (optional)

CREPE DIRECTIONS

1) In a blender, purée all of the crepe ingredients until smooth , adding the melted coconut oil last.

2) Heat an 8" stainless steel skillet over medium-low heat.

3) When the skillet has heated for 1-2 minutes, add 1/2 teaspoon melted coconut oil, and swirl it around.

4) Fill a 1/4 cup dry measuring cup three-quarters full of the batter from the blender, and pour the batter into the skillet.

5) Lift the skillet to swirl the batter, making the crepe slightly larger.

6) Flip the crepe when it's ready, and cook it for only a few seconds on the other side.

7) Repeat the process for the rest of the crepes, adding 1/2 teaspoon melted coconut oil to the skillet before each new crepe.

8) Let the crepes cool completely before adding the filling.

COCONUT CREAM FILLING DIRECTIONS

1) In a mixing bowl, combine the coconut cream/cream concentrate, honey, water, vanilla extract, and liquid vanilla stevia.

TO ASSEMBLE

1) Layer the cooled crepes with the filling, using a very thin layer of filling between crepes.

2) Top the cake with a thin layer of filling and fresh raspberries, and garnish with mint leaves (if using).

3) Serve the cake in thin slices laid on their sides.

4) Cover the cake, and store it on the counter. Do not refrigerate.

Makes 12 or more servings.

The cherry filling combined with the chocolate cake is excellent, but I think the real star here is the frosting. Flecked with vanilla bean and flavored with Olive Nation amaretto extract, it's a show-stopper.

BLACK FOREST CUPCAKES

CUPCAKES DRY INGREDIENTS

3/4 cups (62 g) cocoa powder

1/3 cup (50 g) coconut flour, sifted

1/3 cup (29 g) chia seed meal

1/2 teaspoon baking soda

1/2 teaspoon baking powder

1/4 teaspoon sea salt

CUPCAKES WET INGREDIENTS

5 eggs

1 cup applesauce with no added sugar

1/4 cup honey

1 tablespoon vanilla extract

1/2 teaspoon liquid vanilla stevia

1/4 cup melted coconut oil

FILLING

12 maraschino cherries (I use Tillen Farms) (optional)

1 (9-ounce) jar sour cherry spread (I use Bionaturae, which is free of added sugar)

CHERRY FROSTING INGREDIENTS

1 cup palm shortening

1/2 cup honey

1 vanilla bean, split lengthwise and scraped, seeds reserved

1/4 teaspoon amaretto extract or to taste

1/4 cup (34 g) coconut flour, sifted

1/4 cup (34 g) almond flour

1/8 teaspoon sea salt

Liquid vanilla stevia to taste

CUPCAKES DIRECTIONS

1) Preheat your oven to 325°F.

2) In a mixing bowl, whisk the dry ingredients—cocoa powder, coconut flour, chia seed meal, baking soda, baking powder, and salt.

3) In a separate mixing bowl, use an electric mixer to combine the wet ingredients—eggs, applesauce, honey, vanilla extract, and liquid vanilla stevia, adding the melted coconut oil last.

4) Add the dry ingredients to the wet ingredients, and combine them with the electric mixer.

5) Place 12 unbleached paper liners in a muffin tin and fill liners three-quarters full with the batter.

6) Bake the cupcakes for about 28 minutes or until a toothpick inserted into the center comes out clean. Let them cool completely.

FILLING DIRECTIONS

1) Chop the maraschino cherries (if using) and mix them with the sour cherry spread.

CHERRY FROSTING DIRECTIONS

1) Mix together the palm shortening, honey, seeds from 1 vanilla bean, amaretto extract, coconut flour, almond flour, salt, and liquid vanilla stevia.

TO ASSEMBLE

1) Scoop out about 1 tablespoon of cake from the top of each cupcake.

2) Spoon the cherry filling into the empty space you created on top of each cupcake. *Note: The filling doesn't need to be level with the top of the cupcakes. The frosting will cover it.*

3) Pipe the frosting onto the cupcakes. I use a #1M Open Star Tip for piping. The frosting is even better the day after it's made. The flours absorb some of the moisture, making it slightly thicker.

Makes 12 frosted cupcakes.

Cookies

COCONUT MACAROONS WITH CHOCOLATE DRIZZLE 80

BIRTHDAY COOKIE CAKE 82
EGG-FREE

DARK CHOCOLATE HAZELNUT COOKIES 84
EGG-FREE

WHITE CHOCOLATE CHAI COOKIES 86
EGG-FREE

MINT CHOCOLATE BISCOTTI 88
EGG-FREE

WHITE CHOCOLATE DIPPED MACADAMIA BISCOTTI 90
EGG-FREE

GERMAN CHOCOLATE WHOOPIE PIES 92
EGG-FREE

NO-BAKE CHOCOLATE CHIP "PEANUT BUTTER" COOKIES 94
EGG-FREE

NO-BAKE CHEWY PALEOLEOS 96
EGG-FREE

CHOCOLATE WHIPPED CREAM SUNFLOWER COOKIE SANDWICHES 98

CHOCOLATE BILBERRY FIG COOKIES 100

TOASTED COCONUT CHOCOLATE CHUNK COOKIES 102

CHOCOLATE CHIP COOKIES THREE WAYS 104
EGG-FREE

Shredded coconut has been one of my favorite ingredients since I was little. The first cookie I remember eating was made of shredded coconut. These classic coconut macaroons are lightly sweetened and so good.

COCONUT MACAROONS WITH CHOCOLATE DRIZZLE

MACAROONS INGREDIENTS

4 egg whites

1/2 teaspoon cream of tartar

1/4 cup honey

1/4 teaspoon liquid vanilla stevia

2 teaspoons vanilla extract

1/8 teaspoon sea salt

3 cups (224 g) shredded unsweetened coconut, divided

CHOCOLATE DRIZZLE INGREDIENTS

3 ounces store-bought dark chocolate, melted over a double boiler

1/3 cup canned full-fat coconut milk, heated

1 tablespoon shredded unsweetened coconut for garnish, or more to taste

MACAROONS DIRECTIONS

1) Preheat your oven to 350°F.

2) In a mixing bowl, beat the egg whites with an electric mixer until foamy. Make sure that your mixing bowl and beaters are clean and free of oil.

3) Add the cream of tartar, and beat further to form stiff peaks.

4) Add the honey, liquid vanilla stevia, vanilla extract, and salt. Beat for just a few seconds to combine.

5) Fold in half of the shredded coconut.

6) Fold in the other half of the shredded coconut.

7) Line a baking sheet with unbleached parchment paper.

8) Use a tablespoon to drop the cookies onto the sheet, making them tall and round.

9) Bake the cookies for about 17 minutes, and allow them to cool before adding the Chocolate Drizzle.

CHOCOLATE DRIZZLE DIRECTIONS

1) In a bowl, whisk together the chocolate and coconut milk until completely smooth. Allow the mixture to come to room temperature.

2) Place the chocolate mixture in one corner of a plastic food storage bag, and snip off the tip, making a very small hole.

3) Squeeze the air out of the bag, and pipe the chocolate back and forth across the tops of the cookies.

4) Sprinkle the cookies with shredded unsweetened coconut.

5) You can store the cookies at room temperature, but they are best the day they are made.

Makes about 20 cookies.

Kids of all ages get a big kick out of a giant cookie. My little girls like this cookie "cake" with cacao nibs, which they say taste like coffee beans.

BIRTHDAY COOKIE CAKE

CAKE INGREDIENTS

2 cups (224 g) almond flour

1/4 cup (34 g) arrowroot flour

1/2 cup (80 g) coconut sugar

1/4 teaspoon sea salt

1/4 teaspoon baking soda

1/2 cup palm shortening

1 teaspoon vanilla extract

3 ounces dark chocolate, finely chopped, or 2 & 1/2 ounces cacao nibs

COOKIE DOUGH FROSTING

1/2 cup palm shortening

1/4 cup honey

1 teaspoon vanilla extract

2 tablespoons coconut flour, sifted

2 tablespoons almond flour

1/8 teaspoon sea salt

Liquid vanilla stevia to taste

CAKE DIRECTIONS

1) Preheat your oven to 350°F.

2) In a mixing bowl, whisk together the almond flour, arrowroot flour, coconut sugar, salt, and baking soda.

3) Add the palm shortening and vanilla extract, and beat with an electric mixer.

4) Fold in the chocolate.

5) Line a 12" cast iron skillet with unbleached parchment paper on the bottom only.

6) Spread the cookie dough evenly in the skillet and pack it down.

7) Bake for about 20 minutes or until the edges are beginning to brown slightly.

8) Let the cookie and the skillet cool completely before frosting.

COOKIE DOUGH FROSTING DIRECTIONS

1) Mix together all the ingredients—palm shortening, honey, vanilla extract, coconut flour, almond flour, salt, and liquid vanilla stevia.

2) Decorate the cookie cake with the frosting. I use a #1M Open Star Tip to create stars at the top, and a small round tip to write Happy Birthday. If you don't feel confident writing Happy Birthday, just pipe stars or flowers all around the border of the cookie cake, and fill the middle with candles.

Makes 10 servings.

These are the cookies to reach for when you are craving a dark chocolate cookie with a little crunch. They are not very sweet, especially when made with homemade chocolate bars, but they are satisfying. If sweetness is what you're after, try my S'mores Cookie Parfaits (page 118) or Chocolate Bilberry Fig Cookies (page 100).

DARK CHOCOLATE HAZELNUT COOKIES

DRY INGREDIENTS

3 cups (340 g) hazelnut flour

1/2 cup (45 g) cocoa powder

1/4 cup (23 g) chia seed meal

1/4 cup (40 g) coconut sugar

1/2 teaspoon baking soda

1/4 teaspoon sea salt

WET INGREDIENTS

1 tablespoon water

1/4 cup applesauce with no added sugar

2 ounces (57 g) dark chocolate, melted over a double boiler

1/2 teaspoon liquid vanilla stevia

1) Preheat your oven to 350°F.

2) In a food processor with an S blade, grind hazelnuts to make the flour, or use store-bought flour.

3) In a mixing bowl, whisk together the dry ingredients—hazelnut flour, cocoa powder, chia seed meal, coconut sugar, baking soda, and salt.

4) In a separate mixing bowl, combine the wet ingredients—water, applesauce, chocolate, and liquid vanilla stevia.

5) Add the dry ingredients to the wet ingredients and combine with an electric mixer.

6) Now, you have two options: either lightly flour the dough with cocoa powder and roll it out using any shape or size of cookie cutter you like, or roll the dough tightly in unbleached parchment paper, creating a tube to chill and slice into round cookies later. It all depends on how many cookies you want to make at a time and what shape you want them to be. For heart-shaped cookies that you can put on a mug, see the illustration.

7) Roll the dough to about 1/4" thick and use cookie cutters, or slice it into 1/4" slices if using a refrigerated tube of dough.

8) Line a baking sheet with unbleached parchment paper, and place the cookies close together on the lined sheet, as they don't expand in the oven.

9) Bake the cookies for about 12 minutes, depending on how crunchy you want them to be.

Makes about 20 cookies.

Cut notch before baking

You can substitute dark chocolate for the cookies and the drizzle on top, but all my testers agreed that these cookies are better with white chocolate. My friend Elana (ElanasPantry.com) loved them and said they were unlike any cookies she had ever had. Our favorite way to eat them is straight from the freezer.

WHITE CHOCOLATE CHAI COOKIES

DRY INGREDIENTS

2 cups (224 g) almond flour

1/4 cup (34 g) arrowroot flour

1 teaspoon ground cinnamon

1 teaspoon ground cardamom

1/4 teaspoon sea salt

1/4 teaspoon baking soda

1/8 teaspoon ground cloves

A few cranks of black pepper to taste

WET INGREDIENTS

1/2 cup palm shortening

1/3 cup honey

2 tablespoons melted homemade white chocolate (p. 166)

1 vanilla bean, split lengthwise and scraped, seeds reserved

DRIZZLE

2 ounces homemade white chocolate (p. 166), melted

1) Preheat your oven to 350°F.

2) In a mixing bowl, whisk together the dry ingredients—almond flour, arrowroot flour, cinnamon, cardamom, salt, baking soda, cloves, and pepper.

3) In a separate mixing bowl, use an electric mixer to combine the wet ingredients—palm shortening, honey, white chocolate, and vanilla bean.

4) Add the dry ingredients to the wet ingredients, and combine them with the electric mixer.

5) Line a baking sheet with unbleached parchment paper.

6) Pack the dough into a 3/4-ounce (size 40) scoop with a lever, and level it off. Then use the lever to place each ball of dough on the paper.

7) Wet your hands, and use your palms to flatten each ball to about 2" wide. Leave about 3" of space between the flattened cookies to allow for spreading.

8) Bake the cookies for about 12 minutes or until the edges are slightly golden. They should look a little undercooked, as they will continue to cook slightly after they come out of the oven.

9) Let the cookies cool on the sheet for 5 minutes before using a spatula to transfer them to wire racks to cool completely.

10) Put the cookies in the freezer for 20 minutes.

11) When you remove them from the freezer, immediately drizzle them with the melted white chocolate.

12) Eat the cookies at room temperature, or store them in the freezer and eat them frozen. They crumble less when frozen.

Makes 18 cookies.

Who doesn't love a crunchy mint chocolate cookie? Dipped in white chocolate for contrast, these biscotti are as pretty as they are tasty.

MINT CHOCOLATE BISCOTTI

DRY INGREDIENTS

1 & 1/2 cups (168 g) almond flour

1/4 cup (23 g) cocoa powder

2 tablespoons (17 g) arrowroot flour

2 tablespoons (20 g) coconut sugar

4 tablespoons flax meal

1/2 teaspoon baking soda

WET INGREDIENTS:

1/4 cup applesauce with no added sugar

1/4 teaspoon liquid vanilla stevia

1/2 teaspoon alcohol-free mint extract (if your extract is not alcohol-free, you may need less)

DIP

1 Homemade White Chocolate Bar (p. 166), melted

1) Preheat your oven to 300°F.

2) In a mixing bowl, whisk together the dry ingredients—almond flour, cocoa powder, arrowroot flour, coconut sugar, flax meal, and baking soda.

3) In a separate mixing bowl, combine the wet ingredients—applesauce, liquid vanilla stevia, and mint extract.

4) Add the dry ingredients to the wet ingredients, and combine with an electric mixer until the batter becomes sticky.

5) Line a baking sheet with unbleached parchment paper.

6) Use wet hands to shape the dough into a 4" x 7" log on top of the paper.

7) Bake for 25 minutes. Remove the log from the oven, and let it cool for about an hour.

8) Preheat your oven to 250°F.

9) Using a serrated knife, slice the biscotti on the diagonal into 1" strips.

10) Carefully lay the strips on their sides, and bake them for 25 minutes.

11) Gently flip them over, and bake them for 25 minutes on the other side.

12) Turn off the oven, but leave the biscotti in the oven for another hour.

13) Remove the biscotti from the oven, and leave them on the baking sheet to cool.

14) Freeze the biscotti for an hour before dipping them in the melted white chocolate. (This helps the chocolate dry faster and drip less.)

TO ASSEMBLE

1) Pour the melted white chocolate into a tall, skinny glass.

2) Dip the cold biscotti into the white chocolate, starting with the longest pieces.

3) Hold the biscotti until the chocolate dries. Then dip it a second time.

4) Place the dipped biscotti on unbleached parchment paper to dry.

5) Store the biscotti on the counter for up to a few days or for longer in the freezer. If keeping them on the counter, lightly cover with a kitchen towel. My favorite way to eat them, however, is straight from the freezer. If you freeze them, keep them wrapped in unbleached parchment paper inside a sealed bag.

Makes about 7 cookies.

These addictive biscotti are lightly sweetened with the herbal tincture stevia and dipped in chocolate. They are one of my absolute favorite treats in this book.

WHITE CHOCOLATE DIPPED MACADAMIA BISCOTTI

DRY INGREDIENTS

2 cups (283 g) macadamia flour (from macadamia nuts finely ground in a food processor)

2 tablespoons (17 g) arrowroot flour

1/2 teaspoon baking soda

1 tablespoon white chia seed meal

WET INGREDIENTS

1/4 cup applesauce with no added sugar

1/4 teaspoon liquid vanilla stevia

DIP

1 Homemade White Chocolate Bar (p. 166), melted

1) Preheat your oven to 300°F.

2) In a mixing bowl, whisk together the dry ingredients—macadamia flour, arrowroot flour, baking soda, and chia seed meal.

3) In a separate mixing bowl, combine the wet ingredients—applesauce and liquid vanilla stevia.

4) Add the dry ingredients to the wet ingredients, and combine with an electric mixer until the mixture becomes sticky.

5) Line a baking sheet with unbleached parchment paper.

6) Use wet hands to shape the dough into a 4 & 1/2" x 8" log on top of the paper.

7) Bake the log for 25 minutes.

8) Remove the baking sheet from the oven, and allow the log to cool for about 1 hour.

9) Preheat your oven to 250°F.

10) Using a serrated knife, slice the biscotti on the diagonal into 1" strips.

11) Carefully lay the strips on their sides, and bake them for 25 minutes.

12) Gently flip them over, and bake them for 25 minutes on the other side.

13) Turn off the oven, but leave the biscotti in the oven for another hour.

14) Remove the biscotti from the oven, and leave them on the baking sheet to cool.

15) Freeze the biscotti for 1 hour before dipping them in the melted white chocolate. (This helps the chocolate dry faster and drip less.)

TO ASSEMBLE

1) Pour the melted white chocolate into a tall, skinny glass.

2) Dip the cold biscotti into the white chocolate, starting with the longest pieces.

3) Hold the biscotti until the chocolate dries. Then dip it a second time.

4) Place the dipped biscotti on unbleached parchment paper to dry.

5) Store the biscotti on the counter, lightly covered with a kitchen towel, for up to a few days. My favorite way to eat them, however, is straight from the freezer. If you freeze them, keep them wrapped in parchment paper inside a sealed bag.

Makes about 7 cookies.

I closely associate whoopie pies with my childhood. This version is a much healthier alternative to the convenience store variety, and my kids adore them.

GERMAN CHOCOLATE WHOOPIE PIES

DRY INGREDIENTS

1/2 cup (40 g) coconut sugar

1/4 cup (29 g) flax meal

1/2 cup (44 g) cocoa powder

1/2 cup (69 g) coconut flour, sifted

1/4 cup (34 g) arrowroot flour

1 teaspoon baking soda

1 teaspoon baking powder

WET INGREDIENTS

1 cup canned full-fat coconut milk

1/2 cup applesauce with no added sugar

1 teaspoon vanilla extract

1/4 teaspoon liquid vanilla stevia

1/4 cup melted coconut oil

COCONUT PECAN FROSTING INGREDIENTS

1/2 cup shredded unsweetened coconut

3/4 cup water

1/4 cup (39 g) coconut sugar

1 & 1/2 teaspoons vanilla extract

12 drops liquid vanilla stevia

1/4 teaspoon coconut extract (optional)

1 cup (227 g) melted coconut butter/cream concentrate

3/4 cup chopped pecans

PIE DIRECTIONS

1) Preheat your oven to 325°F.

2) In a mixing bowl, whisk together the dry ingredients—coconut sugar, flax meal, cocoa powder, coconut flour, arrowroot flour, baking soda, and baking powder.

3) In a separate mixing bowl, use an electric mixer to combine the wet ingredients—coconut milk, applesauce, vanilla extract, and liquid vanilla stevia, adding the melted coconut oil last while the mixer is running.

4) Lay a piece of unbleached parchment paper on a baking sheet.

5) Pack the dough into a large (1/3 cup) ice cream scoop with a lever, and level it off. Use the lever to transfer each scoop to the lined sheet, spacing the scoops about 3" apart. Make 10 little cakes.

6) Use wet hands to flatten the scoops to about 3" circles.

7) Bake the cakes for about 25 minutes, and let them cool on the sheet for 5 minutes. Then transfer them to a wire rack to cool completely (at least an hour) before frosting.

COCONUT PECAN FROSTING DIRECTIONS

1) Preheat your oven to 350°F.

2) Spread the shredded coconut evenly on a baking sheet and toast for 5-10 minutes or until golden, stirring once, and keeping a close eye on it so that it doesn't burn.

3) In a small saucepan, add the water and coconut sugar, and simmer until the coconut sugar is just dissolved.

4) In a mixing bowl, place the dissolved sugar, vanilla extract, liquid vanilla stevia, and coconut extract (if using). Stir to combine.

5) Add the melted coconut butter/cream concentrate, pecans, and toasted shredded coconut. Stir to combine.

6) Set the frosting on the counter and let it cool to room temperature (about 30 minutes).

TO ASSEMBLE

1) Lay 5 of the cakes upside down.

2) Top the upside-down cakes with some of the frosting. (You will have a few tablespoons left over.)

3) Top each frosted cake with another cake, and press lightly.

4) Store the whoopie pies on a wire rack on the counter, covered with a kitchen towel. They are best enjoyed soon after they're made. The frosting will be much firmer the next day. Do not refrigerate.

Makes 5 whoopie pies.

Along with hot chocolate, no-bake cookies topped the list of reader requests for recipes in this book. These are our favorite no-bake cookies of all time. They take just minutes to make, last a long time in the refrigerator, and are so handy when cravings strike. Lots of protein and good fat make these treats very satisfying.

NO-BAKE CHOCOLATE CHIP "PEANUT BUTTER" COOKIES

1/2 cup (about 8) soft, pitted Medjool dates

1/2 cup sunflower seed butter with no added sugar

1 & 1/2 cups (126 g) shredded unsweetened coconut

1 teaspoon vanilla extract

1/4 teaspoon sea salt

FOLD IN

2 ounces dark chocolate, chopped, or 1 & 1/2 ounces cacao nibs

1) In a food processor with an S blade, purée the dates until a ball forms.

2) Add the sunflower seed butter, shredded coconut, vanilla extract, and salt, and purée again.

3) Fold in the chocolate.

4) Use a 3/4-ounce (size 40) scoop or your hands to form the dough into about 14 balls, and refrigerate to set. Store the cookies in the refrigerator.

Makes about 14 cookies.

As you may guess from the name of these cookies, they are my soft and chewy version of a certain famous sandwich cookie. This recipe was inspired by the Raw Ice Cream Sandwiches from the website A Dash of Compassion.

NO-BAKE CHEWY PALEOLEOS

COOKIE INGREDIENTS

1 cup (112 g) any nut flour
(I use half walnut flour
and half almond flour)

1/2 cup (46 g) raw cacao powder

1/8 teaspoon sea salt

1/2 cup (about 8) soft, pitted
Medjool dates

1 teaspoon vanilla extract

1 teaspoon water

FILLING INGREDIENTS

1/2 cup melted coconut butter/
cream concentrate

2 tablespoons honey

1 teaspoon vanilla extract

4-6 teaspoons water, as needed

COOKIE DIRECTIONS

1) In a small bowl, combine the nut flour, raw cacao powder, and salt.

2) In a food processor with an S blade, process the dates until a ball forms.

3) Add the vanilla extract, water, and flour mixture to the dates in the food processor, and process for about 20 seconds. (It will look like fine crumbles.)

4) Line a baking sheet with unbleached parchment paper.

5) Transfer the dough to the baking sheet, and lift the sides of the paper to squeeze the dough into a solid mass.

6) Lay another piece of unbleached parchment paper on top, and roll the dough between the 2 pieces of paper to about 8" x 10".

7) Remove the top piece of parchment paper, and use cookie cutters of about 2 & 1/2" (I use the lid of a small mason jar) to cut out cookie shapes.

8) With a spatula, transfer the cookies to a flat plate or cutting board covered with another piece of parchment paper.

9) Press the dough scraps together, and roll the dough between 2 pieces of parchment paper to the same thickness as the first cookies. Continue cutting and rolling until you have 10 large cookies.

10) Freeze the cookies on the paper-covered plate or cutting board for about 45 minutes before adding the filling.

FILLING DIRECTIONS

1) In a small bowl, mix together the coconut butter/cream concentrate, honey, vanilla extract, and water.

2) Add more water as needed until the mixture reaches the consistency of frosting.

TO ASSEMBLE

1) Remove the cookies from the freezer.

2) Turn 5 of the cookies upside down.

3) Divide the filling evenly among the 5 cookies, and spread it across each cookie.

4) Press another cookie on top to complete the sandwiches.

5) Store the cookie sandwiches in the refrigerator.

Makes 5 big cookie sandwiches.

These chilled cookie sandwiches are perfect for summer birthday parties and barbecues. If you like the flavor of peanut butter, then you've gotta give sunflower seed butter a try! Almond butter works here, too, but I think these cookies are much better with SunButter.

CHOCOLATE WHIPPED CREAM SUNFLOWER COOKIE SANDWICHES

DRY INGREDIENTS

1/2 cup (37 g) shredded unsweetened coconut

1/4 cup (34 g) coconut flour, sifted

1/4 cup (39 g) coconut sugar

1/2 teaspoon sea salt

WET INGREDIENTS

1 cup sunflower seed butter with no added sugar

1/2 cup unsweetened almond milk

1 egg

1/2 teaspoon liquid vanilla stevia

1/4 cup melted coconut oil

CHOCOLATE WHIPPED CREAM INGREDIENTS

2 cups coconut cream*

1/2 cup (about 8) soft, pitted Medjool dates

1/4 cup water

2 teaspoons vanilla extract

1/4 cup (23 g) raw cacao powder

*To get coconut cream, refrigerate canned full-fat coconut milk overnight to get it to separate. Open the can, and remove the cream on top. You can also make homemade fresh coconut cream (page 108). Note: Coconut butter/cream concentrate will not work for whipped cream.

COOKIE DIRECTIONS

1) Preheat your oven to 350°F.

2) In a mixing bowl, whisk together the dry ingredients—shredded coconut, coconut flour, coconut sugar, and salt.

3) In a separate mixing bowl, use an electric mixer to combine the wet ingredients—sunflower seed butter, almond milk, egg, and liquid vanilla stevia, adding the melted coconut oil last while the mixer is running.

4) Add the dry ingredients to the wet ingredients, and combine with the electric mixer.

5) Line a baking sheet with unbleached parchment paper.

6) Pack the dough into a 3/4-ounce (size 40) scoop with a lever, and level it off. Then use the lever and your fingers to place each cookie on the paper.

7) Use wet hands to flatten each ball to about 2 & 1/2" wide. (They don't spread in the oven.)

8) Bake the cookies for about 17 minutes for softer cookies (perfect for these sandwiches) or longer for crunchier cookies.

9) Let the cookies cool completely on wire racks before adding the filling.

CHOCOLATE WHIPPED CREAM DIRECTIONS

1) In a blender, purée the coconut cream, dates, water, and vanilla extract until smooth. It will separate, but that's okay.

2) Transfer the mixture to a saucepan, and bring it to a simmer to re-emulsify.

3) Add the raw cacao powder, and whisk until incorporated.

4) Pour the mixture into a mixing bowl, and let it come to room temperature, stirring frequently to prevent a skin from forming.

5) Refrigerate the mixture until cold.

6) Whip the mixture with an electric mixer for 1 minute to make the whipped cream.

TO ASSEMBLE

1) Turn 5 of the cookies upside down.

2) Divide the filling evenly among the 5 cookies, and spread it across each cookie.

3) Place another cookie on top to complete the sandwiches.

4) Freeze the cookie sandwiches for about 2 hours before serving.

Makes 5 cookie sandwiches.

These big, tasty cookies are based on my husband's Christmas Cucidati (Italian fig cookies), which can be found on our blog, www.TheSpunkyCoconut.com. Use the Bionaturae brand spread without added sugar.

CHOCOLATE BILBERRY FIG COOKIES

FILLING INGREDIENTS

1/2 cup dried figs, stems removed, soaked in hot water for 15 minutes

1/2 cup (about 8) soft, pitted Medjool dates, soaked in hot water for 15 minutes

1/2 cup bilberry spread (or raspberry, orange, or any other fruit flavor)

1/2 cup pecans

1/4 cup + 2 tablespoons (60 g) cocoa powder

1/4 cup water

1/8 teaspoon sea salt

DOUGH DRY INGREDIENTS

2 cups (227 g) almond flour

1 cup (136 g) coconut flour, sifted

2 teaspoons baking soda

2 teaspoons baking powder

DOUGH WET INGREDIENTS

1/2 cup melted coconut oil

1/2 cup honey

2 eggs

1/4 teaspoon liquid vanilla stevia

1) Preheat your oven to 350°F.

2) In a food processor with an S blade, purée the filling ingredients—figs, dates, fruit spread, pecans, cocoa powder, water, and salt—for about 15 seconds. Set aside.

3) In a mixing bowl, whisk together the dry dough ingredients—almond flour, coconut flour, baking soda, and baking powder.

4) In a separate mixing bowl, use an electric mixer to combine the wet dough ingredients—coconut oil, honey, eggs, and liquid vanilla stevia.

5) Add the dry ingredients to the wet ingredients, and combine with the electric mixer.

TO ASSEMBLE

1) Lay half of the dough on a sheet of unbleached parchment paper.

2) Lightly flour the top of the paper, and roll the dough into a 7" x 10" rectangle. Use your hands to press the edges in as you roll, making nice, clean edges.

3) Add half the filling in a log shape 1 & 1/2" from one long side of the dough.

4) Use the other side of the parchment paper to lift the dough over the filling so that the 2 long sides meet.

5) Use the side of your hand to press the ends together, sealing the dough. Use a pizza cutter or knife to trim the excess dough.

6) Using the pizza cutter in a back-and-forth motion, cut 1" cookies.

7) Line a baking sheet with unbleached parchment paper.

8) Place the cookies 1" apart on the lined sheet.

9) Repeat the process with the other half of the dough and filling.

10) Bake the cookies for about 12 minutes.

11) Store any leftover cookies on the counter, lightly covered with a cloth napkin.

Makes 18 to 20 cookies.

Toasted coconut goes so well with chocolate. For a special treat, share one of these delicious cookies with someone you love.

TOASTED COCONUT CHOCOLATE CHUNK COOKIES

DRY INGREDIENTS

1 cup (75 g) shredded unsweetened coconut

2 cups (224 g) almond flour

2/3 cup (102 g) coconut sugar

2/3 cup (68 g) flax meal

1 & 1/2 teaspoons baking soda

WET INGREDIENTS

1/2 cup melted coconut oil

2 eggs, brought to room temperature in a bowl of warm water (cold eggs will harden the coconut oil)

1 teaspoon coconut extract

FOLD IN

3 ounces dark chocolate, roughly chopped, or 2 & 1/2 ounces cacao nibs

1) Preheat your oven to 350°F.

2) Spread the shredded coconut evenly on a baking sheet and toast for 5-10 minutes, stirring once, and keeping a close eye on it so that it doesn't burn.

3) Let the toasted coconut cool, and increase the oven temperature to 375°F. Reserve 1 tablespoon of the toasted coconut for the tops of the cookies.

4) In a mixing bowl, whisk together the rest of the cooled toasted coconut, almond flour, coconut sugar, flax meal, and baking soda.

5) In a separate mixing bowl, use an electric mixer to combine the wet ingredients—coconut oil, eggs, and coconut extract.

6) Add the dry ingredients to the wet ingredients, and combine with the electric mixer until dough begins to form.

7) Make sure that the dough isn't warm from the melted coconut oil. Then fold in the chopped chocolate. (If the dough is warm, it will melt the chocolate.)

8) Line a baking sheet with unbleached parchment paper.

9) Use a flexible silicone spatula to divide the dough into 8 balls. Place the balls at least 3" apart on the baking sheet, as they will spread quite a bit in the oven.

10) Using wet hands, flatten the balls into 3" circles.

11) Sprinkle the tops with the reserved toasted shredded coconut, gently patting it down.

12) Bake the cookies for about 15 minutes.

13) Let the cookies cool on the baking sheet for 5 minutes before transferring them to wire racks to cool completely.

Makes 8 huge cookies, perfect for sharing.

These cookies are inspired by my dear friend Elana (ElanasPantry.com) and her famous chocolate chip cookie recipe. There are three ways to make them, depending on what kind of cookie you want. Most of my friends prefer Honeyville almond flour, and I love it too, but these cookies are much better with Bob's Red Mill almond flour (especially Option 3).

CHOCOLATE CHIP COOKIES THREE WAYS

DRY INGREDIENTS

2 cups (224 g) almond flour

1/4 cup (34 g) arrowroot flour

1/4 cup (39 g) coconut sugar

1/4 teaspoon sea salt

1/4 teaspoon baking soda

WET INGREDIENTS

1/2 cup palm shortening

1/4 cup honey

1 teaspoon vanilla extract

FOLD IN

3 ounces dark chocolate, finely chopped, or 2 & 1/2 ounces cacao nibs

Option 1: Follow the recipe as written for medium-thick cookies with a little crunch.

Option 2: For a fatter, slightly softer cookie, omit the honey. Add 2 tablespoons water, and use 1/2 cup coconut sugar.

Option 3: For a thin cookie that is both crunchy and chewy (and really spreads), use 1/2 cup honey and no coconut sugar. If you choose this option, be sure to leave at least 3" of space all the way around the flattened cookies because they will double in size! *Note: They won't spread as much with Honeyville almond flour.*

1) Preheat your oven to 350°F.

2) In a mixing bowl, whisk together the dry ingredients—almond flour, arrowroot flour, coconut sugar, salt, and baking soda.

3) Add the wet ingredients—palm shortening, honey, and vanilla extract—to the dry ingredients, and mix with an electric mixer. (No need to mix the wet ingredients separately first.)

4) Fold in the chocolate.

5) Line a baking sheet with unbleached parchment paper.

6) Pack the dough into a 3/4-ounce (size 40) scoop with a lever, and level it off. Then use the lever to place the ball of dough on the paper.

7) Wet your hands, and use your palms to flatten each ball to about 2" wide. Leave about 2" of space between the flattened cookies to allow for spreading (unless you are making Option 3, in which case you should leave 3").

8) Bake the cookies for about 12 minutes or until the edges are nicely golden. They will continue to cook slightly after they come out of the oven.

9) Let the cookies cool on the baking sheet for 5 minutes before using a spatula to transfer them to wire racks to cool completely.

Makes 20 cookies.

Puddings and Pies

WHIPPED COCONUT CREAM (from store-bought coconut milk) 108
EGG-FREE

WHIPPED COCONUT CREAM (from fresh young coconuts) 110
EGG-FREE

VANILLA & CHOCOLATE BREAD PUDDING 112

MOCK CORNBREAD 112

MINI CHOCOLATE HAZELNUT PIES 114
EGG-FREE

CHOCOLATE PUDDING 116
EGG-FREE

S'MORES COOKIE PARFAITS 118

CHOCOLATE SWIRL CHEESECAKE 120
EGG-FREE

CHOCOLATE PIE WITH RAW GRAHAM CRACKER CRUST 122
EGG-FREE

MOCK PEANUT BUTTER CHEESECAKE 124
EGG-FREE

MULLED WINE POACHED PEARS WITH GANACHE 126
EGG-FREE

CHOCOLATE STRAWBERRY SHORTCAKE TRIFLE 128

STRAWBERRY SEMIFREDDO PIE WITH CHOCOLATE CRUST 130
EGG-FREE

There are two ways to make whipped coconut cream. One way is to use canned full-fat coconut milk that has separated. Not every can will separate, however; it's very frustrating. But if you have cans that have already separated or cans that you know will separate for you when you refrigerate them overnight, this is the easier and less expensive option.

The second way to make whipped coconut cream is to use coconuts (see following pages). Sometimes I do both, making a little bit of each and combining them. Adding some fresh whipped coconut cream to canned whipped coconut cream helps smooth out the texture.

WHIPPED COCONUT CREAM *(from store-bought coconut milk)*

INGREDIENTS

2 (13.5-ounce) cans Natural Value full-fat coconut milk*

1 tablespoon honey

1 teaspoon vanilla extract

Several drops liquid vanilla stevia to taste (optional)

*I use Natural Value coconut milk because it's gum-free and BPA-free. This recipe also works with the 33-ounce carton of Aroy-D Coconut Cream, which is 100% coconut cream and gum-free. If the Aroy-D does not separate in the refrigerator, pour it into a bowl, and freeze it. Then thaw the cream on the kitchen counter. Do not heat it or it will re-emulsify. Now it's ready for Step 2 in the directions.

Note: I have not been able to get brands with gum (such as Thai Kitchen) to separate for more than a year now, though I know of other people who are still able to get them to separate.

1) Chill the cans of coconut milk in the refrigerator overnight.

2) Place a thin cloth napkin over a large mixing bowl, and pour the contents of 1 can over the napkin.

3) Lift the napkin, and squeeze out some of the water. Don't overdo the squeezing, or your coconut cream will be too dry. Just remove most of the water.

4) Repeat Steps 2 and 3 with the second can of coconut milk. When you open the cloth, your coconut cream should look like a ball of soft cheese.

5) In a small mixing bowl, mix together the honey, vanilla extract, and liquid vanilla stevia (to taste).

6) Add the strained cream to the honey-vanilla mixture, and whip with an electric mixer, working up to high speed, for about 1 minute.

Puddings and Pies

To get just over 1 cup of cream, you need at least three whole fresh young coconuts (the white ones with pointy tops). This version costs $12, more or less, depending on where you live, and takes about half an hour to make. If you have the time and the money to make it fresh, the taste is far superior to canned.

WHIPPED COCONUT CREAM *(from fresh young coconuts)*

INGREDIENTS

At least 3 whole fresh young coconuts (the white ones with pointy tops)

1) Lay a coconut on its side, and carefully trim the pointy tip until some brown is showing. Then position it right side up.

2) As a safety measure, put your left hand behind your back (or your right hand if you're left-handed). Doing so will protect you from the knife.

3) Using the heel of a knife, strike the coconut at a 45-degree angle.

4) If the top doesn't open right away, spin the coconut a little bit, put one hand behind your back again, and strike it again. Continue until you are able to pry open the top.

5) Pour the nutritious coconut water into a large glass. I put mine in big mason jars. Store what you don't drink right away in the refrigerator. *Note: The water should be clear or slightly yellow. Pink or purple water means that the coconut has gone bad, and you shouldn't use the water or the meat.*

6) Wedge a flexible silicone spatula between the meat and the inside wall of the coconut. Run the spatula around in a circle, dislodging the coconut meat.

7) Reach inside the coconut, and remove the meat. It usually comes out in 1 piece.

8) Repeat the process with 2 or more coconuts.

9) In a food processor with an S blade, purée the coconut meat, scraping the sides periodically, until it is completely smooth and heavenly.

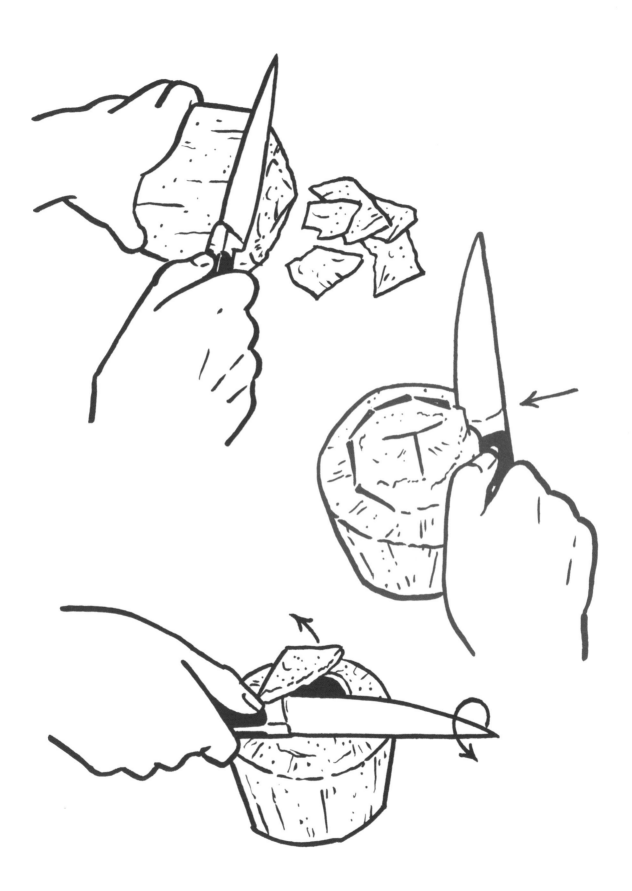

This bread pudding tastes like it has fallen from heaven. I can't remember ever eating a bread pudding this divine—since changing my diet or even before!

VANILLA AND CHOCOLATE BREAD PUDDING

About 3/4 loaf of Mock Cornbread (see below)

7 egg yolks (leftover from making Crepes, p. 74)

1 whole egg

3 cups canned full-fat coconut milk

2 tablespoons honey

1 vanilla bean, split lengthwise and scraped, seeds reserved

1/8 teaspoon liquid vanilla stevia

1/8 teaspoon sea salt

TOPPINGS

1 & 1/2 ounces dark chocolate

Chopped berries for topping (optional)

1) Cut the Mock Cornbread on the diagonal into 4 triangles.

2) Trim the crust on 3 of the 4 cornbread triangles, and cut each of those 3 triangles lengthwise so that they are half as thick.

3) Arrange the bread in a greased 9" x 13" baking dish.

4) Bake the bread at 300°F for about 30 minutes to dry it out. Then allow it to cool. (Otherwise, it won't absorb any liquid.)

5) In a mixing bowl, combine the egg yolks, whole egg, coconut milk, honey, vanilla bean, liquid vanilla stevia, and salt.

6) Pour the mixture over the cooled bread in the baking dish.

7) Cover the dish, and let the bread soak in the refrigerator for about 8 hours.

8) Remove the dish from the refrigerator, and allow it to come to room temperature (approximately 1 & 1/2 hours).

9) Bake the pudding at 325°F for about 30 minutes.

10) Serve the pudding warm, topped with the chopped chocolate and berries.

11) If you need to reheat it, cover it first.

Makes about 10 servings.

MOCK CORNBREAD

DRY INGREDIENTS

1 & 3/4 cups (198 g) almond flour

1/2 cup (68 g) coconut flour, sifted

1/4 cup (34 g) arrowroot flour

1 teaspoon sea salt

3/4 teaspoon baking soda

WET INGREDIENTS

1 cup canned full-fat coconut milk

4 eggs

1/4 cup melted coconut oil*

1 tablespoon apple cider vinegar

1 tablespoon honey

1) Preheat your oven to 350°F.

2) Grease an 8" x 8" baking dish, and set it aside.

3) In a mixing bowl, whisk together the dry ingredients—almond flour, coconut flour, arrowroot flour, salt, and baking soda.

4) In a separate mixing bowl, use an electric mixer to combine the wet ingredients—coconut milk, eggs, coconut oil, apple cider vinegar, and honey.

5) Add the dry ingredients to the wet ingredients, and mix with the electric mixer until just combined.

6) Use a flexible silicone spatula to transfer the batter to the greased baking dish.

7) Even out the batter, and smooth the top with wet hands or the spatula.

8) Bake for about 38 minutes.

Makes about 9 servings.

*Use coconut oil for Bread Pudding, or you can substitute lard if you plan to eat the Mock Cornbread as a side dish.

Puddings and Pies

This chocolate hazelnut filling is based on a recipe in my cookbook Dairy-Free Ice Cream. It has far less sugar than store-bought, and no dairy. It's delicious in anything, but I won't tell if you just eat it with a spoon.

MINI CHOCOLATE HAZELNUT PIES

CHOCOLATE HAZELNUT FILLING INGREDIENTS

1 & 1/2 cups hazelnuts

1 & 1/2 cups canned full-fat coconut milk

1/2 cup (40 g) coconut sugar

1/8 teaspoon sea salt

9 ounces dark chocolate

CRUST DRY INGREDIENTS

1 cup (108 g) walnut flour (from walnuts finely ground in a food processor)

1/2 cup (68 g) coconut flour, sifted

1 & 1/2 tablespoons chia seed meal

1 teaspoon baking soda

1 teaspoon baking powder

CRUST WET INGREDIENTS

1/4 cup + 2 tablespoons applesauce with no added sugar

1 tablespoon honey

10 drops liquid vanilla stevia

1/4 cup melted coconut oil

CHOCOLATE HAZELNUT FILLING DIRECTIONS

1) Preheat your oven to 350°F.

2) Toast the hazelnuts on a baking sheet in the oven for about 15 minutes.

3) Meanwhile, in a small saucepan, heat the coconut milk, coconut sugar, and salt. When the sugar has melted, remove the mixture from the heat, and set it aside.

4) Remove the toasted hazelnuts from the oven, and transfer them to a clean, dry kitchen towel. Rub the hazelnuts in the towel to remove as much of the skin as possible.

5) In a food processor, purée the hazelnuts until they are very fine, then set the food processor aside.

6) Over a double boiler, melt the dark chocolate.

7) Add the melted chocolate to the hazelnut flour in the food processor, and purée until creamy and smooth (about 2 minutes).

8) Add the coconut milk mixture to the chocolate and hazelnuts. Purée until smooth.

CRUST DIRECTIONS

1) In a mixing bowl, whisk together the dry ingredients—walnut flour, coconut flour, chia seed meal, baking soda, and baking powder.

2) In a separate mixing bowl, use an electric mixer to combine the wet ingredients—applesauce, honey, and liquid vanilla stevia, adding the melted coconut oil last while the mixer is running.

3) Add the dry ingredients to the wet ingredients, and combine with the electric mixer.

4) Using a large (1/3 cup) ice cream scoop, divide the batter evenly among six 4" x .75" tart/quiche pans. Press the dough evenly across the bottom of each pan.

5) Put all six pans on a baking sheet and bake the crusts (without the filling) for about 12 minutes.

6) Allow the crusts to cool completely.

TO ASSEMBLE

Pour the chocolate hazelnut filling evenly over the cooled crusts. Sprinkle the top of each pie with chopped hazelnuts, and put the pies in the refrigerator to set. To serve, remove the pies from their pans, and allow them to come to room temperature.

Makes 6 mini pies, with 2 servings per pie.

Stirring a pot of simmering chocolate pudding was one of my first cooking responsibilities; I think I was about eight years old. And my cooking repertoire didn't expand much until I was in my twenties!

CHOCOLATE PUDDING

1 cup unsweetened almond milk

1 cup canned full-fat coconut milk

4 large, soft, pitted Medjool dates

1 vanilla bean, split lengthwise and scraped, seeds reserved

3 ounces store-bought dark chocolate, roughly chopped

1) In a blender or food processor, purée the almond milk, coconut milk, dates, and vanilla bean until completely smooth. The mixture will probably separate, but that's okay.

2) Transfer the mixture to a small saucepan, and bring it to a simmer, watching carefully so that it doesn't boil over.

3) Reduce the heat, and simmer for 10 minutes, whisking frequently.

4) Turn off the heat, and add the chocolate. Stir until the chocolate is melted and incorporated into the pudding.

5) Ladle the pudding into bowls, and serve it warm or cold. It will be thicker after refrigerating.

Makes 2-4 servings, depending on the size of the bowls.

I set out to make a chocolate-dipped meringue "kiss," but I didn't like the sweetness of the cookies with the traditional ratio of 1 egg white to 1/4 cup sugar. Even my husband, who has a much sweeter sweet tooth, said that they were too sweet. Then I made them with half the sugar. Not only were they lighter and airier, but the coconut sugar made them taste just like a marshmallow toasted over a campfire. Yum! They were also more prone to breaking, however, which led to the crumbled S'mores Cookie Parfaits. I can't wait for you to try this one.

S'MORES COOKIE PARFAITS

COOKIE INGREDIENTS

2 large egg whites

1/4 teaspoon cream of tartar

1/4 cup (39 g) coconut sugar, ground in a mini blender or coffee grinder

LAYERS

1 batch of Ganache (p. 72)

1 batch Whipped Coconut Cream (p. 108 or p. 110)

1) Preheat your oven to 220°F.

2) In a small bowl, beat the egg whites with an electric mixer until foamy.

3) Add the cream of tartar, and continue beating until the whites form stiff peaks.

4) Add the ground coconut sugar all at once, and beat it until just incorporated and no longer (a few seconds).

5) Line a baking sheet with unbleached parchment paper, and set it aside.

6) Transfer the meringue to a large plastic food storage bag. Cut about 1/4" off a corner of the bag, and pipe the cookies onto the baking sheet. Smaller cookies will be less likely to break when you remove them from the paper, but you can try any shape you like. These cookies are much more delicate than traditional meringue cookies because they contain half the sugar.

7) Bake the cookies for 2 hours.

8) Turn off the oven, but leave the cookies inside for a couple more hours or until they are completely dry.

9) These cookies are best eaten the day they're made. After that, they start to soften.

TO ASSEMBLE

1) Add a spoonful of Ganache to each small glass.

2) Crumble a handful of the cookies over the Ganache.

3) Add a few spoonfuls of Whipped Coconut Cream.

4) Repeat the process until each glass is full.

Makes 4 parfaits.

I was more crushed when I realized that I had to stop eating dairy than I was when I realized that I had to stop eating gluten. That's when I got into the raw diet. I learned how to make almost every one of my favorite dairy recipes with cashews and coconut. Using many raw food techniques, I created my own dairy-free recipes, and I'm so excited to share some of them with you!

CHOCOLATE SWIRL CHEESECAKE

CRUST INGREDIENTS

1 cup (75 g) shredded unsweetened coconut

1/2 cup (about 8) soft, pitted Medjool dates

2 tablespoons (29 g) raw cacao powder

1 teaspoon vanilla extract

Pinch of sea salt

FILLING

1 cup coconut cream*

1/2 cup (70 g) cashew pieces, soaked for 4-8 hours

1/4 cup honey

1 tablespoon lemon juice

1 teaspoon vanilla extract

1/8 teaspoon liquid vanilla stevia

1/4 cup melted coconut oil

SWIRL IN

1 batch of Ganache (p. 72)

*To get the coconut cream, follow the directions for making whipped cream (page 108), but do not add the honey, vanilla, or stevia.

CRUST DIRECTIONS

1) In a food processor with an S blade, purée the shredded coconut, dates, raw cacao powder, vanilla extract, and salt until the ingredients clump together.

2) Line the walls only of a 7" springform pan by making a ring of unbleached parchment paper. You can staple the paper where the ends meet to help it stay together.

3) Press the crust into the lined pan, and set it aside.

FILLING DIRECTIONS

1) In a food processor with an S blade, purée the coconut cream, cashews, honey, lemon juice, vanilla extract, and liquid vanilla stevia. Add the melted coconut oil last while the processor is running.

2) Continue to purée the mixture for a few minutes. In the beginning, the fat will separate. Then the heat from processing will help it re-emulsify. The filling is done when it's completely smooth and looks like cream sauce.

3) Set aside a few tablespoons of the filling to use when you make the swirl on top of the cheesecake.

4) Pour the rest of the filling over the crust, and set it aside while you make the Ganache.

TO CREATE THE SWIRL

1) The Ganache should be very warm when you add it to the cheesecake. If it isn't, heat it before you begin.

2) When the cream filling is slightly set (like soft cream cheese), drizzle some of the Ganache over the top. *Note: You won't use all the Ganache.*

3) Use a knife to swirl the Ganache in a figure-8 motion.

4) Heat the reserved cream filling, and add it to the top as needed to create a pretty design. This is especially helpful if you end up with a glob of Ganache that you don't like. Just add some of the heated cream filling over the glob, and swirl it around with the knife to fix it.

5) Chill the cheesecake overnight in the refrigerator.

TO SERVE

1) Remove the cheesecake from the refrigerator. Remove the wall of the springform pan, and peel off the paper.

2) Heat a large chef's knife in a glass of very hot water. Run the knife between the crust and the bottom of the pan until the cheesecake has completely separated from the pan. Lift the cheesecake onto a serving plate.

3) Heat the knife again in very hot water, and dry it with a towel. Use the knife to slice the cheesecake while it's still cold from the refrigerator.

4) Allow the cheesecake to come to room temperature for serving. Store it in the refrigerator.

Makes 12 servings.

This chocolate pie is perfect for holidays, and it doesn't take very long to make.

CHOCOLATE PIE ⟍WITH⟋ RAW GRAHAM CRACKER CRUST

CRUST INGREDIENTS

1 cup (100 g) walnut halves and pieces

1/4 cup (about 4) soft, pitted Medjool dates

1 teaspoon ground cinnamon

Pinch of sea salt

FILLING INGREDIENTS

1 cup coconut cream*

1/2 cup (about 8) soft, pitted Medjool dates

3 ounces dark chocolate (preferably homemade, p. 164), melted

1/4 cup melted coconut oil

2 teaspoons vanilla extract

*For the filling, use the cream at the top of a can of separated full-fat coconut milk, such as Natural Value brand (which is BPA-free). To get it to separate, refrigerate a couple of cans overnight. You do not need to squeeze the cream in a cloth napkin for the pie filling as you do to make Whipped Coconut Cream (page 108 or page 110).

1) To make the crust, in a food processor with an S blade, purée the walnuts, dates, cinnamon, and salt for about 20 seconds or until very fine.

2) Transfer the crust mixture to a glass pie dish, and press it across the bottom and halfway up the sides.

3) Rinse the food processor.

4) In a small saucepan, heat the coconut cream just slightly.

5) Add the heated coconut cream, dates, chocolate, coconut oil, and vanilla extract to the food processor, and purée for 1 minute or until the filling is dark and completely smooth.

6) Pour the filling over the crust, and chill to set.

7) When you're ready to serve the pie, top it with Whipped Coconut Cream.

8) Store the pie in the refrigerator.

Makes 8 servings.

If you like cheesecake and the combination of peanut butter and chocolate, you're going to love this dessert. My husband says that it reminds him of a Carvel ice cream cake.

MOCK PEANUT BUTTER CHEESECAKE

COOKIE CRUST DRY INGREDIENTS

1 & 1/2 cups (170 g) any nut flour

1/4 cup (23 g) cocoa powder

2 tablespoons (12 g) chia seed meal

2 tablespoons (20 g) coconut sugar

1/4 teaspoon baking soda

1/8 teaspoon sea salt

COOKIE CRUST WET INGREDIENTS

2 tablespoons applesauce with no added sugar

1 ounce dark chocolate, melted over a double boiler

1/4 teaspoon liquid vanilla stevia

2 teaspoons water

FILLING INGREDIENTS

1/2 cup coconut cream*

1/2 cup sunflower seed butter with no added sugar

3/4 cup (105 g) cashew pieces, soaked for 4-8 hours, then strained

1/4 cup honey

1 tablespoon lemon juice

1 teaspoon vanilla extract

1/8 teaspoon liquid vanilla stevia

1/8 teaspoon sea salt

2 tablespoons melted coconut oil

*To get the coconut cream, follow the directions for making Whipped Coconut Cream (page 108 or page 110), but omit the honey, vanilla, and stevia.

COOKIE CRUST DIRECTIONS

1) Preheat your oven to 350°F.

2) In a food processor with an S blade, grind nuts to make the flour, or use store-bought nut flour.

3) In a mixing bowl, whisk together the dry ingredients—nut flour, cocoa powder, chia seed meal, coconut sugar, baking soda, and salt.

4) In a separate mixing bowl, combine the wet ingredients—applesauce, melted chocolate, liquid vanilla stevia, and water.

5) Add the dry ingredients to the wet ingredients, and use an electric mixer to combine them.

6) Line the bottom of a 7" springform pan with unbleached parchment paper.

7) Press half the cookie mixture (it will be very crumbly) into the bottom of the pan. Save the rest for the filling.

8) Bake the crust for about 14 minutes, and let it cool completely before adding the filling.

TO SERVE

1) Remove the wall of the springform pan, and peel off the paper.

2) Use a thin spatula to remove the cheesecake from the base, and discard the paper.

3) Heat a large chef's knife in a glass of very hot water, and use it to slice the cheesecake.

Makes 12 servings.

FILLING DIRECTIONS

1) In a food processor with an S blade, purée the coconut cream, sunflower seed butter, cashews, honey, lemon juice, vanilla extract, liquid vanilla stevia, and salt, adding the melted coconut oil last while the processor is running. Purée the mixture for a few minutes until it is completely smooth.

2) Line the walls of the springform pan by making a ring of parchment paper. You can staple the paper where the ends meet to help it stay together.

3) Use a flexible silicone spatula to transfer half the filling into the crust, and smooth it out.

4) Sprinkle most of the remaining cookie mixture over the filling, saving a few tablespoons for the very top. Press the cookie mixture lightly into the filling.

5) Drop the rest of the filling by the spoonful over the cookie mixture, and smooth it out with the spatula.

6) Sprinkle the remaining cookie mixture on top to garnish, and chill the cheesecake in the refrigerator overnight to set. Store it in the refrigerator.

I'll be honest: What drew me to poached pears was how beautiful they are. But these lovely pears taste as good as they look.

MULLED WINE POACHED PEARS WITH GANACHE

PEARS

6 cups (about 1 & 1/2 bottles) red wine that you like to drink

6 bags mulling spices, such as R.W. Knudsen Organic Mulling Spices

6 ripe (but not overly ripe) pears (with stems, if possible)

2-4 tablespoons honey to taste

TOPPING

1 batch of Ganache (p. 72)

1) In a 3-quart pot with a lid (I use a Le Creuset pot that is about 9" wide x 4" deep), bring the wine to a simmer.

2) Add the mulling spices to the pot, turn off the heat, and steep for 15 minutes. Remove the bags, and bring the wine back to a simmer.

3) Peel the pears, but leave the stems on. Pick up the peeled pears by the stems, or use a large slotted spoon to carefully lower them into the mulled wine. (It's okay if they lie sideways.)

4) Reduce the heat to low, cover, and poach the pears for about 10 minutes or until tender.

5) Carefully remove the pears, and let the mulled wine cool.

TO SERVE

1) Top the pears with the Ganache.

2) Strain the wine, and serve it with the pears. You can also save it to drink later.

Makes 6 servings.

This trifle is so pretty that making it is worth all the effort. Set it out for your guests to admire when you host a baby shower, bridal shower, birthday party, or Fourth of July celebration.

CHOCOLATE STRAWBERRY SHORTCAKE TRIFLE

1 batch of Bundt Cake batter (p. 72)

1-2 cartons fresh strawberries, depending on the size of your trifle

1 batch of Whipped Coconut Cream (p. 108 or p. 110)

1 batch of Ganache (p. 72)

1) Lightly grease a round cake pan that is as wide as or slightly wider than the trifle bowl you plan to use. Line the bottom of the pan with unbleached parchment paper to make it even easier to remove.

2) Fill the pan about half full of Bundt Cake batter, and bake it until a toothpick inserted into the middle comes out clean. (The time depends on the size of your pan.)

3) Allow the cake to cool in the pan for 15 minutes, and then carefully transfer it to a wire rack.

4) Rinse the strawberries, and remove the stems and leaves. (I like to save the strawberry tops to garnish the trifle as shown in the photo.)

5) In a food processor with an S blade, pulse the strawberries until they resemble chunky jam.

6) Add the strawberries to the bottom of the trifle bowl.

7) Add the Whipped Coconut Cream layer next.

8) Trim the cake so that it fits tightly in the trifle bowl, and put it on top of the whipped cream layer.

9) Top the cake with the Ganache, and garnish with strawberry tops or more whole fresh strawberries.

10) Store the trifle at room temperature.

Makes 6-12 servings, depending on the size of each portion and the size of the trifle dish.

I love the pairing of chocolate and strawberries. This yummy semifreddo (semi-frozen) pie with chocolate crust comes together quickly and looks so pretty.

STRAWBERRY SEMIFREDDO PIE WITH CHOCOLATE CRUST

CRUST INGREDIENTS

1 cup (75 g) shredded unsweetened coconut

1/2 cup (about 8) soft, pitted Medjool dates

2 tablespoons (20 g) raw cacao powder

1 teaspoon vanilla extract

Pinch of sea salt

FILLING INGREDIENTS

2 packages (68 g) freeze-dried strawberries, divided

3 cups Whipped Coconut Cream (p. 108 or p. 110)

1 tablespoon honey

1 tablespoon lemon juice

1 teaspoon vanilla extract

CRUST DIRECTIONS

1) In a food processor with an S blade, purée the coconut, dates, raw cacao powder, vanilla extract, and salt until the ingredients clump together.

2) Press the crust mixture into a 7" springform pan, and set it aside.

FILLING DIRECTIONS

1) Set aside 1/4 cup of the freeze-dried strawberries for garnish.

2) Use a small blender or a food processor (it must be completely dry!) to grind the rest of the strawberries into a powder. Reserve 1 tablespoon of the powder for the top of the pie.

3) In a mixing bowl, combine the Whipped Coconut Cream, honey, lemon juice, and vanilla extract.

4) Add the strawberry powder to the bowl, except for the tablespoon reserved for the top. Whip the filling with an electric mixer for about 1 minute.

5) Use a flexible silicone spatula to transfer the filling to the crust, and spread it evenly.

6) Freeze the pie for 2 hours before serving.

7) Run a knife between the pie and the side wall of the pan to loosen it. Remove the side wall, and run a knife between the base and the crust to loosen it.

8) Transfer the pie to a serving plate.

9) Sift the reserved tablespoon of strawberry powder over the pie just before serving, and garnish it with the freeze-dried strawberries that were set aside.

10) I like to store the pie uncovered in the refrigerator. It dries this way so that the consistency is more like cheesecake.

Makes 10 servings.

Puddings and Pies

Ice Cream

CHOCOLATE FROZEN YOGURT 134
EGG-FREE

FROZEN MISSISSIPPI MUD PIE 136
EGG-FREE

SALTED CARAMEL CHOCOLATE CHUNK ICE CREAM 138
EGG-FREE

FROZEN CHOCOLATE CUSTARD 140

CHOCOLATE VELVET ICE CREAM 142
EGG-FREE

MINT WHIPPED CREAM BITES 144
EGG-FREE

SUNFLOWER CUP PUDDING POPS 146
EGG-FREE

If you like tangy ice cream or frozen yogurt, this recipe is for you. Don't be intimidated; whipping up this treat is surprisingly simple.

CHOCOLATE FROZEN YOGURT

2 (13-ounce) cans full-fat coconut milk

1 tablespoon maple syrup

1/2 cup boiling water

1 tablespoon gelatin

Contents of enough dairy-free probiotics to equal about 50 billion

2 tablespoons raw cacao powder

1/4 cup (about 4) soft, pitted Medjool dates

Liquid stevia to taste

1) In a saucepan, bring the coconut milk and maple syrup to a boil, watching carefully so that it doesn't boil over.

2) Reduce the heat to low, and simmer for 3 minutes.

3) Pour the boiling water into a glass measuring cup, and immediately whisk in the gelatin, whisking until the gelatin is completely dissolved. Add the gelatin to the coconut milk mixture.

4) Pour the liquid into a sterile mixing bowl, and allow it to cool.

5) When the liquid reaches about 92°F, add the probiotics, and whisk very well with a sterile whisk.

6) Add the mixture to a sterile 8" x 8" glass baking dish with a lid.

7) Place the dish on top of a heating pad sandwiched between 2 kitchen towels. (Heating pads without automatic shutoff can be found on Amazon.com.) Turn the heat to low, and let the dish sit on the pad for 18-24 hours. You can also use a yogurt maker. *Note: The gelatin will separate from the cream during this time, and that's okay.*

8) When the yogurt's taste is to your liking, add it to a blender with the raw cacao powder, dates, and liquid stevia, and purée until completely smooth.

9) Freeze the purée for an hour, or refrigerate it until cold.

10) Pour the mixture into your ice cream machine per the manufacturer's instructions.

11) Eat the yogurt straight from the machine, or freeze it further until it is hard enough to make pretty scoops. If it's frozen solid, allow it to sit on the counter for about 20 minutes or until it is as soft as you like.

Makes 6 servings.

Cookie crumbles, coffee ice cream, and fudge are such a great combination. I made this pie while my husband's parents were visiting, and they adored it. Make sure to read the instructions for assembling the pie before making any of the parts of the pie!

FROZEN MISSISSIPPI MUD PIE

GANACHE LAYER

1 batch of Ganache (p. 72)

COFFEE ICE CREAM INGREDIENTS

1 (13-ounce) can full-fat coconut milk

3/4 cup unsweetened hemp milk

1 tablespoon vanilla extract

1/2 cup (about 8) soft, pitted Medjool dates

1/2 cup decaf organic coffee beans

1 cup water, just off the boil

COOKIE CRUST DRY INGREDIENTS

1 & 1/2 cups (170 g) any nut flour

1/4 cup (23 g) cocoa powder

2 tablespoons (12 g) chia seed meal

2 tablespoons (20 g) coconut sugar

1/4 teaspoon baking soda

1/8 teaspoon sea salt

COOKIE CRUST WET INGREDIENTS

2 teaspoons water

2 tablespoons applesauce with no added sugar

1 ounce dark chocolate, melted over a double boiler

1/4 teaspoon liquid vanilla stevia

TO ASSEMBLE

1) Prepare Ganache and set aside, allowing it to come to room temperature.

2) Line a loaf pan with a sheet of unbleached parchment paper large enough to cover the entire inside. Pinch the corners, and fold the edges over to help it stay in place.

3) Mix the Coffee Ice Cream ingredients together (though Step 3) and while it is in the refrigerator/freezer add the Ganache to the lined pan, and put it in the freezer.

4) Make the cookie crust.

5) Continue with making the Coffee Ice Cream in your ice cream machine then transfer the ice cream to the dish containing the chilled Ganache. Leave about 1" at the top for the crust. (There may be some leftover ice cream depending on the size of the pan.)

6) Press about half the cookie crust crumble onto the top of the ice cream, and pack it down. Save the rest to bake as cookies or sprinkle on as a topping.

7) Freeze the mud pie overnight.

8) To serve, place the frozen dish on the kitchen counter for about 30 minutes. Gently remove the pie by lifting the paper, and let it thaw on the serving plate for another 30 minutes before serving.

COFFEE ICE CREAM DIRECTIONS

1) In a blender, purée the coconut milk, hemp milk, vanilla extract, and dates until completely smooth. Keep the mixture in the blender.

2) Grind the coffee beans, and add them to a French press. Cover them with the hot water, and steep for 10 minutes.

3) Press the coffee, add it to the blender with the coconut milk mixture, and purée it again.

4) Freeze the mixture for about 1 hour, or refrigerate it until cold.

5) Pour the mixture into your ice cream machine per the manufacturer's instructions.

COOKIE CRUST DIRECTIONS

1) In a mixing bowl, whisk together the dry ingredients—nut flour, cocoa powder, chia seed meal, coconut sugar, baking soda, and salt.

2) In a separate mixing bowl, combine the wet ingredients—water, applesauce, chocolate, and liquid vanilla stevia.

3) Add the dry ingredients to the wet ingredients and combine with an electric mixer.

4) Shape the leftover crumbles into cookies. Bake at 350°F for about 12 minutes.

This ice cream is out of this world. No one can believe that it's dairy-free and homemade.

SALTED CARAMEL CHOCOLATE CHUNK ICE CREAM

1 (13-ounce) can full-fat coconut milk

1/2 cup (about 8) soft, pitted Medjool dates

1 & 1/4 cups unsweetened hemp milk

1 tablespoon vanilla extract

2 ounces dark chocolate, chopped, or 1 & 1/2 ounces cacao nibs

1/2 batch of Salted Caramel (p. 170), at about room temperature Note: Make the whole batch of caramel, but use only half in the ice cream.

1) Place a 6-cup rectangular glass dish with a lid in the freezer. That way, when you transfer the ice cream to the frozen dish, it will freeze faster.

2) In a blender, purée the coconut milk and dates until completely smooth.

3) Add the hemp milk and vanilla extract to the blender, and purée again.

4) Freeze the mixture for about 1 hour, or refrigerate it until cold.

5) Pour the mixture into your ice cream machine per the manufacturer's instructions.

6) When the ice cream reaches a soft-serve consistency, add the chopped chocolate.

7) Get the Salted Caramel ready to pour (it should be about room temperature).

8) Spread half the ice cream in the freezer dish, and pour the caramel over the ice cream. Add the rest of the ice cream on top, and freeze.

9) When the ice cream is frozen solid, let it thaw on the counter for about 15 minutes or until it reaches the desired firmness.

Makes 6 servings.

Frozen custard or gelato is meant to be eaten warmer than ice cream. The egg yolks give it a certain smoothness that makes it especially enjoyable.

FROZEN CHOCOLATE CUSTARD

2 (13-ounce) cans full-fat coconut milk

1/2 cup (about 8) soft, pitted Medjool dates

6 egg yolks

1/2 cup (80 g) raw cacao powder

1 tablespoon vanilla extract

1/8-1/4 teaspoon liquid vanilla stevia to taste

1) In a blender, purée the coconut milk and dates until completely smooth.

2) Add the egg yolks, raw cacao powder, vanilla extract, and liquid vanilla stevia, and purée again.

3) Freeze the mixture for about 1 hour, or refrigerate it until cold.

4) Pour the mixture into your ice cream machine per the manufacturer's instructions.

5) Eat the custard right away, or freeze it until it's hard enough to make pretty scoops. If it's frozen solid, leave the custard on the counter to thaw until it reaches the desired temperature.

Makes 6 servings.

This ice cream is deep, smooth, and rich, as the name implies. It looks smashing in clear martini glasses for parties, but feel free to eat it in your pajamas any old night of the week.

CHOCOLATE VELVET ICE CREAM

1 (13-ounce) can full-fat coconut milk

10 large, soft, pitted Medjool dates

1/4 cup hemp seeds

1 cup water

1/3 cup (28 g) raw cacao powder

1 tablespoon vanilla extract

1) Add the coconut milk, dates, and hemp seeds to a blender. (A Blendtec or Vitamix works best. If you don't have one of those, you may need to use a food processor for this step.) Purée until completely smooth.

2) Add the water, raw cacao powder, and vanilla extract to the blender. Purée until completely smooth.

3) Pour into a dish, cover, and freeze right away while it still has some air from puréeing.

4) To serve, let it sit on the counter until it is as soft as desired. Scoop into bowls.

Makes about 6 servings.

MINT WHIPPED CREAM BITES

FILLING INGREDIENTS

2 cups Whipped Coconut Cream (p. 108 or p. 110)

2 tablespoons honey

3/4 teaspoon Frontier organic spearmint flavor (You will need less if you use regular peppermint extract. This is the only spearmint flavor I have found.)

1/8 teaspoon liquid vanilla stevia

Several drops yellow and blue India Tree natural food coloring (optional)

COATING

9 ounces homemade* dark chocolate

*You could use store-bought chocolate, but the shells would be much harder and contain much more sugar. You need at least an inch or two of melted chocolate in the jar in order to completely dunk the bites in the coating.

1) In a small bowl, use an electric mixer to whip the Whipped Coconut Cream, honey, spearmint flavor, liquid vanilla stevia, and food coloring (if using).

2) Transfer the filling to one corner of a large plastic food storage bag, and snip about 1/4" off the tip.

3) Squeeze the air out of the bag, and pipe the filling into a truffle mold. Freeze until hard.

4) Pop the filling balls out of the molds, and keep them in the freezer. They probably won't look perfect, but don't worry. When you coat them in the chocolate, they will.

5) Melt the homemade chocolate over a double boiler until just melted.

6) Pour the chocolate into a narrow glass or bowl (I use a small mason jar), and allow it to come to room temperature.

7) Place a piece of unbleached parchment paper on a baking sheet. This is where the bites will dry after you coat them in the chocolate.

8) Take out about 5 frozen filling balls at a time, keeping the rest in the freezer so that they don't melt while you're coating them.

9) Use a toothpick inserted at an angle into the bottom to dip each ball into the melted chocolate.

10) Let the coating dry, twisting the toothpick between your fingers. (This takes only a few seconds).

11) Dip each ball a second time, and let it dry on the toothpick.

12) Ease the ball off of the toothpick by pulling against the surface while pressing gently with your index finger. (See diagram.)

13) Store the bites in the freezer, and let them defrost on the counter for about 20 minutes before serving.

Makes 35 big bites using the Medium Round Truffle Mold from Truffly Made.

Ice Cream

These pudding pops are very fudge-like. The nut butter (or fat) and honey (or sugar content) keep them soft and never icy.

SUNFLOWER CUP PUDDING POPS

LAYERS 1 AND 3 INGREDIENTS

3 ounces dark chocolate, melted over a double boiler

1 cup water

1/2 cup sunflower seed butter with no added sugar

1/4 cup chia seeds

1/4 cup honey

1 tablespoon raw cacao powder

LAYER 2 INGREDIENTS

1/2 cup sunflower seed butter with no added sugar

1/4 cup honey

1 tablespoon water

1/8 teaspoon sea salt

1 & 1/2 ounces chocolate shavings

1) Line a loaf pan with a piece of unbleached parchment paper big enough to cover the bottom and go up every side. Pinch the inside corners, and fold the paper over the edges to help it stay in place.

2) In a blender, purée the Layer 1 and 3 ingredients—melted chocolate, water, sunflower seed butter, chia seeds, honey, and raw cacao powder.

3) Pour a little more than half of the mixture into the prepared loaf pan. Keep the rest in the blender and set aside.

4) Over a double boiler, heat the Layer 2 ingredients (except for the chocolate shavings)—sunflower seed butter, honey, water, and salt—until warm.

5) Pour the Layer 2 mixture over Layer 1, and spread evenly. Add the chocolate shavings. You want the heat of Layer 2 to partially melt the chocolate shavings.

6) Add the rest of the filling from the blender, and spread evenly.

7) Add 8 popsicle sticks, pressing them all the way down, and freeze the pan overnight.

8) To serve, take the pan out of the freezer, and let it sit on the counter for about 20 minutes. Use the parchment paper to lift the block of pudding from the pan, and use a hot chef's knife to cut apart the 8 pops.

9) Store leftovers in the freezer wrapped in parchment paper and sealed in a food storage bag.

Makes 8 servings.

Ice Cream

Drinks

FROZEN CAFE MOCHA 150
EGG-FREE

DECADENT 60-SECOND CHOCO-CHIA MILKSHAKE 152
EGG-FREE

MOLTEN CHOCOLATE AND THE BEST CHOCOLATE MILK EVER 154
EGG-FREE

WHITE CHOCOLATE RASPBERRY SMOOTHIE 156
EGG-FREE

AZTEC HOT CHOCOLATE 158
EGG-FREE

ALMOND BANANA CACAO SMOOTHIE 160
EGG-FREE

In Colorado, we are spoiled by coffee shops that offer coconut, almond, and hemp milk. But you can make healthier dairy-free coffee drinks at home very easily. Just like chocolate, it's important to buy fair trade coffee to ensure that the people who produce it are ethically treated.

FROZEN CAFE MOCHA

1/4 cup organic fair trade coffee beans

1 & 1/2 cups water

1 cup full-fat coconut or other nut milk*

1 tablespoon raw cacao powder

1 tablespoon honey

15 drops liquid vanilla stevia

*You will need extra milk if you aren't using a Blendtec or Vitamix blender.

1) Grind the coffee beans, and add them to a French press.

2) Pour 1 & 1/2 cups water just off the boil over the ground coffee, and steep for 10 minutes. Then press.

3) Pour the coffee into BPA-free freezer trays, and freeze it until hard.

4) In a blender, purée the frozen coffee cubes, the milk, raw cacao powder, honey, and liquid vanilla stevia until completely smooth.

5) Pour evenly between 2 glasses and serve.

Makes 2 servings.

My testers say that this reminds them of the drive-through chocolate milkshakes they used to drink.

DECADENT 60-SECOND CHOCO-CHIA MILKSHAKE

1 cup canned full-fat coconut milk

6 ice cubes

2 tablespoons chia seeds (Grind them in a coffee grinder first if you don't have a Blendtec or Vitamix blender. Otherwise, the shake will be lumpy rather than thick and smooth.)

1 tablespoon raw cacao powder

1 tablespoon honey

10 drops liquid vanilla stevia, or more to taste

1) In a blender, purée the coconut milk, ice cubes, chia seeds, raw cacao powder, honey, and liquid vanilla stevia until smooth.

2) Pour into 1 or 2 glasses and serve.

Makes 1 large or 2 small servings.

Every time I asked my blog readers what chocolate recipe they couldn't live without, at least one person said hot chocolate. I think hot chocolate is like Mom's chicken soup—pure comfort. This recipe also makes the best chocolate milk ever if you use homemade dark chocolate (page 164).

MOLTEN CHOCOLATE and THE BEST CHOCOLATE MILK EVER

4 large, soft, pitted Medjool dates

3 ounces dark chocolate*, melted

1 cup canned full-fat coconut milk

1 vanilla bean, split lengthwise and scraped, seeds reserved or 4 leftover vanilla bean pods

1 & 1/4 cups unsweetened almond milk

*Use homemade dark chocolate (page 164) if you're making chocolate milk. You can use either homemade or store-bought dark chocolate for molten (hot) chocolate. My family prefers molten chocolate made with homemade bars, but it's thicker with store-bought.

OPTION 1 (FOR USING VANILLA BEAN CONTENTS)

1) In a blender, purée the dates, melted chocolate, coconut milk, and contents of vanilla bean until completely smooth. Leave the mixture in the blender.

2) Add the almond milk to the chocolate purée in the blender. Purée again until smooth.

3) Refrigerate the mixture for chocolate milk, or serve it hot for molten chocolate.

OPTION 2 (FOR USING LEFTOVER VANILLA BEAN PODS)

1) In a blender, purée the dates, melted chocolate, and coconut milk until completely smooth. Leave the mixture in the blender.

2) Bring the almond milk and leftover pods to a boil in a small saucepan. Reduce the heat to low, and simmer for 5 minutes with the lid on, slightly cracked. (This step will infuse the milk with the vanilla). Keep a close eye on it so that it doesn't boil over. Remove the pods from the saucepan.

3) Add the almond milk to the chocolate purée in the blender. Purée again until smooth.

4) Refrigerate the mixture for chocolate milk, or serve it hot for molten chocolate. (Pictured with Dark Chocolate Hazelnut Cookies, page 84.)

Makes 2 large or 4 small servings.

This pretty smoothie has a surprise ingredient: cacao butter. I think it goes very well with the bright flavor of the raspberries.

WHITE CHOCOLATE RASPBERRY SMOOTHIE

1 ounce cacao butter

1 heaping cup (5 ounces) frozen raspberries

1 cup unsweetened almond or canned full-fat coconut milk (I like to use 1/2 cup of each)

Juice of half a lemon

1 tablespoon chia seeds

1 tablespoon honey

1 tablespoon egg white protein powder (optional)

1) Over a double boiler, heat the cacao butter until just melted. Remove it from the heat.

2) In a blender, add the raspberries, milk, lemon juice, chia seeds, honey, and egg white protein powder (if using). Add the melted cacao butter last, just before blending, and purée until smooth.

Makes 1 large or 2 small smoothies.

California chilies add sweetness and a vibrant color that makes this hot drink beautiful. My Aztec Hot Chocolate is presented in two layers and served with a spoon for stirring.

AZTEC HOT CHOCOLATE

1 cup canned full-fat coconut milk

1 cup unsweetened almond milk

1/4 cup honey

1/8 teaspoon ground cayenne pepper

1 vanilla bean, split lengthwise and scraped, seeds reserved or 4 leftover vanilla bean pods

2 dried California chilies

3 ounces dark chocolate, melted over a double boiler

TOPPING

Chocolate shavings (optional)

OPTION 1 (FOR USING VANILLA BEAN CONTENTS)

1) In a blender, add the coconut milk, almond milk, honey, cayenne pepper, and vanilla bean contents. Set aside.

2) Remove the seeds from the chilies, and grind them in a mini blender or coffee grinder.

3) Add the ground chilies to the milk mixture in the blender, and purée.

4) Pour the mixture into a small saucepan and bring to a simmer over low heat. Set aside.

5) Add the melted chocolate to the glasses, then ladle the hot milk mixture over the top to create 2 layers. Top with chocolate shavings, if desired.

6) Serve with a spoon for stirring the chocolate into the milk after presentation.

OPTION 2 (FOR USING LEFTOVER VANILLA BEAN PODS)

1) In a blender, add the coconut milk, almond milk, honey, and cayenne pepper. Set aside.

2) Remove the seeds from the chilies, and grind them in a mini blender or coffee grinder.

3) Add the ground chilies to the milk mixture in the blender, and purée.

4) Pour the mixture into a small saucepan, and add the leftover vanilla pods.

5) Bring to a boil, reduce the heat to low, and simmer for 5 minutes with the lid on, slightly cracked. (Doing so will infuse the milk with the vanilla.) Remove the pods from the saucepan.

6) Add the melted chocolate to the glasses, then ladle the hot milk mixture over the top to create 2 layers. Top with chocolate shavings, if desired.

7) Serve with a spoon for stirring the chocolate into the milk after presentation.

Makes 2 servings.

The banana in this smoothie is there more for thickening than for flavor. If you want a stronger banana taste, use a whole banana. This smoothie is also excellent with organic SunButter in place of the almond butter (for a peanut butter-like flavor).

ALMOND BANANA CACAO SMOOTHIE

1 (13-ounce) can full-fat coconut milk, chilled

1/2 banana, refrigerated

4 ice cubes

2 tablespoons raw almond butter

1-2 tablespoons raw cacao powder to taste

1 teaspoon honey

5 drops liquid vanilla stevia

Pinch of sea salt

1) In a blender, purée all the ingredients—coconut milk, banana, ice cubes, almond butter, raw cacao powder, honey, liquid vanilla stevia, and salt—until completely smooth.

2) Serve in 1 or 2 glasses.

Makes 1 large or 2 small smoothies.

Candy

HOMEMADE DARK CHOCOLATE BAR 164
EGG-FREE

HOMEMADE WHITE CHOCOLATE BAR 166
EGG-FREE

CHOCOLATE CARAMEL APPLES WITH SLICED ALMONDS 168
EGG-FREE

SALTED CARAMEL 170
EGG-FREE

SALTED CARAMEL BACON BARK 170
EGG-FREE

ALMOND COCONUT CANDIES 172
EGG-FREE

CHOCOLATE FUDGE 174
EGG-FREE

WHITE CHOCOLATE FUDGE 176
EGG-FREE

CHERRY CORDIALS TWO WAYS 178
EGG-FREE

CHOCOLATE-DIPPED CRANBERRY-ORANGE NUT BARS 180
EGG-FREE

SUNFLOWER CUPS 182
EGG-FREE

WHITE CHOCOLATE BACON CANDIES 184
EGG-FREE

CHOCOLATE TRUFFLES 186
EGG-FREE

MOCHA TRUFFLES 186
EGG-FREE

STRAWBERRY TRUFFLES 188
EGG-FREE

MATCHA TRUFFLES 188
EGG-FREE

ALMOND AND CHOCOLATE-STUFFED BACON-WRAPPED DATES 190
EGG-FREE

PISTACHIO-DATE FREEZER CANDIES 192
EGG-FREE

Not only are these chocolate bars easy to make, healthy, and crazy delicious, but they're low on the glycemic index, too. Sweetened with a small amount of coconut sugar and stevia, they won't spike your blood sugar levels like junk food candy does. Unless store-bought is specified, you can use this bar as an ingredient in any of my recipes.

HOMEMADE DARK CHOCOLATE BAR

1/2 cup (85 g) cacao butter

1 vanilla bean, split lengthwise and scraped, seeds reserved

1 tablespoon + 2 teaspoons (28 g) melted coconut butter/ cream concentrate

2/3 cup (57 g) cocoa/raw cacao powder*

1/4 cup (39 g) coconut sugar

10 drops liquid vanilla stevia, or to taste (the more you add, the softer the bars will be)

*If you plan to eat your bars like candy or heat them only slightly, use raw cacao powder.

1) Make sure that your bowl, spoons, and all other equipment are completely dry, or the chocolate will separate!

2) Place a mixing bowl over a pot of barely simmering water. The bottom of the bowl should sit a few inches above the water level.

3) Add the cacao butter to the bowl. As soon as the butter has melted, remove the bowl from the heat.

4) Add the vanilla, coconut butter/cream concentrate, and cocoa/raw cacao powder to the bowl. Stir to combine, and set the bowl aside.

5) Grind the coconut sugar into a powder in a coffee grinder or mini blender.

6) Stir the powdered coconut sugar into the rest of the ingredients. You don't need to mix it well.

7) In a small blender, purée the lumpy mixture for 1 minute. (You can use a food processor or stick blender, but a mini blender works best for a single batch.)

8) Add the liquid vanilla stevia a few drops at a time until the chocolate is sweet enough for you. Make sure that the tasting spoons are dry!

9) Line an 8" x 6" x 2" (6 cup) glass dish with a piece of unbleached parchment paper big enough to cover the bottom and go up the sides. Pinch the corners to help the paper stay in place. You can use candy molds instead, if desired.

10) Pour the chocolate into the lined dish, and allow it to cool to room temperature.

11) Refrigerate the bar until it hardens completely. Keep it in the refrigerator in a glass container with a lid until you're ready to use it.

Makes 1 bar, about 7 ounces.

Creating a white chocolate bar without powdered white sugar or milk powder is difficult. I developed three substitutions for white sugar and milk powder.

HOMEMADE WHITE CHOCOLATE BAR

1/2 cup (85 g) melted cacao butter

1 tablespoon + 2 teaspoons (28 g) melted coconut butter/cream concentrate

3 tablespoons 100% egg white protein powder, or 3 tablespoons coconut flour, or 3 tablespoons powdered coconut sugar

1 vanilla bean, split lengthwise and scraped, seeds reserved

20 drops liquid vanilla stevia, or to taste (optional)

100% egg white protein powder: This is a great option because it keeps the chocolate bar white. Use up to 20 drops of liquid vanilla stevia to sweeten.

Coconut flour: If you can't use egg white protein powder, coconut flour works, too. The only problem is that it gives the bar a grainy texture. You likely won't notice it when you use the white chocolate to dip biscotti or drizzle on cookies. (None of our testers noticed.) For white chocolate bars to be eaten alone, use powdered coconut sugar instead. Sweeten your coconut flour bars with up to 20 drops of liquid vanilla stevia.

Powdered coconut sugar: Grind coconut sugar into a powder using a dry mini blender or coffee grinder. This bar tastes amazing and is caffeine-free, but it isn't white. Omit the stevia for this option.

1) Make sure that your bowl, blender, and all other equipment are completely dry, or the chocolate will separate!

2) Place a mixing bowl over a pot of barely simmering water. The bottom of the bowl should sit a few inches above the water level.

3) Add the cacao butter to the bowl. As soon as the cacao butter has melted, remove it from the heat.

4) In a small blender, purée the coconut butter/cream concentrate, protein powder/coconut flour/coconut sugar, and vanilla for 1 minute. (A mini blender works best for a single batch.)

5) Add your liquid vanilla stevia a few drops at a time until the chocolate is sweet enough for you. Make sure that the tasting spoons are dry!

6) Line an 8" x 6" x 2" (6 cup) glass dish with a piece of unbleached parchment paper big enough to cover the bottom and go up the sides. Pinch the corners to help the paper stay in place. You can use candy molds* instead, if desired.

7) Pour the chocolate into the lined dish, and freeze it until the chocolate sets.

8) Keep the bar in the refrigerator in a glass container with a lid until you are ready to use it.

*For using molds: Place the mold in the freezer, and let the white chocolate cool on the counter for an hour and a half. Stir well then pour into the cold mold. Freeze immediately to set quickly and prevent the vanilla or coconut sugar from settling.

Makes 1 bar, about 5 ounces.

Candy

These sweet treats make me want to go for a hayride and pick a pumpkin in a pumpkin patch.

CHOCOLATE CARAMEL APPLES
WITH SLICED ALMONDS

EQUIPMENT

Popsicle sticks

3 ice cream-sized bowls (for chocolate, caramel, and nuts)

2 empty egg cartons

INGREDIENTS

4 apples

6 ounces store-bought dark chocolate

Sliced almonds

1 batch of Salted Caramel (p. 170)

1) Press a popsicle stick into the top of each apple, and chill the apples in the refrigerator overnight.

2) Make two 1/4" slits, at least 4" apart, in the top of each closed egg carton. (These will hold the apples upside down as they dry.)

3) Melt the chocolate over a double boiler, and carefully pour the melted chocolate into one of the ice cream-sized bowls.

4) Dip each cold apple in the chocolate, and swirl it around. Hold the apple over the bowl, and twist it until the chocolate begins to dry.

5) Place the apple stick in one of the slits in the egg carton, and let it sit upside down to dry completely.

6) Repeat with the other 3 apples.

7) Fill another ice cream-sized bowl about half full with sliced almonds. Set it aside.

8) Heat the leftover Salted Caramel as directed at the end of the recipe (page 170). *Note: The caramel should be fairly thick and cool, as you can tell by the photo. If the caramel is too thin and hot, it will just run off the apple, taking the chocolate with it.*

9) Dip a chocolate-covered apple in the caramel, and swirl it around. You can also use a butter knife to spread the caramel around the apple. Only a small amount of caramel is needed for each apple.

10) Dip the coated apple in the sliced almonds.

11) Place the apple stick in one of the slits in the egg carton, and let it sit upside down to dry completely.

12) Repeat with the other 3 apples.

Makes about 4 caramel apples.

The tricks to making this caramel are to watch it carefully and be patient. The ingredients and the method couldn't be simpler. Store covered at room temperature.

SALTED CARAMEL

1 cup canned full-fat coconut milk

1 cup (156 g) coconut sugar

1/4 teaspoon sea salt

1) In a heavy-bottomed pot that is about 7" wide x 3" deep, add the coconut milk, coconut sugar, and salt.

2) Whisk to combine the ingredients, and turn on the heat. Bring the mixture to a boil, watching carefully so that it doesn't boil over. Boil over medium heat for 15 minutes.

3) Reduce the heat to low, and simmer for 5 minutes, watching carefully to make sure that it doesn't burn. If it begins to burn, the edges will turn dry and black.

4) Wear gloves to pour the caramel into a small bowl, and stir periodically as it cools to room temperature. Don't wash the pot just yet; you may need it again.

5) If the caramel isn't thick (similar to molasses) when it reaches room temperature (after about 20 minutes), pour it back into the pot, and let it simmer over the lowest heat possible for another 3-5 minutes.

6) Wear gloves to pour the caramel back into the small bowl, and stir periodically as it cools to room temperature. Store covered at room temperature.

7) To reheat leftover caramel (such as for dipping apples or pouring over ice cream), put the dish of caramel in a larger dish of very hot water, and cover it for 15 minutes. If needed, add more hot water, and repeat.

Makes about 1 cup.

SALTED CARAMEL BACON BARK

1/2 batch of Salted Caramel (above)*

6 ounces dark chocolate

4 strips of crisp cooked bacon

*Make the whole batch of caramel, but use only half in the bacon bark.

1) Make the Salted Caramel, and let it cool almost to room temperature.

2) Line an 8" x 8" dish with a piece of unbleached parchment paper big enough to cover the bottom and go up the sides. Pinch the corners to help it stay in place, and set the dish aside.

3) Over a double boiler, melt the chocolate, and pour it into the prepared dish.

4) Allow the chocolate to cool to room temperature on the counter. Then place it in the freezer until hard.

5) Drizzle the caramel over the chocolate, and sprinkle the top with crumbled crisp bacon.

6) Freeze the candy until it is hard enough to break into bark. You can then store it in the freezer or the refrigerator.

Makes 8 servings.

Candy

Inspired by a certain famous candy, this distant cousin is infinitely healthier, more satisfying, and more attractive.

ALMOND COCONUT CANDIES

1/4 cup melted coconut butter/ cream concentrate

2 tablespoons melted coconut oil

2 tablespoons honey

1/4 teaspoon almond extract

1/4 teaspoon coconut extract

Pinch of sea salt

3/4 cup (56 g) shredded unsweetened coconut

2 tablespoons coconut flour, sifted

6 ounces dark chocolate, melted over a double boiler

30 almonds

1) In a small mixing bowl, combine the coconut butter/cream concentrate, coconut oil, honey, almond extract, coconut extract, and salt.

2) Add the shredded coconut and coconut flour to the bowl, and stir to combine.

3) Press the mixture into a 30-cavity silicone peanut butter cup mold so that each cavity is two-thirds full.

4) Place the mold in the freezer for about 20 minutes.

5) Remove the mold from the freezer, and top each cavity with a spoonful of the melted chocolate or enough to fill each cavity.

6) Give the mold a little jiggle to smooth out the chocolate.

7) Let the candies sit on the counter for 5 minutes so that the chocolate comes to room temperature. Then refrigerate them until firm.

8) Pop each candy out of the mold, and flip the mold over so that the chocolate is on the bottom.

9) Add a drop of melted coconut oil to each cold candy and secure an almond on the top. The coconut oil will harden from the cold candy and act as a "glue" for the almonds.

10) Store the candies in the refrigerator or in a cool spot in the kitchen.

Makes 30 candies.

A couple years ago, I dreamed of selling this fudge and variations of it in cute little boxes, especially around the holidays. Then baby #3 arrived, we moved, and I started writing this cookbook. But this recipe is too good to keep it a secret any longer!

CHOCOLATE FUDGE

1 & 1/2 cups water

3/4 cup (119 g) coconut sugar

2 cups melted coconut butter/ cream concentrate

3/4 cup (62 g) raw cacao powder

2 teaspoons vanilla extract

1/2 teaspoon liquid vanilla stevia

1) In a small saucepan, heat the water over medium heat. Add the coconut sugar, stir until the sugar has just dissolved, and turn off the heat.

2) In a food processor with an S blade, purée the sugar water, coconut butter/cream concentrate, raw cacao powder, vanilla extract, and liquid vanilla stevia for 20 seconds, stopping once to scrape the sides.

3) Line an 8" x 8" dish with a piece of unbleached parchment paper large enough to cover the bottom and go up the sides. Pinch the corners of the paper to help it stay in place.

4) Using a flexible silicone spatula, transfer the fudge mixture to the lined dish, and spread it out evenly.

5) Refrigerate the fudge to set, and store it in the refrigerator.

6) Cut the fudge into bite-sized pieces to serve.

VARIATIONS

Mint Chocolate Fudge: Add 1/2 teaspoon mint extract.
Mocha Fudge: Add 4 teaspoons ground decaf coffee.
Cherry Cordial Fudge: Add 1 teaspoon amaretto extract (I use Olive Nation brand).

Makes about 16 servings.

*Something about this **White Chocolate Fudge** makes me want to curl up on the couch and watch the snow falling outside my window.*

WHITE CHOCOLATE FUDGE

1/2 cup (85 g) cacao butter

3/4 cup Whipped Coconut Cream (p. 108 or p. 110)

1/2 cup melted coconut butter/ cream concentrate

1/3 cup honey

1/2 a vanilla bean, split lengthwise and scraped, seeds reserved

1/8 teaspoon liquid vanilla stevia

1/4 cup coconut flour, sifted

1) Over a double boiler, heat the cacao butter until just melted. Set it aside.

2) In a food processor with an S blade, purée the Whipped Coconut Cream, melted coconut butter/cream concentrate, honey, vanilla, and liquid vanilla stevia.

3) While puréeing, add the melted cacao butter.

4) Turn off the food processor, and add the coconut flour. Purée for 10 seconds.

5) Line a 6-cup rectangular dish with a piece of unbleached parchment paper large enough to cover the bottom and go up the sides. Pinch the corners of the paper to help it stay in place.

6) Using a flexible silicone spatula, transfer the fudge mixture to the lined dish, and spread it evenly.

7) Refrigerate the fudge to set, and store it in the refrigerator.

8) Cut the fudge into bite-sized pieces to serve.

Makes about 16 servings.

CHERRY CORDIALS TWO WAYS

MARASCHINO CHERRY CORDIALS

1 (9-ounce) jar sour cherry spread (I use Bionaturae, which is free of added sugar)

9 maraschino cherries

4 ounces homemade* dark chocolate (p. 164), melted over a double boiler

*Store-bought chocolate also works, but creates a harder shell. You won't use all the chocolate.

1) Fill 9 cavities of the truffle mold about half full with the sour cherry spread.

2) Press 1 whole maraschino cherry into each cavity, and top it with extra sour cherry spread as needed.

3) Insert a toothpick into the middle of each cavity, through the maraschino cherry.

4) Freeze the filling in the mold for at least 8 hours. It will not harden completely.

5) Remove the mold from the freezer, and press each cavity from the bottom up to gently pop the fillings out of the mold. If a little bit remains in the cavity, scoop it out, and then press it back into place. Once it's dipped in chocolate, no one will ever know. Do not try to pull them out by the toothpicks, which are for dipping the candies in chocolate.

6) Dip each candy into the melted chocolate, and allow it to dry as you hold it by the toothpick. (This only takes a few seconds.) Twist the toothpick between your fingers while the chocolate dries. Then dip it a second time, once again allowing it to dry as you hold it.

7) Carefully remove the toothpick, and place the candy on a sheet of unbleached parchment paper.

8) Allow the chocolate-coated candies to thaw to room temperature, or refrigerate them for firmer candies.

Makes 9 cherry cordials.

SOUR CHERRY CORDIALS

1 (9-ounce) jar sour cherry spread (I use Bionaturae, which is free of added sugar)

4 ounces homemade* dark chocolate (p. 164), melted over a double boiler

*Store-bought chocolate also works, but it creates a harder shell. You won't use all the chocolate.

1) Fill 7 cavities of the truffle mold with the sour cherry spread.

2) Insert a toothpick into the middle of each filled cavity. If your spread isn't thick enough to hold a toothpick, then freeze the filling in the mold for 30 minutes or until it will hold a toothpick.

3) Freeze the filling in the mold for at least 8 hours. It will not harden completely.

4) Remove the mold from the freezer, and press each cavity from the bottom up to gently pop the fillings out of the mold. Do not try to pull them out by the toothpicks, which are for dipping the candies in chocolate.

5) Dip each candy into the melted chocolate, and allow it to dry as you hold it by the toothpick. (This only takes a few seconds.) Twist the toothpick between your fingers while the chocolate dries. Dip it a second time, once again allowing it to dry as you hold it.

6) Carefully remove the toothpick and place the candy on a sheet of unbleached parchment paper.

7) Allow the chocolate-coated candies to thaw to room temperature, or refrigerate them for firmer candies.

Makes 7 cherry cordials.

Cherry cordials were my favorite candies when I was younger. Finding dairy-free versions is almost impossible, so I'm excited to share these recipes with you!

I have two ways of making them. One uses the classic maraschino cherry. I didn't want to make my own maraschino cherries, so I ordered cherries that are free of red dye online, from a company called Tillen Farms.

The filling for option two is made with pure sour cherry spread. These cherry candies are both sweet and sour—a great combination. If the filling is too sour for you, it's easy to sweeten it with a little liquid stevia.

For both versions, I use the 63-Cavity Medium Round Truffle Mold by Truffly Made (purchased on Amazon.com). For cherry cordials it's important that the mold is made of silicone so you can get the filling out once it's frozen. If you're making the maraschino cherry version, the mold also needs to be deep enough to hold a whole pitted cherry.

These candy bars are perfect to take to the movies or to enjoy on movie night at home.

CHOCOLATE-DIPPED CRANBERRY-ORANGE NUT BARS

BAR INGREDIENTS

1 cup whole almonds

1 & 1/4 cups sliced almonds

1 cup walnuts

3/4 cup dried cranberries

2 tablespoons black sesame seeds

Coconut oil to grease the dish

1/4 cup shredded unsweetened coconut

1/2 cup honey

1 teaspoon vanilla extract

3 tablespoons orange zest (from about 2 whole oranges)

1/4-1/2 teaspoon sea salt to taste

DIP

6 ounces dark chocolate, melted

1) Preheat your oven to 350°F.

2) In a mixing bowl, combine the whole almonds, sliced almonds, walnuts, dried cranberries, and sesame seeds. Set the mixture aside.

3) Line a 9" x 13" baking dish with a piece of unbleached parchment paper large enough to cover the bottom and go up the sides. Pinch the corners of the paper to help keep it in place.

4) Grease the bottom of the paper with coconut oil, and sprinkle it with the shredded coconut. Set the dish aside.

5) In a small saucepan over medium-low heat, add the honey, vanilla extract, orange zest, and salt. As soon as the honey begins to simmer, remove it from the heat.

6) Pour the honey mixture over the dry ingredients in the bowl, and stir to coat the dry ingredients evenly.

7) Using a flexible silicone spatula, transfer the nut mixture to the prepared baking dish, and spread it evenly.

8) Bake for about 20 minutes. (The longer it bakes, the crunchier the bars will be. If you prefer a crunchy bar, bake a little longer so that the nuts are more golden brown.)

9) Remove the dish from the oven, and allow it to cool. Slice into 12 bars, and refrigerate until cold.

10) Over a double boiler, melt the dark chocolate. Dip each refrigerated bar halfway into the melted chocolate, and return it to the parchment paper.

11) Return the dipped bars to the refrigerator to set before serving.

VARIATION

Chocolate-Dipped Cherry-Ginger Nut Bars: Substitute 1/2 cup dried sour cherries for the cranberries. Add 1/4 cup crystallized ginger, rinsed and finely chopped. Omit the orange zest.

Makes 12 bars.

You won't use all of the chocolate, but it's better to have too much than too little. Save whatever you don't use for another recipe.

SUNFLOWER CUPS

6 ounces dark chocolate

1/2 cup sunflower seed butter with no added sugar

1 tablespoon honey

1 vanilla bean, split lengthwise and scraped, seeds reserved

Pinch of sea salt

1) Melt the chocolate. When it is the consistency of frosting use a silicone basting brush to coat the inside of 8 miniature baking cups. When all are coated rinse the brush in hot water and dry with a towel.

2) Freeze for 5 minutes then brush on another coat of chocolate. Freeze the chocolate-coated cups while you make the filling. Rinse the brush in hot water and dry with a towel.

3) In a mixing bowl combine the sunflower seed butter, honey, vanilla, and salt.

4) Remove the chocolate cups from the freezer. Roll the sunflower seed mixture into balls and press into the cups.

5) Brush chocolate over the top of the filled cups and freeze to set. Rinse the brush in hot water and dry with a towel. When the top coat is solid brush a final coat of chocolate on top.

6) Store the Sunflower Cups in the refrigerator and enjoy cold or at room temperature.

Makes 8 miniature sunflower cups.

My little girls love these candies. I hope you do, too!

WHITE CHOCOLATE BACON CANDIES

CANDY BASE INGREDIENTS

1 & 1/2 ounces cacao butter

1 & 1/2 ounces melted coconut butter/cream concentrate

2 teaspoons honey

1 vanilla bean, split lengthwise and scraped, seeds reserved

10 drops liquid vanilla stevia

1-2 teaspoons lard to taste

TOPPINGS

Crisp bacon crumbles

Ground pink Himalayan salt

1) Place a mixing bowl over a pot of barely simmering water. The bottom of the bowl should sit a few inches above the water level.

2) Add the cacao butter to the bowl. As soon as the cacao butter has melted, remove it from the heat.

3) In a mini blender, purée the coconut butter/cream concentrate, honey, vanilla, liquid vanilla stevia, and lard.

4) Let the mixture come to room temperature, then stir well, pour into molds and freeze to set.

5) Top the candies with crisp bacon crumbles and ground pink Himalayan salt. Store in the refrigerator.

*The bacon candies in the photo were made in a spiral cone silicone chocolate mold that I got from Amazon.com. You can also make them in a truffle mold and dip them in dark chocolate.

Makes 12 spiral cone candies.

Thanks to truffle molds, these candies are fast and simple to make. They're also completely delicious.

CHOCOLATE TRUFFLES

1/2 cup (85 g) cacao butter

1/3 cup (85 g) melted coconut butter/cream concentrate

1-2 tablespoons honey to taste

1-2 tablespoons raw cacao powder to taste

1 vanilla bean, split lengthwise and scraped, seeds reserved

20 drops liquid vanilla stevia

3 ounces dark chocolate

1) Place a mixing bowl over a pot of barely simmering water. The bottom of the bowl should sit a few inches above the water level.

2) Add the cacao butter to the bowl. As soon as the cacao butter has melted, remove it from the heat.

3) In a mini blender, purée the cacao butter, coconut butter/cream concentrate, honey, raw cacao powder, vanilla, and liquid vanilla stevia.

4) Pour the mixture into a truffle mold, and freeze until cold (several hours or more).

5) Place the dark chocolate in a bowl, and place the bowl over a pot of barely simmering water for 1-2 minutes until the chocolate has just barely melted.

6) Remove the bowl from the heat, and transfer the melted chocolate to a small dish for dipping.

7) Place a piece of unbleached parchment paper on a baking sheet. (This is where the truffles will dry after you coat them in the chocolate.)

8) Remove the truffles from the mold, and use a toothpick inserted at an angle into the bottom to dip each truffle into the chocolate.

9) Let the excess chocolate run off into the bowl, and ease it off the toothpick by pulling the truffle against the surface while pressing gently with your index finger. (See diagram, page 144.)

10) Let the truffles dry and come to room temperature before serving. Store them in a dark place at 70°F or lower.

Makes 15 or more truffles, depending on the size of the mold.

This chocolate and coffee flavor is amazing, and I love the way these truffles look when you bite into them.

MOCHA TRUFFLES

1) Same as above, but in step three omit the cacao powder and add 2-3 teaspoons ground organic decaf coffee, to taste.

The kids have a lot of fun dipping these truffles in melted chocolate. The only hard part is waiting until they cool to eat them.

STRAWBERRY TRUFFLES

1/2 cup (85 g) cacao butter

1/3 cup (85 g) melted coconut butter/cream concentrate

1 tablespoon honey

1 vanilla bean, split lengthwise and scraped, seeds reserved

20 drops liquid vanilla stevia

4 teaspoons Frontier alcohol-free strawberry extract

1-2 teaspoons India Tree red food coloring, depending on how dark you want the color

3 ounces dark chocolate

1) Place a mixing bowl over a pot of barely simmering water. The bottom of the bowl should sit a few inches above the water level.

2) Add the cacao butter to the bowl. As soon as the cacao butter has melted, remove it from the heat.

3) In a mini blender, purée the cacao butter, coconut butter/cream concentrate, honey, vanilla, liquid vanilla stevia, strawberry extract, and food coloring.

4) Pour the mixture into a truffle mold, and freeze until cold (several hours or more).

5) Place the dark chocolate in a bowl, and place the bowl over a pot of barely simmering water for 1-2 minutes until the chocolate has just barely melted.

6) Remove the bowl from the heat, and transfer the melted chocolate to a small dish for dipping.

7) Place a piece of unbleached parchment paper on a baking sheet. (This is where the truffles will dry after you coat them in the chocolate.)

8) Remove the truffles from the mold, and use a toothpick inserted at an angle into the bottom to dip each truffle into the chocolate.

9) Let the excess chocolate run off into the bowl, and ease it off the toothpick by pulling the truffle against the surface while pressing gently with your index finger. (See diagram, page 144.)

10) Let the truffles dry and come to room temperature before serving. Store them in a dark place at 70°F or lower.

Makes 15 or more truffles, depending on the size of the mold.

Matcha, or green tea powder, makes the prettiest truffles. I created this flavor for my husband, who is an avid tea drinker.

MATCHA TRUFFLES

1) Same as above, but in step three omit the strawberry extract and food coloring. Replace with 1-2 teaspoons Matcha powder, to taste. (The color will be dark at first, but will lighten after the mixture solidifies.)

Candy

I was first introduced to bacon-wrapped stuffed dates at my bridal shower in 2001. I thought then, and still think, that they are one of the most heavenly treats in the world. Rather than stuffing these with whole almonds, however, I've made a filling of almond butter and cocoa powder. I think they're divine.

ALMOND and CHOCOLATE-STUFFED BACON-WRAPPED DATES

1/4 cup almond butter

3 tablespoons cocoa powder

1 & 1/2 teaspoons honey

1/8 teaspoon sea salt

Water, as needed

20 large, soft Medjool dates

About 8 ounces uncooked bacon

1) Preheat your oven to 400°F.

2) In a small mixing bowl, combine the almond butter, cocoa powder, honey, and salt. Add a splash or two of water as needed to properly combine. The mixture should be just dry enough to roll into balls with your hands.

3) Roll the mixture into 20 balls about 3/4" wide.

4) Carefully make an incision down the long side of each date, and remove the pit. (Split it open; don't cut it in half.)

5) Stuff each date with an almond-chocolate ball. Close the dates around the filling so that they look as if they had never been cut.

6) Cut each uncooked bacon strip into thirds.

7) Keeping the cut sides of the dates up, wrap the cut bacon tightly around the stuffed dates so that the ends of the bacon meet or overlap on the bottom. Secure each with a toothpick straight through the middle.

8) Bake the candies on a baking sheet for about 24 minutes or until the bacon is crisp. (You will need more or less baking time depending on the leanness of the bacon.)

9) Let cool for at least 5 minutes before serving.

Makes 20 candies.

These candies have a great balance of pistachio and chocolate, and I just love to look at them (and then eat them).

PISTACHIO-DATE FREEZER CANDIES

CANDY INGREDIENTS

10 large, soft, pitted Medjool dates

1/2 cup shelled dry-roasted pistachios (such as Eden Organic brand)

1/4 cup raw cashew butter

3 tablespoons water

2 tablespoons raw cacao powder

2 tablespoons coconut flour, sifted

COATING INGREDIENTS

1/4 cup shelled dry-roasted pistachios

3 ounces dark chocolate

1) In a food processor with an S blade, purée the dates, 1/2 cup pistachios, cashew butter, and water for about 5 minutes or until smooth, stopping to scrape the sides a few times when it gets stuck.

2) Add the raw cacao powder and coconut flour to the food processor, and purée until combined.

3) Use a flexible silicone spatula to transfer the dough to a small dish, and chill it in the refrigerator for a few hours.

4) Using your hands or a 3/4-ounce (size 40) scoop with a lever, shape the dough into about 11 balls.

5) Freeze the balls on a baking sheet covered with unbleached parchment paper for about an hour.

TO COAT

1) To make the coating, grind 1/4 cup pistachios in a coffee grinder or mini blender until fine. Set them aside in a small dish for dipping.

2) Over a double boiler, melt the dark chocolate for 1-2 minutes. Remove it from the heat, and transfer it to a small dish for dipping.

3) Insert a toothpick into the bottom of each ball and dip it into the melted chocolate, and then quickly into the ground pistachios before the chocolate dries.

4) Store the candies wrapped in unbleached parchment paper in a sealed bag in the freezer. You can eat them at room temperature, but they are most delightful straight from the freezer.

Makes about 11 candies.

Savory Dishes

ANCHO CHILI BEEF STEW 196
EGG-FREE

SALADE DU JOUR WITH VINAIGRETTE AU CHOCOLAT 198
EGG-FREE

CHILI WITH ROASTED BUTTERNUT SQUASH 200
EGG-FREE

SPICY CHOCOLATE MASSAMAN 202
EGG-FREE

COCOA AND SPICE-RUBBED RIBS 204
EGG-FREE

CHICKEN IN MOLE SAUCE 206
EGG-FREE

BARBECUE SAUCE 208
EGG-FREE

OVEN-ROASTED BARBECUE DRUMSTICKS 208
EGG-FREE

TOMATO AND CHERRY CHICKEN CUTLETS 210
EGG-FREE

CAULI-RICE 210
EGG-FREE

SLOW-COOKED CHICKEN 212
EGG-FREE

You can make this rich stew with any type of meat or vegetables. It's very versatile and hearty. Mock Cornbread (page 112) tastes great with this stew.

ANCHO CHILI BEEF STEW

1 cup water

2 dried ancho chilies

1 cup tomatoes, cored

1 tablespoon coconut oil

1 small yellow onion, roughly chopped

2 cloves garlic, peeled

1 teaspoon ground cinnamon

1 & 1/2 teaspoons ground cumin

2-4 tablespoons honey to taste

1/2 to 1 teaspoon sea salt to taste

1 quart beef broth (homemade or Imagine Organic brand), divided

1 pound stew beef, at room temperature

3 ounces dark chocolate, chopped

1/2 cup canned full-fat coconut milk

Sliced cherry tomatoes for garnish

1) Boil the water. Pour the water into a bowl, place the dried chilies in the water, cover, and let them soften for about 20 minutes.

2) Squeeze the cored tomatoes to remove the excess liquid, and roughly chop them. Set them aside.

3) Place a large pot over medium-low heat. Add the coconut oil, and sauté the tomatoes, onion, and garlic in the oil for about 5 minutes.

4) Transfer the tomatoes, onion, and garlic to a blender, and set aside.

5) Take the chilies out of the water, reserving the soaking water. Remove the stems, cut the chilies in half, and scrape out the seeds. Add the chilies and soaking water to the blender with the tomatoes, onions, and garlic. Wash your hands right away so that you don't touch your eyes with chili juice.

6) Add the cinnamon, cumin, honey, salt, and 1 cup of the beef broth to the blender, and purée.

7) Place the stew beef in the pot, and pour the purée from blender, as well as the rest of the beef broth, on top.

8) Bring the stew almost to a boil, and reduce the heat. Simmer with the lid on, slightly cracked, for about 1 hour.

9) Turn off the heat, and add the chopped chocolate and coconut milk.

10) Serve with lots of sliced cherry tomatoes.

Makes about 4 servings.

I love using cacao nibs in this sensational salad. Figs and berries are a feast for your eyes and your palate.

SALADE DU JOUR ⚌ VINAIGRETTE AU CHOCOLAT

VINAIGRETTE INGREDIENTS

2 tablespoons water

1/4 cup apple cider vinegar

1/4 cup cashew pieces

1/4 teaspoon sea salt

A few cranks of black pepper

1 tablespoon honey

1/2 cup extra-virgin olive oil

1 tablespoon cacao nibs

SALAD INGREDIENTS

Fresh figs

Blackberries

Blueberries

Lettuce

Cacao nibs for garnish

1) In a mini blender, purée the water, apple cider vinegar, and cashew pieces until creamy and smooth.

2) Add the salt, pepper, honey, olive oil, and cacao nibs and purée for just a few seconds. If you purée it longer, your vinaigrette may become the consistency of mayonnaise. It will be just as good, but extremely thick.

3) Assemble the salad to your liking, pour the vinaigrette over it, and enjoy.

Makes about 1 & 1/2 cups of dressing.

If you've never cooked with dried chilies, you're in for a real treat. They take the flavor of a dish to a whole new level, and they're so easy to use. Mock Cornbread (page 112) tastes great with this recipe.

CHILI WITH ROASTED BUTTERNUT SQUASH

1 cup water

2 dried chipotle chilies

1 dried ancho chili

1 pound uncooked butternut squash, diced

Coconut oil for cooking

1/8 teaspoon sea salt + 1/2 to 1 teaspoon to taste

1/8 teaspoon garlic powder

2 cups chopped yellow onion

4 cloves garlic, chopped

1 pound grass-fed ground beef

1 cup beef broth (homemade or Imagine Organic)

1 (15-ounce) can fire-roasted diced tomatoes (I use Muir Glen)

1 (7-ounce) jar tomato paste (I use Bionaturae)

2 tablespoons honey

2 teaspoons dried oregano

2 teaspoons ground cumin

1 teaspoon paprika

1/2 teaspoon ground cinnamon

2 ounces dark chocolate, chopped

Juice of half a lime (about 1 tablespoon)

1) Boil the water. Pour the water into a bowl, place the dried chipotle and ancho chilies in the water, cover, and let them soften for about 20 minutes.

2) Preheat your oven to 400°F.

3) Drizzle the squash with coconut oil. Sprinkle it with 1/8 teaspoon salt and 1/8 teaspoon garlic powder, and toss to coat.

4) Spread the squash in a single layer on a baking sheet, and roast it for about 1 hour or until nicely browned.

5) In a large pot over medium-low heat, combine 1 tablespoon coconut oil and the onion and chopped garlic. Sauté for about 5 minutes.

6) Add the ground beef to the pot, and break it up with a spatula as it cooks for about 5 minutes.

7) Meanwhile, take the chilies out of the water, remove the stems, cut them in half, and scrape out the seeds. Wash your hands right away so that you don't touch your eyes with chili juice.

8) In a blender, purée the chilies and beef broth.

9) Add the purée, tomatoes, tomato paste, honey, oregano, cumin, paprika, cinnamon, and 1/2 to 1 teaspoon salt to the beef in the pot.

10) Bring the beef mixture to a boil, reduce the heat to low, and simmer, uncovered, for about 20 minutes.

11) Turn off the heat, and stir in the chopped chocolate.

12) Top the chili with the roasted butternut squash and lime juice, and serve.

Makes about 4 servings.

A faster, easier version of Massaman curry, my Spicy Chocolate Massaman doesn't disappoint. To make a milder version, cut the ancho chili powder, garlic, and ginger in half. We like to eat our curry over Cappello's grain-free fettuccine (www.cappellosglutenfree.com) or Sweet Potato Noodles (see below).

SPICY CHOCOLATE MASSAMAN

SAUCE INGREDIENTS

Coconut oil for cooking

1 cup finely chopped onion

1 tablespoon minced garlic

1 tablespoon minced fresh ginger

1 tablespoon ancho chili powder

1 (13-ounce) can full-fat coconut milk

2 tablespoons coconut sugar

2 tablespoons cocoa powder

1 tablespoon tamarind paste (I use Aunt Patty's Organic)

1 tablespoon sunflower seed butter with no added sugar

1 teaspoon fine lemon zest (from about half a lemon)

1/2 teaspoon sea salt

1/2 teaspoon ground cinnamon

1/2 teaspoon ground cardamom

1/8 teaspoon ground cloves

About 2 pounds chicken breasts (4 chicken breast halves) or stew meat

1/4 cup packed fresh basil

SWEET POTATO NOODLES INGREDIENTS

2 peeled sweet potatoes

Lard or coconut oil for cooking

Sea salt and freshly ground black pepper to taste

SAUCE DIRECTIONS

1) In a 12" skillet, add a few tablespoons of coconut oil. Sauté the onion, garlic, and ginger in the oil for about 3 minutes.

2) Add the chili powder, coconut milk, coconut sugar, cocoa powder, tamarind paste, sunflower seed butter, lemon zest, salt, cinnamon, cardamom, and cloves to the pan. Bring the mixture to a simmer, and reduce the heat to low.

3) Massaman curry is often eaten with stew beef, but we usually use boneless, skinless chicken breast. Whatever meat you choose, cut it into cubes or strips. Stir the meat into the sauce, and simmer (uncovered) until the meat is cooked through.

4) Top each serving with fresh basil, chopped first if you prefer.

SWEET POTATO NOODLES DIRECTIONS

1) Use a spiralizer (I adore my Benriner Turning Slicer) or a food processor with a julienne attachment to create the sweet potatoes noodles.

2) Cook the noodles in 1–2 tablespoons of lard or coconut oil over medium heat for 5-10 minutes, stirring frequently.

3) Season with salt and pepper.

Makes 4 servings.

These ribs are fast and easy to prepare. The only hard part is waiting for them to slow cook!

COCOA AND SPICE-RUBBED RIBS

EQUIPMENT

A pan with a lid that is long enough to hold ribs (Tip: The bottom tray of a broiler pan is usually big enough to hold a rack of ribs, and you can use an upside-down baking sheet as a lid.)

INGREDIENTS

2 tablespoons cocoa powder

2 tablespoons coconut sugar

1 tablespoon ancho chili powder

1 & 1/2 teaspoons sea salt

1 tablespoon onion powder

1 & 1/2 teaspoons garlic powder

1 & 1/2 teaspoons dried oregano

1 & 1/2 teaspoons mustard powder

1 teaspoon ground ginger

1 teaspoon ground cinnamon

1/2 cup red wine

1/2 cup water

2 & 1/2 pounds beef or pork baby back ribs, at room temperature

1) Preheat your oven to 300°F.

2) In a small bowl, combine the cocoa powder, coconut sugar, ancho chili powder, salt, onion powder, garlic powder, oregano, mustard powder, ginger, and cinnamon. Set aside.

3) Coat the bottom side of the ribs with about 1/4 cup of the spice mixture.

4) Lay the ribs in the pan, right side up.

5) Coat the tops of the ribs with the rest of the spice mixture.

6) Pour the wine and water in the pan around the ribs, and cover with the lid.

7) Bake for 1 hour, and then check the level of the liquids. If the lid isn't tight-fitting, add another 1/2 cup each of wine and water.

8) Bake for another 30 minutes.

9) If the lid is tight-fitting, remove it at this point. If it isn't tight-fitting, leave it on.

10) Bake for another 30 minutes.

11) Check the ribs for an internal temperature of 160°F, then transfer to a platter, and pour the juices over top.

Makes 2 to 4 servings.

This recipe is based on the chicken mole in my first cookbook, The Spunky Coconut Cookbook, 2nd Edition. Although not a Paleo cookbook (it was first published in 2009), I still use many of the recipes in that book that are naturally Paleo, and I modify others.

CHICKEN IN MOLE SAUCE

1 cup chopped yellow onion

2 cloves garlic, minced

1 tablespoon lard or coconut oil

1 cup chicken stock

2 tablespoons tomato paste

2 tablespoons cocoa powder

1/2 cup raisins

1/4 cup sesame seeds + 2 tablespoons for garnish

2 tomatoes, cored and chopped

1 teaspoon chili powder

1/2 teaspoon cumin

1/2 teaspoon ground cinnamon

1/2 teaspoon sea salt

About 2 pounds chicken breasts (4 chicken breast halves)

Herbamare or sea salt and freshly ground black pepper to taste

1) Preheat your oven to 350°F.

2) In a large Dutch oven, sauté the onion and garlic in the lard or coconut oil for about 5 minutes. Then turn off the heat.

3) Add the chicken stock, tomato paste, cocoa powder, raisins, 1/4 cup sesame seeds, tomatoes, chili powder, cumin, cinnamon, and salt. Stir to combine the ingredients.

4) Season the chicken with Herbamare or salt and pepper on both sides, and sink the chicken breasts down under the sauce.

5) Cover the Dutch oven with its lid, and bake for about 45 minutes or until the chicken is cooked through.

6) To serve, garnish with the remaining 2 tablespoons of sesame seeds.

Makes 4 servings.

You may not ordinarily keep tamarind paste, fish sauce, and celery seed powder in your kitchen, but trust me, you should pick them up to make this crazy-good barbecue sauce. This recipe makes enough sauce to freeze half so that you won't run out of sauce anytime soon. And you can use the tamarind paste again soon when you make my Spicy Chocolate Massaman (page 202).

BARBECUE SAUCE

1/3 cup apple cider vinegar

1 (14-ounce) jar organic tomato paste

1/2 cup honey

1 ounce dark chocolate, melted over a double boiler

1 teaspoon tamarind paste (I use Aunt Patty's Organic)

1 teaspoon gluten-free fish sauce

3/4 teaspoon chili powder (for medium sauce; add more for a hotter sauce)

1/2 teaspoon garlic powder

1/4 teaspoon celery seed powder

3/4 teaspoon sea salt

1/8 teaspoon freshly ground black pepper

1) In a blender, purée the apple cider vinegar, tomato paste, honey, chocolate, tamarind paste, fish sauce, chili powder, garlic powder, celery seed powder, salt, and pepper until smooth.

2) Store the sauce in mason jars in the refrigerator, or freeze it for later use. If you freeze it, leave an inch of space at the top of the jar for expansion.

Makes 3 cups.

Here's a great way to put that newly made barbecue sauce to good use!

OVEN-ROASTED BARBECUE DRUMSTICKS

12 chicken drumsticks

Barbecue Sauce (see above)

1) Preheat your oven to 425°F.

2) Lightly grease a broiler pan, and lay the drumsticks on the pan.

3) Brush the drumsticks on both sides with the barbecue sauce.

4) Bake for 40 minutes, taking the drumsticks out and brushing them with more sauce every 10 minutes. (I brush only the tops and sides when I take them out of the oven.)

5) Turn off the oven, and leave the drumsticks in the oven for another 10 minutes or until the meat is cooked through.

6) Serve with extra sauce.

Makes 12 drumsticks.

This is one of my family's favorite chicken recipes, and it's also one of the fastest to make!

TOMATO AND CHERRY CHICKEN CUTLETS

About 2 pounds chicken breasts (4 chicken breast halves)

3/4 cup crushed tomatoes

3/4 cup sour cherry spread with no added sugar (I use Bionaturae)

2 tablespoons cocoa powder

1 tablespoon apple cider vinegar

1/4 teaspoon sea salt + a pinch for seasoning

10 drops liquid vanilla stevia

A few cranks of black pepper

Coconut oil for cooking

1/4 cup toasted sliced almonds for garnish

1) Slice the 4 chicken breast halves into cutlets. Set them aside.

2) In a large liquid measuring cup, combine the tomatoes, sour cherry spread, cocoa powder, apple cider vinegar, 1/4 teaspoon salt, and liquid vanilla stevia.

3) Add a few tablespoons of coconut oil to a 12" stainless steel skillet, and preheat it over medium-low heat.

4) Add the chicken to the heated skillet (it's okay if the cutlets overlap a little), and season the meat lightly with salt and pepper.

5) Pour the sauce from the measuring cup over the chicken.

6) Cover the skillet with a lid, slightly cracked, and reduce the heat to low.

7) Cook for 20 minutes or until the chicken is cooked through.

8) Serve over Cauli-Rice (see below), and garnish with toasted sliced almonds.

Makes 4-8 servings.

CAULI-RICE

1 large head of cauliflower

1/2 cup chopped yellow onion

2 tablespoons lard or coconut oil

Herbamare or sea salt and freshly ground black pepper to taste

1) Roughly chop the cauliflower.

2) In a food processor with an S blade, purée one-quarter of the chopped cauliflower until it is fine like rice. Transfer it to a mixing bowl.

3) Add another quarter of the chopped cauliflower to the food processor, along with the chopped onion, and purée until fine like rice. Transfer it to the mixing bowl.

4) Shred the remaining 2 batches of cauliflower as before.

5) In a 12" stainless steel or cast iron skillet over medium heat, add the lard or coconut oil. Cook the Cauli-Rice in the lard or oil for about 20 minutes, stirring every 5 minutes.

6) Season with Herbamare or salt and pepper.

Makes about 6 servings.

Slow-cooking creates meat that is tender and moist. Once you make this chicken, I guarantee that you will be eager to slow cook more often. This rub is also fantastic with pork shoulder.

SLOW-COOKED CHICKEN

1 tablespoon cocoa powder

2 teaspoons whole green peppercorns

2 teaspoons whole coriander seeds

2 teaspoons sea salt

2 teaspoons ground cinnamon

1/2 teaspoon ground nutmeg

1 & 1/2 pounds sweet potatoes

1 & 1/2 pounds carrots

1 tablespoon melted coconut oil

1 whole uncooked chicken (3-5 pounds)

1) Preheat your oven to 300°F.

2) Grind the cocoa powder, peppercorns, coriander seeds, salt, cinnamon, and nutmeg in a mini blender or coffee grinder. Let the spices settle before opening.

3) Scrub the sweet potatoes and carrots, and chop them into bite-sized pieces. Add them to a greased Dutch oven, large enough to hold the whole chicken, and then toss them in 1 tablespoon of the spice mixture and the oil. Set aside.

4) Rub 1 tablespoon of the spice mixture on the back side of the chicken. Rub another tablespoon between the chicken breast and the skin. Finally, add the rest of the spice mixture to the top of the skin.

5) Lay the chicken on top of the sweet potatoes and carrots. Tuck the wings under, and tie the legs together.

6) Put the lid on and bake for 2 hours.

7) Check the chicken for an internal temperature of 165°F. Then untie the legs, slice into pieces, and serve.

Makes 4 servings.

INDEX

hemp milk, 136, 138

hemp seeds, 142

Herbamare, 206, 210

L

lard, 184, 202, 206, 210

lemon, 58, 72, 120, 124, 130, 156, 202

lime, 200

M

macadamia flour, 90

macadamia nuts, 40, 60, 68, 90

maple syrup, 134

maraschino cherries, 76, 178

Medjool dates, 46, 50, 94, 96, 98, 100, 116, 120, 122, 130, 134, 136, 138, 140, 142, 154, 190, 192

mint extract, 88

mint leaves, 74

Mock Cornbread, 30, 112

mulling spices, 126

mustard powder, 204

N

nutmeg, 212

O

olive oil, 198

onion, 196, 200, 202, 204, 206, 210

orange zest, 180

oregano, 200, 204

P

palm shortening, 54, 64, 70, 76, 82, 86, 104

paprika, 200

pears, 126

pecans, 52, 92, 100

peppermint extract, 68, 144

pink Himalayan salt, 184

pistachios, 192

pork baby back ribs, 204

R

raisins, 206

raspberries, 42, 74, 156

raw cacao powder, 40, 46, 64, 96, 98, 120, 130, 134, 140, 142, 146, 150, 152, 160, 164, 174, 186, 192

red wine, 126, 204

rose water, 58

S

Salted Caramel, 138, 168, 170

sesame seeds, 180, 206

sour cherry spread, 76, 178, 210

stew beef, 196

strawberries, 50, 64, 128, 130

strawberry extract, 188

sunflower seed butter, 94, 98, 124, 146, 182, 202

sweet potatoes, 202, 212

T

tamarind paste, 202, 208

tomato paste, 200, 206, 208

tomatoes, 196, 200, 206, 210

U

unsweetened coconut, 40, 52, 80, 92, 94, 98, 102, 120, 130, 172, 180

V

vanilla bean pods, 154, 158

W

walnut flour, 42, 96, 114

walnuts, 42, 114, 180

Whipped Coconut Cream, 118, 122, 124, 128, 130, 144, 176

white chia seed meal, 36, 90

white chocolate, 58, 86, 88, 90

White Chocolate Bar, 88, 90

Y

yellow onion, 196, 200, 206, 210

Z

zucchini, 38

101 BIBLE CROSSWORDS

VOLUME 4

**Puzzles Created by
N. Teri Grottke
David K. Shortess
John Hudson Tiner
Tonya Vilhauer**

BARBOUR
PUBLISHING

Published by Barbour Publishing, Inc., P.O. Box 719, Uhrichsville, Ohio 44683
www.barbourbooks.com

Our mission is to publish and distribute inspirational products offering exceptional value and biblical encouragement to the masses.

ecpa Member of the Evangelical Christian Publishers Association

Printed in the United States of America.
5 4 3 2 1

101
BIBLE
CROSSWORDS

1

ACROSS

1 Heber's son (1 Chronicles 4:18)
6 "Lest at any time we should let them _____" (Hebrew 2:1)
10 "O daughter of _____" (Lamentations 4:21)
14 Moses' father (Exodus 6:20)
15 Detest
16 Smelling orifice
17 "That thou _____ him" (1 Kings 8:25)
19 "Punish the men that are settled on their _____" (Zephaniah 1:12)
20 Your thigh is connected to this
21 "_____ shall see God" (Matthew 5:8)
22 Idols
24 "There is but a _____ between me and death" (1 Samuel 20:3)
25 "_____, Hizkijah, Azzur" (Nehemiah 10:17)
26 "Let him _____ evil" (1 Peter 3:11)
29 "For thou _____ certain strange things to our ears" (Acts 17:20)
33 Jahath's son (1 Chronicles 4:2)
34 Shoham's brother (1 Chronicles 24:27)
35 Always
36 A son of Shem (Genesis 10:22)
37 The son of Eliadah (1 Kings 11:23)
38 Mud
39 "Ye shall in no _____ enter" (Matthew 5:20)
40 First garden
41 "The head slippeth from the _____" (Deuteronomy 19:5)
42 "The children of Eden which were in _____" (2 Kings 19:12)
44 We have five of these
45 "_____ the death of the cross" (Philippians 2:8)
46 "She _____ in her body that she was healed of that plague" (Mark 5:29)
47 Roman emperor
50 Snare
51 "_____ that ye refuse not" (Hebrews 12:25)
54 "Nevertheless _____ heart" (1 Kings 15:14)
55 "And the chief priests and scribes stood and _____ accused him" (Luke 23:10)
58 Young human female
59 Belonging to Eli
60 Elevate
61 "Knowledge is _____ unto him that understandeth" (Proverbs 14:6)
62 "That dippeth with me in the _____" (Mark 14:20)
63 Tear repeatedly

DOWN

1 A giant (2 Samuel 21:18)
2 Ahab's father (1 Kings 16:28)
3 Harvest product
4 A son of Noah
5 Left out
6 Fleecy ruminant
7 "The elect _____" (2 John 1:1)
8 Possessive pronoun
9 "What is thy _____" (Esther 9:12)
10 "Shall there _____ and deliverance arise" (Esther 4:14)
11 "When _____ the Edomite was there" (1 Samuel 22:22)
12 "As he saith also in _____" (Romans 9:25)
13 Chaos
18 Show (arch.)
23 "For do I now persuade _____, or God?" (Galatians 1:10)
24 "As one of the vain fellows _____ uncovereth himself" (2 Samuel 6:20)
25 "River _____: behold" (Deuteronomy 2:24)
26 Selected ones

by N. Teri Grottke

27 Eber's father (Genesis 10:24)
28 Pursue
29 "Namely, _____ in the wilderness" (Deuteronomy 4:43)
30 "For innumerable _____ have compassed me" (Psalm 40:12)
31 Wait on
32 "_____ whose fruit" (Jude 1:12)
34 "Sent Jerubbaal, and _____" (1 Samuel 12:11)
37 "_____ in heaven for you" (1 Peter 1:4)
41 "Greet Priscilla and Aquila my _____ in Christ Jesus" (Romans 16:3)
43 Area near Babylon (2 Kings 17:24)
44 Jesus' coat didn't have one
46 "So can no fountain both yield salt water and _____" (James 3:12)

47 Prison
48 Largest continent
49 Hearing organs
50 "What. . .hath been done to Mordecai for _____?" (Esther 6:3)
51 Mix
52 Otherwise
53 Looked at
56 Hophni's father (1 Samuel 4:4)
57 After Micah (abbr.)

2

A Righteous Husband

ACROSS

1 Mary's husband (Matthew 1:16)
5 Gym class (abbr.)
7 The Son of God: "The holy _____" (Luke 1:35 NIV)
8 "The winds and the waves _____ him" (Matthew 8:27 NIV)
10 "Every _____ his parents went to Jerusalem for the Feast of the Passover" (Luke 2:41 NIV)
12 Paul desired to change his _____ with the Galatians (Galatians 4:20)
13 What the Magi saw in the east (Matthew 2:1–2 NIV)
15 "Glory to God. . .and _____ earth peace" (Luke 2:14)
17 God caused the star to _____ "over the place where the child was" (Matthew 2:9 NIV)
19 Greater London police, New Scotland _____ (abbr.)
21 The Ocean State (abbr.)
23 Matching coat and trousers
25 Source from which valuable matter is extracted
27 "Like the blind we _____ along" (Isaiah 59:10 NIV)
29 Ordered; "Job has not _____ his words against me" (Job 32:14 NIV)
31 Airman (abbr.)
32 Elizabeth's cousin (Luke 1:36, 38)

DOWN

1 "The angel said. . . , 'I bring you good news of great _____' " (Luke 2:10 NIV)
2 Jesus warned against causing little _____ to sin (Matthew 18:6)
3 "Pharisees. . .love the most important _____ in the synagogues" (Luke 11:43 NIV)
4 A south wind precedes _____ weather (Luke 12:55)
5 A coin (Mark 12:42 NIV)
6 "The _____ is the lamp of the body" (Matthew 6:22 NIV)
9 Used to startle or frighten
11 The Philistines made "five gold _____" as part of a guilt offering (1 Samuel 6:4 NIV)
14 "A strong wind was blowing and the waters grew _____" (John 6:18 NIV)
16 "We are to God the _____ of Christ" (2 Corinthians 2:15 NIV)
18 "_____ king of Jarmuth" (Joshua 10:3 NIV)
20 Industrious
22 Formerly Persia
24 Rearrange the letters of the second highest voice part in a 4-part chorus
26 Final destination of an ambulance (abbr.)
28 "One beka _____ person, that is, half a shekel" (Exodus 38:26)
30 "Why am I _____ favored" (Luke 1:43)

by John Hudson Tiner

3

ACROSS

1 The son of Asaph, the recorder (Isaiah 36:22)
5 Too
9 "The _____ tree" (Joel 1:12)
14 Father (Galatians 4:6)
15 Opposite of *front*
16 "_____ up a child" (Proverbs 22:6)
17 "All the hills shall _____" (Amos 9:13)
18 Uncovered
19 Weary
20 A quality that makes one able to be tricked
23 Detest
24 Tiny insect
25 Female sheep
28 Enticed
31 A son of Noah
34 Jesus is the prince of this
36 King of Assyria (2 Kings 15:19)
37 Opposite of *despair*
38 "Pitched beside the well of _____" (Judges 7:1)
39 Likely
40 "For as _____ was three days" (Matthew 12:40)
41 Always
42 "And _____ lay at his feet until the morning" (Ruth 3:14)
43 "_____, and Accad, and Calneh" (Genesis 10:10)
44 Color of blood
45 "O thou _____ among women?" (Song of Solomon 6:1)
48 Exclamation of affirmation
49 Transgression
50 "The women. . .brought that which they had _____" (Exodus 35:25)
52 "If the _____ came to thee" (Obadiah 1:5)
59 Bellybutton
60 Charge
61 "Collar of my _____" (Job 30:18)
63 Make a correction

64 "Of _____, the family of Arodites" (Numbers 26:17)
65 Jesus' grandfather (Luke 3:23)
66 "He that ministered to my _____" (Philippians 2:25)
67 To refuse to take responsibility
68 "As he saith also in _____" (Romans 9:25)

DOWN

1 Like jelly
2 Ruth's son (Ruth 4:13–17)
3 Strong and _____
4 Break out of a shell
5 Paarai was one (2 Samuel 23:35)
6 "To open before him the two _____ gates" (Isaiah 45:1)
7 "Through faith also _____ herself received strength to conceive seed" (Hebrews 11:11)
8 "The heads of _____ and Zeeb" (Judges 7:25)
9 Pay attention to
10 "Put my finger into the _____ of the nails" (John 20:25)
11 Cut back
12 Untruths
13 Opposite of *begins*
21 Comforted
22 Eliasaph's father (Numbers 3:24)
25 A son of Midian (Genesis 25:4)
26 "They that _____ networks" (Isaiah 19:9)
27 "_____ nor sown" (Deuteronomy 21:4)
29 In the _____ Room
30 Slice
31 Bee product
32 "Kings of armies did flee _____" (Psalm 68:12)
33 "Their dwelling was from _____. . . unto Sephar" (Genesis 10:30)
35 The first First and Second of the NT (abbr.)
37 "Ye shall point out for you mount _____" (Numbers 34:7)

by N. Teri Grottke

39 Son of Abdiel (1 Chronicles 5:15)
40 Ishmael's son (1 Chronicles 1:31)
42 "They _____ his praise"
    (Psalm 106:12)
45 "Who have reaped down your
    _____" (James 5:4)
46 Paseah's father (1 Chronicles 4:12)
47 "For he shall make even a _____
    riddance of all them"
    (Zephaniah 1:18)
49 "The night is far _____, the day is
    at hand" (Romans 13:12)
51 A pharaoh of Egypt
    (2 Chronicles 35:20)
52 Chew a bone
53 "In _____ was there a voice"
    (Matthews 2:18)
54 City in Egypt (Hosea 10:8)
55 "_____ the Canaanite"
    (Numbers 21:1)

56 Type of weed
57 Two or more deer
58 "_____ of his patrimony"
    (Deuteronomy 18:8)
62 Bind

4

God's Greatest Gift

This is how God showed his love among us:
He sent his one and only Son into the world that we might live through him.

1 JOHN 4:9 NIV

ACROSS

1 "To die in the _____"
   (1 Corinthians 4:9 NIV)
6 "Even as _____ obeyed Abraham"
   (1 Peter 3:6)
10 Highland topper, for short
13 Anklebone
14 "For he had _____" (Acts 18:18)
   (2 words)
15 "And they returned _____ again"
   (Acts 21:6)
16 Start of a **VERSE** of gratitude to the
   Lord (2 Corinthians 9:15) (4 words)
19 "That they may _____ whole month"
   (Numbers 11:21) (2 words)
20 "Enlarge the place of thy _____"
   (Isaiah 54:2)
21 "Let us _____"
   (Exodus 14:12)
22 "Honest" politician of old
23 Part 2 of the **VERSE**
24 "How _____ art thou?" (Genesis 47:8)
25 It may show you the way to go
26 "And of such as _____ cattle"
   (Genesis 4:20)
28 Part 3 of the **VERSE**
31 "Eat nothing containing _____"
   (Exodus 13:3 NIV)
34 "Sheba and _____ shall offer gifts"
   (Psalm 72:10)
35 "And Peter said, _____ am not"
   (Luke 22:58) (2 words)
36 Part 4 and end of the **VERSE**
   (2 words)
39 Does yard work
40 Actress Hayworth
41 Ancient Greek city
42 Enzyme ending
43 "And Jesus went _____ him"
   (Mark 5:24)
44 "And the _____ saw the angel of the
   LORD" (Numbers 22:23)
45 "Like a crane _____ swallow"
   (Isaiah 38:14) (2 words)
46 Agent (abbr.)

47 Day-care denizen
50 "To sharpen every man his _____"
   (1 Samuel 13:20)
53 Scarlet's home
55 "And said, _____ it, O LORD"
   (Jeremiah 11:5) (2 words)
56 Start of the **GIFT** in 2 Corinthians
   9:15 (John 3:16) (3 words)
59 "The daughter of _____ the Hittite"
   (Genesis 26:34)
60 "The high hills _____ refuge for the
   wild goats" (Psalm 104:18) (2 words)
61 "And in three days I will _____ it up"
   (John 2:19)
62 End of the **GIFT**
63 "I will _____ you with filth"
   (Nahum 3:6 NIV)
64 "_____ the friends by name"
   (3 John 1:14)

DOWN

1 Where the queen often is around 4:00
   p.m. (2 words)
2 The faithful harlot (Joshua 2:1–24)
3 Buoy up
4 "The son of _____ young man"
   (Exodus 33:11) (2 words)
5 "Ye know not what ye _____"
   (Mark 10:38)
6 Cavalry sword
7 "From the plain of _____" (Amos 1:5)
8 "Shoot your arrows and _____ them"
   (Psalm 144:6 NIV)
9 Grain spikelet
10 "_____ by day and night"
   (Exodus 13:21) (2 words)
11 Josiah's father (2 Chronicles 33:25)
12 "In the first year of Darius the _____"
   (Daniel 11:1)
15 "_____ not thy peace" (Psalm 109:1)
17 Greek portico
18 "The _____ of the bricks"
   (Exodus 5:8)
23 "Children, their _____ is the sword"
   (Job 27:14 NIV)

by David K. Shortess

24 Famous DC office
25 "The cruel venom of _____ "
    (Deuteronomy 32:33)
26 "The _____ in the desert"
    (Jeremiah 17:6)
27 "_____, Father"
    (Galatians 4:6)
28 Secretary of State under Pres. Reagan
29 The scoop, for short
30 "The great prostitute, who _____ on
    many waters" (Revelation 17:1 NIV)
31 City on the Colorado
32 Son of Seth (Genesis 5:6)
33 "_____ forgive our debtors"
    (Matthew 6:12) (2 words)
34 Short, light drama
35 Department heads (abbr.)
37 La Scala highlight
38 "In the land of Nod, on the _____ of
    Eden" (Genesis 4:16)
43 Architect of London's Saint Paul's
    Cathedral

44 Captured king of the Amalekites
    (1 Samuel 15:8)
45 "In any tree, _____ the ground"
    (Deuteronomy 22:6) (2 words)
46 "And _____ their wit's end"
    (Psalm 107:27) (2 words)
47 "We've come _____ you up"
    (Judges 15:12 NIV) (2 words)
48 More than chubby
49 Belief
50 "_____ the right one for me"
    (Judges 14:3 NIV)
51 Hawaiian port
52 "On them, _____ us at the
    beginning" (Acts 11:15) (2 words)
53 Hiram's kingdom (2 Samuel 5:11)
54 Seth was his stead (Genesis 4:25)
55 "And I will give him the morning
    _____" (Revelation 2:28)
57 "Gourds his _____ full"
    (2 Kings 4:39)
58 Kin to com and edu

5

ACROSS

1 "We cannot speak unto thee _____ or good" (Genesis 24:50)
4 Eve was made from Adam's
7 Chop (arch.)
10 "Tower of _____" (Genesis 35:21)
12 Haniel's father (1 Chronicles 7:39)
14 "_____ of Judah" (2 Samuel 6:2)
16 Son of Zerah (1 Chronicles 2:6)
17 King Hoshea's father (2 Kings 15:30)
18 Asher didn't drive out the inhabitants of this town (Judges 1:31)
19 "Shimei, and _____, and the mighty men" (1 Kings 1:8)
20 "Hamath, Berothah, _____, which is between the border" (Ezekiel 47:16)
22 Appendage
25 "_____ king of Hamath" (2 Samuel 8:9)
26 Right hand (abbr.)
29 "As a thread of _____ is broken" (Judges 16:9)
31 Commerce
36 Be in debt to (arch.)
38 Highly respected
41 "Rinnah, Ben-hanan, and _____" (1 Chronicles 4:20)
42 Untruth
43 "Shilshah, and Ithran, and _____" (1 Chronicles 7:37)
45 "And Kattath, and _____, and Shimron" (Joshua 19:15)
47 Below
48 A son of Gad (Genesis 46:16)
49 Luke (abbr., var.)
51 "_____ down here" (Ruth 4:1)
52 Battle where Goliath's brother was slain (2 Samuel 21:19)
55 Peleg's son (Genesis 11:18)
57 "And _____, and Zilthai, and Eliel" (1 Chronicles 8:20)
61 Slice
64 "_____ it, and smote the Philistine in his forehead" (1 Samuel 17:49)

65 Had intimate relations (arch.)
68 Son of Dishan (Genesis 36:28)
70 "As free, and not _____ your liberty" (1 Peter 2:16)
71 "Land from _____ to the wilderness" (Isaiah 16:1)
72 Green citrus
73 Color of blood
74 "To meet the Lord in the _____" (1 Thessalonians 4:17)
75 Became acquainted

DOWN

1 Sleeping place
2 Twelfth Hebrew month (Esther 9:1)
3 "Even _____ to die" (Romans 5:7)
4 "For ye tithe mint and _____" (Luke 11:42)
5 Sick
6 "By the _____ of God they perish" (Job 4:9)
7 "Helkath, and _____, and Beten" (Joshua 19:25)
8 A son of Shem (Genesis 10:22)
9 Spider's art
11 Revile
13 A son of Jehiel (1 Chronicles 9:37)
14 Barrier
15 "Against Jerusalem, _____" (Ezekiel 26:2)
21 "That shall _____ thee" (Habakkuk 2:7)
23 A son of Helah (1 Chronicles 4:7)
24 Opposite of *stay*
26 Decay
27 Esau and Jacob were these
28 One of the wives of Ashur, the father of Tekoa (1 Chronicles 4:5)
30 Water source
32 Correction
33 So be it
34 Works
35 "Og the king of Bashan, which dwelt at Astaroth in _____" (Deuteronomy 1:4)

by N. Teri Grottke

37 Elihu's father (1 Samuel 1:1)
39 "The children of _____" (Nehemiah 7:47)
40 "_____ me whether ye sold the land for so much?" (Acts 5:8)
44 Are (arch.)
46 "As the trees of _____ aloes" (Numbers 24:6)
50 Abram's birthplace
53 Strong trees
54 Moza's son (1 Chronicles 8:37)
56 "Even unto Ithiel and _____" (Proverbs 30:1)
57 Otherwise
58 "Have _____ a wound" (Obadiah 1:7)
59 Motel
60 Produced by a chicken
62 Thummim's partner (Deuteronomy 33:8)

63 Gentle
64 A temple gate (2 Kings 11:6)
66 Hophni's father (1 Samuel 4:4)
67 Fight between countries
69 Rope web

6

ACROSS

1 "_____ hath forsaken me" (2 Timothy 4:10)
5 "The _____ looks of man shall be humbled" (Isaiah 2:11)
8 "Sinners shall be converted _____ thee" (Psalm 51:13)
10 Factory
11 "Came unto Caesarea to salute _____" (Acts 25:13)
13 "The three _____ followed Saul" (1 Samuel 17:14)
16 Budge
17 Abdomen
19 Ardent
21 "Abimelech took an _____ in his hand" (Judges 9:48)
23 Dine
25 "Eber, Peleg, _____" (1 Chronicles 1:25)
26 _____ loving care
29 "Consider the _____ of the field" (Matthew 6:28)
31 "I will settle you after your old _____" (Ezekiel 36:11)
33 "Thou _____ me against him" (Job 2:3)
34 "The _____ shall inherit the earth" (Psalm 37:11)
35 "The land is as the garden of _____" (Joel 2:3)
36 "Which was the son of _____" (Luke 3:35)
39 "Shall we be consumed with _____" (Numbers 17:13)
41 "And fought against _____" (2 Kings 12:17)
45 Cainan's father (Genesis 5:9)
46 "Seven times a day do I praise _____" (Psalm 119:164)
47 "By faith _____ was translated" (Hebrews 11:5)
48 "Also I shook my _____" (Nehemiah 5:13)
50 "Nabal did _____ his sheep" (1 Samuel 25:4)
51 Level
52 "House of Millo, which goeth down to _____" (2 Kings 12:20)
54 "Glean _____ of corn" (Ruth 2:2)
55 Legislature
57 Atonement
59 "Shuthelah: of _____, the family" (Numbers 26:36)
60 "They gave them in full _____ to the king" (1 Samuel 18:27)
61 "All _____, and all men of valour" (Judges 3:29)
62 "Thou _____ make me hope" (Psalm 22:9)

DOWN

2 Meditate
3 "Go to the _____, thou sluggard" (Proverbs 6:6)
4 Uproot
5 "And the _____ of the valleys" (Song of Solomon 2:1)
6 Antique
7 "The people _____ upon the spoil" (1 Samuel 14:32)
9 "As he saith also in _____" (Romans 9:25)
10 Liquefy
11 "The little _____, that spoil the vines" (Song of Solomon 2:15)
12 "That one _____ happeneth to them all" (Ecclesiastes 2:14)
14 "Their inheritance was unto _____" (Joshua 19:10)
15 Timber
16 Spouse
18 Flog
20 "Whose mouths _____ be stopped" (Titus 1:11)
22 "The same measure that ye _____ withal" (Luke 6:38)
24 Dwell
27 Natives of Damascus
28 "The _____ and flags shall wither" (Isaiah 19:6)
29 House

by Tonya Vilhauer

30 "Thy days may be _____ in the land" (Deuteronomy 25:15)

32 Firmament

33 "The young _____ from their music" (Lamentations 5:14)

36 "Of Gad the king's _____" (2 Chronicles 29:25)

37 "_____ and Caiaphas being the high priests" (Luke 3:2)

38 Free

40 Nathan's son (2 Samuel 23:36)

42 Leading

43 "Being mindful of thy _____" (2 Timothy 1:4)

44 "Restore all that was _____" (2 Kings 8:6)

48 "Though ye have _____ among the pots" (Psalm 68:13)

49 "Cast him into the _____ of ground" (2 Kings 9:26)

52 Tarry

53 "Alammelech, and _____, and Misheal" (Joshua 19:26)

56 "Thou _____ cursed above all cattle" (Genesis 3:14)

58 "Samuel arose and went to _____" (1 Samuel 3:5)

7

ACROSS

1 Repulsive
5 "By his name _____" (Psalm 68:4)
8 A son of Benjamin (Genesis 46:21)
12 Goods
13 "_____ there yet the treasures" (Micah 6:10)
14 Paradise
15 "He built _____, and restored it to Judah" (2 Chronicles 26:2)
16 "Ye shall point out for you mount _____" (Numbers 34:7)
17 He forsook Paul (2 Timothy 4:10)
19 Joshua's father (Exodus 33:11)
20 Asked (arch.) (Ruth 3:6)
22 A false god of Shechem (Judges 9:46)
23 "Otherwise it is of no strength at all while the _____ liveth" (Hebrews 9:17)
25 Abram's birthplace
26 "God created _____ heaven" (Genesis 1:1)
27 Single
28 Sadoc's father (Matthew 1:14)
30 "Go to the _____" (Proverbs 6:6)
33 Resounded
36 A son of Jehaleleel (1 Chronicles 4:16)
40 "I will make thy _____ brass" (Micah 4:13)
43 This name is taken from the Greek *deuteronomion* (abbr.)
44 Listened
45 "Argob and _____" (2 Kings 15:25)
46 Female sheep
48 Insane
49 What you do with clothes
51 A king of Midian (Numbers 31:8)
54 "_____ that ye refuse not" (Hebrews 12:25)
57 Astatine (sym.)
58 By oneself
63 "Weeping may _____ for a night" (Psalm 30:5)
65 "So they _____ it up" (Micah 7:3)
66 Buzzing stinger
67 "He...is _____ than an infidel" (1 Timothy 5:8)
68 Opposite of *good*
69 A Harodite guard of David's (2 Samuel 23:25)
71 Prophet
72 Before (poet.)
73 "The horse and his _____ hath he thrown into the sea" (Exodus 15:1)
74 Snake sound
75 Saul's grandfather (1 Chronicles 8:33)
76 "They shall _____ like torches" (Nahum 2:4)

DOWN

1 "Ye are of more _____ than many sparrows" (Luke 12:7)
2 Put these in the fire
3 Allow
4 Dishon's son (Genesis 36:26)
5 Jeshishai's father (1 Chronicles 5:14)
6 These cities are forsaken (Isaiah 17:2)
7 "_____ mouth is smoother than oil" (Proverbs 5:3)
8 "Ajalon, and _____, and Shocho" (2 Chronicles 28:18)
9 "Mahli, and _____, and Jeremoth" (1 Chronicles 23:23)
10 Release from the guilt or penalty of sin
11 Shamgar's father (Judges 3:31)
12 "Their sound _____ into all the earth" (Romans 10:18)
18 "And _____ lay at his feet until the morning" (Ruth 3:14)
21 "_____, Hizkijah, Azzur" (Nehemiah 10:17)
22 A son of Nahor (Genesis 22:21–23)
24 Turn over (abbr.)
28 A chill
29 "But the wheat and the _____ were not smitten" (Exodus 9:32)

by N. Teri Grottke

30 "Against Jerusalem, _____"
   (Ezekiel 26:2)
31 "_____ was an hair of"
   (Daniel 3:27)
32 "When _____ king"
   (2 Samuel 8:9)
34 "Arad, and _____"
   (1 Chronicles 8:15)
35 Opposite of *old*
37 A male sheep
38 "Helez the Paltite, _____"
   (2 Samuel 23:26)
39 Increase
41 Not many
42 Sheep clippers
47 "Land from _____ to" (Isaiah 16:1)
50 Partook
52 Venomous snakes
53 Teletypewriter (abbr.)
54 To stitch

55 "Adam, Sheth, _____"
   (1 Chronicles 1:1)
56 "Og the king of Bashan, which
   dwelt at Astaroth in _____"
   (Deuteronomy 1:4)
58 Take an oath (biblical sp.)
59 "Set in _____ the things that are
   wanting" (Titus 1:5)
60 Live with
61 A prince of Midian (Joshua 13:21)
62 365 days
64 Makes use of
68 "Zechariah, _____"
   (1 Chronicles 15:18)
70 Untruth

8

A Comforting Promise

*"And surely I am with you always,
to the very end of the age."*

MATTHEW 28:20 NIV

ACROSS

1 "Into the _____ of fire"
(Revelation 20:14)

5 "Respond to their _____ and heal
them" (Isaiah 19:22 NIV)

10 "The LORD _____ great victory
for all" (1 Samuel 19:5 NIV)
(2 words)

14 Ireland to Yeats

15 Serf

16 "These things saith the _____"
(Revelation 3:14)

17 "And what, the son of my _____?"
(Proverbs 31:2)

18 "And if a man shall _____ pit"
(Exodus 21:33) (2 words)

19 *The Forsyte* _____ (PBS miniseries)

20 Start of a portion of a **VERSE** from
Hebrews 13:5 (3 words)

22 "Went before _____, till it came and
stood" (Matthew 2:9)

23 Greek market

24 **VERSE**, cont'd from 20 Across

25 Caniff's Canyon

28 Lukewarm

31 **VERSE**, cont'd from 24 Across

32 Pruninghooks' precursors (Micah 4:3)

34 "In purple now lie on _____ heaps"
(Lamentations 4:5 NIV)

37 Familiar e-mail server (abbr.)

38 Mimic

39 An unclean animal
(Leviticus 11:29 NIV)

40 "And it shall be as the chased
_____" (Isaiah 13:14)

41 Word with school or station

42 Thin and tall

44 "They did _____ me" (Psalm 35:15)

45 "Choice fruits, with _____ and nard"
(Song of Songs 4:13 NIV)

46 "To sharpen every man his _____"
(1 Samuel 13:20)

47 Auras

50 Count of jazz

53 Decorative pitcher

54 **VERSE**, cont'd from 31 Across
(2 words)

59 "The rod of Aaron was among their
_____" (Numbers 17:6)

60 Shallot kin

61 Epochs

62 Dust bowl victim

63 "They cast four anchors out of the
_____" (Acts 27:29)

64 Follows the book of John

65 "And lay them down in their _____"
(Psalm 104:22)

66 Like Swiss cheese

67 End of **VERSE**, cont'd from 54 Across

DOWN

1 Simeon's close younger brother
(Genesis 29:33–34)

2 "And _____ of new timber"
(Ezra 6:4) (2 words)

3 Fuzzy brown fruit

4 "I will _____ you to your enemies"
(Jeremiah 15:14 NIV)

5 LP player, briefly

6 "But he was a _____" (2 Kings 5:1)

7 "Was it a sin for me to lower myself in
order to _____ you by preaching"
(2 Corinthians 11:7 NIV)

8 "Ho, such _____!" (Ruth 4:1)
(2 words)

9 "There shall come a _____ out of
Jacob" (Numbers 24:17)

10 "The field is _____" (Joel 1:10)

11 Cow town in Nebraska

12 Judean desert (Judges 1:16 NIV)

13 "And he had _____ written, that no
man knew" (Revelation 19:12)
(2 words)

21 Not sml. or med. (abbr.)

24 "This is the _____ of the Israelites"
(1 Chronicles 27:1 NIV)

by David K. Shortess

25 "He prophesies, his own parents will
_____ him" (Zechariah 13:3 NIV)
26 "Surely _____ art my bone and my
flesh" (Genesis 29:14)
27 Scaleless fishes
29 British rank below a marquis
30 "But when ye _____" (Matthew 6:7)
32 "Goliath, of Gath, whose height
was six cubits and a _____"
(1 Samuel 17:4)
33 Quaker colonizer
34 "The Jews who lived in that _____"
(Acts 16:3 NIV)
35 "Though you _____ like the eagle"
(Obadiah 1:4 NIV)
36 "Master, it is good for us to be
_____" (Mark 9:5)
38 "By Christ Jesus throughout all
_____" (Ephesians 3:21)
43 Mary's angelic messenger
(Luke 1:26–27)

44 "I am a God, I sit in _____ of God"
(Ezekiel 28:2) (2 words)
45 "Some trust in chariots, and some in
_____" (Psalm 20:7)
46 "And I said unto him, _____, thou
knowest" (Revelation 7:14)
47 "The leaven of _____" (Mark 8:15)
48 "So I _____" (Genesis 41:21)
49 "They are _____ with joy and
gladness" (Psalm 45:15 NIV)
(2 words)
51 "For _____ the harvest" (Isaiah 18:5)
52 Cher's erstwhile partner
54 Eat a snack
55 "And pass _____ Zin"
(Numbers 34:4) (2 words)
56 Part of a foot
57 *Kiss Me*, _____
58 *They*, in Roma

9

ACROSS

1 "_____ of blue" (Exodus 39:31)
5 "The children of _____"
(Nehemiah 7:58)
10 "Cheeks, and the _____"
(Deuteronomy 18:3)
13 A great distance
14 Thief
15 Galatians, _____, Philippians,
Colossians (abbr.)
16 Seir was of this nationality
(Genesis 36:20)
18 "Tappuah, and _____"
(Joshua 15:34)
19 "Shimei, and _____" (1 Kings 1:8)
20 King of Damascus
(2 Corinthians 11:32)
21 Third book (abbr.)
22 Opposite of *slow*
23 Places of very little rain
25 Forgive
27 Observe (arch.)
29 "_____, and Idbash"
(1 Chronicles 4:3)
32 Sack
35 "Down in _____" (Acts 27:27)
37 "For he oft refreshed me, and was
not ashamed of my _____"
(2 Timothy 1:16)
38 "_____, and Shema"
(Joshua 15:26)
40 A son of Bela (1 Chronicles 7:7)
41 Greek form of *Sinai* (Acts 7:30)
42 "And Hazarshual, and _____, and
Azem" (Joshua 19:3)
44 Biggest part of the hands
47 "All these were _____ of war"
(Judges 20:17)
48 A Harodite guard of David's
(2 Samuel 23:25)
49 "To abstain from _____"
(1 Timothy 4:3)
51 Phaltie's father (2 Samuel 3:15)
54 Joseph's brothers called him this
(Genesis 37:17–19)
58 Ruth's second husband (Ruth 4:13)

60 "After that the full corn in the
_____" (Mark 4:28)
62 "Will _____ them as silver"
(Zechariah 13:9)
63 Utilize
64 Ahab's father (1 Kings 16:28)
65 Chooses
66 Large lake
67 Jumped
69 You (arch.)
70 Zephaniah's son (Zechariah 6:14)
71 Ate in style
72 "The linen _____ at a price"
(1 Kings 10:28)

DOWN

1 Jahath's son (1 Chronicles 4:2)
2 Before (arch.)
3 Concerns
4 Descendants of Eri
5 Female version of Joe
6 Cain's victim
7 Saul's first cousin (1 Samuel 14:50)
8 "Not to _____ thee" (Ruth 1:16)
9 Attached to the shoulder
10 "Go up against the land of _____"
(Jeremiah 50:21)
11 Larger than monkeys
12 Bit (arch.)
14 This is what the Jews did on the
Sabbath
17 A son of Micah
(1 Chronicles 8:35)
22 Community in New York, _____
Eddy
24 Peel
26 Contemporary of Hosea and Isaiah
(abbr.)
28 A king of Tyre (1 Chronicles 14:1)
30 Belonging to me
31 "And Ahijah, Hanan, _____"
(Nehemiah 10:26)
32 "The _____ lying in a manger"
(Luke 2:16)
33 "Shelesh, and _____"
(1 Chronicles 7:35)

by N. Teri Grottke

34 "He asked whether the man were a
   _____" (Luke 23:6)
36 Was ill
39 "The son of Dekar, in _____"
   (1 Kings 4:9)
43 "Between Bethel and _____"
   (Genesis 13:3)
45 Damaged
46 "The bow of _____" (Job 20:24)
50 "Peace and _____; then sudden
   destruction cometh"
   (1 Thessalonians 5:3)
52 A son of Joseph (Luke 3:26)
53 A brother of Abram (Genesis 11:26)
55 Mephibosheth's son (2 Samuel 9:12)
56 Come in
57 "And _____ between"
   (Genesis 10:12)
58 "An angel of the Lord in a flame of
   fire in a _____" (Acts 7:30)

59 "As he saith also in _____"
   (Romans 9:25)
61 "Harvest is _____" (Joel 3:13)
64 Elderly
68 An altar (Joshua 22:34)

Spy to the Promised Land

ACROSS

1 Agreed with Joshua that the people could take the land (Numbers 13:30 NIV)

5 Joshua, Caleb, and ten others went into Canaan to _____ out the land (Deuteronomy 1:22–23 NIV)

8 A son of Jether (1 Chronicles 7:38 NIV)

9 "Iron is taken from the earth, and copper is smelted from _____" (Job 28:2 NIV)

10 Moses gave Hoshea the _____ Joshua (Numbers 13:16 NIV)

11 First human to die (Genesis 4:8 NIV)

12 Those afraid to enter the Promised Land said, "Wouldn't it _____ better for us to go back to Egypt?" (Numbers 14:3 NIV)

13 Because Caleb followed God wholeheartedly, _____ descendants would inherit the Promised Land (Numbers 14:24 NIV)

14 "See what the land _____ like" (Numbers 13:18 NIV)

15 The LORD said, "Send some _____ to explore Canaan" (Numbers 13:2 NIV)

16 Negative

17 The clock in London is Big _____

18 The frightened spies said that all the people they _____ were of great size (Numbers 13:32)

19 Gorillas and orangutans are examples

21 Book that follows Leviticus (abbr.)

22 The manna stopped the very day that the Israelites _____ the produce of Canaan (Joshua 5:11–12 NIV)

23 "Jesus _____ many who had diseases, sicknesses and evil spirits" (Luke 7:21 NIV)

25 Name of the land God gave the Israelites (Numbers 13:2 NIV)

26 Caleb said, "_____ here I am today, eighty-five years old!" (Joshua 14:10 NIV)

DOWN

1 Caleb said, "We _____ certainly do it" (Numbers 13:30 NIV)

2 People of the Arabia peninsula

3 "The blind receive sight, the _____ walk" (Matthew 11:5 NIV)

4 Barium (sym.)

5 Loud weeping

6 Before

7 Color between orange and green; slang for being cowardly

11 A southernmost town of the tribe of Judah in the Negev (Joshua 15:32 NIV)

13 Female chicken

14 God made an oath to Abraham, _____, and Jacob (Genesis 50:24 NIV)

15 *My* (Fr.)

16 Numbers 13:4–15 lists the _____ of the men sent to explore the land

17 Joshua "had _____ Moses' aide since youth" (Numbers 11:28 NIV)

18 Jehoiada assigned a third of the men to the _____ Gate (2 Kings 11:6 NIV)

20 Organization for parents and teachers

21 Joshua was the son of _____ (Numbers 13:16 NIV)

23 Circa (abbr.)

24 "What kind of towns _____ they live in?" (Numbers 13:19 NIV)

by John Hudson Tiner

11

ACROSS

1 Prison
5 Told
9 A son of Ephraim (Numbers 26:35)
14 Son of Naum (Luke 3:25)
15 Haniel's father
   (1 Chronicles 7:39)
16 Idol
17 Market
18 "Thou shalt not _____ the harlot"
   (Hosea 3:3)
19 "A _____ of sedition" (Acts 24:5)
20 Guilty or not guilty
21 "The tongue can no man tame; it is
   an unruly evil, full of deadly _____"
   (James 3:8)
23 An altar (Joshua 22:34)
24 "I _____ not" (Luke 17:9)
26 Opposite of *near*
28 Rhymers
30 The second Hebrew month
   (1 Kings 6:1)
32 Hearing organs
36 Attached to the shoulder
37 The seventeenth order of the
   priesthood (1 Chronicles 24:15)
39 A chill
40 Look
42 He forsook Paul (2 Timothy 4:10)
44 Little color
45 "The fourth to _____"
   (1 Chronicles 25:11)
46 A son of Caleb (1 Chronicles 2:18)
48 "Hundred and _____ years old"
   (Joshua 24:29)
49 Chaos
50 Hophni's father (1 Samuel 4:4)
51 "Nevertheless the men _____ hard"
   (Jonah 1:13)
53 A dreidel is a type of _____
55 Apples grow on this
56 Beryllium (sym.)
58 "_____ with the villages thereof"
   (2 Chronicles 28:18)
61 "_____, Hizkijah, Azzur"
   (Nehemiah 10:17)

65 "And Hazarshual, and _____, and
   Azem" (Joshua 19:3)
67 What the wind did at the parting of
   the Red Sea
68 Grapes grow here
69 "Mint and _____" (Matthew 23:23)
70 Comfort
71 Esau's father-in-law (Genesis 26:34)
72 "Ziha and _____ were over the
   Nethinims" (Nehemiah 11:21)
73 Colored
74 "Give thyself no _____"
   (Lamentations 2:18)

DOWN

1 "And compassed the _____ of the
   saints about" (Revelation 20:9)
2 "Imna, and Shelesh, and _____"
   (1 Chronicles 7:35)
3 To pierce with horns
4 "Who remembered us in our low
   _____" (Psalm 136:23)
5 "For he _____ his brethren would
   have understood" (Acts 7:25)
6 Permit
7 "_____ the Ahohite"
   (1 Chronicles 11:29)
8 Weeks are made of these
9 Amalek's mother (Genesis 36:12)
10 American Maritime Officers (abbr.)
11 Has ownership
12 Old
13 Saul's grandfather
   (1 Chronicles 8:33)
22 "And king Ahaz cut _____ the
   borders of the bases" (2 Kings 16:17)
25 Right hand (3-letter abbr.)
27 Harvest
28 Reward
29 Manna was measured in _____
   (Exodus 16:16–18)
30 The son of Salu (Numbers 25:14)
31 Enoch's son (Genesis 4:18)
33 A gem on the third row of the
   ephod (Exodus 28:19)
34 Reigned

by N. Teri Grottke

35 "For thee have I _____"
   (Genesis 7:1)
36 "And _____, and Pharah"
   (Joshua 18:23)
38 "Yea, what _____, yea, what
   revenge!" (2 Corinthians 7:11)
41 Know (arch.)
43 Grieved
47 Greek form of *Noah*
   (Matthew 24:38)
50 One of Paul's churches in Asia
   (abbr.)
52 "I have cut off like a _____ my life"
   (Isaiah 38:12)
54 "And Moses called _____ the son
   of Nun Jehoshua" (Numbers 13:16)
55 "Thought on _____ things"
   (Matthew 1:20)
56 A mighty man of David
   (2 Samuel 23:36)

57 Belonging to Eli
59 Ruth's son (Ruth 4:13–17)
60 Potter's material
62 "Thou also, son of man, take thee a
   _____" (Ezekiel 4:1)
63 Seth's son (Genesis 4:26)
64 Lease
65 Sack
66 Type of snake

12

One of Another

To the chief Musician, A Psalm of David the servant of the Lord.

PREFACE TO PSALM 36

ACROSS

1 "Each man _____ a sword to his side" (Exodus 32:27 NIV)
6 "The love of many shall wax _____" (Matthew 24:12)
10 Soften up
14 "He is able to _____" (Daniel 4:37)
15 "The ruler of that _____, saw her" (Genesis 34:2 NIV)
16 "Then Jacob _____ up" (Genesis 31:17)
17 Craze
18 "Set me as a _____ upon thine heart" (Song of Solomon 8:6)
19 "These _____ smoke in my nose" (Isaiah 65:5) (2 words)
20 **THESE OF THAT:** Oreb and Zeeb (Judges 8:3) (3 words)
23 "Now _____ was very old" (1 Samuel 2:22)
24 "And _____ the sacrifices of the dead" (Psalm 106:28)
25 "Ye shall in no _____ enter" (Matthew 5:20)
29 Gold purity units
32 Colonel's subordinate (abbr.)
35 "In the house of the _____" (Ezra 6:1)
37 Nobody won the game. It was _____ (2 words)
38 Anger
39 **THIS OF THOSE:** Abram's old home (Genesis 11:31) (4 words)
43 Ike's battleground (abbr.)
44 "And Ahab _____, and went to Jezreel" (1 Kings 18:45)
45 Jean Sebelius's countrymen
46 "Also I shook my _____" (Nehemiah 5:13)
47 Not caring about right or wrong

50 Italian noble family
51 Jeanne d'Arc, e.g. (abbr.)
52 "The _____ of Joppa" (Ezra 3:7)
54 **THESE OF HIM:** The Baptist's followers (Luke 7:18) (3 words)
63 "He went up _____ a mountain" (Matthew 5:1)
64 Seine feeder
65 Fibula's partner
66 "In the land of Nod, on the east of _____" (Genesis 4:16)
67 Soaks flax
68 "Horns of ivory and _____" (Ezekiel 27:15)
69 "The burden of _____" (Isaiah 23:1)
70 Retirement accounts (abbr.)
71 "The paper _____ by the brooks" (Isaiah 19:7)

DOWN

1 Cornmeal mush
2 Ski lift
3 "Yet they _____: have not spoken to them" (Jeremiah 23:21) (2 words)
4 "_____ water face" (Proverbs 27:19) (2 words)
5 "When I come again in _____" (Judges 8:9)
6 "And _____, out of the ivory palaces" (Psalm 45:8)
7 Nabisco's black and white treat
8 "His _____ also shall not wither" (Psalm 1:3)
9 "Titus unto _____" (2 Timothy 4:10)
10 "And as many as _____ by sea" (Revelation 18:17)
11 "Shaphat the son of _____" (Numbers 13:5)

by David K. Shortess

12 "There was _____ of glass"
   (Revelation 4:6) (2 words)
13 "But _____ incorruptible"
   (1 Corinthians 9:25) (2 words)
21 Deer kin
22 "And of the truth _____"
   (3 John 1:12)
25 "Wrath is _____, and anger is
   outrageous" (Proverbs 27:4)
26 It connects to the heart
27 Single-masted sailboat
28 Folklore prankster
30 Black snake
31 He or she finisher (3-letter abbr.)
32 Bearings
33 "Then both the new maketh
   _____" (Luke 5:36) (2 words)
34 Obed's son (Ruth 4:22)
36 Low cloud layers
40 A ship's base (2 words)

41 Tokyo, once
42 "Sick, and ready to _____"
   (Luke 7:2)
48 Estimate value
49 Former Dodger manager Durocher
51 British biscuit
53 "And with your seed _____ you"
   (Genesis 9:9)
54 "And for his _____, there was a
   continual diet" (Jeremiah 52:34)
55 The "500"
56 British money (abbr.)
57 "But his _____ shall not be so"
   (Isaiah 16:6)
58 ¿Como _____ usted?
59 Agree
60 Poignant reed
61 "Naphtali is a _____ let loose"
   (Genesis 49:21)
62 No votes

13

ACROSS
1 "One day is with the Lord as a thousand _____" (2 Peter 3:8)
6 "_____ against the fenced cities" (Zephaniah 1:16)
11 Jehoshaphat's father (2 Chronicles 20:31–32)
14 Phares's son (Luke 3:33)
15 A city on Crete (Acts 27:7–8)
16 Opposite of *women*
17 "In whatsoever _____" (Philippians 4:11)
18 Esarhaddon was king here (Ezra 4:2)
19 Became acquainted
20 "All _____, and all men of valour" (Judges 3:29)
22 Snake sound
23 Metal pegs
26 "_____ the devil, and he will flee from you" (James 4:7)
29 "There went out a _____ from Caesar Augustus" (Luke 2:1)
30 Noah was this person (2 Peter 2:5)
31 "_____, and Calneh, in the land of Shinar" (Genesis 10:10)
32 Uncontrolled anger
33 Type of snake
36 "And your feet _____ with the preparation of the gospel of peace" (Ephesians 6:15)
37 Farm buildings
39 "Of Harim, _____" (Nehemiah 12:15)
40 "Ye shall point out for you mount _____" (Numbers 34:7)
41 David wrote Psalms 57 and 142 in one
42 A son of Caleb (1 Chronicles 2:18)
43 "And _____ it with slime" (Exodus 2:3)
45 "Two of them went that same day to a village called _____" (Luke 24:13)
46 What the angel had done to Joseph (Matthew 1:24)

47 "To _____ his brethren the children of Israel" (Acts 7:23)
48 Take care of
49 Say hello
52 _____ salad
53 Jerusalem
55 "The _____ of Ethiopia shall not equal it" (Job 28:19)
60 Before Matthew (abbr.)
61 "Came to_____" (Isaiah 30:4)
62 Cognizant
63 No matter which
64 Bend
65 Inside

DOWN
1 "_____ verily, their sound" (Romans 10:18)
2 Mordecai's charge (abbr.)
3 Jether's son (1 Chronicles 7:38)
4 Decay
5 "And the LORD _____ a sweet savour" (Genesis 8:21)
6 "_____ for the day" (Joel 1:15)
7 Final
8 "Behold, the _____ was a cedar" (Ezekiel 31:3)
9 Peleg's son (Genesis 11:18)
10 Disfigure
11 Ahiezer's father (Numbers 1:12)
12 "What thou _____, write in a book" (Revelation 1:11)
13 Picnic pests
21 Utilize
22 Strike
23 A pharaoh of Egypt (2 Chronicles 35:20)
24 "_____ he will repay" (Isaiah 59:18)
25 Enoch's son (Genesis 4:18)
27 They are good scrambled
28 "_____ lay at his feet until the morning" (Ruth 3:14)
29 Race
30 Made a mistake
34 Nose of a pig

by N. Teri Grottke

35 "Baked it in _____" (Numbers 11:8)
37 "The _____ lying in a manger" (Luke 2:16)
38 "Praise ye the LORD for the _____ of Israel" (Judges 5:2)
39 Weapons
41 Cows chew this
42 Jonah's father (Jonah 1:1)
44 Increase
45 Adam's wife
46 Started
48 A son of Ishmael (Genesis 25:13–15)
50 "They _____ to and fro" (Psalm 107:27)
51 Otherwise
53 "Against Jerusalem, _____" (Ezekiel 26:2)
54 "_____ greedily after the error" (Jude 1:11)

56 Have possession
57 Cooking vessel
58 "_____ there yet the treasures" (Micah 6:10)
59 "The fenced cities are Ziddim, _____, and Hammath" (Joshua 19:35)

14

ACROSS

1 Aside from
5 Timber
10 "She hath also born. . ._____"
(Genesis 22:20, 22)
12 "Ye have _____ treasure together"
(James 5:3)
14 "The plowman shall overtake the
_____" (Amos 9:13)
15 "Thou lovest. . .lying _____ than to
speak righteousness" (Psalm 52:3)
16 Stumble
17 "They had _____" (John 21:15)
19 "The wheat and the _____ were
not smitten" (Exodus 9:32)
20 "There come two _____ more
hereafter" (Revelation 9:12)
22 Oath
23 "He was desirous to see him of a
_____ season" (Luke 23:8)
24 "The face of the deep is _____"
(Job 38:30)
26 "The _____ of gold" (1 Kings 7:49)
27 Faster than a walk
28 "It was _____ painful for me"
(Psalm 73:16)
29 Turret
32 Three
35 "Duke _____" (Genesis 36:15)
36 "The children of _____"
(Nehemiah 7:47)
37 Chair
39 "His body was _____ with the dew
of heaven" (Daniel 4:33)
40 "And there were seven sons of one
_____" (Acts 19:14)
42 "They. . ._____ the sacrifices of the
dead" (Psalm 106:28)
43 "The king of _____"
(Joshua 12:13)
45 "He reigned _____ years in
Jerusalem" (Jeremiah 52:1)
47 Gad's son (Genesis 46:16)
48 "Wherefore then _____ thou a
snare for my life" (1 Samuel 28:9)
49 Fastener

50 "He _____ him away to his house"
(Mark 8:26)

DOWN

1 "The branches _____ are made
white" (Joel 1:7)
2 "A _____ of the word"
(James 1:23)
3 "The sucking child shall play on the
hole of the _____" (Isaiah 11:8)
4 Lack
5 "They. . ._____ dust into the air"
(Acts 22:23)
6 Construe
7 Dine
8 "The border. . .went out to the cities
of mount _____" (Joshua 15:9)
9 "Jesus _____ their faith said, . . .Be
of good cheer" (Matthew 9:2)
10 Team
11 "The ships. . .are _____ of fierce
winds" (James 3:4)
13 "Thou hast drunken the _____"
(Isaiah 51:17)
18 "_____ his son, Jehoshua his son"
(1 Chronicles 7:27)
21 "Of how much _____ punishment. . .shall he be thought worthy"
(Hebrews 10:29)
23 "Thou shalt make _____ of blue"
(Exodus 26:4)
25 "Jehiel. . .and his firstborn son
Abdon, then _____"
(1 Chronicles 9:36)
26 "_____ king of Hamath"
(2 Samuel 8:9)
28 Journey
29 Haul
30 "I am Alpha and _____"
(Revelation 22:13)
31 "Seek him that. . .calleth for the
_____ of the sea" (Amos 5:8)
32 Bind
33 "Seven days shall there be no
_____ found in your houses"
(Exodus 12:19)

by Tonya Vilhauer

34 "In the day that thou _____ thereof thou shalt surely die" (Genesis 2:17)
36 "Carry neither purse, nor _____, nor shoes" (Luke 10:4)
38 Tabernacle
40 "Send ye the lamb. . .from _____ to the wilderness" (Isaiah 16:1)
41 "They shall say in all the highways, _____ " (Amos 5:16)
44 Cave
46 Vision

15

ACROSS

1. Petroleum product
4. Salah's son (Genesis 10:24)
8. To stitch
11. A son of Helem (1 Chronicles 7:35)
12. "For if ye do these things, ye shall _____ fall" (2 Peter 1:10)
14. A son of Benjamin (Genesis 46:21)
15. Tear apart
16. Oily fruit
17. "I have stretched out my hands _____ thee" (Psalm 88:9)
18. Caleb's son (1 Chronicles 4:15)
19. Solomon's great-grandson (1 Kings 15:8)
20. Son of Joktan (Genesis 10:26–29)
22. "The _____ with the tongs. . . worketh in the coals" (Isaiah 44:12)
24. Loaded (arch.)
26. Before (arch.)
27. What Lot did in the gate of Sodom
29. Force
32. "Through faith also _____ herself received strength to conceive seed" (Hebrews 11:11)
34. Saul's grandfather (1 Chronicles 8:33)
35. "He. . .sent _____ unto them" (Genesis 43:34)
36. Ontario Basketball Association (abbr.)
37. Instructor
39. Bind
40. "They. . .brought him up to the king of Babylon to _____" (2 Kings 25:6)
42. Not lukewarm or cold but _____
43. When Peter doubted, he began to _____
44. Stories
45. King Saul's father
46. "And it went out to. . .Maaleha-crabbim, and passed along to _____" (Joshua 15:3)
47. "She crieth. . .at the _____ of the city" (Proverbs 8:3)
49. Go get
51. Darling
52. After Jonah (abbr.)
53. Connected to the foot
55. The earth was destroyed by a flood this many times
58. Belshazzar's kingdom was to be given to them (Daniel 5:28)
60. "Then will the LORD be jealous for his land, and _____ his people" (Joel 2:18)
61. Entrance
62. Shamgar's father (Judges 3:31)
63. Shoe bottom
64. Ground moisture
65. Seeing organs
66. No matter which

DOWN

1. Sheaves of barley offered in Jewish temple worship on the second day of Passover
2. Too many to count
3. Boy
4. "Adam, Sheth, _____" (1 Chronicles 1:1)
5. Another name for *Zoar* (Genesis 14:2)
6. A king of Midian (Numbers 31:8)
7. Rebel
8. "Joel the _____ of Pethuel" (Joel 1:1)
9. Xerxes's second queen (abbr.)
10. "_____ hath woe?" (Proverbs 23:29)
11. A son of Bela (1 Chronicles 7:7)
13. A prince of Midian (Numbers 31:8)
14. "For _____ are not a terror to good works" (Romans 13:3)
19. Partook
21. A type of venomous snake
23. "_____ the son of Ikkesh" (2 Samuel 23:26)
25. "A _____ in the sounds" (1 Corinthians 14:7)
27. Large lake

by N. Teri Grottke

28 "Borders of _____ to Ataroth" (Joshua 16:2)
30 Blood vessel
31 Well of strife (Genesis 26:20)
32 Classify
33 Asa's father (1 Chronicles 3:10)
34 Rebuilt Jerusalem (abbr.)
35 Became acquainted
37 Flavor
38 Faithful husband (abbr.)
41 "The borrower is servant to the _____" (Proverbs 22:7)
43 "_____ down here" (Ruth 4:1)
45 The Simon from here carried the cross
46 Zechariah (abbr.)
48 "In _____ was there a voice" (Matthew 2:18)
49 _____ Eddy, a community in New York

50 With heat
52 Measure (arch.)
54 "But the _____ of their God was upon the elders" (Ezra 5:5)
55 Strange
56 Greek form of Noah (Luke 17:26)
57 Bovine
59 "Even the _____ of the LORD is near" (Ezekiel 30:3)
60 Public service announcement (abbr.)

God's Tender Mercies

For the LORD *is good; his mercy is everlasting;*
and his truth endureth to all generations.

PSALM 100:5

ACROSS

1 It walks on pseudopods (var.)
6 "He. . .put them under _____"
(2 Samuel 12:31)
10 "By this time there is a bad _____"
(John 11:39 NIV)
14 Uproar
15 Give off
16 VIP transporter
17 "And he turned _____" (Ruth 4:1)
18 Perform again
19 The Jairite, the Tekoite, and the
Ithrite (2 Samuel 20:26; 23:26, 38)
20 Start of a **QUOTE** from
Lamentations 3:23 describing the
puzzle theme (4 words)
23 "_____ me away, that I may go unto
mine own place" (Genesis 30:25)
24 Compass point halfway between NE
and E
25 "_____ for the day" (Joel 1:15)
29 "And _____ thy kids beside the
shepherds' tents"
(Song of Solomon 1:8)
31 "And as many as _____ by sea,
stood afar off" (Revelation 18:17)
35 Italian noble family
37 "Kill it at the _____ of the
tabernacle" (Leviticus 3:2)
39 _____ *Miserables*
40 **QUOTE**, cont'd from 20 Across
42 **QUOTE**, cont'd from 40 Across
(2 words)
44 "Lead _____ Benjamin"
(Hosea 5:8 NIV) (2 words)
45 So-so grades
47 Threat
48 Chinese cabbage
50 Threat
52 _____ *bien*
53 Passport, driver's license, etc. (abbr.)

55 "Take thee a _____, and lay it
before thee" (Ezekiel 4:1)
57 End of the **QUOTE**, cont'd from
42 Across (2 words)
65 Atoll item
66 Christmas
67 Small ship crane
68 _____ Roberts University
69 "He could not heal you, nor _____
you of your wound" (Hosea 5:13)
70 Sidestep
71 "But he _____ the chains apart and
broke the irons" (Mark 5:4 NIV)
72 Emergency Response Notification
System (abbr.)
73 "_____ our days as of old"
(Lamentations 5:21)

DOWN

1 "In _____ pasture shall they feed"
(Ezekiel 34:14) (2 words)
2 Iditarod command
3 Lake, city, or canal
4 "Shall I give. . .the fruit of my
_____ for the sin of my soul?"
(Micah 6:7)
5 "Now these are the _____ the
Israelites received" (Joshua 14:1 NIV)
6 Composed
7 Improved
8 "The gates of thy land shall be set
_____ open" (Nahum 3:13)
9 *Uncle Tom's Cabin* author
10 _____ Wendell Holmes Jr.
11 "A _____ vision has been shown to
me" (Isaiah 21:2 NIV)
12 Son of Eliphaz (Genesis 36:11)
13 Optimistic
21 "I. . .will _____ them as silver"
(Zechariah 13:9)
22 Main dinner dish

by David K. Shortess

25 "The children of _____" (Amos 1:13)
26 First name of hotel fame
27 "Behold, the nations are as _____ of a bucket" (Isaiah 40:15) (2 words)
28 "Stand in awe, and _____ not" (Psalm 4:4)
30 "A living _____ is better than a dead lion" (Ecclesiastes 9:4)
32 "And the horns of the _____ shall be cut off" (Amos 3:14)
33 Remove rime
34 Marks of satisfaction? Perhaps, "Marks for satisfactory grades"
36 Seventeen-year locust
38 Fake gold
41 "_____ thee down to the floor" (Ruth 3:3)
43 Pismire
46 Ann _____, movie and TV actress of yesteryear

49 Nonsense
51 Remingtons
54 "_____ those days were" (Haggai 2:16)
56 "Rebuke not an _____, but entreat him as a father" (1 Timothy 5:1)
57 Between a walk and a run
58 "The Philistines saw that their _____ was dead" (1 Samuel 17:51 NIV)
59 "Both of the first _____" (Leviticus 9:3)
60 Organized trip
61 Cathedral center
62 John in Wales
63 "Thou stoodest on the other _____" (Obadiah 1:11)
64 "When he returned, he cut them up into the pot of _____" (2 Kings 4:39 NIV)

17

ACROSS

1 "Shallum, and Telem, and _____" (Ezra 10:24)
4 One of Shaharaim's wives (1 Chronicles 8:8)
9 "Nevertheless _____ heart was perfect" (1 Kings 15:14)
13 "He _____ down with sleep" (Acts 20:9)
15 Part of the preistly garb (Leviticus 8:7)
16 Son of Shimei (1 Chronicles 23:10)
17 "According to thine _____" (Numbers 18:16)
19 Ahira's father (Numbers 1:15)
20 Rocks
21 Speaking
23 Abijah's brother (2 Chronicles 11:20)
26 Consume food
27 "That which _____ been is named already" (Ecclesiastes 6:10)
30 "_____ down here" (Ruth 4:1)
31 "A voice was heard. . ._____ weeping" (Jeremiah 31:15)
33 A tree (Isaiah 44:14)
34 43,560 sq. ft. x 2
36 An altar (Joshua 22:34)
38 "But the wheat and the _____ were not smitten" (Exodus 9:32)
39 Opposite of *within*
41 Barrier
42 Physical education (abbr.)
43 Eliud's father (Matthew 1:14)
44 Adam's wife
45 Big
48 Before Habakkuk (abbr.)
50 Killed (arch.)
51 Buzzing stinger
52 "He shall _____ with his teeth" (Psalm 112:10)
54 Deep red
58 "The Philistines. . .had taken. . ._____" (2 Chonicles 28:18)
62 Load (arch.)

63 "He saw the wind _____" (Matthew 14:30)
66 Joseph mourned for Jacob at this threshing floor (Genesis 50:10)
67 "A Certain woman. . .had an _____ of blood twelve years" (Mark 5:25)
68 Type of weed that was sown with the wheat in Jesus' parable (Matthew 13:24–30)
69 Will not take responsibility
70 "This only would I _____ of you" (Galatians 3:2)
71 Bind

DOWN

1 Utilizes
2 Decomposing metal
3 "He had cast _____ the waters" (Exodus 15:25)
4 Wild animals
5 Capable
6 Son of Abdiel (1 Chronicles 5:15)
7 "_____ of Jesse" (Isaiah 11:10)
8 "Of Harim, _____" (Nehemiah 12:15)
9 "The LORD. . .smote them to _____" (Joshua 10:10)
10 "The Hivite, and the Arkite, and the _____" (Genesis 10:17)
11 Ahira's father (Numbers 1:15)
12 "They _____ his praise" (Psalm 106:12)
14 "_____, and Dimonah, and Adadah" (Joshua 15:22)
18 Became acquainted
22 Smallest
24 "He is come to _____" (Isaiah 10:28)
25 "Having _____ ears" (2 Timothy 4:3)
27 "The joy of the _____ ceaseth" (Isaiah 24:8)
28 Jehu's great-grandfather (1 Chronicles 4:35)
29 "God created _____ heaven" (Genesis 1:1)

by N. Teri Grottke

31 Peleg's son (Genesis 11:18)
32 "Intreat me not to _____ thee" (Ruth 1:16)
35 Rulers' nationality at Jesus' time
37 "This man. . ._____ away much people after him" (Acts 5:37)
39 Employment pay
40 "Out of whose womb came the _____?" (Job 38:29)
41 False god of Babylon (Isaiah 46)
46 Gideoni's son (Numbers 1:11)
47 Cure
49 Hurry
50 The devil knows his time is this
53 "_____ lay at his feet until the morning" (Ruth 3:14)
54 Clothed
55 Charge
56 Ishmaelite camel driver (1 Chronicles 27:30)

57 Smelling orifice
59 "Collar of my _____" (Job 30:18)
60 Jaroah's son (1 Chronicles 5:14)
61 "As he saith also in _____" (Romans 9:25)
64 After Song of Songs (abbr.)
65 Temple gate (2 Kings 11:6)

ACROSS

1 "Lest at any time thou _____ thy foot against a stone" (Matthew 4:6)
5 "Adonijah, Bigvai, _____" (Nehemiah 10:16)
9 "A sore _____ that cannot be healed" (Deuteronomy 28:35)
14 Shammah's father (2 Samuel 23:11)
15 "I am the _____ of Sharon" (Song of Solomon 2:1)
16 "The sons of _____ the Netophathite" (Jeremiah 40:8)
17 "In _____ was there a voice heard" (Matthew 2:18)
18 Suffer
19 Briar
20 Jesus _____ upon the cross
21 King of the Amalekites (1 Samuel 15:8)
22 "The son of _____, in Aruboth" (1 Kings 4:10)
23 Often translated *dill* (Matthew 23:23)
25 "Messengers. . .make the _____ Ethiopians afraid" (Ezekiel 30:9)
27 "The LORD. . .delivered me out of the _____ of the lion" (1 Samuel 17:37)
30 Flog
31 Taxi
34 "_____ the Bethelite" (1 Kings 16:34)
36 "The plain of _____" (Joshua 13:9)
41 Hushim's father (1 Chronicles 7:12)
43 Caleb's son (1 Chronicles 4:15)
45 "The brook of _____" (Psalm 83:9)
46 A shade of purple
48 "A _____ and a flower" (Exodus 25:33)
50 "The son of _____" (Luke 3:35)
51 "The Egyptians shall _____ to drink" (Exodus 7:18)
53 "They did so at the going up to _____" (2 Kings 9:27)
54 "And the men of _____ made Nergal" (2 Kings 17:30)
55 "His truth _____ to all generations" (Psalm 100:5)

56 "The shipmen _____ that they drew near" (Acts 27:27)
60 Some
61 Limbs
65 "The _____ of the sea" (Esther 10:1)
66 Lifetime
67 Superior
68 "Rejoicing in himself _____" (Galatians 6:4)
69 "Mordecai. . .had taken _____ for his daughter" (Esther 2:15)
70 "Fine linen, and coral, and _____" (Ezekiel 27:16)
71 Boundaries
72 One on which they laded the corn (Genesis 42:26)
73 "Shallum, and _____, and Uri" (Ezra 10:24)

DOWN

1 "Chalcol, and _____, the sons of Mahol" (1 Kings 4:31)
2 Repeat
3 "Mattathias, which was the son of _____" (Luke 3:26)
4 "They bowed their _____, and worshipped" (Nehemiah 8:6)
5 "And they gave them the city of _____" (Joshua 21:11)
6 "Then answered _____ the Edomite" (1 Samuel 22:9)
7 Rebekah's husband
8 "The men of Cuth made _____" (2 Kings 17:30)
9 "The north side of _____" (Joshua 19:27)
10 "The Nethinims dwelt in _____" (Nehemiah 3:26)
11 "Let all _____ that seek thee rejoice" (Psalm 40:16)
12 "_____ of this life" (Luke 21:34)
13 "He maketh my feet like _____ feet" (2 Samuel 22:34)
24 NT book after Galatians (abbr.)
26 "Take. . .a _____ of three years old" (Genesis 15:9)

by Tonya Vilhauer

28 "On the east side of _____" (Numbers 34:11)
29 Frail
31 "Whosoever shall _____ on the name of the Lord" (Acts 2:21)
32 "And _____ went before the ark" (2 Samuel 6:4)
33 Beor's son (Genesis 36:32)
35 Dialects
37 Emission
38 "I gave unto _____ mount Seir" (Joshua 24:4)
39 Lock
40 One of Esau's mothers-in-law (Genesis 36:2)
42 Rodent
44 "And the _____ go about the streets" (Ecclesiastes 12:5)
47 "Carry these ten _____ unto the captain" (1 Samuel 17:18)

49 Victim
52 "I am with you always, even unto the _____" (Matthew 28:20)
56 Indicator
57 "The son of _____, which was the son of Nagge" (Luke 3:25)
58 "And _____, and Thimnathah, and Ekron" (Joshua 19:43)
59 "_____, TEKEL, UPHARSIN" (Daniel 5:25)
62 Genuine
63 Spouse
64 Bine
66 "_____, she is broken" (Ezekiel 26:2)
67 "Moses. . ._____ him up into the mount" (Exodus 24:18)

19

ACROSS

1 Jephthah fled to there (Judges 11)
4 "_____ king of Hamath"
   (2 Samuel 8:9)
7 43,560 sq. ft. x 2
12 "And in process of _____"
   (Genesis 4:3)
13 Attached to the shoulder
14 Sofa
15 Jerahmeel's son (1 Chronicles 2:25)
16 Turning away from sin
19 "We...shall...meet the Lord in the
   _____" (1 Thessalonians 4:17)
20 Lived (arch.)
21 Tikvath's father
   (2 Chronicles 34:22)
24 To plant small seed
25 Partook
28 Outfield (abbr.)
29 Seminary (abbr.)
30 Ground moisture
31 "Earth, blood, and fire, and pillars of
   _____" (Joel 2:30)
33 "Do ye _____ to reprove words"
   (Job 6:26)
37 Omri bought this hill (1 Kings 16:24)
39 "The mirth of _____ ceaseth"
   (Isaiah 24:8)
40 Famous
41 "Jozabad, and _____"
   (2 Chronicles 31:13)
42 Abraham's nephew
43 "God saw that it _____ good"
   (Genesis 1:21)
45 "_____ reigned nine and twenty
   years in Jerusalem"
   (2 Chronicles 29:1)
46 A tree (Isaiah 44:14)
47 Child's favorite seat
48 "Doeth not any of those
   _____, but even hath eaten upon
   the mountains" (Ezekiel 18:11)
52 "I brought you to possess the land of
   the _____" (Amos 2:10)
55 "I _____ alone because of thy
   hand" (Jeremiah 15:17)

56 "Roebucks, and _____, and fatted
   fowl" (1 Kings 4:23)
59 Land measurement
60 Giants (Deuteronomy 2:11)
61 "A _____ of dove's dung"
   (2 Kings 6:25)
62 Peaceful
63 Did (arch.)
64 Before (arch.)
65 "So shall _____ seed be"
   (Romans 4:18)

DOWN

1 A son of Jehaleleel
   (1 Chronicles 4:16)
2 Manna was measured this way
3 "Zechariah, _____"
   (1 Chronicles 15:18)
4 "They...pitched at _____"
   (Numbers 33:27)
5 "They...brought the heads of
   _____ and Zeeb" (Judges 7:25)
6 "It shall not be lawful to _____
   toll, tribute, or custom, upon
   them" (Ezra 7:24)
7 The only NT history book
8 "Collar of my _____" (Job 30:18)
9 Sprint
10 Book of time (abbr.)
11 "And _____ lay at his feet until the
   morning" (Ruth 3:14)
12 Zuph's son
   (1 Chronicles 6:34–35)
17 Joram smote these people
   (2 Kings 8:21)
18 "No man putteth _____ wine into
   old bottles" (Mark 2:22)
22 Rulers' nationality at Jesus' time
23 Before (arch.)
25 Maasiai's father (1 Chronicles 9:12)
26 Cloth shelter
27 Female sheep
29 "The mercy _____ were the faces
   of the cherubims" (Exodus 37:9)
31 "The _____ with the tongs"
   (Isaiah 44:12)

by N. Teri Grottke

32 Relatives
34 Last book of the OT (abbr.)
35 A son of Aaron (Exodus 6:23)
36 Say hello
37 "Land from _____ to the wilderness" (Isaiah 16:1)
38 Son of Naum (Luke 3:25)
44 Each
47 "All the daughters of musick shall be brought _____" (Ecclesiastes 12:4)
48 A city of Lycaonia (Acts 14:6)
49 Milcah's brother (Genesis 11:29)
50 "Wherefore now rise up _____ in the morning" (1 Samuel 29:10)
51 Originate
52 Charity
53 "Priest of the _____ high God" (Hebrews 7:1)
54 Rip

56 Gave food to
57 A family of returned exiles (Ezra 2:57)
58 "Jehoiada. . .bored a hole in the _____ of it" (2 Kings 12:9)
59 College entrance exam

20

ACROSS

1 "The _____ of thy life shall be increased" (Proverbs 9:11)
6 Feline
9 Holler
13 "The battle at _____" (Numbers 21:33)
14 Aram's brother (1 Chronicles 7:34)
15 "The son of _____" (Luke 3:31)
16 Repeat
17 Club
18 "Though I forbear, what am I _____" (Job 16:6)
19 Crimson
20 Coz's son (1 Chronicles 4:8)
22 Tension
23 Indicator
24 Time
25 Appointment
28 "Neither shall ye touch it, lest ye _____" (Genesis 3:3)
29 "Ye _____ a pit for your friend" (Job 6:27)
32 Sharar's son (2 Samuel 23:33)
34 "These made war with _____" (Genesis 14:2)
35 Citron
36 "By me princes rule, and _____" (Proverbs 8:16)
37 Bani's son (Ezra 10:34)
38 "From _____, and from all the mountains" (Joshua 11:21)
39 "Thou. . ._____ not look on iniquity" (Habakkuk 1:13)
40 Affirmative
41 Jonathan's father (1 Chronicles 11:34)
42 "Naaman, _____, and Rosh" (Genesis 46:21)
43 "_____ is confounded" (Jeremiah 50:2)
45 Hushim's father (1 Chronicles 7:12)
46 Close
48 Thirty-six inches
50 "He sat him down in a _____ of the city" (Judges 19:15)
53 Cupola
54 Jitney
57 "The river of _____" (Ezra 8:21)
58 "_____, Elah, and Naam" (1 Chronicles 4:15)
59 "Make a joyful _____ unto the LORD" (Psalm 100:1)
61 "The heathen _____" (Psalm 46:6)
62 Tin
63 "Boaz had _____ and drunk" (Ruth 3:7)
64 "_____ with her suburbs" (1 Chronicles 6:70)
65 "Or if he shall ask an _____" (Luke 11:12)
66 "They that are unlearned and unstable _____" (2 Peter 3:16)

DOWN

1 Twelve months
2 Rim
3 "South of _____" (Judges 1:16)
4 "_____, and the mighty men" (1 Kings 1:8)
5 The LORD spoke to Moses in Mount _____ (Leviticus 25:1)
6 "_____ on the left" (Joshua 19:27)
7 Ahaziah's father (1 Kings 22:49)
8 _____ for tat
9 Strong desire
10 Besides
11 "A feast of wines on the _____" (Isaiah 25:6)
12 Male youngsters
15 "The same measure that ye _____ withal it shall be measured to you again" (Luke 6:38)
21 "He said, _____; but I will die here" (1 Kings 2:30)
22 "Jashub, and _____, and Ramoth" (Ezra 10:29)
23 Bargains
24 "Cut it into _____" (Exodus 39:3)
25 "Let them praise his name in the _____" (Psalm 149:3)

by Tonya Vilhauer

26 "Abishua, and Naaman, and
   _____" (1 Chronicles 8:4)
27 Ginath's son (1 Kings 16:21)
28 Eliasaph's father (Numbers 1:14)
29 Leah's daughter (Genesis 34:1)
30 Statue
31 Uri's son (1 Kings 4:19)
33 "God _____ Balaam"
   (Numbers 23:4)
35 Ahumai's brother
   (1 Chronicles 4:2)
40 "_____ they shall flee away"
   (Nahum 2:8)
43 Yet
44 Barrage
46 Separate
47 "The _____, even Christ"
   (Ephesians 4:15)
48 "The _____ man. . .told him,
   Whence art thou?" (2 Samuel 1:13)

49 "_____ a right spirit within me"
   (Psalm 51:10)
50 "Through faith also _____ herself
   received strength" (Hebrews 11:11)
51 Aside from
52 Fury
53 Pull
54 "Surely the serpent will _____
   without enchantment"
   (Ecclesiastes 10:11)
55 "Maintain good works for necessary
   _____" (Titus 3:14)
56 "He _____ him away to his house"
   (Mark 8:26)
58 Frozen water
60 Row

21

ACROSS

1 Son of Abdiel (1 Chronicles 5:15)
4 To stitch
7 "_____, and Magog" (Revelation 20:8)
10 Elevate
12 Should
14 Simon Peter's father (John 1:42)
15 "Imna, and Shelesh, and _____" (1 Chronicles 7:35)
16 "Fathers, provoke not your children to _____" (Colossians 3:21)
17 Ruth's son (Ruth 4:13–17)
18 "We. . .shall. . .meet the Lord in the _____" (1 Thessalonians 4:17)
20 "I have _____ unto thy testimonies" (Psalm 119:31)
22 Increase
23 Consume food
24 Home of the Rockies (abbr.)
26 Boy
27 "_____, so would we have it" (Psalm 35:25)
29 Abraham's brother (Genesis 11:27)
31 "To _____ is reserved the blackness of darkness for ever" (Jude 1:13)
33 "Let the _____ return with his brothers" (Genesis 44:33 NIV)
35 "That at the _____ of Jesus every knee should bow" (Philippians 2:10)
36 "Tyrus hath said against Jerusalem, _____" (Ezekiel 26:2)
38 A gem on the third row of the ephod (Exodus 28:19)
40 "The men of Israel answered the _____ of Judah" (2 Samuel 19:43)
41 Weeks are made of these
43 "God saw that it _____ good" (Genesis 1:21)
44 People
47 The first Hebrew month (Esther 3:7)
49 Gym class (abbr.)
50 Before (arch.)
51 A Moabite border city (Numbers 21:15)
52 Oath
54 To make a mistake
55 "Ephraim is joined to _____" (Hosea 4:17)
58 Fuss
59 So be it
62 One who consumes food
64 Lease
68 "They _____ his praise" (Psalm 106:12)
69 "It hath no _____: the bud shall yield no meal" (Hosea 8:7)
70 Foot covering
71 Naaman's brother (Numbers 26:40)
72 A son of Gad (Genesis 46:16)
73 Motel

DOWN

1 Jether's son (1 Chronicles 7:38)
2 "And some began to spit on _____" (Mark 14:65)
3 Prophet for King Hezekiah (abbr.)
4 Biggest star in our solar system
5 "As the partridge sitteth on _____" (Jeremiah 17:11)
6 "Do not _____ the edge" (Ecclesiastes 10:10)
7 Battle where Goliath's brother was slain (2 Samuel 21:19)
8 Single
9 A son of Jacob (Genesis 35:26)
11 Tahath's son (1 Chronicles 7:20)
12 Boat paddle
13 Not false
14 Peleg's brother (Genesis 10:25)
19 Zechariah's father (Ezra 5:1)
21 Is able
22 "Giving thanks _____ for all things" (Ephesians 5:20)
24 "_____ up before me" (Jonah 1:2)

by N. Teri Grottke

25 Jerahmeel's son
(1 Chronicles 2:25)
27 To humble
28 "The king's commandment
was urgent, and the furnace
exceeding _____"
(Daniel 3:22)
30 Jael used this to kill Sisera
32 "They shall give. . .cheeks, and the
_____" (Deuteronomy 18:3)
34 Even
36 "Of Harim, _____"
(Nehemiah 12:15)
37 Delilah cut Samson's
39 "Stand in the _____"
(Ezekiel 22:30)
42 "None. . .was cleansed, _____
Naaman the Syrian" (Luke 4:27)
45 Pay attention to

46 Mistakes
48 East of Eden (Genesis 4:16)
53 "There come two _____ more
hereafter" (Revelation 9:12)
56 "Even of _____ my people is risen
up as an enemy" (Micah 2:8)
57 Night sky illuminator
58 Where the mercy seat was
59 Solomon's great-grandson
(1 Kings 15:8)
60 Disfigure
61 "The latter _____" (Ruth 3:10)
63 Phinehas's father (1 Samuel 4:4)
65 A son of Benjamin (Genesis 46:21)
66 Jehoshua's father (1 Chronicles 7:27)
67 "Joshua. . .died, being an hundred
and _____ years old"
(Joshua 24:29)

22

King After King

Therefore if any man be in Christ, he is a new creature:
old things are passed away; behold, all things are become new.

2 CORINTHIANS 5:17

ACROSS

1 "Is it _____ for you to flog a Roman"
   (Acts 22:25 NIV)
6 "And the third beast had _____ as a
   man" (Revelation 4:7) (2 words)
11 "Sir, come down _____ my child die"
   (John 4:49)
14 "To _____ for wickedness"
   (Daniel 9:24 NIV)
15 Soft drinks
16 "When anyone went to a wine _____
   to draw" (Haggai 2:16 NIV)
17 "Go _____ possess the land"
   (Deuteronomy 1:8) (2 words)
18 Lock
19 Kin to Ltd. (abbr.)
20 Three successive evil **KINGS** of Israel
   (1 Kings 15:25–16:14) (3 words)
23 Over there
24 So long
25 "The proud have _____ snare for me"
   (Psalm 140:5) (2 words)
29 "Giving all diligence, _____ your
   faith virtue" (2 Peter 1:5) (2 words)
32 "Let thy servant abide instead of the
   _____ bondman to my lord"
   (Genesis 44:33) (2 words)
36 "An _____ pleasing to the LORD"
   (Leviticus 1:13 NIV)
38 "_____ that my words were now
   written! _____ that they were printed
   in a book" (Job 19:23) (2 words)
40 *Its*, in Paris
41 Two successive evil **KINGS** of Israel
   (2 Kings 15:17–26) (2 words)
45 _____ Arbor, Michigan
46 Away from the wind
47 Walk like a crab
48 "The Lord hath _____ of them"
   (Matthew 21:3)
50 Where Saul's medium lived
   (1 Samuel 28:7)
53 Hardy heroine
54 "The. . .child shall play on the hole of
   the _____" (Isaiah 11:8)

56 "I tell you, _____" (Luke 13:3)
58 Three successive, **KINGS** of Israel
   (1 Kings 16:16–22:53) (3 words)
67 Snow, English, or split
68 "No _____ shall come on his head"
   (Judges 13:5)
69 "He. . .cannot _____ much"
   (Leviticus 14:21) (2 words)
70 Work unit
71 Something taboo (2 words)
72 Very angry
73 "We. . . passed to the _____ of
   Cyprus" (Acts 27:4 NIV)
74 Spread about
75 "My _____ for me"
   (1 Chronicles 22:7) (2 words)

DOWN

1 "Where the body of Jesus had
   _____" (John 20:12)
2 Sicilian volcano
3 "Shamgar. . .slew six hundred men
   with an ox _____" (Judges 3:31)
4 "There was one _____, a prophetess"
   (Luke 2:36)
5 "Being _____ the hand of them. . .,
   I came into Damascus" (Acts 22:11)
   (2 words)
6 "Instead, he puts it on _____"
   (Luke 8:16 NIV) (2 words)
7 "Not seeing the sun _____ season"
   (Acts 13:11) (2 words)
8 Summer drinks
9 Ledger, at times
10 English 101 paper
11 "Ye thought _____ against me"
   (Genesis 50:20)
12 American bullfrog genus
13 What acid does on glass
21 Python, for example
22 Snaky fish
25 "So they hanged _____ on the
   gallows" (Esther 7:10)
26 Actress Dunne
27 He wrote, "No man is an island"

by David K. Shortess

28 "I _____ poor man" (1 Samuel 18:23) (2 words)
30 Lacquered the cloth on an airplane's skin
31 "_____ Lord is at hand" (Philippians 4:5)
33 "They are all gone _____" (Psalm 14:3)
34 "Two tenth _____ unto one ram" (Numbers 28:28)
35 "And he sat down among the _____" (Job 2:8)
37 "_____! I am warm" (Isaiah 44:16 NIV)
39 "My heart _____ turned to wax" (Psalm 22:14 NIV)
42 Proboscidean pachyderm
43 "Blessed are ye, when _____ shall revile you" (Matthew 5:11)
44 "And the archers _____ him" (1 Chronicles 10:3)

49 Southeast Asia language group
51 "Set them in two rows, six _____" (Leviticus 24:6) (3 words)
52 Cry at the stadium
55 The woman named in Hebrews 11:11 and her namesakes (var.)
57 Horizontal, multi-element antennas
58 German auto
59 "You, a _____ man" (John 10:33 NIV)
60 "I know. . .thy _____ against me" (Isaiah 37:28)
61 "_____ begat Sadoc" (Matthew 1:14)
62 "A _____ of a man" (Numbers 19:16)
63 Not a one
64 "Make _____ oil" (Exodus 30:25) (2 words)
65 Pooch in The Thin Man
66 Cultivates, at times

23

ACROSS

1 Captain of David's army
   (1 Chronicles 11:6)
5 First letter of the Greek alphabet
10 Zuph's father
   (1 Chronicles 6:34–35)
14 A child of Gad (Numbers 26:16–18)
15 "Judgment is come. . .upon _____"
   (Jeremiah 48:21)
16 Uncontrolled anger
17 Caused to go to a destination
18 "A tower of _____"
   (Song of Solomon 7:4)
19 Jerahmeel's son (1 Chronicles 2:25)
20 First book of the Gospels
22 "_____ wings of a great eagle"
   (Revelation 12:14)
24 South Africa (abbr.)
25 A deliverer of Israel (Judges 3:15)
26 To beat
27 "For if God _____ not the angels"
   (2 Peter 2:4)
30 A son of Zophah
   (1 Chronicles 7:36–37)
34 "I am meek and _____ in heart"
   (Matthew 11:29)
35 Give for temporary use
36 Indebted
37 "He removeth _____ the speech of
   the trusty" (Job 12:20)
38 "Not _____ your liberty"
   (1 Peter 2:16)
40 Son of Joktan (Genesis 10:26–29)
41 Saul's grandfather
   (1 Chronicles 8:33)
42 "Ahijah, Hanan, _____"
   (Nehemiah 10:26)
43 Talked (arch.)
44 "To the twelve tribes which are
   scattered abroad, _____"
   (James 1:1)
46 "Then went Abimelech to
   _____"(Judges 9:50)
47 Bag
48 Son of Shammai (1 Chronicles 2:45)
49 *I* in French

51 Fuss
52 Going without food
55 Daniel had a vision by this river
57 Cook
59 "Moses drew _____"
   (Exodus 20:21)
61 "The plain of _____" (Daniel 3:1)
62 A caretaker in sickness
63 "I will send a fire on the wall of
   _____" (Amos 1:7)
64 Type of trees
65 In place of
66 "_____. . .begat sons and
   daughters" (Genesis 11:11)

DOWN

1 More than one Jo
2 A brother of David
   (1 Chronicles 2:15)
3 Temple prophetess in Jesus' time
   (Luke 2:36)
4 "Peter went out, and wept _____"
   (Luke 22:62)
5 "The prince of the tribe of the
   children of Asher" (Numbers 34:27)
6 "Thou hast _____ righteousness"
   (Hebrews 1:9)
7 Till
8 "Ye shall point out for you mount
   _____" (Numbers 34:7)
9 "If we ask _____ according to his
   will, he heareth us" (1 John 5:14)
   (2 words)
10 "Now gather thyself in _____"
   (Micah 5:1)
11 Boat paddle
12 Generations
13 "_____, and Ivah" (Isaiah 37:13)
21 "_____ shall see God"
   (Matthew 5:8)
23 "Thou, being a _____ olive tree,
   wert grafted in among them"
   (Romans 11:17)
26 At a certain time
27 "David. . ._____ it, and smote the
   Philistine" (1 Samuel 17:49)

by N. Teri Grottke

28 "Force and _____" (Ezra 4:23)
29 Cognizant
30 David used this to defeat Goliath
31 Moses' brother-in-law (Numbers 10:29)
32 "Nor _____ my love, until he please" (Song of Solomon 8:4)
33 Eleasah's father (1 Chronicles 2:39)
38 "The _____ shall come down" (Isaiah 34:7)
39 This happened to the Egyptians in the Red Sea
40 "She crieth in the. . ._____ of the gates" (Proverbs 1:21)
42 Joseph mourned for Jacob the threshingfloor of _____ (Genesis 50:10)
43 "The archers _____ at King Josiah" (2 Chronicles 35:23)
45 Greek form of *Isaiah* (Matthew 3:3)

46 Experienced flavor
48 A son of Ishmael (1 Chronicles 1:30–31)
49 Brother of Jesus (Matthew 13:55; Jude 1:1)
50 Nehemiah's wall was finished in this month (Nehemiah 6:15)
52 "_____ ye well" (Acts 15:29)
53 The border went to here from Remmonmethoar (Joshua 19:13)
54 Look at
56 Attached to the shoulder
58 "The frogs died _____ of the houses" (Exodus 8:13)
60 A male sheep

24

ACROSS

1 Plenty
5 "_____ and Caiaphas being the high priests" (Luke 3:2)
10 Hushai's son (1 Kings 4:16)
12 "Friend, lend me three _____" (Luke 11:5)
14 "We sailed under Crete, over against _____" (Acts 27:7)
15 "They. . ._____ the Holy One of Israel" (Psalm 78:41)
17 Maim
18 Cay
20 Colonize
21 "_____, and Thimnathah, and Ekron" (Joshua 19:43)
22 Rent
23 "The sorrows of _____ compassed me" (2 Samuel 22:6)
24 Left
27 "So shall the _____ be calm unto you" (Jonah 1:12)
28 "_____ them with brass" (Exodus 27:6)
31 Strive
32 Simon's father (John 1:42)
34 "Hewed stones, _____ with saws" (1 Kings 7:9)
35 "The Syrians of _____" (2 Samuel 10:6)
37 Cave
38 "_____ shall we escape" (Hebrews 2:3)
41 "Behold now _____, which I made with thee" (Job 40:15)
44 "The way of the plain from _____" (Deuteronomy 2:8)
46 "Alammelech, and _____, and Misheal" (Joshua 19:26)
47 "Eber, Peleg, _____" (1 Chronicles 1:25)
49 Zoheth's father (1 Chronicles 4:20)
50 Sup
51 Statute
53 Gait

54 "Nethaneel the fourth, _____ the fifth" (1 Chronicles 2:14)
57 Mail
59 "To _____ the most Holy" (Daniel 9:24)
60 "Paul departed from _____" (Acts 18:1)
61 "Benjamin's _____ was five times" (Genesis 43:34)
62 Storage building

DOWN

1 "Gird yourselves, and _____" (Joel 1:13)
2 "Children of Lod, Hadid, and _____" (Ezra 2:33)
3 Cistern
4 Linen
5 "_____ power is given unto me" (Matthew 28:18)
6 "Make a joyful _____ unto the LORD" (Psalm 100:1)
7 "His _____ shall be called Wonderful" (Isaiah 9:6)
8 "The name of his city was _____" (Genesis 36:35)
9 "Thou _____ a crown of pure gold on his head" (Psalm 21:3)
10 "David. . .went. . .from _____ of Judah" (2 Samuel 6:2)
11 "_____ with her suburbs" (Joshua 21:18)
13 Vendor
14 "They _____ the Ammonites" (1 Samuel 11:11)
16 Deferment
19 "For _____ is the kingdom of God" (Luke 6:20)
25 "The King. . .brought men. . . from Cuthah, and from _____" (2 Kings 17:24)
26 "The tower of _____" (Ezekiel 29:10)
28 Atarah's son (1 Chronicles 2:26)
29 Male youngster
30 Reverence

by Tonya Vilhauer

32 Careah's son (2 Kings 25:23)
33 "The house of _____ the Gittite" (2 Samuel 6:10)
35 "The sons of Becher; _____" (1 Chronicles 7:8)
36 "They. . ._____ the sacrifices of the dead" (Psalm 106:28)
38 Accelerate
39 "Leave their wealth to _____" (Psalm 49:10)
40 "My father chastised you with _____" (2 Chronicles 10:11)
41 Evil
42 "Praise him with stringed instruments and _____" (Psalm 150:4)
43 One of Aram's sons (Genesis 10:23)
45 Tabulated
48 "If he. . ._____ thee ought, put that on mine account" (Philemon 1:18)

52 "They shall say in all the highways, _____" (Amos 5:16)
55 "Neither shall ye touch it, lest ye _____" (Genesis 3:3)
56 "That which groweth of _____ own accord" (Leviticus 25:5)
58 "Restore unto me _____ joy" (Psalm 51:12)

25

ACROSS

1 First place
5 Requested (arch.) (Ruth 3:6)
9 "_____ body also was like the beryl" (Daniel 10:6)
12 "Girded with fine gold of _____" (Daniel 10:5)
14 Generations
15 Arabian city (Job 6:19)
16 "They were much perplexed _____" (Luke 24:4)
18 "The joy of the _____ ceaseth" (Isaiah 24:8)
19 Not false
20 Daughter of Asher (Genesis 46:17)
21 Jacob's God-given name
24 The daughter of Solomon (1 Kings 4:15)
27 Tied
28 "Jedidah, the daughter of Adaiah of _____" (2 Kings 22:1)
29 Decay
30 Color of a horse
31 To make a mistake
32 "He that overcometh shall _____ all things" (Revelation 21:7)
35 "The word of God is. . .a discerner of the thoughts and _____ of the heart" (Hebrews 4:12)
39 "The beauty of old _____ is the grey head" (Proverbs 20:29)
40 "_____ according to the law" (Deuteronomy 17:11)
41 Son of Abdiel (1 Chronicles 5:15)
42 Sickness
44 Foreigner
46 Under
47 Eliphaz's son (Genesis 36:12)
48 "Hali, and _____" (Joshua 19:25)
49 "One. . ._____ about" (Revelation 1:13)
50 Jerahmeel's son (1 Chronicles 2:25)
51 "All the days that he _____ himself unto the LORD" (Numbers 6:6)
57 Bird home
58 "The mountains shall reach unto _____" (Zechariah 14:5)
59 Menan's son (Luke 3:31)
60 Consume food
61 "It. . .shall be eaten: as a _____ tree" (Isaiah 6:13)
62 Circle

DOWN

1 "_____ upon mount Zion shall be deliverance" (Obadiah 1:17)
2 The heathens of these people worshiped Diana (abbr.)
3 "_____ lay at his feet until the morning" (Ruth 3:14)
4 "_____ came unto Ashdod" (Isaiah 20:1)
5 "They. . .found. . .the _____ lying in a manger" (Luke 2:16)
6 Time past
7 Book of laws (abbr., var.)
8 This queen prevented a Babylonian holocaust (abbr.)
9 Fireplace
10 A son of Zophah (1 Chronicles 7:36)
11 A giant (2 Samuel 21:18)
13 "We went over the brook _____" (Deuteronomy 2:13)
15 "They rushed with one accord into the _____" (Acts 19:29)
17 American University in London (abbr.)
20 Hurt
21 A son of Merari (1 Chronicles 24:27)
22 "A bishop must be. . .not _____ angry" (Titus 1:7)
23 Boaz's wife
24 "She placed the _____ under one of the shrubs" (Genesis 21:15 NKJV)
25 Arsenic (sym.)
26 Light smell
28 Winged rodent
30 Moza's son (1 Chronicles 8:37)
33 Famous

by N. Teri Grottke

34 "And _____ between Nineveh and Calah" (Genesis 10:12)
35 "Out of whose womb came the _____" (Job 38:29)
36 Crucifixion instrument
37 You (arch.)
38 When Peter doubted, he began to _____
40 A tree (Isaiah 44:14)
42 Despise
43 Astatine (sym.)
44 Moses' father (Exodus 6:20)
45 Later (arch.)
46 Paul and Silas were sent by night here (Acts 17:10)
47 "To meet the Lord in the _____" (1 Thessalonians 4:17)
48 Skeletal component
49 "A root that bareth _____ and wormwood" (Deuteronomy 29:18)

51 "The same day went Jesus out of the house, and _____ by the sea side" (Matthew 13:1)
52 Saw spinning wheels (abbr.)
53 "The name of his city was _____" (1 Chronicles 1:50)
54 Hophni's father (1 Samuel 4:4)
55 "Hundred and _____ years old" (Joshua 24:29)
56 Prophet who called the Israelites to finish rebuilding the temple (abbr.)

26

Biblical Big Boys

*And there we saw the giants. . .
and we were in our own sight as grasshoppers,
and so we were in their sight.*

NUMBERS 13:33

ACROSS

1 Its capital has been Agana
5 "In _____ also is his tabernacle" (Psalm 76:2)
10 "And he _____ the sin of many" (Isaiah 53:12)
14 Taj Mahal city
15 North Florida city
16 Son of Seth (Genesis 4:26)
17 "_____ in the earth in those days" (Genesis 6:4) (3 words)
20 Help a felon
21 *Dead*, in Paris
22 "Surely in vain the _____ is spread" (Proverbs 1:17)
25 "And they filled them up to the _____" (John 2:7)
27 In abundance
31 "And _____ of oil" (Leviticus 14:21) (2 words)
33 Company head
35 "Able was I _____ saw Elba" (2 words)
36 Slightest
39 Home of the Mets
42 Japanese volcano
43 "There went out a champion. . .named _____, whose height was six cubits and a span" (1 Samuel 17:4) (3 words)
46 Pale
47 Malayan sailboat (var.)
48 Treble clef guys
50 "The _____ are a people not strong" (Proverbs 30:25)
52 Swift boat from Vietnam War (abbr.)
54 Three in Thüringen
55 Put away
58 Kind of hoop
61 1,760 equal 1 mi. (abbr.)
62 "He. . .measured the _____ all around" (Ezekiel 42:15 NIV)
64 "How much _____ shall I answer him" (Job 9:14)

66 "With all Bashan, which was called _____" (Deuteronomy 3:13) (4 words)
73 "Wherein I _____ erred" (Job 6:24)
74 Tapeworm (var.)
75 "_____ certain man was sick" (John 11:1) (2 words)
76 "And Abraham lifted up his _____" (Genesis 22:13)
77 Fishhook leader
78 "The nations are as a _____ of a bucket" (Isaiah 40:15)

DOWN

1 "And Moses _____ him into the camp" (Numbers 11:30)
2 Cry of disgust
3 "_____ not my days few" (Job 10:20)
4 "Call me not Naomi, call me _____" (Ruth 1:20)
5 "Hear ye therefore the parable of the _____" (Matthew 13:18)
6 Acid found in vinegar
7 Roman household god or spirit
8 Primary school (abbr.)
9 "And I will send a fire on _____" (Ezekiel 39:6)
10 George Harrison was one
11 New England Cape
12 "But the name of the wicked shall _____" (Proverbs 10:7)
13 Ogee shape
18 "As their lives _____ away in their mothers' arms" (Lamentations 2:12 NIV)
19 "Was _____ the son of Ikkesh" (1 Chronicles 27:9)
22 Viet _____
23 Appealing to refined taste
24 Blue Jays' home
26 Furnace survivor (Daniel 3:26)
28 Public speaking
29 Tear up again
30 Old MacDonald's refrain ending

by David K. Shortess

32 Hair goop
34 Expression of discovery
37 A little drink
38 "Now the Valley of Siddim was full of _____ pits" (Genesis 14:10 NIV)
40 Newt
41 "He is of _____; ask him" (John 9:23)
44 "From the _____ of the rocks I see him" (Numbers 23:9)
45 "_____ the Word was made flesh" (John 1:14)
46 "There _____ a man sent from God" (John 1:6)
49 Bro's sib
51 Marshlands
53 "I am not come to destroy, but to _____" (Matthew 5:17)
56 Baseball stat
57 Fender blemishes
59 "It must be settled in a _____ assembly" (Acts 19:39 NIV)

60 "As many _____ love, I rebuke and chasten" (Revelation 3:19) (2 words)
63 "Ye have made it _____ of thieves" (Luke 19:46) (2 words)
65 "I shall multiply my days as the _____" (Job 29:18)
66 "_____ LORD is my light" (Psalm 27:1)
67 "The _____ is withered away" (Isaiah 15:6)
68 "Adam was. . .formed, then _____" (1 Timothy 2:13)
69 "I am _____ that bear witness of myself" (John 8:18)
70 "Fight neither with small _____ great" (1 Kings 22:31)
71 "No man can serve _____ masters" (Matthew 6:24)
72 "The trees. . .are full of _____" (Psalm 104:16)

27

ACROSS

1 Rabbit
5 Perished
9 "Girded with fine gold of_____"
   (Daniel 10:5)
14 "Nevertheless _____ heart was
   perfect" (1 Kings 15:14)
15 "I will _____ all that afflict thee"
   (Zephaniah 3:19)
16 This Hararite was father to Jonathan
   in David's army (1 Chronicles 11:34)
17 "They looked unto him, and were
   _____" (Psalm 34:5)
19 The father of Sychem (Acts 7:16)
20 Flavor
21 Seth's son (Genesis 4:26)
23 The valley of craftsmen
   (Nehemiah 11:35)
24 Manna measurement
26 One who charges interest
29 Samuel's mother
32 Eshcol's brother (Genesis 14:13)
33 "_____ there yet the treasures"
   (Micah 6:10)
34 Simeon was called this (Acts 13:1)
37 Jacob's daughter (Genesis 34:1)
41 Teacher of Judaism
43 Jether's son (1 Chronicles 7:38)
44 Idol
45 "The devil, as a roaring lion, walketh
   _____, seeking whom he may
   devour" (1 Peter 5:8)
46 Boundary
48 Adam was the first
49 "Yea, what _____, yea, what
   revenge" (2 Corinthians 7:11)
51 Jael killed him (Judges 4:18–21)
53 "_____ the devil, and he will flee
   from you" (James 4:7)
56 Son of Shammai
   (1 Chronicles 2:45)
57 Tenth NT book (abbr.)
58 Nagge's son (Luke 3:25)
61 "They. . .came into an harlot's
   house, _____ Rahab" (Joshua 2:1)
65 Allotment
68 "Rejoice not thou, whole _____"
   (Isaiah 14:29)
70 Opposite of *giver*
71 Micaiah's father (2 Chronicles 18:7)
72 Potter's material
73 Strainer
74 Bird home
75 Edges of garments

DOWN

1 Stop
2 Largest continent
3 Worn-out clothing
4 Paseah's father (1 Chronicles 4:12)
5 Payment
6 Inside
7 First garden
8 Father of Puah (Judges 10:1)
9 Utilize
10 People's Health Movement (abbr.)
11 Shechem's father (Genesis 33:19)
12 "Three days _____ I fell sick"
   (1 Samuel 30:13)
13 The son of Bechorath
   (1 Samuel 9:1)
18 "Husham of the land of the _____
   reigned in his stead"
   (1 Chronicles 1:45)
22 Biggest star in our solar system
25 A son of Benjamin
   (Genesis 46:21)
27 "Wrath, strife, _____, heresies"
   (Galatians 5:20)
28 Thummim's partner
29 "Habor, and _____"
   (1 Chronicles 5:26)
30 "_____, and Dumah"
   (Joshua 15:52)
31 "The other _____"
   (Nehemiah 7:33)
32 A son of Shem (Genesis 10:22)
35 "It is the _____ of asps within him"
   (Job 20:14)
36 A son of Gad (Genesis 46:16)
38 "At the _____ of Jesus"
   (Philippians 2:10)

by N. Teri Grottke

39 Greek form of *Hagar* (Galatians 4:24)
40 "_____, and Ivah" (Isaiah 37:13)
42 Ezekiel's father
47 OT prophet who served four kings (abbr.)
50 Partook
52 "And he shall _____" (Isaiah 9:20)
53 Takes a break
54 This man was a Netophathite (Jeremiah 40:8)
55 "_____ off the dust under your feet" (Mark 6:11)
56 Grinds flour
59 Turn quickly
60 Crippled
62 "Whosoever shall compel thee to go a _____, go with him twain" (Matthew 5:41)

63 "Tappuah, and _____" (Joshua 15:34)
64 Weeks are made of these
66 Prophetic end book (abbr.)
67 Before (poet.)
69 Consume

28

Ark Builder

ACROSS

1 By faith he built an ark to save his family
4 Sick people wanted to touch the _____ of Jesus' cloak (Matthew 14:36 NIV)
8 "At the _____ of the hundred and fifty days the water had gone down" (Genesis 8:3 NIV)
9 "So make yourself an _____ of cypress wood" (Genesis 6:14 NIV)
10 To kill
12 "Every good _____ bears good fruit" (Matthew 7:17 NIV)
13 Herod had been quarreling with the people of _____ and Sidon (Acts 12:20 NIV)
14 Cuts with blows of a heavy cutting instrument
15 A sailor's word for *yes*
16 Skirmish
19 Used to catch fish
23 One of Noah's sons (Genesis 5:32)
24 "These _____ the generations of Noah" (Genesis 6:9)
25 "So the LORD was sorry he had _____ made them" (Genesis 6:6 NLT)
27 Russian ruler, generally
28 Daniel interpreted the writing on the wall, which was "_____, MENE, TEKEL, PARSIN" (Daniel 5:25 NLT)
29 A kind of cultural revolution, one person at a time

DOWN

1 "Your _____ is set in a rock" (Numbers 24:21 NIV)
2 After the flood, "_____ Noah was left, and those with him in the ark" (Genesis 7:23 NIV)
3 A month in the Jewish calendar (Ezra 6:15)
5 Moses did not _____ to look on the face of God (Acts 7:32 NIV)
6 "Nimrod. . ._____ to be a mighty warrior" (Genesis 10:8 NIV)
7 Supplements income
11 The flood began in the six hundredth _____ of Noah's life (Genesis 7:11)
12 The dove returned with an olive leaf! "_____ Noah knew that the water had receded from the earth" (See Genesis 8:11 NIV)
16 One of Noah's sons (Genesis 5:32)
17 Lay the way
18 Word to end a prayer
20 "My couch will _____ my complaint" (Job 7:13 NKJV)
21 Otherwise known as a streetcar (Brit.)
22 Threadbare (arch.)
26 In regard to (abbr.)
27 Signifying company's ownership (abbr.)

1	2	3			4	5	6	7
8						9		
10			11		12			
13					14			
			15					
16	17	18			19	20	21	22
23						24		
25			26		27			
28					29			

by John Hudson Tiner

29

ACROSS

1 Burial place
5 Too
9 "And he called them the land of _____ unto this day" (1 Kings 9:13)
14 Son of Joktan (Genesis 10:26–28)
15 "Every man should _____ rule" (Esther 1:22)
16 Absalom's captain (2 Samuel 17:25)
17 Another name for *Zoar* (Genesis 14:2)
18 "The king's _____" (Genesis 14:17)
19 Loaded (arch.)
20 Able to be tricked
23 "Every _____ should bow" (Philippians 2:10)
24 OT book prior to Jonah (abbr.)
25 Fight between countries
28 Opposite of *newness*
31 He met a friendly fish (abbr., var.)
34 Abraham's heir
36 Utilize
37 Dwelling
38 "In the _____ day" (Leviticus 23:32)
39 Are (arch.)
40 Pumpkins grow on these
41 Furthest part
42 Opposite of *hers*
43 Idol
44 "_____ that ye refuse not" (Hebrews 12:25)
45 "Burst into song. . .you _____" (Psalm 29:2)
48 "He _____ horns" (Habakkuk 3:4)
49 A knight
50 "What. . .hath been done to Mordecai for _____" (Esther 6:3)
52 "For the _____ of this service" (2 Corinthians 9:12)
59 "For in him we live, and move, and have our _____" (Acts 17:28)
60 Jerahmeel's son (1 Chronicles 2:25)
61 Sadoc's father (Matthew 1:14)
63 David would do this before the ark
64 7 days
65 "_____, and Ivah" (Isaiah 37:13)
66 "Nor _____ the thing" (Psalm 89:34)
67 Peter fished with these
68 So be it

DOWN

1 Jephthah fled to there (Judges 11:3)
2 Ruth's son (Ruth 4:13–17)
3 Not female
4 "The one with the _____ horses is going toward the north country" (Zechariah 6:6 NIV)
5 Guni's son (1 Chronicles 5:15)
6 "To open before him the two _____ gates" (Isaiah 45:1)
7 Heber's father (Luke 3:35)
8 "They. . .brought the heads of _____ and Zeeb" (Judges 7:25)
9 "And Othniel the son of Kenaz, _____ younger brother" (Judges 1:13)
10 "Look from the top of _____" (Song of Solomon 4:8)
11 Asked (arch.) (Ruth 3)
12 Utilizes
13 Boys
21 Father of Methuselah (Genesis 5:21)
22 "We _____ not" (2 John 1:8)
25 "A feast of _____ on the lees" (Isaiah 25:6)
26 Digression
27 Realm
29 A caretaker in sickness
30 Underwent beauty treatments in the palace before attaining a higher position (abbr.)
31 Undigested whale food
32 The ending
33 "The son of _____" (1 Kings 4:10)
35 Partook
37 "One shall then open _____ the gate" (Ezekiel 46:12)
39 "To meet the Lord in the _____" (1 Thessalonians 4:17)

by N. Teri Grottke

40 "To _____ his brethren the children of Israel" (Acts 7:23)
42 Lotan's son (1 Chronicles 1:39)
45 "Jesus. . .with his _____ wrote on the ground" (John 8:6)
46 Lane
47 "But rather giving of _____" (Ephesians 5:4)
49 "For _____ the fathers fell asleep, all things continue" (2 Peter 3:4)
51 "The children of _____" (Ezra 2:44)
52 Adoniram's father (1 Kings 4:6)
53 "Lookest thou upon them that _____ treacherously" (Habakkuk 1:13)
54 "For ye tithe _____ and rue and all manner of herbs" (Luke 11:42)
55 "The fruit of righteousness is _____ in peace" (James 3:18)
56 Cherries grow on this

57 David's brother (1 Chronicles 2:15)
58 Not any
62 "They have. . ._____ greedily after the error" (Jude 1:11)

30

ACROSS

1 Compassion
5 They shall divide it into seven _____" (Joshua 18:5)
10 "She bare a son, and called his name _____" (Genesis 4:25)
14 "_____, lama sabachthani" (Mark 15:34)
15 "Nadab and _____ died" (1 Chronicles 24:2)
16 "He. . .brought them unto Halah, and Habor, and _____" (1 Chronicles 5:26)
17 Exchange for price
18 "Behold, thou art _____ than Daniel" (Ezekiel 28:3)
19 "Nevertheless _____ heart was perfect" (1 Kings 15:14)
20 Cultivate
21 "They shall be as though they had not _____" (Obadiah 1:16)
22 Hyssop
23 "Thy god, O _____, liveth" (Amos 8:14)
26 Each
28 "He. . .smote them with _____" (1 Samuel 5:6)
31 "The emptiers have. . ._____ their vine branches" (Nahum 2:2)
32 Exchanged
33 Expose
35 "Thou _____ cursed above all cattle" (Genesis 3:14)
36 Bind
37 God _____ blessed me
40 "If an ox _____ a man or a woman" (Exodus 21:28)
42 Drag
43 Jewish confession of faith
45 "Thou shalt not rule over him with _____" (Leviticus 25:43)
47 "Goshen, and _____, and Giloh" (Joshua 15:51)
48 Abyss
49 "He might know how much every man had gained by _____" (Luke 19:15)
51 "Thou art the God that _____ wonders" (Psalm 77:14)
54 At this present place
55 Lodging
56 Lion's cry
60 Point of former attachment of the umbilical cord
63 Soil
64 "Sinners shall be converted _____ thee" (Psalm 51:13)
65 "He _____ them from the judgment seat" (Acts 18:16)
66 Lack
67 Strike

DOWN

1 Bane
2 "_____ the Ahohite" (1 Chronicles 11:29)
3 Fee
4 "Ye have _____ your members" (Romans 6:19)
5 "The LORD. . .delivered me out of the _____ of the lion" (1 Samuel 17:37)
6 "Observe the month of _____" (Deuteronomy 16:1)
7 Ascend
8 "Seven times a day do I praise _____" (Psalm 119:164)
9 "Another shall. . ._____ himself" (Isaiah 44:5)
10 "He was buried in _____" (Judges 10:2)
11 "It is _____ for heaven and earth to pass" (Luke 16:17)
12 Daze
13 "They were troubled, and _____ away" (Psalm 48:5)
24 "By grace ye _____ saved" (Ephesians 2:5)
25 "Cain. . .dwelt in the land of _____" (Genesis 4:16)
27 "In a _____ it shall be made with oil" (Leviticus 6:21)
28 Mistake

by Tonya Vilhauer

29 "The family of _____ was taken" (1 Samuel 10:21)
30 Sod
32 License plate
34 "The son of _____, sons of Reuben" (Numbers 16:1)
36 Peat
37 "Joseph, . . .the son of _____" (Luke 3:23)
38 Josiah's father (Jeremiah 1:2)
39 "Then Israel _____ this song" (Numbers 21:17)
41 "He that eateth of their _____ dieth" (Isaiah 59:5)
42 King of Assyria (2 Kings 15:19)
43 Ahiam's father (2 Samuel 23:33)
44 "The children of _____" (Nehemiah 7:43)
46 "The other disciple did _____ Peter" (John 20:4)

50 "I. . .will _____ the caul of their heart" (Hosea 13:8)
51 Platter
52 "Children of Lod, Hadid, and _____" (Ezra 2:33)
53 Terminate
57 "Thou believest that there is _____ God" (James 2:19)
58 "They. . ._____ the sacrifices of the dead" (Psalm 106:28)
59 Pole
61 "_____, and Rekem, and Zur" (Joshua 13:21)
62 Allow

31

ACROSS

1 "Two cheeks, and the _____" (Deuteronomy 18:3)
4 Nineteenth OT book (abbr.)
7 A male sheep
10 A son of Ulla (1 Chronicles 7:39)
12 "He must bring two _____ lambs and one ewe lamb" (Leviticus 14:10 NIV)
13 A servant of the church at Cenchrea (Romans 16:1)
15 "The _____ after his kind" (Leviticus 11:14)
16 A son of Judah (1 Chronicles 2:3)
17 Sisera was captain of this host (Judges 4:2)
18 "Mahli, and _____" (1 Chronicles 23:23)
19 Gaddi's father (Numbers 13:11)
20 Not dead
21 Not easily found
22 Ahira's father (Numbers 1:15)
23 Battles are drawn on these
24 "I have come into my garden, my _____, my bride" (Song of Songs 5:1 NIV)
26 Throw
28 Son of Joktan (Genesis 10:28)
30 Should
34 Out of danger
36 "As he saith also in _____" (Romans 9:25)
39 "For ye tithe mint and _____" (Luke 11:42)
40 "Of _____, the family of the Arodites" (Numbers 26:17)
41 Sixteenth letter of the Hebrew alphabet (heading for Psalm 119:121–128)
42 A king of Tyre (1 Chronicles 14:1)
44 Son of Eliphaz (Genesis 36:11)
45 "_____ the waters" (Exodus 15:25)
46 "At the _____ of the city" (Proverbs 8:3)
47 "And I will purge out from among you the _____" (Ezekiel 20:38)
49 Beach surface
51 Strong trees
54 Roman emperor
58 "A great well that is in _____" (1 Samuel 19:22)
62 The border went to here from Remmonmethoar (Joshua 19:13)
64 Elevate
65 Made a mistake
66 Hand-driven boat propellers
67 Dirt prepared for crops
68 Test
69 Guilty or not guilty
70 In other words, no

DOWN

1 "They shall go to confusion together that are _____ of idols" (Isaiah 45:16)
2 A son of Haman (Esther 9:9)
3 The Spirit of God moved upon the face of this
4 Zalaph's son (Nehemiah 3:30)
5 A son of Pashur (Ezra 10:22)
6 "Hodijah, Bani, _____" (Nehemiah 10:13)
7 King of Syria (Isaiah 7:1)
8 Opposite of *below*
9 "Tarshish, _____, Marsena" (Esther 1:14)
11 "Being absent now I write to them which _____ have sinned" (2 Corinthians 13:2)
12 "Jaakan to _____" (Deuteronomy 10:6)
13 A son of Reuben (Genesis 46:9)
14 "Their border was Helkath, and _____" (Joshua 19:25)
25 Gaal's father (Judges 9:26)
27 Small deer
29 "The _____ which is lent" (1 Samuel 2:20)
31 Teeth
32 Injured
33 Rip
34 Identical

by N. Teri Grottke

35 "_____, and Dumah"
(Joshua 15:52)
37 "_____ down here" (Ruth 4:1)
38 Seth's son (Genesis 4:26)
42 "_____, and Ivah?" (Isaiah 37:13)
43 Relating to me
44 "Either good _____ bad"
(Genesis 31:24)
45 This prophet appears on the Sistine
Chapel (abbr.)
48 "All the country wept with a _____
voice" (2 Samuel 15:23)
50 Daughter of Caleb
(1 Chronicles 2:49)
52 "A _____ and a flower"
(Exodus 25:33)
53 Closure
55 "Come out of _____"
(Romans 11:26)
56 China's continent

57 Depend on
58 To place
59 To violate an accepted standard of
conduct
60 Weep
61 "_____ will reign for ever and ever"
(Revelation 11:15 NIV)
63 "_____ there yet the treasures"
(Micah 6:10)

32

Biblical Succession

A melange of children, servants, robes, and retinues.
What do these have in common?
It doesn't take special training to find out.

ACROSS

1 "The seventh _____" (Revelation 8:1)
5 Letters at O'Hare (abbr.)
9 Job side benefits
14 "Eloi, Eloi, _____ sabachthani?" (Mark 15:34)
15 "Their hope will become a dying _____" (Job 11:20 NIV)
16 "Men condemned to die in the _____" (1 Corinthians 4:9 NIV)
17 "And she came to Jerusalem with _____" (1 Kings 10:2) (4 words)
20 _____ cavae (the two major veins)
21 Rani's wrap-around
22 British Inc. (abbr.)
23 Third tones of diatonic scales
25 "So shall thy _____ be" (Genesis 15:5)
28 "He armed his _____" (Abram's impromptu army, in Genesis 14:14) (2 words)
36 Heavy frost
37 Muscle spasm
38 Cancel a mission
39 Dentists organization (abbr.)
40 Billy Graham Center location
43 Film actress West
44 Metric prefix (hundredth)
46 "_____ voice from heaven" (Matthew 3:17) (2 words)
47 Green _____ plum
48 "_____ the way he should go" (Solomon's advice in Proverbs 22:6) (5 words)
52 "I was at _____" (Job 16:12)
53 "_____ not vain repetitions" (Matthew 6:7)
54 Colorado tribe
57 Book after Nehemiah (abbr., var.)
60 Coherent light

64 "And his train _____" (What Isaiah saw in Isaiah 6:1) (3 words)
68 Satellite path
69 Former monetary unit of Italy
70 Gaelic
71 "The chief _____ in the synagogues" (Matthew 23:6)
72 "_____ was a cunning hunter" (Genesis 25:27)
73 "_____ garments" (Isaiah 63:1)

DOWN

1 Eastern European
2 Roof overhang
3 "Even so, _____" (Revelation 1:7)
4 Wyoming city
5 "If he asks for an _____?" (Luke 11:12 NIV)
6 Short for tarpaulins (sailors)
7 "And I saw as it were _____ of glass" (Revelation 15:2) (2 words)
8 Growing thinly
9 Tamp
10 "They do alway _____ in their heart" (Hebrews 3:10)
11 "For my flesh is _____ food" (John 6:55 NIV)
12 "_____ together in love" (Colossians 2:2)
13 "I stood upon the _____ of the sea" (Revelation 13:1)
18 "Glory _____ his holy name" (1 Chronicles 16:10) (2 words)
19 One who knots
24 "Adam. . .called his name _____" (Genesis 5:3)
26 John in Wales
27 Brylcreem quantity, usually
28 "The _____ of land that Jacob bought" (Joshua 24:32 NIV)
29 "His _____ shall fall backward" (Genesis 49:17)

by David K. Shortess

30 "Look from the top of _____"
(Song of Solomon 4:8)

31 "Lest ye _____" (Genesis 3:3)

32 *La* _____ (Milan opera house)

33 "You. . .sat like a _____ in the desert" (Jeremiah 3:2 NIV)

34 _____-comedy play

35 Seventeenth-century Dutch painter

40 "You travel. . .to _____ single convert" (Matthew 23:15 NIV) (2 words)

41 Tic-_____ (says the clock)

42 Hawaiian island

45 "_____ them about thy neck" (Proverbs 6:21)

47 "Their feet. . ._____ like burnished bronze" (Ezekiel 1:7 NIV)

49 "They have _____ deceit" (Romans 3:13)

50 "Bray. . .with a _____" (Proverbs 27:22)

51 "Which had wintered in the _____" (Acts 28:11)

54 Andromedan transports? (abbr.)

55 "Bind the _____ of thine head" (Ezekiel 24:17)

56 Island of exile

58 "_____ I say then" (Galatians 5:16)

59 "To make _____ public example" (Matthew 1:19) (2 words)

61 Lively

62 "Or _____ I die" (Genesis 30:1)

63 "A _____ shaken with the wind" (Matthew 11:7)

65 "He. . ._____ the torches" (Judges 15:4–5 NIV)

66 Parisian ands

67 The nineteenth letter in the Greek alphabet

33

ACROSS

1 To clothe
6 Father of Rachel and Leah (Genesis 29:16)
11 "_____ is like your people Israel" (2 Samuel 7:23 NIV)
14 Place at the edge of the wilderness (Exodus 13:20)
15 Cognizant
16 Hebrew for *embrace* (abbr.)
17 "The one with the _____ horses toward the west" (Zechariah 6:6 NIV)
18 Place in wilderness of Etham where the Israelites camped (Numbers 33:5–8)
19 When the Hebrew women gave birth in relation to midwives (Exodus 1:19)
20 "The parts of _____" (Acts 2:10)
22 "Of _____, the family of Arodites" (Numbers 26:17)
23 Distributed cards
26 "He shall be _____ away" (Job 20:8)
29 Walls of shrubs
30 "He. . .burnt up both the _____" (Judges 15:5)
31 Zorobabel's son (Matthew 1:13)
32 "All the hills shall _____" (Amos 9:13)
33 Means "the Lord's servant" in Hebrew (abbr.)
36 Birth 'til death
37 "Destitute of _____ food" (James 2:15)
39 Act
40 A son of Gad (Genesis 46:16)
41 Sister of a parent
42 A bird that is forbidden to be eaten (Leviticus 11:13–15)
43 Johanan's father (2 Kings 25:23)
45 Jael killed him (Judges 4:18–21)
46 "Thou _____ in the throne judging right" (Psalm 9:4)
47 Amasa's father (2 Samuel 17:25)
48 Detest
49 This place is on the left hand of Damascus (Genesis 14:15)
52 Hophni's father (1 Samuel 4:4)
53 Before (arch.)
55 Chalcol's father (1 Kings 4:31)
60 He was a prophet to the Northern Kingdom but a native of the Southern Kingdom (abbr., var.)
61 "See, here is _____" (Acts 8:36)
62 Chief among the captains of David's mighty men (2 Samuel 23:8)
63 Cooking vessel
64 The son of Zerah (1 Chronicles 6:41)
65 "Now faith is the substance of things _____ for" (Hebrews 11:1)

DOWN

1 Ground moisture
2 Book of Ruth (abbr., var.)
3 A son of Benjamin (Genesis 46:21)
4 "The king _____ upon his royal throne" (Esther 5:1)
5 "And the LORD _____ a sweet savour" (Genesis 8:21)
6 Baby sheep
7 "I will take _____ the chariots from Ephraim" (Zechariah 9:10 NIV)
8 Elihu's father (Job 32:2)
9 Jether's son (1 Chronicles 7:38)
10 Jerusalem was this man's main concern (abbr.)
11 "_____ the body is, thither will the eagles be gathered together" (Luke 17:37)
12 "Gideon. . .pitched beside the well of _____" (Judges 7:1)
13 Ruth's son (Ruth 4:13–17)
21 Possessive pronoun
22 Question
23 "Name of _____" (Judges 1:11)
24 The building up of one's faith
25 A chill
27 Pure
28 Take action
29 "Lest he _____ thee to the judge" (Luke 12:58)

by N. Teri Grottke

30 "The _____ with the tongs" (Isaiah 44:12)
34 "Shilshah, and Ithran, and _____" (1 Chronicles 7:37)
35 "Of Harim, _____" (Nehemiah 12:15)
37 Render therefore to all their _____" (Romans 13:7)
38 "Get thee to _____, unto thine own fields" (1 Kings 2:26)
39 Race
41 "_____ there yet the treasures" (Micah 6:10)
42 "They. . .pitched in _____" (Numbers 33:18)
44 Partook
45 "The children of _____" (Nehemiah 7:47)
46 Nahshon's son (1 Chronicles 2:11)

48 "For in so doing thou shalt _____ coals of fire on his head" (Romans 12:20)
50 Jerahmeel's son (1 Chronicles 2:25)
51 A son of Zophah (1 Chronicles 7:36)
53 Reverent fear
54 Obese
56 Fuss
57 Your thigh is connected to this
58 Single
59 "_____, Hadid, and Ono" (Ezra 2:33)

34

ACROSS

1 Adage
4 Dine
7 "Make thee an _____ of gopher wood" (Genesis 6:14)
10 Blackbird
12 Exceed
14 "_____ with joy receiveth it" (Matthew 13:20)
15 "Strangers of _____" (Acts 2:10)
16 "Solomon's servants: the children of _____" (Ezra 2:55)
17 Menahem's father (2 Kings 15:17)
18 "Jezreel, and Ishma, and _____" (1 Chronicles 4:3)
20 Mart
22 "Cut off from Ahab him that _____" (2 Kings 9:8)
24 "The _____, and the box tree together" (Isaiah 41:19)
25 "_____, lama sabachthani" (Mark 15:34)
26 "My lips shall _____ praise" (Psalm 119:171)
30 Libel
32 "Found him sitting under an _____" (1 Kings 13:14)
34 "Lest at any time thou _____ thy foot against a stone" (Matthew 4:6)
36 "Even with a _____ destruction" (Micah 2:10)
37 Gera's son (Judges 3:15)
40 "The word of God was preached of Paul at _____" (Acts 17:13)
41 "The children of _____ of Hezekiah" (Ezra 2:16)
42 Merodachbaladan's father (Isaiah 39:1)
44 Flurries
46 "The two and twentieth to _____" (1 Chronicles 24:17)
47 Platter
50 "A _____ of three years old" (Genesis 15:9)
51 Cleft

53 "_____ power is given unto me" (Matthew 28:18)
54 "Over the camels also was _____ the Ishmaelite" (1 Chronicles 27:30)
56 "Rejoicing in himself _____" (Galatians 6:4)
58 "They gave them the city of _____" (Joshua 21:11)
60 Facts
61 "God _____ it unto good" (Genesis 50:20)
62 Panorama
63 Storage building
64 "Like _____, who obeyed Abraham" (1 Peter 3:6)
65 Verily

DOWN

1 "Carry neither purse, nor _____, nor shoes" (Luke 10:4)
2 "Shuni, and Ezbon, Eri, and _____" (Genesis 46:16)
3 "The LORD. . .closed up all the _____" (Genesis 20:18)
4 Flight (abbr.)
5 "The LORD shall. . .bring to pass his _____" (Isaiah 28:21)
6 Pekoe
7 "Talmai, the children of _____" (Joshua 15:14)
8 "And they _____ upon the camels" (Genesis 24:61)
9 "Being _____ together in love" (Colossians 2:2)
11 Pekan
12 Bethrapha's father (1 Chronicles 4:12)
13 Boundary
14 Correspond
19 "From _____ to the wilderness" (Isaiah 16:1)
21 "Go to the _____, thou sluggard" (Proverbs 6:6)
23 Perdu
24 Handbags

by Tonya Vilhauer

27 "Judah shall yet again take _____"
   (2 Kings 19:30)
28 Brother of Jamin (1 Chronicles 2:27)
29 "Make their nobles like _____"
   (Psalm 83:11)
30 "What will ye see in the _____"
   (Song of Solomon 6:13)
31 Lug
33 "By grace ye _____ saved"
   (Ephesians 2:5)
35 "He that _____ a matter wisely
   shall find good" (Proverbs 16:20)
36 "And cut them with _____"
   (1 Chronicles 20:3)
38 "The children of _____"
   (Ezra 2:45)
39 Barrage
40 "She. . .crushed _____ foot against
   the wall" (Numbers 22:25)
43 "I _____ this well" (Genesis 21:30)

45 Lubricant
48 Malchijah's father (Nehemiah 3:11)
49 "His sword _____ in his hand"
   (Numbers 22:23)
50 "Thrice was I beaten with _____"
   (2 Corinthians 11:25)
52 "Between blood and blood, between
   _____" (Deuteronomy 17:8)
53 "There was one _____, a
   prophetess" (Luke 2:36)
55 Youngster
57 Row
58 "From Cuthah, and from _____"
   (2 Kings 17:24)
59 "For the _____ that is in the land
   of Assyria" (Isaiah 7:18)

35

ACROSS

1 Filth
5 Increase
8 One of the Hebrew midwives (Exodus 1:15)
12 King Hoshea's father (2 Kings 15:30)
13 "They shall _____ God" (Matthew 5:8)
14 "For thy name's sake, O LORD, _____ mine iniquity; for it is great" (Psalm 25:11)
16 Employment pay
18 A son of Aaron (Exodus 6:23)
20 Fuss
21 Descendant of Jacob
23 "The _____ of truth shall be established for ever" (Proverbs 12:19)
24 To make a mistake
25 "They. . ._____ greedily after the error" (Jude 1:11)
26 Zibeon's son (1 Chronicles 1:40)
27 "And after him _____, Sallai" (Nehemiah 11:8)
30 "Jeremiah of _____" (Jeremiah 52:1)
32 To carry out directions
33 "Drink of _____ wine" (Song of Solomon 8:2)
35 Bind
36 The archangel (Jude 1:9)
38 "How is the gold become _____" (Lamentations 4:1)
41 Inside
42 These kind of men came from the east to find the King of the Jews
43 "_____ with the villages thereof" (2 Chronicles 28:18)
45 "They. . .were all baptized of him in the river of _____" (Mark 1:5)
47 "He that hath a _____ nose, or any thing superfluous" (Leviticus 21:18)
48 "Destroy _____ kings and people" (Ezra 6:12)

50 Son of Abdiel (1 Chronicles 5:15)
51 Boat paddle
52 "Coasts of Geshuri and _____" (Deuteronomy 3:14)
56 First mother
57 "Chalcol, and _____" (1 Kings 4:31)
58 Works
60 The spy from the tribe of Asher (Numbers 13)
62 A king of Midian (Numbers 31:8)
64 Riverbank (Exodus 2:5)
65 Foot covering
66 "As a lion in his _____" (Psalm 10:9)
67 "I _____ not" (Luke 17:9)

DOWN

1 Ground moisture
2 "_____ the Ahohite" (1 Chronicles 11:29)
3 Worn-out clothing
4 "That the Son of God might be glorified _____" (John 11:4)
5 Arsenic (sym.)
6 "Lookest thou upon them that _____ treacherously" (Habakkuk 1:13)
7 "Name of _____" (Judges 1:11)
8 "His city was _____" (Genesis 36:39)
9 Abram's birthplace
10 A son of Haman (Esther 9:8–10)
11 Sister of Naham (1 Chronicles 4:19)
14 "They passed through _____" (Acts 15:3)
15 "_____ shall have distresses" (Ezekiel 30:16)
17 "Through faith also _____ herself received strength to conceive seed" (Hebrews 11:11)
19 Someone from Italy
22 A son of Gad (Genesis 46:16)
26 "Joshua was clothed with filthy garments, _____ stood" (Zechariah 3:3)
27 Received

by N. Teri Grottke

28 King Hezekiah's mother
(2 Kings 18:1–2)
29 "The _____ that is in the land of
Assyria" (Isaiah 7:18)
31 God of Babylon (Isaiah 46)
33 Good student
34 Twenty-first letter of the Greek
alphabet
36 Prophet whose name means "Who
is like the Lord?" (abbr.)
37 A son of Aaron (Exodus 6:23)
38 "God _____ tempt Abraham"
(Genesis 22:1)
39 Biblical book of sixty-six chapters
(abbr.)
40 Opposite of *women*
41 "_____ ye not"
(Romans 11:2)
42 "For thou _____ bitter things
against me" (Job 13:26)

43 "Chariots, and _____, and souls of
men" (Revelation 18:13)
44 "David. . .came into the forest of
_____" (1 Samuel 22:5)
45 "By his name _____" (Psalm 68:4)
46 "Jamin, and _____"
(Genesis 46:10)
47 Enemies
49 Loaded (arch.)
53 David hid from Saul here
54 Person who inherits
55 Zechariah's father (Ezra 5:1)
57 Payment owed
59 Famous Betsy could do this
61 "_____, every one that thirsteth"
(Isaiah 55:1)
63 Indium (sym.)

36

A Comforting Promise

And surely I am with you always, to the very end of the age
MATTHEW 28:20 NI

ACROSS

1 "The sky is _____" (Matthew 16:2)
4 "Epicurean and _____ philosophers" (Acts 17:18 NIV)
9 "They _____ him" (Numbers 21:35)
14 "Shimei son of _____ —in Benjamin" (1 Kings 4:18 NIV)
15 "But _____ man answers harshly" (Proverbs 18:23 NIV) (2 words)
16 Emanations
17 Start of a **QUOTE** (Psalm 62:5 NIV) (5 words)
20 Member of an American Indian people originally from Utah
21 Clear the board
22 "To abide _____ ever" (1 Kings 8:13) (2 words)
25 "You who _____ about the law" (Romans 2:23 NIV)
26 "And a _____ the breadth thereof" (Exodus 39:9)
30 British snack time
31 Uniform decoration
34 Third son of Jether (1 Chronicles 7:38)
35 "The _____ is a great city" (Genesis 10:12)
37 Robert Louis Stevenson initials
38 A bit crazy
40 **QUOTE**, cont'd from 17 Across (2 words)
42 **QUOTE**, cont'd from 40 Across
43 "He removed his _____" (Ruth 4:8 NIV)
45 Little Women author's monogram
46 Chedorlaomer was its king (Genesis 14:1)
49 "That _____ their tongues" (Jeremiah 23:31)
50 Glacial deposit
53 Seen at JFK
54 Atlantis org.
56 Georgia Office of Homeland Security (abbr.)

57 "Ye that. . .are heavy _____" (Matthew 11:28)
59 Young pigeon
61 Defunct orbiter
62 **QUOTE**, cont'd from 42 Across (4 words)
69 "I shall _____ sorrow" (Revelation 18:7) (2 words)
70 Refuse
71 "Prop" or "prof" ending
72 Ahasuerus's chief aide (Esther 3:1)
73 Hot South American music
74 End of the **QUOTE**, cont'd from 62 Across

DOWN

1 Official on the field (abbr.)
2 Father of Phinehas (1 Samuel 1:3)
3 Son of Bilhah (Genesis 35:25)
4 *No Exit* playwright
5 "And under every green _____" (1 Kings 14:23)
6 Quebecer's ending, in Quebec
7 Jaundice
8 Choir-related
9 "Say only what the LORD _____?" (Numbers 24:13 NIV)
10 Ruminates
11 Cortez's quest
12 Sigma follower
13 Course for new arrivals (abbr.)
18 Two of a kind
19 Strait joining the Atlantic and Pacifi
22 "Of _____ own accord" (Leviticus 25:5)
23 Teachers organization (abbr.)
24 "And there shall be _____" (Matthew 24:7)
25 "Every head shall be _____" (Jeremiah 48:37)
27 "Living in your _____ houses" (Haggai 1:4 NIV)

by David K. Shortess

28 "We. . ._____ come to worship him" (Matthew 2:2)
29 "And he said, _____; but thou didst laugh" (Genesis 18:15)
32 Play introduction
33 "Is there any thing _____ hard for me?" (Jeremiah 32:27)
36 "Alway, even unto the _____" (Psalm 119:112)
39 "Even thou wast as _____ of them" (Obadiah 1:11)
41 Herd of whales
42 Friends in Paris
43 "The _____ waxed hot" (Exodus 16:21)
44 "All hold John _____ prophet" (Matthew 21:26) (2 words)
45 "For a _____ kid" (Numbers 15:11) (3 words)
47 "They. . ._____ the sacrifices of the dead" (Psalm 106:28)
48 "And have put on the new _____" (Colossians 3:10)

51 Reciprocates
52 Elijah gave him his mantle (1 Kings 19:19)
55 "And engrave on it _____ seal" (Exodus 28:36 NIV) (3 words)
58 Sandy's two-cent's worth
60 M–R reverse connection
61 "A _____ of meat from the king" (2 Samuel 11:8)
62 Intermedin, initially
63 "_____, though I walk" (Psalm 23:4)
64 "Round about the _____ thereof" (Exodus 28:33)
65 Last OT book (abbr.)
66 Stadium cheer
67 "I put it _____ have washed my feet" (Song of Solomon 5:3) (2 words)
68 Word preceding Psalm 119:97

37

ACROSS

1 "Zechariah, _____, and Jaaziel"
   (1 Chronicles 15:18)
4 "Who layeth the _____ of his
   chambers" (Psalm 104:3)
9 "_____ lay at his feet until the
   morning" (Ruth 3:14)
12 "Doth God take care for _____"
   (1 Corinthians 9:9)
14 Bathsheba's first husband
   (2 Samuel 11:3)
15 "_____ not unto thine own
   understanding" (Proverbs 3:5)
17 Dimensions
18 Pagan goddess of the Ephesians
19 Otherwise
20 Mountain where Jesus liked to pray
22 "Prove me now _____"
   (Malachi 3:10)
24 "They _____ against me"
   (Hosea 7:14)
25 "Ye shall point out for you mount
   _____" (Numbers 34:7)
26 "All the _____ of it" (Numbers 9:3)
30 Bird homes
34 Staff
37 "Of Hena, and _____?"
   (2 Kings 19:13)
39 A judge of Israel (Judges 3:15)
41 Snare
43 A son of Japheth (Genesis 10:2)
45 Weed of grain fields especially of
   biblical times
46 "Restore all that was _____"
   (2 Kings 8:6)
47 "_____ not the world" (1 John 2:15)
48 "I saw a _____ heaven"
   (Revelation 21:1)
49 One of Shaharaim's wives
   (1 Chronicles 8:8)
52 "And he must _____ go through
   Samaria" (John 4:4)
55 Jether's son (1 Chronicles 7:38)
57 This many souls were saved in the ark
61 "Azariah, Raamiah, _____"
   (Nehemiah 7:7)

66 "Mattithiah, and Shema, and
   _____" (Nehemiah 8:4)
67 Was indebted to
68 "They set the altar upon his _____"
   (Ezra 3:3)
70 "Helkath, and _____, and Beten"
   (Joshua 19:25)
71 Farm building
72 Son of Ribai (1 Chronicles 11:31)
73 "Ahijah, Hanan, _____"
   (Nehemiah 10:26)
74 Exclamation of affirmation
75 Enan's son (Numbers 1:15)
76 "God created _____ heaven"
   (Genesis 1:1)

DOWN

1 Baalam's father (2 Peter 2:15)
2 Banish
3 "Jiphtah, and Ashnah, and _____"
   (Joshua 15:43)
4 Flower beginnings
5 A son of Gad (Genesis 46:16)
6 Zibeon's son (1 Chronicles 1:40)
7 "Fifteen shekels, shall be your
   _____" (Ezekiel 45:12)
8 "I am the rose of _____"
   (Song of Solomon 2:1)
9 Killed (arch.)
10 Jesus' grandfather (Luke 3:23)
11 From _____ to west
13 "For if ye do these things, ye shall
   _____ fall" (2 Peter 1:10)
16 Restored the walls in just fifty-two
   days (abbr.)
21 Phinehas's father (1 Samuel 4:4)
23 Before (poet.)
27 Letter written by Paul to one person
   (abbr.)
28 Great wickedness
29 "At Lydda and _____" (Acts 9:35)
31 To place
32 "Now the serpent was more subtil
   _____ any beast" (Genesis 3:1)
33 Certain
34 Not left hand but _____ (abbr.)

by N. Teri Grottke

35 "The heads of _____ and Zeeb" (Judges 7:25)
36 Son of Zerah (1 Chronicles 2:6)
38 Has ownership
40 Ground moisture
42 David wrote these (abbr., var.)
44 "_____ that ye refuse" (Hebrews 12:25)
50 A male sheep
51 "Mount Sinai in _____" (Galatians 4:25)
53 "A lion in his _____" (Psalm 10:9)
54 Returning exiles—the children of _____ (Ezra 2:44)
56 Shamgar's father (Judges 3:31)
58 Goliath was one
59 The king of Assyria took Israel here in their captivity (2 Kings 17:6)
60 Yours (arch.)
61 A city of the priests (1 Samuel 22:19)

62 "Then he was no more, because God took him _____" (Genesis 5:24 NIV)
63 In this place
64 "Of Harim, _____" (Nehemiah 12:15)
65 Rephaiah's father (1 Chronicles 4:42)
66 Largest continent
69 "O Lord, let your _____ be attentive" (Nehemiah 1:11 NIV)

38

ACROSS

1 "Zur, and Hur, and _____, which were dukes" (Joshua 13:21)
5 "Used curious _____ brought their books" (Acts 19:19)
9 Buns
10 "_____ the chancellor" (Ezra 4:8)
12 "The vine of _____" (Isaiah 16:8)
13 "Shalt not be to him as an _____" (Exodus 22:25)
15 "They _____ in the dry places like a river" (Psalm 105:41)
16 "The pen of the _____ is in vain" (Jeremiah 8:8)
18 "_____ joy of the LORD" (Nehemiah 8:10)
20 "Thou shalt not approach to his wife: she is thine _____" (Leviticus 18:14)
22 "The brook of _____" (Psalm 83:9)
23 "Thy rod and thy staff _____ comfort me" (Psalm 23:4)
24 "Worthy is the Lamb that was _____" (Revelation 5:12)
26 Dine
27 "Esther _____, and stood before the king" (Esther 8:4)
28 "Malchishua, Abinadab, and _____" (1 Chronicles 8:33)
30 Ruler of the half part of Keilah (Nehemiah 3:18)
32 Coxa
33 "Bethel on the west, and _____ on the east" (Genesis 12:8)
34 "The people gat them by _____" (2 Samuel 19:3)
38 "The Beerothites fled to _____" (2 Samuel 4:3)
42 Army
43 Frozen water
45 "The _____ that the king rideth upon" (Esther 6:8)
46 "God had sworn with an _____ to him" (Acts 2:30)
47 Nail heads
49 Mellow
50 Wood
51 "As when one _____ out water" (Proverbs 17:14)
53 "I _____ down under his shadow with great delight" (Song of Solomon 2:3)
54 "Husham of the land of _____" (Genesis 36:34)
56 "The merchants of Sheba and _____" (Ezekiel 27:22)
58 "Whose soever sins ye _____, they are remitted unto them" (John 20:23)
59 Nathan's father (1 Chronicles 2:36)
60 "Straightway the spirit _____ him" (Mark 9:20)
61 Reck

DOWN

1 "Will a man _____ God?" (Malachi 3:8)
2 "Under oaks and poplars and _____" (Hosea 4:13)
3 Ebony
4 "_____, whom she bear" (1 Chronicles 7:14)
5 "The son of Hesed, in _____" (1 Kings 4:10)
6 "_____ between Nineveh and Calah" (Genesis 10:12)
7 "_____ saith thy son Joseph" (Genesis 45:9)
8 "At the gate of _____" (2 Kings 11:6)
9 "Amnon, and _____, Benhanan" (1 Chronicles 4:20)
11 Procedure
12 "_____ uncle said unto him" (1 Samuel 10:14)
14 "Joanna, which was the son of _____" (Luke 3:27)
15 Level
17 A prophet son of Amoz (2 Kings 19:20) (abbr.)
19 "Saul _____ David" (1 Samuel 18:9)

by Tonya Vilhauer

21 "Likewise from _____, and from Chun" (1 Chronicles 18:8)
23 "Judas Iscariot, which also was the _____" (Luke 6:16)
25 "His _____ of brass" (Daniel 7:19)
27 Father of Shamgar (Judges 3:31)
29 Prone
31 "Naaman, _____, and Rosh" (Genesis 46:21)
34 "The Chaldeans, Pekod, and _____" (Ezekiel 23:23)
35 Sippet
36 "_____ put on her royal apparel" (Esther 5:1)
37 "Send me Uriah the _____" (2 Samuel 11:6)
38 "Sharaim, and Adithaim, and _____" (Joshua 15:36)
39 "Parmashta, and _____, and Aridai" (Esther 9:9)

40 "Michael, and _____, and Joha" (1 Chronicles 8:16)
41 Assemble
44 Saw
47 "Fir trees of _____" (Ezekiel 27:5)
48 "All my _____ shall Tychicus declare unto you" (Colossians 4:7)
51 "Eloi, Eloi, _____ sabachthani?" (Mark 15:34)
52 "If the world _____ you" (John 15:18)
55 "And God _____ Balaam" (Numbers 23:4)
57 Very angry

39

ACROSS

1 The city Lot fled to (Genesis 19:22–23)
5 A great distance
9 "She. . .daubed it with slime and with _____" (Exodus 2:3)
14 Along with
15 "_____ the door after her" (2 Samuel 13:17)
16 Amasa's father (2 Samuel 17:25)
17 Hold back (arch.)
19 Bed covering
20 Area near Babylon (2 Kings 17:24)
21 "We _____ not those things which we have wrought" (2 John 1:8)
22 "Thou. . .hast fenced me with bones and _____" (Job 10:11)
23 "The children of _____" (Ezra 2:52)
25 She left Peter at the door (Acts 12:13–14)
27 Brother of Shammai (1 Chronicles 2:28)
29 Conspicuous
33 "Hammoleketh bare _____" (1 Chronicles 7:18)
36 Son of Micah (1 Chronicles 8:35)
38 Exclamation of affirmation
39 "_____ not unto thine own understanding" (Proverbs 3:5)
40 "_____ wings of a great eagle" (Revelation 12:14)
41 Spiders spin these
42 To perform
43 Saw
45 One of David's priests (1 Kings 1:8)
46 Son of Aaron (Exodus 6:23)
48 Mix
50 Son of Jahdai (1 Chronicles 2:47)
52 High respect (var.)
56 Make unclean
59 Symbol of power
61 Make good _____ of
62 Another name for Jerusalem (Isaiah 29:1)
63 Former inhabitants of Jerusalem
65 Spear
66 "Nevertheless _____ heart was perfect" (1 Kings 15:14)
67 "Give thyself no _____" (Lamentations 2:18)
68 Finished
69 "All the hills shall _____" (Amos 9:13)
70 "Many. . .used curious _____" (Acts 19:19)

DOWN

1 Sibling of Jeush (2 Chronicles 11:19)
2 Oily fruit
3 "Children of _____" (Ezra 2:50)
4 Staff
5 In an overseas country
6 Enemies
7 "Nor _____ the thing that is gone out of my lips" (Psalm 89:34)
8 Most people use their _____ of the two (2 words) (abbr.)
9 "They came to Antioch in _____" (Acts 13:14)
10 "Kedesh, and Hazor, and _____" (Joshua 15:23)
11 You (arch.)
12 Team
13 Headcovers
18 "_____ and Medad" (Numbers 11:27)
22 "Let fall also _____ of the handfuls" (Ruth 2:16)
24 "Smote _____, and Dan" (1 Kings 15:20)
26 "Joanna the wife of Chuza _____ steward" (Luke 8:3)
28 Clothing
30 Looked at
31 "Men of the other _____" (Nehemiah 7:33)
32 Job
33 "_____ the Ahohite" (1 Chronicles 11:29)

by N. Teri Grottke

34 Adherents of creed
35 "That which _____ been is named already" (Ecclesiastes 6:10)
37 Reverent fear
41 To tell about danger
43 "The LORD _____ a sweet savour" (Genesis 8:21)
44 Little color
45 "For _____ sake will I not hold my peace" (Isaiah 62:1)
47 Each
49 "He would _____ out a little from the land" (Luke 5:3)
51 "He thought on _____ things" (Matthew 1:20)
53 "Cast ye the unprofitable servant into _____ darkness" (Matthew 25:30)
54 Utilizes (arch.)
55 Takes a break

56 "Valley of Shaveh, which is the king's _____" (Genesis 14:17)
57 "Shuthelah: of _____" (Numbers 26:36)
58 Opposite of *lose*
60 Son of Joktan (Genesis 10:26–29)
63 Like jelly
64 "_____ the son of Ikkesh" (2 Samuel 23:26)

40

Fortified on All Sides

Uzziah built towers in Jerusalem. . .and fortified them.

2 CHRONICLES 26:9

ACROSS

1 "As the deer _____ for streams of water" (Psalm 42:1 NIV)
6 Tolkien creature
9 WW II battle site in France (2 words) (abbr.)
13 Howdy in HI
14 "He shall not go out to _____" (Deuteronomy 24:5)
15 "And _____ went before the ark" (2 Samuel 6:4)
16 **FIRST SIDE:** "And there stood a watchman on the _____" (2 Kings 9:17) (3 words)
19 "And the king sat upon his _____ at other times" (1 Samuel 20:25) (2 words)
20 Military address (abbr.)
21 "They brought the _____" (Mark 12:16 NIV)
23 Units of resistance
25 Home of the Globe and Mail
27 "He is _____ creature" (2 Corinthians 5:17) (2 words)
30 "_____, our eye hath seen it" (Psalm 35:21)
32 "But the _____ charged them" (Mark 7:36) (2 words)
33 "Are you not _____ men" (1 Corinthians 3:4 NIV)
34 "_____ shadow of death" (Job 34:22)
35 "The _____ of man" (Psalm 144:3)
36 "_____ of all creatures" (Genesis 7:15 NIV)
38 "The street of the city _____ pure gold" (Revelation 21:21)
40 "And _____ out heaven with the span" (Isaiah 40:12)
44 "And all that handle the _____" (Ezekiel 27:29)
46 Big snake
48 Designated part
49 "For with my _____ passed over" (Genesis 32:10) (2 words)

52 "There _____ in a window" (Acts 20:9)
53 "Each has its _____" (Song of Songs 6:6 NIV)
54 "Thou shalt not _____ unto him" (Deuteronomy 13:8)
56 Perform again
58 "His _____ also was like the beryl" (Daniel 10:6)
59 "They neither _____ nor reap" (Luke 12:24)
61 "When the _____ comes" (Matthew 19:28 NCV) (2 words)
65 **SECOND SIDE:** "Israel. . .spread his tent beyond _____" (Genesis 35:21) (4 words)
68 Whet
69 "For if _____ not away" (John 16:7) (2 words)
70 "_____ trying to please men" (Galatians 1:10 NIV) (3 words)
71 British gun
72 "Eat _____ of it raw" (Exodus 12:9)
73 German steel center

DOWN

1 Servings of butter
2 Burn balm
3 "_____ certain man was sick" (John 11:1) (2 words)
4 **THIRD SIDE:** "From _____ even unto the border of Ethiopia" (Ezekiel 29:10) (4 words)
5 Wife of Abraham (Genesis 17:15)
6 "After their _____ lusts" (2 Peter 3:3)
7 Indian prince
8 "Men _____ in unawares" (Jude 1:4)
9 Old patriotic organization (abbr.)
10 **FOURTH SIDE:** "Fortified cities and against _____" (Zephaniah 1:16 NIV) (3 words)
11 "Neither _____ to another" (Leviticus 19:11) (2 words)

by David K. Shortess

12 Small round bodies set within sedimentary rock
17 "What _____ the better" (Ecclesiastes 6:11) (2 words)
18 Runs fast
22 "In the days of _____" (Luke 17:26)
24 "Who will _____ us any good" (Psalm 4:6)
26 "And yet there is _____" (Luke 14:22)
27 Power booster
28 Teachers organization (abbr.)
29 "Of _____, the family of the Erites" (Numbers 26:16)
31 "Cretans and _____—we hear" (Acts 2:11 NIV)
37 "But for you it is _____" (Philippians 3:1)
39 "Though you _____ like the eagle" (Obadiah 1:4 NIV)
41 "They are quenched as _____" (Isaiah 43:17)
42 Samuel's "dad"
43 "A _____ of dragons" (Jeremiah 10:22)

45 Oxydol rival
47 "I _____ pleasant bread" (Daniel 10:3) (2 words)
49 Non-arts degree, sometimes (abbr.)
50 "Let him go free for his _____ sake" (Exodus 21:27)
51 "The anger _____ displeasure" (Deuteronomy 9:19) (2 words)
55 "I became like a Jew, _____ the Jews" (1 Corinthians 9:20 NIV) (2 words)
57 Robinson Crusoe author
60 "Lord, to whom shall _____" (John 6:68) (2 words)
62 Cities in Ohio and Oklahoma
63 "Eat some of my _____" (Genesis 27:31 NIV)
64 The Emerald Isle
66 "Joseph's _____ brethren went" (Genesis 42:3)
67 "A tree that will not _____" (Isaiah 40:20)

41

ACROSS

1 "_____ was of the king's seed in Edom" (1 Kings 11:14)
3 Cooking vessel
6 Attached to the shoulder
9 "The name thereof _____" (Judges 1:26)
10 "Anab, and Eshtemoh, and _____" (Joshua 15:50)
12 "His spirit came _____" (Judges 15:19)
14 A son of Gad (Genesis 46:16)
15 "We came to Myra, a city of _____" (Acts 27:5)
17 Hurry
18 "The melody of thy _____" (Amos 5:23)
20 Elderly
21 "Of the _____ Ruth" (Ruth 1:4)
22 No
23 Humanity
25 Get older
26 Nobelium (sym.)
27 "While their feast _____" (Judges 14:17)
31 One of three postexilic prophets (abbr.)
32 A son of Pashur (Ezra 10:22)
35 Vision-impaired priest (1 Samuel 3:2)
36 After Nahum (abbr.)
37 The father of Ethan (1 Chronicles 6:44)
38 Appendage
39 Single
40 The home of the Hebrews in Egypt
41 "Against Jerusalem, _____" (Ezekiel 26:2)
42 "Who hath _____ you to flee from the wrath to come" (Luke 3:7)
44 Arsenic (sym.)
45 A son of Jacob (Genesis 35:26)
46 Joab's brother (2 Samuel 2:18)
49 A temple gate (2 Kings 11:6)
50 A city in Benjamin (Joshua 18:21–28)
53 To consume
54 "Thou settest a print upon the _____ of my feet" (Job 13:27)
57 Abraham's father (Luke 3:34)
58 "Have I received any _____ to blind mine eyes" (1 Samuel 12:3)
60 Large lake
61 David fought the Syrians here (2 Samuel 10:17)
62 Prophet
63 "He _____ horns" (Habakkuk 3:4)
64 "Shimei, and _____, and the mighty men" (1 Kings 1:8)
65 Commanded militarily
66 "Say in their hearts, _____" (Psalm 35:25)

DOWN

1 Jaroah's son (1 Chronicles 5:14)
2 "Encamped at _____" (Numbers 33:35)
3 "The sick of the _____" (Mark 2:9)
4 No matter which
5 "Be diligent to come unto me to _____" (Titus 3:12)
6 Type of quartz (pl.)
7 Hasty
8 "Very last _____" (Luke 12:59)
9 Book of ceremonial laws (abbr.)
11 "Whosoever shall compel thee to go a _____, go with him twain" (Matthew 5:41)
12 Aholibah's sister (Ezekiel 23:4)
13 Saul's grandfather (1 Chronicles 8:33)
16 Fuss
19 Eliasaph's father (Numbers 3:24)
24 "The _____ of Jericho" (2 Kings 25:5)
25 "Look from the top of _____" (Song of Solomon 4:8)
26 "The children of _____, six hundred fifty and two" (Ezra 2:60)
28 "Telmelah, _____, Cherub, Addon" (Nehemiah 7:61)
29 A son of Zabad (1 Chronicles 7:21)

by N. Teri Grottke

30 Bore
33 Burnt residue
34 Zerubbabel's father (Haggai 1:1)
36 "_____ shall we escape"
   (Hebrews 2:3)
40 A son of Jahdai (1 Chronicles 2:47)
41 A chill
43 Ezbai's son (1 Chronicles 11:37)
47 The author of this NT book is
   unknown (abbr.)
48 Hearing organs
49 "A _____ to take fire"
   (Isaiah 30:14)
50 Right hand (abbr.)
51 "Sons of _____" (1 Chronicles 7:12)
52 "Kill every _____ among the little
   ones" (Numbers 31:17)
55 Rachel's sister
56 Unhappy
59 Buzzing stinger

42

ACROSS

1 "Even with a _____ destruction" (Micah 2:10)
5 A great distance
9 "From _____ to the wilderness" (Isaiah 16:1)
13 Wrongdoing
14 Cush's son (Genesis 10:7)
15 "They shall say in all the highways, _____" (Amos 5:16)
16 To make right
17 "Adonijah, Bigvai, _____" (Nehemiah 10:16)
18 Fewer
19 "Gave the _____" (Nehemiah 8:8)
20 Group
21 Geuel's father (Numbers 13:15)
22 "He sold them into the hand of _____" (1 Samuel 12:9)
24 Level
26 Alchitran
27 Hymns
29 Voyage
30 "The son of _____" (Nehemiah 11:13)
35 Faultless
39 "To the moon, and to the _____" (2 Kings 23:5)
40 Individually
41 Sick
42 "Goeth out to Remmonmethoar to _____" (Joshua 19:13)
43 "Tread down the wicked in _____ place" (Job 40:12)
44 "At the name of Jesus every _____ should bow" (Philippians 2:10)
45 "The son of _____" (Luke 3:28)
46 Book of creation (abbr.)
48 Buss
50 "Esau was a cunning _____" (Genesis 25:27)
53 "They. . ._____ the sacrifices of the dead" (Psalm 106:28)
54 Reverence
57 Confident
58 "With a _____ round about the hole" (Exodus 39:23)
60 Mutineer
62 "He that eateth of their _____ dieth" (Isaiah 59:5)
63 "The burning _____" (Leviticus 26:16)
64 Gad's son (Genesis 46:16)
65 Assemble
66 "Rulers of _____" (Exodus 18:21)
67 "The cattle upon a thousand _____" (Psalm 50:10)

DOWN

1 "Mattathias, which was the son of _____" (Luke 3:26)
2 "Upon thy people, and into thine _____" (Exodus 8:3)
3 "It shall be both scoured, and _____ in water" (Leviticus 6:28)
4 "Submit yourselves unto the _____" (1 Peter 5:5)
5 "Nevertheless _____ heart was perfect" (1 Kings 15:14)
6 _____ government
7 Shephatiah's father (2 Samuel 3:4)
8 "They _____ in the dry places like a river" (Psalm 105:41)
9 "The son of _____" (Luke 3:35)
10 "The faith of God's _____" (Titus 1:1)
11 "Zeboim, even unto _____" (Genesis 10:19)
12 "The son of _____" (1 Chronicles 6:37)
16 "Thy King cometh, sitting on an _____ colt" (John 12:15)
21 King of Moab (2 Kings 3:4)
23 Swiftly
25 "Are ye unworthy to judge the _____ matters" (1 Corinthians 6:2)
28 "Ye that _____ in judgment" (Judges 5:10)
29 Arcane
31 "There was one _____, a prophetess" (Luke 2:36)

by Tonya Vilhauer

32 "In the morning sow thy _____"
   (Ecclesiastes 11:6)
33 "They came to the threshingfloor
   of _____" (Genesis 50:10)
34 Zoheth's father
   (1 Chronicles 4:20)
35 Noddle
36 NT book after Galatians (abbr.)
37 "Wheat and the _____ were not
   smitten" (Exodus 9:32)
38 "Thou _____ them out of thine
   own heart" (Nehemiah 6:8)
39 "Canst thou bind the sweet
   influences of _____" (Job 38:31)
41 "I would not write with paper and
   _____" (2 John 1:12)
47 Jeroboam's father (2 Kings 15:18)
49 "Beriah, and _____ their sister"
   (Genesis 46:17)
50 Gigantic

51 "The Pharisees began to _____
   him vehemently" (Luke 11:53)
52 Fury
54 Cain's brother
55 Healthy
56 Asked for a double portion of
   Elijah's spirit (abbr., var.)
57 "The son of _____, which was the
   son of Noe" (Luke 3:36)
59 Joshua's father (Joshua 2:1)
61 "Of _____, the family of the
   Erites" (Numbers 26:16)

43

ACROSS

1 Panhandle
4 A Canaanite city (Joshua 11:21)
8 "Dwelling was from _____" (Genesis 10:30)
13 Sadoc's father (Matthew 1)
15 Elihu's father (1 Samuel 1:14)
16 Fire product
17 "The glory of the _____ is one" (1 Corinthians 15:40)
19 "Only the _____ of Dagon was left to him" (1 Samuel 5:4)
20 "Ard, the family of the _____" (Numbers 26:40)
21 "_____ sister was Timna" (Genesis 36:22)
23 "Sister in law is _____ back" (Ruth 1:15)
24 Not dry
25 "God _____ be tempted with evil" (James 1:13)
28 "The howling thereof unto _____" (Isaiah 15:8)
33 Kish's father (1 Samuel 9:1)
34 "_____ of spices" (Song of Solomon 6:2)
35 Prophet father of Maher-shalal-hash-baz (abbr.)
36 Real estate
37 A son of Jahdai (1 Chronicles 2:47)
38 A child of Shobal (Genesis 36:23)
39 Archenemy of Haman (three letter abbr.)
40 A son of Judah (1 Chronicles 2:3)
41 "Saul leaned upon his _____" (2 Samuel 1:6)
42 "But if any man think that he _____ himself" (1 Corinthians 7:36)
45 "From _____ come wars and fightings among you" (James 4:1)
46 Abraham's nephew
47 A city of Hadarezer (1 Chronicles 18:8)
48 Hunger
51 "He was of the house and _____ of David" (Luke 2:4)

55 Azor's son (Matthew 1:14)
56 Done away with
58 Get up
59 Thorny flower
60 Exhaust
61 "I saw the _____" (Habakkuk 3:7)
62 Female sheep
63 Boat paddle

DOWN

1 "Valley of _____" (Psalm 84:6)
2 Jeshua's son (Nehemiah 3:19)
3 Precious metal
4 *Attention* (Dutch)
5 "The _____ of a whip" (Nahum 3:2)
6 "Against Jerusalem, _____" (Ezekiel 26:2)
7 A male bovine
8 Lord
9 "Who remembered us in our low _____" (Psalm 136:23)
10 Ostracize
11 Edges of garments
12 Type of snake
14 "Ye have _____ as kings without us" (1 Corinthians 4:8)
18 Small chair
22 Be indebted to (arch.)
25 A faithful spy (Numbers 14:6)
26 To humble
27 "In the _____ day" (Leviticus 23:32)
28 A son of Benjamin (Genesis 46:21)
29 First garden
30 Flax cloth
31 Abraham's heir
32 Abram lived in this plain (Genesis 13:18)
34 Not straight
37 Rhymers
38 "Thou _____ thine hand" (Psalm 104:28)
41 A son of Gad (Genesis 46:16)
43 "_____ thou persuadest me to be a Christian" (Acts 26:28)

by N. Teri Grottke

44 "The _____ of them and of the chief priests prevailed" (Luke 23:23)
45 "And _____ I was speaking" (Daniel 9:20)
47 "They sailed _____ by Crete" (Acts 27:13)
48 "_____ ye well" (Acts 15:29)
49 Returned exiles—children of _____ (Ezra 2:15)
50 Rabbit
52 A son of Abinadab (2 Samuel 6:3)
53 A son of Benjamin (Genesis 46:21)
54 "Mahli, and _____" (1 Chronicles 23:23)
55 "The Egyptians _____ at their own table" (Genesis 43:32 NLT)
57 Arrow ejector

44

Man's Way or God's Way

All the ways of a man are clean in his own eyes;
but the Lord weigheth the spirits.

PROVERBS 16:2

ACROSS

1 Git outta here!
6 Relating to style or manner
11 What will be, will be—*Che sarà,*
   _____
15 Start of a **QUOTE** from Proverbs
   14:12 NIV
16 "And behold, _____ horse"
   (Revelation 6:8) (2 words)
17 "In heaven _____ earth"
   (Deuteronomy 3:24) (2 words)
18 Capital of Morocco
19 "And _____ foot" (Mark 6:33 NIV)
   (2 words)
20 "She opened it and saw the _____"
   (Exodus 2:6 NIV)
21 **QUOTE**, cont'd from 15 Across
   (5 words)
24 "One beka _____ person, that is"
   (Exodus 38:26 NIV)
25 "The _____ of hell and of death"
   (Revelation 1:18)
26 "He that planted the _____"
   (Psalm 94:9)
27 "And wilt thou _____ it up in three
   days?" (John 2:20)
28 "That which was _____"
   (Matthew 18:11)
30 "The fourth part of a _____"
   (2 Kings 6:25)
33 Tribal Kenyans
36 "The son of _____" (Job 25:6)
37 "Children of _____ men"
   (Job 30:8)
38 **QUOTE**, cont'd from 21 Across
   (6 words)
42 July times in NY
43 "Stricken in _____" (Joshua 23:1)
44 "And _____ rod that budded"
   (Hebrews 9:4)
45 _____ Plaines, Illinois
46 "So Tibni died, and _____ reigned"
   (1 Kings 16:22)
48 Use a crystal ball
49 *Angle* or *pod* prefix
50 Swiss river
51 Sound of pleasure

54 **QUOTE**, cont'd from 38 Across
   (5 words)
59 Greek god of war
60 "It is _____ am Alpha and Omega"
   (Revelation 21:6) (2 words)
61 "Not for your _____ do I this"
   (Ezekiel 36:32)
62 "Even where Satan's _____ is"
   (Revelation 2:13)
63 _____ Island, one-time immigrant
   exam station
64 "One jot _____ tittle"
   (Matthew 5:18) (2 words)
65 "And _____ for your flocks"
   (Numbers 32:24 NIV)
66 End of the **QUOTE**, cont'd from 54
   Across
67 Slang expression of disgust

DOWN

1 "Lest I _____ her naked" (Hosea 2:3)
2 "And let the angel of the LORD _____
   them" (Psalm 35:5)
3 Steel in concrete
4 "I got _____ deal!" (unfair treatment)
   (2 words)
5 "And he said unto _____, and eat it
   up" (Revelation 10:9) (3 words)
6 "Antipas was my faithful _____"
   (Revelation 2:13)
7 Moonfish
8 "Of the tribe of _____ craftsman"
   (Exodus 38:23 NIV) (2 words)
9 "There was also _____" (Joshua 17:1)
   (2 words)
10 Magnifiers
11 "Be ye therefore _____" (1 Peter 4:7)
12 "And _____ on every altar"
   (Numbers 23:14) (2 words)
13 "And he took one of his _____"
   (Genesis 2:21)
14 "Is _____ thing too hard for the
   LORD" (Genesis 18:14)
22 "Eat nothing made with _____"
   (Exodus 12:20 NIV)
23 "For thou shalt _____ the labour of
   thine hands" (Psalm 128:2)

by David K. Shortess

27 Stadium cheers
28 "And the _____ walk" (Matthew 11:5)
29 "Put it _____ reed"
    (Matthew 27:48) (2 words)
30 Roman politician who was opposed to
    Julius Caesar
31 "For _____ the days that were before
    the flood" (Matthew 24:38) (2 words)
32 Hur, -Gay, and Franklin
33 TV's talking horse (2 words)
34 "Joshua son of Nun, Moses' _____"
    (Joshua 1:1 NIV)
35 Ranking NCOs (abbr.)
36 "_____ from the east came to
    Jerusalem" (Matthew 2:1 NIV)
37 "Canaan, there shalt thou _____ me"
    (Genesis 50:5)
39 "And all that handle the _____, the
    mariners" (Ezekiel 27:29)
40 Mother-of-pearl
41 "And she conceived, and _____"
    (Isaiah 8:3) (3 words)
46 "And my people the _____"
    (Jeremiah 6:27 NIV)

47 "For to be carnally _____ is death"
    (Romans 8:6)
48 British Columbia First Nation tribe
49 "The LORD _____ the heart"
    (Proverbs 17:3 NIV)
50 "And _____ up" (Revelation 10:10)
    (2 words)
51 "Above all that we _____ think"
    (Ephesians 3:20) (2 words)
52 "When a man dieth in _____"
    (Numbers 19:14) (2 words)
53 Gardening accessories
54 "Behold, I am a dry _____"
    (Isaiah 56:3)
55 "And there builded _____ altar unto
    the LORD" (Genesis 12:7) (2 words)
56 "They will _____ out the bread"
    (Leviticus 26:26 NIV)
57 Terry Gilliam film, *Lost _____
    Mancha*
58 "Some would even _____ to die"
    (Romans 5:7)
59 "On the hole of the _____" (Isaiah 11:8)

45

ACROSS

1 "God hath not given us the spirit of
_____" (2 Timothy 1:7)
5 "Punish the men that are settled on
their _____" (Zephaniah 1:12)
9 "If she have _____ strangers"
(1 Timothy 5:10)
11 Simon Peter (John 1:42)
13 Opposite of *me*
14 "Abiezer the _____"
(1 Chronicles 27:12)
16 Have possession
17 Forgive
18 Motel
20 Goat baby
21 "See, here is _____; what doth
hinder me to be baptized"
(Acts 8:36)
23 "Ye shall in no _____ enter"
(Matthew 5:20)
24 "Till I make thine _____ thy
footstool" (Luke 20:43)
27 "_____ of Berea" (Acts 20:4)
29 "It will _____ him to powder"
(Luke 20:18)
30 "_____ whose fruit" (Jude 12)
31 "Forasmuch as _____ excellent
spirit" (Daniel 5:12)
32 We
33 Subdued
36 Trap
39 "He shall give thee the _____ of
thine heart" (Psalm 37:4)
41 Peresh's brother (1 Chronicles 7:16)
43 Ahira's father (Numbers 1:15)
44 Ammihud's son (1 Chronicles 9:4)
46 Article
47 "_____ was an hair of their head
singed" (Daniel 3:27)
48 "The elements shall melt with
fervent heat, the _____ also"
(2 Peter 3:10)
50 "Out of whose womb came the
_____" (Job 38:29)
51 "Shemaiah the _____"
(Jeremiah 29:31)

55 Staff
56 Singed
57 Biblical den dweller, for a time
59 Told an untruth
60 "The Lord is at _____"
(Philippians 4:5)

DOWN

1 "His mother. . .gave them to the
_____" (Judges 17:4)
2 An altar (Joshua 22:34)
3 Greek form of *Hagar*
(Galatians 4:24)
4 Made new again
5 Allow
6 A book of four written by Paul in
prison (abbr.)
7 A son of Benjamin (Genesis 46:21)
8 "And I will _____ the soul of the
priests" (Jeremiah 31:14)
9 Calling for a calf (arch.)
10 He forsook Paul (2 Timothy 4:10)
11 "_____ for flocks"
(2 Chronicles 32:28)
12 We have five of these
13 Wooden collar
15 One of Paul's most trusted
missionary friends (abbr.)
19 Saul's grandfather
(1 Chronicles 8:33)
22 Decay
23 Roman emperor
25 A son of Parosh (Ezra 10:25)
26 Opposite of *outer*
28 Dried plum
33 "Two _____ shall there be in one
board" (Exodus 26:17)
34 Son of Jehaleleel (1 Chronicles 4:16)
35 This book is a series of speeches by
Moses (abbr.)
36 "The cedar, the _____ tree, and the
myrtle" (Isaiah 41:19)
37 Went to bed
38 Mamre's brother (Genesis 14:13)
39 "As a lion in his _____"
(Psalm 10:9)

by N. Teri Grottke

40 In place of
41 Zebulun's border was to this city
   (Joshua 19:12)
42 Pay attention to
45 A son of Noah
49 "_____, and Ivah?" (Isaiah 37:13)
52 "Between Bethel and _____"
   (Genesis 13:3)
53 Before (arch.)
54 Commanded militarily
58 Indium (sym.)

46

ACROSS

1 Wrote last book of the NT (Revelation 1:1)
5 "We are being called to account today for _____ act of kindness" (Acts 4:9 NIV)
7 "The fields. . ._____ ripe for harvest" (John 4:35 NIV)
8 Not mixed with anything else; John saw a "city of _____ gold" (Revelation 21:18 NIV)
10 "Come, follow _____, Jesus said" (Mark 1:17 NIV)
11 A small private room for prayer; also an enclosed place for hanging clothes
12 Jacob's brother (Genesis 25:26)
14 Simon and Andrew fished in the _____ of Galilee (Mark 1:16)
15 "Can. . .the leopard change its _____" (Jeremiah 13:23)
18 *Tank* or *truck* (abbr.)
19 The *yellowhammer* is the state bird here (abbr.)
20 Shau's grandson (Genesis 38:2–3)
21 "God. . ._____ all things" (Revelation 4:11 NIV)
24 Distance across; length, _____, height
25 Possessive of nonhuman pronoun; "The world and _____ desires pass away" (1 John 2:17 NIV)
27 "I _____ the Alpha and the Omega" (Revelation 1:8 NIV)
28 OT prophet of righteousness

DOWN

1 Brother of John, son of Zebedee (Matthew 4:21)
2 Minerals that contain metals
3 "Going on from there, _____ saw two other brothers" (Matthew 4:21 NIV)
4 John was an _____, one of 12 disciples Jesus chose (Matthew 10:2)
5 An enclosed space; "Jesus spoke. . . while teaching in the temple _____" (John 8:20 NIV)
6 John used this to catch fish (Matthew 4:21)
9 "A man of knowledge _____ words with restraint" (Proverbs 17:27 NIV)
11 "Can you drink the _____ I drink" (Mark 10:38 NIV)
13 "How can this be? Nicodemus _____" (John 3:9 NIV)
16 "Do not break your _____" (Matthew 5:33 NIV)
17 Jesus had the people sit down on the _____ (John 6:10)
18 To clip
21 Organization started by Beverly LaHaye to bring biblical principles into public policy
22 John "took the little scroll from the angel's hand and _____ it" (Revelation 10:10 NIV)
23 Lacking brightness
26 "They had Peter and John brought before them and began _____ question them" (Acts 4:7)

by John Hudson Tiner

47

ACROSS

1 Prophet sent to King Ahab (abbr., var.)
4 Soft infant food (pl.)
8 Very young person
13 Bird home
15 Asa's father (1 Chronicles 3:10)
16 Gomer's husband (Hosea 1:2–3)
17 This priest rebuilt the temple
18 Transgression
19 Situated down or below
20 Ehud escaped here (Judges 3:26)
22 "_____ that ye refuse not" (Hebrews 12:25)
23 Predicted Assyrian invasion of Judah (abbr.)
24 "Neither _____ they the king's laws" (Esther 3:8)
25 "Mine eyes fail with looking _____" (Isaiah 38:14)
28 Child's favorite seat
29 "Give _____ to His command-ments" (Exodus 15:26 NKJV)
30 Son of Joktan (Genesis 10:26–29)
34 Twenty-first letter of the Greek alphabet
36 "_____, Hadid, and Ono" (Ezra 2:33)
39 Eve was made from Adam's
41 A son of Benjamin (Genesis 46:21)
42 Abraham's nephew
43 Before (arch.)
44 Disfigure
45 "Dip the _____ of his finger in water" (Luke 16:24)
46 Female sheep
47 "She. . ._____ down across from him at a distance of about a bowshot" (Genesis 21:16 NKJV)
48 "And _____ lay at his feet until the morning" (Ruth 3:14)
49 Book presents God's faithfulness and love for His people (abbr.)
50 As well
52 "A _____ of dove's dung" (2 Kings 6:25)
54 "Against Jerusalem, _____" (Ezekiel 26:2)
56 "I am _____ than thou" (Isaiah 65:5)
59 Ripped
61 A family of returned exiles (Ezra 2:57)
64 Writing tool
65 Abraham's firstborn (Genesis 21:3)
68 "And the shekel shall be twenty _____" (Ezekiel 45:12)
70 Songs of praise, forgiveness, thankfulness, and power are a few themes in this book (abbr., var.)
71 Father (Galatians 4:6)
72 "_____, Nekeb, and Jabneel"
73 "Sons of _____" (1 Chronicles 7:12)
74 "Gilalai, _____, Nethaneel" (Nehemiah 12:36)
75 Penuel's son (1 Chronicles 4:4)
76 A son of Helem (1 Chronicles 7:35)
77 Kept from detection

DOWN

1 "Day of _____ birth" (Ecclesiastes 7:1)
2 "They slew of them in _____ ten thousand men" (Judges 1:4)
3 "And of Asriel, the family of the _____" (Numbers 26:31)
4 Opposite of *future*
5 A son of Aaron (Exodus 6:23)
6 Bowling target
7 Known as The Rainbow Country (abbr.)
8 "Then were they all of good _____" (Acts 27:36)
9 "This bread of ours we took _____ for our provision" (Joshua 9:12 NKJV)
10 Rephaiah's father (1 Chronicles 4:42)
11 "Punish the men that are settled on their _____" (Zephaniah 1:12)
12 Son of Zerah (1 Chronicles 2:6)
14 A son of Micah (1 Chronicles 8:35)
19 Shemaiah's son (1 Chronicles 3:22)
21 Round, red fruits

by N. Teri Grottke

22 "I will send _____ of flies upon thee" (Exodus 8:21)
26 The seventeenth letter of the Hebrew alphabet
27 Accomplish
31 "Passed along by the north of _____" (Joshua 15:6)
32 A son of Jehiel (1 Chronicles 9:37)
33 Parts of the mouth
34 Guilty or not guilty
35 "Awake, ye drunkards, and weep; and _____" (Joel 1:5)
37 "Unto them were committed the _____ of God" (Romans 3:2)
38 "Though thou _____ me, I will not eat of thy bread" (Judges 13:16)
40 "He giveth to all life, and _____, and all things" (Acts 17:25)
51 This state's name comes from the Iroquois, meaning "good river" (abbr.)

53 Beryllium (sym.)
55 Lotan's son (1 Chronicles 1:39)
57 "The queen in gold of _____" (Psalm 45:9)
58 "Christ. . ._____ again" (Acts 17:3)
60 "Hariph, Anathoth, _____" (Nehemiah 10:19)
61 Samuel killed this Amelekite king (1 Samuel 15:32–33)
62 Darius was one (Daniel 11:1)
63 Enoch's son (Genesis 4:18)
66 "Through faith also _____ herself received strength to conceive seed" (Hebrews 11:11)
67 "They. . .have _____ a wound" (Obadiah 1:7)
69 Advanced Medical Optics (abbr.)
70 Talks about Onesimus, the slave, in this book (abbr., var.)
73 Conquered by Joshua (Joshua 8:1–3)

48

Love Never Fails

And now abide faith, hope, love, these three;
but the greatest of these is love.

1 CORINTHIANS 13:13 NKJV

ACROSS

1 Ruffled shirt front
6 "Put it upon a _____" (Numbers 21:9)
10 "The _____ facing Joppa" (Joshua 19:46 NIV)
14 Islands greeting
15 "Cast her _____ heaps" (Jeremiah 50:26) (2 words)
16 "**LOVE** is _____" (A characteristic of love from 1 Corinthians 13 NKJV)
17 Grinding tooth
18 "_____ they faint in the way" (Matthew 15:32)
19 French _____-China
20 "**LOVE**. . ._____" (A characteristic of love from 1 Corinthians 13:4–7 NKJV) (3 words)
23 German auto
24 "It is _____ on fire of hell" (James 3:6)
25 "They. . .took no _____ with them" (Matthew 25:3)
28 In _____ (In its place)
30 Sale inducement
35 Shapeless mass
37 A long, long time
39 Excessive zeal
40 A characteristic of **LOVE** from 1 Corinthians 13:4 NKJV (3 words)
43 "There is one _____ unto all" (Ecclesiastes 9:3)
44 "Much _____ gold" (Psalm 19:10)
45 "His teeth shall be set on _____" (Jeremiah 31:30)
46 More crimson
48 In charge of airport security (abbr.)
50 *Auction* or *profit* follower
51 "A _____ for a burnt offering" (Leviticus 16:3)
53 Suitable for chuch use (abbr.)

55 "**LOVE**. . ._____" (A characteristic of love from 1 Corinthians 13:4–7 NKJV) (3 words)
62 "Casting all your _____ upon him" (1 Peter 5:7)
63 "Over Edom will I cast out my _____" (Psalm 60:8)
64 _____ Gay, famous WWII bomber
65 Get things ready, for short
66 Vietnam neighbor
67 "He looked like glowing _____" (Ezekiel 1:27 NIV)
68 Follower of Joel
69 Fraternal fellows
70 Wear away

DOWN

1 Door post
2 Healing succulent
3 Gaucho's cowcatcher
4 Actress Maureen
5 "Then departed Barnabas to _____" (Acts 11:25)
6 Succeed (3 words)
7 German auto
8 "For his anger _____ only a moment" (Psalm 30:5 NIV)
9 Hadassah (Esther 2:7)
10 Similar
11 "Put a _____ on his hand, and shoes on his feet" (Luke 15:22)
12 "The Creator of the _____ of the earth" (Isaiah 40:28)
13 "Why make ye this _____, and weep?" (Mark 5:39)
21 *Good-bye*, in Lyon
22 List components
25 One who leers
26 "Gaius, whom _____ in the truth" (3 John 1:1) (2 words)
27 "I have _____ thee" (Isaiah 43:4)

by David K. Shortess

29 "Disobedient and _____ for doing anything good" (Titus 1:16 NIV)
31 Unit of cotton
32 Positive electrode
33 Slight color
34 "The very thing I was _____ to do" (Galatians 2:10 NIV)
36 "For, lo, the wicked _____ their bow" (Psalm 11:2)
38 "The _____ man does not know" (Psalm 92:6 NIV)
41 Cubic meter
42 Respond to a stimulus
47 Fight playfully (dial.)
49 "And you will devise an evil _____" (Ezekiel 38:10 NIV)
52 Taj _____
54 Ocean vessel
55 "Do thyself no _____: for we are all here" (Acts 16:28)

56 Sandwich cookie
57 Energizes (with up)
58 "Which things the angels desire to _____ into" (1 Peter 1:12)
59 "It teaches us to say _____ ungodliness and worldly passions" (Titus 2:12 NIV) (2 words)
60 "Therefore my heart is _____" (Psalm 16:9)
61 "Then let him count the years of the _____ thereof" (Leviticus 25:27)
62 He presents his numbers well (abbr.)

49

ACROSS

1 What you do to a drum
5 "The seed should spring and _____" (Mark 4:27)
9 "In Asher and in _____" (1 Kings 4:16)
14 Likewise
15 Salathiel's father (Luke 3:27)
16 Henadad's son (Nehemiah 3:18)
17 Yell
18 So be it
19 Things
20 "Woe to the land _____ with wings" (Isaiah 18:1)
22 "The Amorites would dwell in mount _____" (Judges 1:35)
23 Not dry
24 Hebrew eighth month
25 "Every _____ fled away" (Revelation 16:20)
29 "God created _____ heaven" (Genesis 1:1)
31 "The linen _____ at a price" (1 Kings 10:28)
35 Allotment
36 "Barley, and _____, and lentiles" (Ezekiel 4:9)
38 "But the wheat and the _____ were not smitten" (Exodus 9:32)
39 Cephas
40 Boat paddle
41 Rebuke
43 King Hezekiah's mother (2 Kings 18:2)
44 Honed
46 "The son of _____" (1 Kings 4:10)
47 Suspend
49 Possessive pronoun
50 Tall buildings
51 Have possession
53 "He became the first of the herdsmen _____ live in tents" (Genesis 4:20 NLT)
54 Hurry
57 Looks at (arch.)

63 A gem on the third row of the ephod (Exodus 28:19)
64 "Mahli, and _____" (1 Chronicles 23:23)
65 "_____ the Ahohite" (1 Chronicles 11:29)
66 Reigned
67 "_____ not unto thine own understanding" (Proverbs 3:5)
68 Shoe bottom
69 "If by any _____ I may provoke" (Romans 11:14)
70 Picnic pests
71 "At his holy _____" (Psalm 99:9)

DOWN

1 "The earth with her _____ was about me for ever" (Jonah 2:6)
2 King Hoshea's father (2 Kings 15:30)
3 Largest continent
4 Spoke
5 Chewed
6 Forgive
7 Jerahmeel's son (1 Chronicles 2:25)
8 "The one _____ of the cherub" (1 Kings 6:24)
9 A son of Aaron (Exodus 6:23)
10 "Aquila, born in Pontus, _____ come from Italy" (Acts 18:2)
11 Opposite of *under*
12 Gentle
13 Snake sound
21 "The life of the _____ thereof" (Proverbs 1:19)
24 "Zechariah, _____, and Jaaziel" (1 Chronicles 15:18)
25 A son of Beriah (1 Chronicles 8:16)
26 The visiting queen at Solomon's court was from here
27 Dead language
28 "_____ there yet the treasures" (Micah 6:10)
29 Product of weeping
30 "The joy of the _____ ceaseth" (Isaiah 24:8)

by N. Teri Grottke

32 Get up

33 "The horse and his _____ hath he thrown into the sea" (Exodus 15:1)

34 "And he must _____ go through Samaria" (John 4:4)

36 "None other _____ there" (John 6:22)

37 Instructional place

42 Chop

45 A liquid measure (Leviticus 23:13)

48 "It cannot be _____ for gold" (Job 28:15)

50 "And some fell among _____" (Mark 4:7)

52 Troublesome plants

53 Small bread grain

54 Hurt

55 A chill

56 Heber's father (Luke 3:35)

57 Another name for *Zoar* (Genesis 14:2)

58 First garden

59 "That dippeth with me in the _____" (Mark 14:20)

60 Jesus cried this on the cross

61 Having great height

62 "_____ the Bethelite" (1 Kings 16:34)

50

ACROSS

1 Twelve months
5 Kudos
9 "Kingdom was Babel, and Erech, and _____" (Genesis 10:10)
14 "We _____ bear record" (3 John 1:12)
15 "The curse upon mount _____" (Deuteronomy 11:29)
16 Nahash's son (2 Samuel 17:27)
17 Wander
18 "He caused an east _____ to blow in the heaven" (Psalm 78:26)
19 "The stork, the _____ after her kind" (Leviticus 11:19)
20 "It came to pass in the month _____" (Nehemiah 2:1)
22 Framework for carrying (arch.)
24 "A _____, and a stone lay upon it" (John 11:38)
25 "_____ his son, Jehoshua his son" (1 Chronicles 7:27)
27 Spotted
29 Run after
32 "I gave unto _____ mount Seir" (Joshua 24:4)
33 "Thou believest that there is _____ God" (James 2:19)
34 Report
36 "Your old men shall dream _____" (Joel 2:28)
41 "Take thee a _____" (Ezekiel 4:1)
43 "My people _____ know that thou art a virtuous woman" (Ruth 3:11)
45 "The sons of _____ the Netophathite" (Jeremiah 40:8)
46 Fashion
48 Close
50 "Which is the _____, even Christ" (Ephesians 4:15)
51 A prophet son of Amoz (abbr.)
53 Indicator
55 "The wheat and the _____ were not smitten" (Exodus 9:32)
56 Emote
59 Terminate
60 Uproar
62 "All their _____ shall be scattered" (Jeremiah 10:21)
65 Mareshah's father (1 Chronicles 4:21)
69 Obtain
70 "Where the women _____ hangings for the grove" (2 Kings 23:7)
73 "Let all _____ that seek thee rejoice" (Psalm 40:16)
74 Level
75 Salah's son (Genesis 10:24)
76 "Thou _____ cast me into the deep" (Jonah 2:3)
77 Lease
78 Unique
79 "Adam, Sheth, _____" (1 Chronicles 1:1)

DOWN

1 "Merchants received the linen _____ at a price" (1 Kings 10:28)
2 "_____, lama sabachthani?" (Mark 15:34)
3 "Nevertheless _____ heart was perfect" (1 Kings 15:14)
4 "The _____ shall come" (John 11:48)
5 Not many
6 "Observe the month of _____" (Deuteronomy 16:1)
7 "But hath in due times _____ his word" (Titus 1:3)
8 "Let him call for the _____ of the church" (James 5:14)
9 Wood
10 Verify
11 Polyp
12 Over
13 "So when they had _____" (John 21:15)
21 Substantive
23 Construe
26 Lack

by Tonya Vilhauer

28 Remedy

29 "Whether it be oven, or ranges for
_____" (Leviticus 11:35)

30 Monad

31 Depend on

35 "Out of the spoils _____ in battles"
(1 Chronicles 26:27)

37 Tenth NT book (abbr.)

38 Hushim's father (1 Chronicles 7:12)

39 "Gilalai, _____, Nethaneel, and
Judah" (Nehemiah 12:36)

40 Edge

42 "Samuel arose and went to _____"
(1 Samuel 3:6)

44 "If a man have long _____"
(1 Corinthians 11:14)

47 "He called the name of the well
_____" (Genesis 26:20)

49 Rant

52 Response

54 "The Egyptians shall _____ to
drink" (Exodus 7:18)

56 "Going _____ strange flesh"
(Jude 1:7)

57 "Ruth _____ unto her" (Ruth 1:14)

58 Symbol

61 "_____, the family of the
Tahanites" (Numbers 26:35)

63 Coin

64 Always

66 Eleazar's father (2 Samuel 23:9)

67 "Thy King cometh, sitting on an
_____ colt" (John 12:15)

68 "Ephron dwelt among the children
of _____" (Genesis 23:10)

71 Minor OT prophet (abbr., var.)

72 In time

51

ACROSS

1 Shallum's father (1 Chronicles 9:19)
5 A brother of Arad (1 Chronicles 8:15)
9 _____ and hers towels, for example
12 The Israelites filled _____ with manna (Exodus 16:32)
14 Dwell
15 Arrived
16 King of Syria (Isaiah 7:1)
17 "Brought the heads of _____" (Judges 7:25)
18 "Of Harim, _____" (Nehemiah 12:15)
19 In time past
20 Sister of a parent
22 Joshaviah's father (1 Chronicles 11:46)
24 "They were _____ upon the trees until the evening" (Joshua 10:26)
26 Beg
27 Elderly
28 Abiel's son (1 Samuel 9:1)
29 Female sheep
32 Furious driver (2 Kings 9:20)
35 Garden in Babylon
37 Judge after Jephthah (Judges 12:7–8)
39 "The Spirit of God was hovering _____ its surface" (Genesis 1:2 NLT)
40 Shaving tool
42 Give for temporary use
43 "Traitors, _____, highminded, lovers of pleasures" (2 Timothy 3:4)
45 Grapes grow on this
46 "Used curious _____" (Acts 19:19)
47 "Garments, _____ stood" (Zechariah 3:3)
48 Asa's father (1 Chronicles 3:10)
50 He is good
52 A son of Zebulun (Genesis 46:14)
54 In the opposite direction
58 "_____ sister was Timna" (Genesis 36:22)
60 "Let fall also _____ of the handfuls" (Ruth 2:16)
61 Capable
62 Naum's son (Luke 3:25)
63 Not short
65 A son of Benjamin (1 Chronicles 8:2)
67 A lot
68 Idol
69 Trap
70 "_____ there yet the treasures" (Micah 6:10)
71 "With three _____ of great stones" (Ezra 6:4)
72 The tenth part of an ephah (Exodus 16:36)

DOWN

1 A son of Esau (Genesis 36:5)
2 The end
3 Eliadah's son (1 Kings 11:23)
4 A son of Gad (Genesis 46:16)
5 "Her maidens walked _____ by the river's side" (Exodus 2:5)
6 Filth
7 First mother
8 "I will purge out from among you the _____" (Ezekiel 20:38)
9 Rehob's son (2 Samuel 8:3)
10 A son of Helem (1 Chronicles 7:35)
11 Jesus' coat didn't have one (John 19:23)
13 "As a _____ which melteth" (Psalm 58:8)
15 Jesus' first miracle was here (John 2:11)
21 Below
23 Location of the spring called Enhakkore (Judges 15:19)
25 It provided shade for Jonah (Jonah 4:6)
26 A duke of Edom (Genesis 36:41)
28 A daughter of Job (Job 42:14)
30 Desire

by N. Teri Grottke

31 "Pride _____ in humiliation, while humility brings honor" (Proverbs 29:23 NLT)
32 Jediael's brother (1 Chronicles 11:45)
33 "_____ the death of the cross" (Philippians 2:8)
34 "He shall bring forth the _____ thereof" (Zechariah 4:7)
36 A son of Jesse (1 Samuel 17:12)
38 "First the _____, then the ear" (Mark 4:28)
41 A son of Jahdai (1 Chronicles 2:47)
44 "The linen _____ at a price" (1 Kings 10:28)
49 "Thou shalt _____ thyself: for then shall the LORD go" (2 Samuel 5:24)
51 Bread bakes in these
53 Opposite of *hard*

54 "House of the _____" (Ezra 6:1)
55 Jorkoam's father (1 Chronicles 2:44)
56 Meager
57 "Libnah, and _____" (Joshua 15:42)
58 Tibetan monk
59 A son of Eliphaz (Genesis 36:11)
60 "They are not _____ in giving birth like Egyptian women" (Exodus 1:19 NLT)
64 Fuss
66 "Lod, and _____, the valley of craftsmen" (Nehemiah 11:35)

52

Christmas Greetings

And the Word was made flesh, and dwelt among us. . .
full of grace and truth.

JOHN 1:14

ACROSS

1 "And _____ the father of Canaan" (Genesis 9:18) (2 words)
6 "And death rather _____ my life" (Job 7:15)
10 "And after three days _____ again" (Mark 8:31)
14 "Thy neck _____ tower of ivory" (Song of Solomon 7:4) (3 words)
15 "Jesus died and _____ again" (1 Thessalonians 4:14)
16 "_____ in the path of your commands" (Psalm 119:32 NIV) (2 words)
17 "Thy _____ perish with thee" (Acts 8:20)
18 *Mila 18* author
19 "For God did _____ me before you" (Genesis 45:5)
20 Start of a good holiday **REMINDER** for this year (3 words)
23 "Four days _____ I was fasting" (Acts 10:30)
25 Giants' Mel
26 "A bushel, or _____ a bed?" (Mark 4:21)
30 "I have found my lost _____" (Luke 15:9 NIV)
32 Town on the Delaware River
36 "_____ no man any thing" (Romans 13:8)
37 Like a fork
39 Wampum
40 High school equivalent exam (abbr.)
41 **REMINDER**, cont'd from 20 Across (2 words)
45 "And lead us _____ into temptation" (Matthew 6:13)
48 "_____ is this day" (Deuteronomy 4:38) (2 words)
49 Book after Micah
53 "Because they _____ not" (Matthew 2:18)
54 "And to give his life a _____ for many" (Matthew 20:28)
57 "We came to _____, a city of Lycia" (Acts 27:5)

58 "And bread made without _____" (Exodus 12:8 NIV)
60 New (prefix)
62 "_____ her a double portion" (Revelation 18:6 NIV)
63 End of **REMINDER**, cont'd from 41 Across
68 "I know it _____ of a truth" (Job 9:2) (2 words)
71 "Know that it is _____" (Matthew 24:33)
72 "And bound _____ his son" (Genesis 22:9)
75 "His flesh shall wax _____" (Isaiah 17:4)
76 "So Jesus came again into _____" (John 4:46)
77 Nickname for a very timid person: Nervous _____
78 "To sit up _____" (Psalm 127:2)
79 "And in him _____" (2 Corinthians 1:20)
80 Shows shock

DOWN

1 "And saith unto _____" (Matthew 4:6)
2 Mount _____, Japan
3 "Durst no _____ himself to them" (Acts 5:13) (2 words)
4 "When _____ the blood" (Exodus 12:13) (2 words)
5 "Let not the king _____" (2 Chronicles 18:7) (2 words)
6 "Do not _____ neighbor" (Micah 7:5 NIV) (2 words)
7 "Shaphat the son of _____" (Numbers 13:5)
8 "But such _____ common to man" (1 Corinthians 10:13) (2 words)
9 "And make her _____ on high?" (Job 39:27)
10 "For he is _____" (Matthew 28:6)
11 Anger
12 "Neither light of the _____" (Revelation 22:5)

by David K. Shortess

13 "Even unto the _____" (Psalm 119:112)
21 The Beehive State (abbr.)
22 "And his body is _____ a tree" (Deuteronomy 21:22 NIV) (2 words)
23 "His strange _____" (Isaiah 28:21)
24 "Let me _____ pray thee" (Jeremiah 40:15) (2 words)
27 "Am I a _____" (1 Samuel 17:43)
28 "Save one little _____ lamb" (2 Samuel 12:3)
29 "His eyes shall be _____ with wine" (Genesis 49:12)
31 "And Abner the son of _____" (2 Samuel 2:12)
33 "Or the leopard his _____?" (Jeremiah 13:23)
34 "Even _____ men with him" (Jeremiah 41:1)
35 Lummox
38 "Because of the _____" (Nehemiah 5:3)
42 Jehoshaphat's father (1 Kings 22:41)
43 "Stand in awe, and _____ not" (Psalm 4:4)
44 "A _____ without blemish out of the flock" (Leviticus 6:6)
45 "And he said, _____" (Joshua 5:14)

46 "And my people the _____" (Jeremiah 6:27 NIV)
47 Herbal, for one
50 They are often on the backs of pews
51 "_____, the son of Hur" (Exodus 31:2)
52 Physicist and Nobelist Planck
55 "And _____ and filled a sponge" (Mark 15:36) (2 words)
56 "Create in _____ clean heart" (Psalm 51:10) (2 words)
59 "Cast a _____ upon me" (Lamentations 3:53)
61 "_____ unto the LORD a new song" (Psalm 96:1) (2 words)
64 Empire conquered by Pizarro
65 "The coat was without _____" (John 19:23)
66 Rational
67 "Why was it, _____" (Psalm 114:5 NIV) (2 words)
68 "It shall be _____ with him" (Isaiah 3:11)
69 "Said unto the _____" (Mark 4:39)
70 "And they _____ down" (Ruth 4:2)
73 High mountain
74 Baseball's Young and namesakes

53

ACROSS

1 Solomon's great-grandson
(1 Kings 15:8)
4 "Suburbs, and _____"
(1 Chronicles 6:73)
8 Zechariah's father (Ezra 5:1)
12 "Used curious _____" (Acts 19:19)
13 Measured (arch.)
15 Action
16 Ebed's son (Judges 9:26)
17 Ribai's son (1 Chronicles 11:31)
18 Give for temporary use
19 "Og the king of Bashan, which
dwelt at Astaroth in _____"
(Deuteronomy 1:4)
21 "Because of his _____ for wicked
men" (Job 34:36)
23 "Tobiah, and _____ the Arabian"
(Nehemiah 6:1)
26 Another name for stannum
27 "Thou inhabitant of _____"
(Micah 1:11)
28 Best
31 Anub's father (1 Chronicles 4:8)
32 Jacob's God-given name
34 "Set it between Mizpeh and
_____" (1 Samuel 7:12)
36 "_____, Hizkijah, Azzur"
(Nehemiah 10:17)
38 Tiny insect
39 Certain
40 Uncovered
41 A sweet spice (Exodus 30:34)
44 Prophecy book for Nineveh and the
Assyrians (abbr.)
45 "And every _____ fled away"
(Revelation 16:20)
47 A daughter of Zelophehad
(Numbers 26:33)
49 Hophni's father (1 Samuel 4:4)
50 "Righteousness as a mighty _____"
(Amos 5:24)
51 "Ziph, and Telem, and _____"
(Joshua 15:24)
54 "The waters of _____"
(Isaiah 15:9)

57 Boys
58 Belonging to Shem's father
61 Eat formally
62 "As he saith also in _____"
(Romans 9:25)
63 A son of Joseph (Luke 3:26)
64 Night sky illuminator
65 Take care of
66 "_____ shall offer gifts"
(Psalm 72:10)
67 "Hundred and _____ years old"
(Joshua 24:29)

DOWN

1 "_____ the Canaanite"
(Numbers 21:1)
2 "The astrologers, the _____,
the monthly prognosticators"
(Isaiah 47:13)
3 Slumbering
4 Patriarch of a family of returned
exiles (Ezra 2)
5 Old-time fishers' tool
6 In the edge of the wilderness
(Exodus 13:20)
7 "What _____ ye to weep"
(Acts 21:13)
8 Laziness
9 "The fallow _____"
(Deuteronomy 14:5)
10 Homes of wild animals
11 Strange
12 Get older
14 "Which the clouds do drop and
_____ upon man abundantly"
(Job 36:28)
20 Rephaiah's father (1 Chronicles 4:42)
22 Christians want to _____ souls for
Christ
24 "Behold, Rachel _____ daughter
cometh with the sheep"
(Genesis 29:6)
25 "I have an _____ to thee, O
captain" (2 Kings 9:5)
27 One of Solomon's servants
(Nehemiah 7:57)

by N. Teri Grottke

28 "_____ a calf tender and good" (Genesis 18:7)
29 "Found Abishag a _____" (1 Kings 1:3)
30 Abraham's father
31 "A _____ of dove's dung" (2 Kings 6:25)
33 No matter which
35 If he was your boss, you could carry your weapon to work (abbr.)
37 Let go
41 "The leeks, and the _____, and the garlick" (Numbers 11:5)
42 "Ye shall point out for you mount _____" (Numbers 34:7)
43 Old
46 "Destroy _____ kings and people" (Ezra 6:12)
48 "Thou _____ affliction upon our loins" (Psalm 66:11)

50 Disgrace
51 "In presence am _____ among you" (2 Corinthians 10:1)
52 Adam and Eve were cast out of here
53 The giant had six of these (2 Samuel 21:20)
55 A son of Judah (1 Chronicles 2:3)
56 Saul's grandfather (1 Chronicles 8:33)
57 Abraham's nephew
59 This NT book has an anonymous author and an unknown time of writing (abbr.)
60 "Of Keros, the children of _____" (Nehemiah 7:47)

Prince of Egypt

ACROSS

1 "She named him _____, saying, 'I drew him out of the water'" (Exodus 2:10 NIV)
5 Helps solve mysteries (abbr.)
7 "Let there _____ strife" (Genesis 13:8) (2 words)
8 A cry of despair; "_____! I am fainting" (Jeremiah 4:31 NIV)
10 Type of deer
11 Near Ai and east of Bethel: Beth _____ (Joshua 7:2 NIV)
12 "A new king. . .came to power _____ Egypt" (Exodus 1:8 NIV)
13 Paul put many of the _____ in prison (Acts 26:10 NIV)
15 King of Judea, called "that fox" by Jesus (Luke 13:32 NIV)
16 "Is there _____ in the white of an egg?" (Job 6:6 NIV)
18 Another name for Dad
19 A grain offering was baked in one (Leviticus 2:4 NIV)
20 Group of cheerleaders, _____ squad
21 Of the burning bush, Moses said, "I will go _____ and see this strange sight" (Exodus 3:3 NIV)
22 Horn sound
23 Pharaoh's daughter felt sorry for baby Moses because _____ was crying (Exodus 2:6 NIV)
24 Pharaoh was ruler of this country

DOWN

1 "The LORD said to Moses, 'Come up to _____ the mountain'" (Exodus 24:12 NIV) (2 words)
2 Pharaoh's daughter said, "This is _____ of the Hebrew babies" (Exodus 2:6 NIV)
3 "Let my people go, _____ that they may hold a festival to me in the desert" (Exodus 5:1 NIV)
4 "In the town of David a _____ has been born to you" (Luke 2:11 NIV)
5 Breathe rapidly
6 "The place where you are standing _____ holy ground" (Exodus 3:5 NIV)
7 "The mirth of the wicked is _____" (Job 20:5 NIV)
9 Give for temporary use; Jesus says to _____ to enemies without expecting to get anything back (Luke 6:35 NIV)
11 Moses' brother (Exodus 4:14)
13 A _____ famine struck the distant country where the younger, wasteful son had gone (Luke 15:14 NIV)
14 "Strike you hands together and _____ your feet" (Ezekiel 6:11 NIV)
15 "Invite him to _____ something to eat" (Exodus 2:20 NIV)
17 The Lord is "slow to anger, abounding in _____ and faithfulness" (Exodus 34:6 NIV)
18 A person who writes verse
20 Energy
21 Moses said, "_____, what a great sin these people have committed!" (Exodus 32:31 NIV)
22 Close to; Moses met Zipporah _____ a well in Midian (Exodus 2:15–21)

by John Hudson Tiner

ACROSS

1 An idol of Babylon (Isaiah 46:1)
4 Make a correction
9 Possesses
12 "Prepare war, _____ up the mighty men" (Joel 3:9)
13 Priests had to wash here
14 King Hezekiah's mother (2 Kings 18:2)
15 "Abiezer the _____" (1 Chronicles 27:12)
17 "_____ the door after her" (2 Samuel 13:17)
19 Knight
20 "Let him down by the _____ in a basket" (Acts 9:25)
21 A son of Haman (Esther 9:9)
23 A son of Zophah (1 Chronicles 7:36)
24 "If well, why _____ thou me?" (John 18:23)
25 Bed coverings
28 Visiting queen at Solomon's court was from here (2 Chronicles 9:1)
29 "Abraham gave a _____ part of all" (Hebrews 7:2)
30 "Do not _____ the edge" (Ecclesiastes 10:10)
31 Weed of grain fields especially of biblical times
35 Zibeon's daughter (Genesis 36:2)
36 Alemeth's father (1 Chronicles 9:42)
37 Enoch's son (Genesis 4:18)
38 Male sheep
39 "God made a wind to pass _____ the earth" (Genesis 8:1)
40 "They _____ him" (Mark 11:4)
41 "Son of _____, in Aruboth" (1 Kings 4:10)
43 "They shall _____ from sea to sea" (Amos 8:12)
44 Changed
47 "Heavens shall _____ away with a great noise" (2 Peter 3:10)
48 "They who _____ to be somewhat in conference" (Galatians 2:6)
49 Flow

50 A son of Bela (1 Chronicles 7:7)
53 "Helkath, and _____" (Joshua 19:25)
54 Adrammelech and Sharezer's brother (2 Kings 19:37)
57 "Rachel had taken the images. . . and _____ upon them" (Genesis 31:34)
58 Stop
59 Esau's father-in-law (Genesis 26:34)
60 "God created _____ heaven" (Genesis 1:1)
61 Baanah's son (1 Chronicles 11:30)
62 "They are _____ with the showers of the mountains" (Job 24:8)

DOWN

1 Mighty man of David (2 Samuel 23:36)
2 A son of Ram (1 Chronicles 2:27)
3 Allow
4 Places of sacrifice
5 A son of Merari (Numbers 3:20)
6 Great wickedness
7 Restaurant workers sometimes put a _____ over their hair
8 "As when a thirsty man _____" (Isaiah 29:8)
9 Places to live
10 Stayed in a place
11 Paul's missionary partner
12 "God saw that it _____ good" (Genesis 1:21)
16 Be in debt to (arch.)
18 This NT author took messages to the Corinthian church (abbr.)
22 Eve was made from Adam's
23 "Cart came into the field of Joshua, a _____" (1 Samuel 6:14)
24 "Laban went to _____ his sheep" (Genesis 31:19)
25 Night sky illuminator
26 "_____, and Ivah?" (Isaiah 37:13)
27 "Tappuah, and _____" (Joshua 15:34)
28 Tear repeatedly

by N. Teri Grottke

30 "May be _____ for a wave offering before the LORD" (Leviticus 7:30)
32 "Of _____, the family" (Numbers 26:17)
33 "Who said, _____ it" (Psalm 137:7)
34 "Mahli, and _____" (1 Chronicles 23:23)
36 Joshua's father (Haggai 1:1)
40 "Even unto _____" (Genesis 10:19)
42 Before (arch.)
43 "Sow that was _____ to her wallowing in the mire" (2 Peter 2:22)
44 Type of tree (Isaiah 44:14)
45 Smallest
46 A descendant of Ephraim (1 Chronicles 7:22–25)
47 "No scrip, no bread, no money in their _____" (Mark 6:8)

49 Ebed's son (Judges 9:26)
50 Lazy
51 "_____ of Jesse" (Isaiah 11:10)
52 Motel
55 "_____ that ye refuse" (Hebrews 12:25)
56 Ground moisture

Listen Up

Hear diligently my speech
and my declaration with your ear

JOB 13:1

ACROSS

1 "If a man _____, will he live again?" (Job 14:14 NIV)
5 Average grades
9 "And let _____ man hearken unto me" (Job 34:34) (2 words)
14 "Sweeter _____ than honey" (Psalm 19:10)
15 "Within as it were an half _____ of land" (1 Samuel 14:14)
16 "That the island was called _____" (Acts 28:1 NIV)
17 Start of Jesus' closing **WORDS** to each of the seven churches (Revelation 2–3) (5 words)
20 If he _____ satisfy his soul when he is hungry" (Proverbs 6:30) (2 words)
21 "As _____ gone by" (Malachi 3:4 NIV) (2 words)
22 Mineral spring site
23 Town on Lake Murray, NW of Columbia, S.C.
25 **WORDS**, cont'd from 17 Across (4 words)
32 "Eden who were in _____ Assar?" (Isaiah 37:12 NIV)
33 "_____ of faith" (Trust in the unseen) (2 words)
34 What Ezekiel saw in the wall in Ezekiel 8:7 (2 words)
35 "Forgive their sin, and will _____ their land" (2 Chronicles 7:14)
37 "We shall be _____ by his life" (Romans 5:10)
39 "Fine _____ have been poured upon me" (Psalm 92:10 NIV)
40 "Is this how you _____ king over Israel?" (1 Kings 21:7 NIV) (2 words)
42 Trait bearers
44 "The people _____ down to eat and to drink" (Exodus 32:6)

45 **WORDS**, cont'd from 25 Across (3 words)
48 "Can a devil _____ the eyes of the blind?" (John 10:21)
49 Government river project (abbr.)
50 "For they might not be _____ come into the city" (2 Samuel 17:17) (2 words)
54 Mild earthquakes
58 End of **WORDS**, cont'd from 45 Across (3 words)
61 Avant-garde French composer Erik
62 Volunteer service for women in WWI (abbr.)
63 "The body is a _____" (1 Corinthians 12:12 NIV)
64 "And to make _____ of sins" (Daniel 9:24) (2 words)
65 Give off
66 Coal units

DOWN

1 Dits' companions
2 "In a basket was _____ down by the wall" (2 Corinthians 11:33) (2 words)
3 *This* in Torreon (Sp.)
4 "_____ thou also them that hold" (Revelation 2:15) (2 words)
5 Marsh plants
6 "The woodwork will _____ it" (Habakkuk 2:11 NIV)
7 Mound stat (abbr.)
8 "And _____ them in their place" (Nehemiah 13:11)
9 "If an ox gore _____ woman" (Exodus 21:28) (4 words)
10 Magician's stick
11 Intestinal segments
12 "Neither _____ thou in all the plain" (Genesis 19:17)
13 "His fingers into his _____" (Mark 7:33)

by David K. Shortess

18 "I am _____ and Omega" (Revelation 1:8)
19 "For I will make _____ great nation" (Genesis 21:18) (2 words)
23 "Upon the great confidence which _____ you" (2 Corinthians 8:22) (3 words)
24 "Except they _____ of their deeds" (Revelation 2:22)
25 "The _____ has two daughters" (Proverbs 30:15 NIV)
26 Make glad
27 *Scant* in Sussex (Brit.)
28 "And _____ will go for us?" (Isaiah 6:8)
29 Crane
30 God of Islam
31 "_____ everything. Hold on to the good" (1 Thessalonians 5:21 NIV)
32 "There be many _____ say" (Psalm 4:6)
36 _____ Cruces, NM
38 Intentionally destroy

41 "Hating even the garment _____ by the flesh" (Jude 1:23)
43 Frugal person
46 City north of Kuala Lumpur, Malaysia
47 "Then I said, _____ off" (Lamentations 3:54) (3 words)
50 "An edict was issued in _____" (Esther 9:14 NIV)
51 "Ahira the son of _____" (Numbers 1:15)
52 Follows *sermon* or *kitchen* (suffix)
53 "_____ no wise" (Romans 3:9) (2 words)
54 Siamese language
55 Expression of incredulity (2 words)
56 "Give free _____ to my complaint" (Job 10:1 NIV)
57 Concordes, for example (abbr.)
59 "Save one little _____ lamb" (2 Samuel 12:3)
60 Moving machine component

ACROSS

1 Having great height
5 Possessive pronoun
8 What you do with clothes
12 "As he saith also in _____" (Romans 9:25)
13 Large lake
14 Damaged
16 Curses
18 43,560 sq. ft. x 2
20 He was a shepherd from Tekoa in Judah (abbr.)
21 Hushim's husband (1 Chronicles 8:8)
23 Book written by John while exiled on Patmos (abbr.)
24 "_____ upon mount Zion" (Obadiah 1:17)
25 Steal
26 "Even of _____ my people is risen up as an enemy" (Micah 2:8)
27 Whole
30 Tenth Jewish month (Esther 2:16)
32 There was none at the inn
33 Ghost
35 A son of Gad (Genesis 46:16)
36 "Ungodly sinners have spoken _____ him" (Jude 1:15)
38 Writing tool
41 Opposite of *autumn*
42 "Whosoever shall say to his brother, _____, shall be in danger of the council" (Matthew 5:2)
43 One of David's wives (1 Chronicles 3:3)
45 "_____ out into the deep" (Luke 5:4)
47 Hananiah's father (Jeremiah 28:1)
48 "Who gave himself _____ our sins" (Galatians 1:4)
50 Abdiel's son (1 Chronicles 5:15)
51 Nahor's firstborn (Genesis 22:20–21)
52 Broken pieces
56 King Hezekiah's mother (2 Kings 18:2)
57 "Dwelling was from _____" (Genesis 10:30)
58 "Plucked up by the _____" (Jude 1:12)
60 "My sword shall be _____ in heaven" (Isaiah 34:5)
62 This prophet's name means "God strengthens" (abbr.)
64 Daniel had a vision by this river
65 Basketball team Miami _____
66 Boy
67 "Through faith also _____ herself received strength to conceive seed" (Hebrews 11:11)

DOWN

1 Also
2 "Nevertheless _____ heart" (1 Kings 15:14)
3 "A _____ek of barley" (Hosea 3:2 NIV)
4 A son of Mizraim (Genesis 10:13)
5 Rhode _____ (abbr.)
6 Rip
7 Ahiam's father (1 Chronicles 11:35)
8 "God saw that it _____ good" (Genesis 1:21)
9 Judah's firstborn (Numbers 26:19)
10 Resting place of Noah's ark
11 "And _____, and Engannim" (Joshua 19:21)
14 "Your lusts that war in your _____?" (James 4:1)
15 Bird from the ark sent out three times
17 "Wilderness of _____" (Exodus 15:22)
19 "Not in _____ and drunkenness" (Romans 13:13)
22 Partook
26 Allow
27 Before (arch.)
28 "_____ was an hair of their head" (Daniel 3:27)
29 "When _____ king" (2 Samuel 8:9)
31 This is used to control a horse

by N. Teri Grottke

33 "The company in ships, and
_____" (Revelation 18:17)
34 Bowling target
36 Capable
37 "Wert _____ in among them"
(Romans 11:17)
38 Cooking vessel
39 The author of this book calls himself
"the Preacher" (abbr.)
40 Jonah would have loved this biblical
book (abbr.)
41 Knight
42 "It shall be a _____ heap"
(Isaiah 17:1)
43 Caleb's wife (1 Chronicles 2:18)
44 "Elihu the son of Barachel the
_____" (Job 32:2)
45 Book by the weeping prophet (abbr.)
46 "Sons of _____"
(1 Chronicles 7:12)

47 Jezebel's husband
49 "_____ weeping for her children"
(Jeremiah 31:15)
53 "I will send a fire on the wall of
_____" (Amos 1:6)
54 Puah's son (Judges 10:1)
55 Night sky illuminator
57 Became acquainted
59 "Of Keros, the children of _____"
(Nehemiah 7:47)
61 Used to express joy
63 An altar (Joshua 22:34)

58

ACROSS

1 Save
5 "The sons of _____"
(1 Chronicles 7:39)
9 "I reap where I _____ not"
(Matthew 25:26)
14 "_____ the Ahohite"
(1 Chronicles 11:29)
15 "Goeth out to Remmonmethoar to
_____" (Joshua 19:13)
16 Reprove
17 Neb
18 "Prepare war, _____ up the mighty
men" (Joel 3:9)
19 Grassland
20 "There was a continual _____
given him" (Jeremiah 52:34)
21 Thought
22 "Stingeth like an _____"
(Proverbs 23:32)
23 Agreement
25 Lade
27 Flog
30 Holler
33 "_____ ye, and believe the gospel"
(Mark 1:15)
38 "Her children _____ up"
(Proverbs 31:28)
40 "Dwelt at Michmash, and _____"
(Nehemiah 11:31)
42 "Whom thou slewest in the valley of
_____" (1 Samuel 21:9)
43 Hyssop
44 "What _____ thee, O thou sea"
(Psalm 114:5)
45 Citron
46 "Sons of Merari by Jaaziah; _____"
(1 Chronicles 24:27)
47 Esau's mother-in-law
(Genesis 36:2)
48 Old-time anesthesia
49 "He carried into the land of _____"
(Daniel 1:2)
51 "From the vessels of _____"
(Isaiah 22:24)
53 Utilize
54 Cainan's father (Genesis 5:9)

56 "Samuel arose and went to _____"
(1 Samuel 3:6)
58 "_____ the sacrifices of the dead"
(Psalm 106:28)
61 "I would not write with paper and
_____" (2 John 1:12)
62 Carmine
66 "The inhabitants of _____"
(Isaiah 10:31)
68 Zoheth's father (1 Chronicles 4:20)
70 Maim
71 "Absalom made _____ captain of
the host" (2 Samuel 17:25)
72 Gera's son (Judges 3:15)
73 "They shall say in all the highways,
_____!" (Amos 5:16)
74 "Bakbakkar, Heresh, and _____"
(1 Chronicles 9:15)
75 A son of Cush (Genesis 10:7)
76 Male red deer

DOWN

1 "Be ye _____ one to another"
(Ephesians 4:32)
2 "_____, lama sabachthani?"
(Mark 15:34)
3 "Woe to them that are at _____ in
Zion" (Amos 6:1)
4 Devotion
5 "O foolish people and _____?"
(Deuteronomy 32:6)
6 Guide
7 Salina is one
8 Leading
9 "He took him a potsherd to _____
himself" (Job 2:8)
10 "Jemuel, and Jamin, and _____"
(Genesis 46:10)
11 "He caused an east _____ to blow
in the heaven" (Psalm 78:26)
12 Rim
13 Whitetail
24 Look at
26 "Unto Enoch was born _____"
(Genesis 4:18)
27 "The _____ are for thy clothing"
(Proverbs 27:26)

by Tonya Vilhauer

8 "King's house, with Argob and
_____" (2 Kings 15:25)
9 "The kingdoms of Ararat, _____,
and Ashchenaz" (Jeremiah 51:27)
1 "I have _____ still and been quiet"
(Job 3:13)
2 Syringa
4 Beat
5 Barachel's son (Job 32:2)
6 "I will take away the _____ of
Baalim" (Hosea 2:17)
7 Yonder
9 Gem
1 Hanani's son (1 Kings 16:1)
4 "Is not _____ the Levite thy
brother?" (Exodus 4:14)
8 "The son of _____, which was the
son of Nagge" (Luke 3:25)
0 Bestial
2 "Sophereth, the children of _____"
(Nehemiah 7:57)

55 "Thick clouds of the _____"
(2 Samuel 22:12)
57 Micaiah's father (1 Kings 22:8)
58 King of the Amalekites
(1 Samuel 15:8)
59 "The troops of _____" (Job 6:19)
60 "The curse upon Mount _____"
(Deuteronomy 11:29)
62 "All the mingled people, and
_____" (Ezekiel 30:5)
63 "Which was the son of _____"
(Luke 3:35)
64 "Duke Teman, duke _____"
(Genesis 36:15)
65 "Thou shouldest make thy _____ as
high as the eagle" (Jeremiah 49:16)
67 A prophet son of Amoz (abbr.)
69 "But if _____ bear a maid child"
(Leviticus 12:5)

59

ACROSS

1 Retained
5 "_____, and Shema" (Joshua 15:26)
9 Binea's son (1 Chronicles 8:37)
14 "_____ the Ahohite" (1 Chronicles 11:29)
15 Travel other than on foot
16 "_____ whose fruit" (Jude 1:12)
17 "In whose eyes a vile person is _____" (Psalm 15:4)
19 The king of Assyria took Israel here in their captivity (2 Kings 17:6)
20 Ethan's father (1 Chronicles 6:44)
21 "And _____ away much people after him" (Acts 5:37)
23 "As the serpent beguiled _____ through his subtilty" (2 Corinthians 11:3)
24 Chicken products
26 Idols
29 Ahijah's son (2 Kings 9:9)
32 Joseph mourned for Jacob at his threshing floor (Genesis 50:10)
33 "To meet the Lord in the _____" (1 Thessalonians 4:17)
34 "For three transgressions of _____, and for four" (Amos 1:9)
37 Burdened
41 Teacher of Judaism
43 "_____ there yet the treasures" (Micah 6:10)
44 "Like a _____ or a swallow" (Isaiah 38:14)
45 Allotment
46 "The well of _____" (2 Samuel 3:26)
48 Not cooked
49 "And with the _____" (Deuteronomy 28:27)
51 "_____ builders did hew them" (1 Kings 5:18)
53 Shinrath's father (1 Chronicles 8:21)
56 Greek form of *aware* (Acts 14:6)

57 "They departed from _____, and pitched in Dibongad" (Numbers 33:45)
58 "_____ shall offer gifts" (Psalm 72:10)
61 Absalom's captain (2 Samuel 17:25)
65 A raisin is first this
68 "From Mithcah, and pitched in _____" (Numbers 33:29)
70 Ishmael's mother (Genesis 16:16)
71 "I have stretched out my hands _____ thee" (Psalm 88:9)
72 "And in the _____" (Deuteronomy 1:7)
73 Belonging to them
74 Perished
75 Salah's son (Genesis 10:24)

DOWN

1 Strike with the foot
2 Jesus cried this on the cross (Mark 15:34)
3 "Baked it in _____" (Numbers 11:8)
4 "In _____ and offerings" (Malachi 3:8)
5 This is attached to the shoulder
6 "Lest ye be wearied and faint in your _____" (Hebrews 12:3)
7 A brother of Arad (1 Chronicles 8:15)
8 Darius was one
9 "If thou depart to the _____, then I will go to the left" (Genesis 13:9) (2 words) (abbr.)
10 A son of Jether (1 Chronicles 7:38)
11 A son of Eber (Genesis 10:25)
12 Haul
13 Fire product
18 "The four hundred and _____ year" (1 Kings 6:1)
22 "To _____, that God was in Christ, reconciling the world unto himself" (2 Corinthians 5:19)
25 Happy (arch.)
27 "_____ also, and Pedaiah" (1 Chronicles 3:18)

by N. Teri Grottke

28 Twelfth Hebrew month (Esther 3:7)
29 "The earth with her _____ was about me for ever" (Jonah 2:6)
30 A son of Zibeon (1 Chronicles 1:40)
31 Anak's father (Joshua 15:13)
32 Greek form of *Asher* (Revelation 7:6)
35 Hasty
36 "Shallum, and Telem, and _____" (Ezra 10:24)
38 A son of Zerah (1 Chronicles 2:6)
39 "Tappuah, and _____" (Joshua 15:34)
40 Current events
42 "And they filled them up to the _____" (John 2:7)
47 "Against Jerusalem, _____" (Ezekiel 26:2)
50 King Saul's father (Acts 13:21)
52 "Though I have all faith, so that I could _____ mountains, and have not charity, I am nothing" (1 Corinthians 13:2)

53 Vision
54 "A certain Adullamite, whose name was _____" (Genesis 38:1)
55 Idol
56 Garbage
59 A judge of Israel (Judges 3:15)
60 Mighty man of David (2 Samuel 23:36)
62 A Canaanite city (Joshua 11:21)
63 "_____ of his patrimony" (Deuteronomy 18:8)
64 "Sons of _____" (1 Chronicles 7:12)
66 "Name of his city was _____" (1 Chronicles 1:50)
67 Make a mistake
69 "Bezer, and _____" (1 Chronicles 7:37)

Career Change

Therefore if any man be in Christ, he is a new creature: old things are passed away; behold, all things are become new.

2 CORINTHIANS 5:17

ACROSS

1 Messy people
6 "Put it into a _____ with holes" (Haggai 1:6)
9 "Ye shall offer _____ your own will" (Leviticus 19:5) (2 words)
13 "_____ Israel: the LORD" (Deuteronomy 6:4) (2 words)
14 "And Joseph _____ goodly person" (Genesis 39:6) (2 words)
15 "From the _____ of his foot unto his crown" (Job 2:7)
16 "And he shall _____ the left hand" (Isaiah 9:20) (2 words)
17 "Things the angels desire to look _____" (1 Peter 1:12)
18 "The _____ of this command is love" (1 Timothy 1:5 NIV)
19 Start of **QUOTE** taken from Mark 1:17 NIV (3 words)
22 DeMille's *Ten Commandments*, for example
25 Folklore little guy
26 Add on
27 Reduced in rank
29 "Laid he up in the _____" (Genesis 41:48)
31 "That dress doesn't _____ for you." (3 words)
32 Metric foot
33 Occupants of UFOs (abbr.)
36 **QUOTE**, cont'd from 19 Across (5 words)
39 Wind direction (abbr.)
40 Blue dye
41 "He marketh it out with a _____ fitteth it" (Isaiah 44:13) (2 words)
42 An NCO (abbr.)
43 "Since you _____ all my advice" (Proverbs 1:25 NIV)
44 Alter to advantage
47 "It _____ meat offering" (Leviticus 2:6) (2 words)

48 "Shew _____ pray thee" (Judges 1:24) (2 words)
49 End of **QUOTE**, cont'd from 36 Across (3 words)
53 "Even in laughter the heart may _____" (Proverbs 14:13 NIV)
54 Sicilian peak
55 It may go with tea
59 Brain canal
60 "For a _____ of shoes" (Amos 2:6)
61 "According to the _____ of these words" (Genesis 43:7)
62 "More _____ than the gold of Ophir" (Isaiah 13:12 NIV)
63 "Brass, _____ tinkling cymbal" (1 Corinthians 13:1) (2 words)
64 "Knit together _____ man" (Judges 20:11) (2 words)

DOWN

1 "_____ seeketh wool" (Proverbs 31:13)
2 Meadow in a poem
3 Dobbin's morsel
4 Plant from which buds are eaten
5 "But will do _____ more" (Job 27:19 NIV) (2 words)
6 Alberta resort
7 "I speak _____ wise men" (1 Corinthians 10:15) (2 words)
8 British pokey
9 "The thing _____ from me" (Daniel 2:5) (2 words)
10 "And came _____ large flocks" (Genesis 30:43 NIV) (2 words)
11 "A blind man, or _____" (Leviticus 21:18) (2 words)
12 This preceded the fax
14 "As if a rod were to _____ him who lifts it up" (Isaiah 10:15 NIV)
20 "Even the solemn _____" (Isaiah 1:13)
21 Dear small child
22 Collections of old Norse poems

by *David K. Shortess*

3 Unskilled laborers in Mexico

4 "_____ me great works"
(Ecclesiastes 2:4) (2 words)

8 "They will begin _____ away under
the oppression" (Hosea 8:10 NIV)
(2 words)

9 America's uncle

0 Mercury alloy often found in the
mouth

2 "Or have any _____ blemish"
(Deuteronomy 15:21)

3 Oglers

4 "Any that can skill _____ timber"
(1 Kings 5:6) (2 words)

5 Soft-napped leather

7 "Your lightning _____ up the world"
(Psalm 77:18 NIV)

8 Pronounces with great clarity

2 Domain

3 "But their heart _____ from me"
(Matthew 15:8) (2 words)

44 "She was a woman of _____
countenance" (2 Samuel 14:27)
(2 words)

45 Pronouncements

46 "And she called his name _____"
(Genesis 30:13)

47 Region in ancient western Asia Minor

50 It may be the result of a payment
default (slang)

51 "Shall come a _____ out of Jacob"
(Numbers 24:17)

52 ¿*Cómo* _____ *usted?*

56 "March _____ warriors—men of
Cush" (Jeremiah 46:9 NIV) (2 words)

57 "_____ his son, Jehoshua his son"
(1 Chronicles 7:27)

58 "_____ it was chewed"
(Numbers 11:33)

61

ACROSS

1 "So many _____ of voices in the world" (1 Corinthians 14:10)
6 Drinking vessels
10 Father (Galatians 4:6)
14 Abraham's heir
15 Zibeon's daughter (Genesis 36:2)
16 "Rewardeth the proud _____" (Psalm 31:23)
17 "Found Abishag a _____" (1 Kings 1:3)
19 Shammai's brother (1 Chronicles 2:28)
20 "And the Midianites sold _____ into Egypt unto Potiphar" (Genesis 37:36)
21 "The whole world _____ in wickedness" (1 John 5:19)
22 A son of Jerahmeel (1 Chronicles 2:25)
23 "Jonah was in the _____ of the fish three days" (Jonah 1:17)
24 "_____ nor sown" (Deuteronomy 21:4)
25 Military clergyman, for example (abbr.)
27 Make good _____ of time
28 Complete
29 Depend
31 "Resen between Nineveh and _____" (Genesis 10:12)
33 "We _____ our bread" (Lamentations 5:9)
36 A son of Jether (1 Chronicles 7:38)
37 Jorkoam's father (1 Chronicles 2:44)
38 Make a mistake
39 The book that started it all (abbr.)
40 A son of Bela (1 Chronicles 8:5)
41 Jacob's brother
42 Spirit
44 A son of Bani (Ezra 10:34)
46 Its capital is Augusta (abbr.)
47 "_____ great bulwarks" (Ecclesiastes 9:14)
48 "The children of _____, the children of Meunim" (Nehemiah 7:52)

50 Prepared
51 Peter's mother-in-law was healed ⊙ this
52 Sharp-toothed tool
55 "_____ him vehemently" (Luke 11:53)
56 "There was no _____ in the land" (Judges 18:7)
58 "Punish the men that are settled o⊙ their _____" (Zephaniah 1:12)
59 "Shelesh, and _____" (1 Chronicles 7:35)
60 "In _____ for all Israel" (Malachi 4:4)
61 "The third river. . .goeth toward th⊙ _____ of Assyria" (Genesis 2:14)
62 Peter's occupation required these
63 "One day is with the Lord as a thousand _____" (2 Peter 3:8)

DOWN

1 Saul's father (1 Samuel 9:1–2)
2 Rephaiah's father (1 Chronicles 4:4⊙
3 Amos's father (Luke 3:25)
4 A son of Jacob
5 "His _____ are his pride" (Job 41:15)
6 Humpbacked animal
7 Accord
8 Way
9 "And _____ lay at his feet until t⊙ morning" (Ruth 3:14)
10 Charge with an oath (Matthew 26:63)
11 Sons of thunder (Mark 3:17)
12 Hadad's father (Genesis 36:35)
13 A son of Ulla (1 Chronicles 7:39)
18 "Shall compel thee to go a _____ go with him twain" (Matthew 5:4⊙
22 Place to get clean
23 Purchase
24 "The rock _____" (Judges 15:11⊙
25 Rocky outcropping
26 In this place
28 A son of Sheresh (1 Chronicles 7:16)

by N. Teri Grottke

30 "O people, nations, and _____"
(Daniel 3:4)
31 Small wagon
32 "Against Jerusalem, _____"
(Ezekiel 26:2)
34 A son of Shem (Genesis 10:22)
35 Not false
37 Decomposing metal
40 Pure
41 Taught the child Samuel
(1 Samuel 3:1)
43 Obscure from sight (arch.)
44 Makes use of
45 "The first man is of the earth,
_____" (1 Corinthians 15:47)
47 Paul and Silas were sent by night
here (Acts 17:10)
48 "Of his own will _____ he us
with the word of truth"
(James 1:18)

49 "For innumerable _____ have
compassed me" (Psalm 40:12)
50 "According to this _____"
(Galatians 6:16)
51 Reknown
52 "Through faith also _____ herself
received strength to conceive seed"
(Hebrews 11:11)
53 "_____, Hizkijah, Azzur"
(Nehemiah 10:17)
54 Spiders spin these
56 Adam was the first
57 Small deer

62

ACROSS
1 Call on
6 "Jerusalem shall become _____" (Micah 3:12)
11 "The Syrians of Zoba, and of Rehob, and _____" (2 Samuel 10:8)
14 "The son of _____, keeper of the wardrobe" (2 Chronicles 34:22)
15 "Parmashta, and _____, and Aridai" (Esther 9:9)
16 Undivided
17 Thrash
18 "The prophets of God _____ them" (Ezra 5:2)
21 "The son of _____, which was the son of Noe" (Luke 3:36)
22 "Of Gad the king's _____" (2 Chronicles 29:25)
24 "Micah his son, _____ his son" (1 Chronicles 5:5)
25 "In the wilderness of mount _____" (Acts 7:30)
26 Eliasaph's father (Numbers 3:24)
28 Dark
29 Lease
30 "_____ the son of a Canaanitish woman" (Exodus 6:15)
32 "He cast four _____" (Exodus 38:5)
33 Spume
34 Remnants
35 Entry
39 "The priest's office shall be _____" (Exodus 29:9)
43 Single
44 "And _____ him up into the mount" (Exodus 24:18)
46 Gullet
47 Blemish
48 "Perform unto the Lord thine _____" (Matthew 5:33)
50 Rescue
51 Venomous snakes
53 Bed covering
54 Shammah's father (2 Samuel 23:11)

55 "The children of Ziha, the children of _____" (Ezra 2:43)
57 Clothing
59 "If any be a _____ of the word" (James 1:23)
60 "The _____ of the people" (Hebrews 9:7)
61 "Pekod, and _____" (Ezekiel 23:23)
62 Effortless

DOWN
1 Phials
2 "One of the king of _____ servants" (2 Kings 3:11)
3 Jonathan's father (2 Samuel 21:21)
4 "That which groweth of _____ own accord" (Leviticus 25:5)
5 "The son of Eliel, the son of _____" (1 Chronicles 6:34)
6 Loll
7 Established (abbr.)
8 "The king _____ from the banquet" (Esther 7:7)
9 Mothers and fathers
10 Jewish confession of faith
12 Feretory
13 Restore
14 "The gods of Sepharvaim, _____, and Ivah? (2 Kings 18:34)
19 "Thou in thy mercy hast _____ forth the people" (Exodus 15:13)
20 "Baalah, and _____, and Azem" (Joshua 15:29)
23 Ratiocinate
25 "Gave the _____" (Nehemiah 8:8)
27 "Not given to filthy _____" (Titus 1:7)
29 Dextral
31 "They of Persia and of _____ and of Phut" (Ezekiel 27:10)
32 Rodent
35 "And the trumpet in _____" (Hosea 5:8)
36 Shaphan's son (Jeremiah 29:3)
37 Cadavers
38 Charge

by Tonya Vilhauer

40 Statues

41 Blackbirds

42 "The mountains shall drop _____ wine" (Amos 9:13)

44 "The children of Giddel, the children of _____" (Ezra 2:47)

45 Yonder

48 Nun's son (Numbers 13:8)

49 Gaze

50 "The next day we arrived at _____" (Acts 20:15)

52 "The sons of Zophah; _____" (1 Chronicles 7:36)

56 Expert

58 "_____ also the Jairite" (2 Samuel 20:26)

ACROSS

1 Market
5 Fleecy ruminant
10 Cain's victim
14 King Hoshea's father
    (2 Kings 15:30)
15 A son of Reuben (Exodus 6:14)
16 "_____; God hath numbered thy
    kingdom, and finished it"
    (Daniel 5:26)
17 Dwell
18 "But _____ foolish questions"
    (Titus 3:9)
19 At once (Mark 1:30)
20 A son of Ram (1 Chronicles 2:27)
21 "The _____ chamber was five
    cubits broad" (1 Kings 6:6)
23 A baptismal site of John the Baptist
    (John 3:23)
25 "Wilt thou _____ the prey for the
    lion?" (Job 38:39)
26 Enemies
29 A son of David
    (2 Samuel 5:13–14)
34 "_____, Reuse, Recycle"
37 Wound covering
39 "_____ him vehemently"
    (Luke 11:53)
40 "And he will take your daughters to
    be _____" (1 Samuel 8:13)
45 Melchi's father (Luke 3:28)
46 "Say unto them which _____ it"
    (Ezekiel 13:11)
47 Became acquainted
48 "_____, O isles, unto me"
    (Isaiah 49:1)
51 "Being _____ together"
    (Colossians 2:2)
53 Heber's father (Luke 3:35)
56 "He shall _____ his flesh in water"
    (Numbers 19:7)
60 "The outgoings thereof are in the
    valley of _____" (Joshua 19:14)
66 "Set it between Mizpeh and
    _____" (1 Samuel 7:12)
67 Daniel had a vision by this river
68 To the side
69 "And in process of _____"
    (Genesis 4:3)
70 Verbalize
71 This Hararite was father to Jonathan
    in David's army (1 Chronicles 11:34)
72 "Tappuah, and _____"
    (Joshua 15:34)
73 Exhaust
74 "Came to_____" (Isaiah 30:4)
75 Refuse to admit

DOWN

1 Menan's son (Luke 3:31)
2 Similar
3 First bird out of the ark
4 "They shall give account _____ in
   the day of judgment"
   (Matthew 12:36)
5 Breadth
6 Own
7 "He built _____, and restored it to
   Judah" (2 Chronicles 26:2)
8 Elkanah's grandfather
   (1 Samuel 1:1)
9 "Eubulus greeteth thee, and _____,
   and Linus" (2 Timothy 4:21)
10 "_____, and Shema"
    (Joshua 15:26)
11 A brother of Shoham
    (1 Chronicles 24:27)
12 Seth's son (Genesis 4:26)
13 Gave a loan
22 Not left hand but _____ (abbr.)
24 Smelling orifice
27 This book's key verse: "Vanity of
    vanities; all is vanity" (abbr.)
28 "A certain blind man _____ by the
    way side begging" (Luke 18:35)
30 "Altogether for _____ sakes?"
    (1 Corinthians 9:10)
31 "And they filled them up to the
    _____" (John 2:7)
32 Shammah's father (2 Samuel 23:11)

by N. Teri Grottke

33 First place
34 "Even unto Ithiel and _____"
(Proverbs 30:1)
35 Gaddiel's father (Numbers 13:10)
36 "The LORD will judge the _____ of
the earth" (1 Samuel 2:10 NKJV)
38 Send (Zephaniah 1:7)
41 "To the plough and looking back,
is _____ for the kingdom of God"
(Luke 9:62)
42 Strong wood
43 Joshua's father
44 First Hebrew month (Exodus 34:18)
49 Aka Hadassah (abbr.)
50 Saul defeated him in his first battle
as king (1 Samuel 11)
52 Experienced flavor
54 "Even unto _____" (Genesis 10:19)
55 A son of Shemidah
(1 Chronicles 7:19)

57 Yours (arch.)
58 "_____, and Chalcol"
(1 Kings 4:31)
59 Foe
60 Fair
61 "_____ the Ahohite"
(1 Chronicles 11:29)
62 Couple
63 Pelt
64 Furthest part
65 "Punish the men that are settled on
their _____" (Zephaniah 1:12)

It's All Relative

Each theme answer (17, 26, 47, and 61 Across) describes one of the four people listed in the clue. The circled letter in the answer provides the identity of the correct person.

ACROSS

1 Kind of metabolism
6 Ex-New York governor Mario
11 Mr. Baba
14 Godly love
15 Late Chilean-born pianist Claudio
16 "That he might _____ him out of their hands" (Genesis 37:22)
17 A. Bathsheba
   B. Abigail
   C. Ahinoam
   D. Michal
20 Fencing weapon
21 "Round about the _____ thereof" (Exodus 28:33)
22 Pond plant
23 Olympic gold medal runner Sebastian
25 Leeds trolly
26 A. Jehu
   B. Ahab
   C. Ahaziah
   D. Jehoshaphat
34 Prefix for the birds
35 "According to the _____ of the king" (Esther 1:7)
36 Indonesian island
37 Engrossed
39 Bergen's dummy Mortimer
41 Royal address
42 Figure of speech
44 "He has a _____" (Matthew 11:18 NIV)
46 Agency that issues nine-digit ID numbers (abbr.)
47 A. Rachel
   B. Bilhah
   C. Zilpah
   D. Leah
50 *Trinity* author Leon
51 "Then answered I, and said, So be _____ LORD" (Jeremiah 11:5) (2 words)
52 Sports stadiums
55 "He said, _____ is a lion's whelp" (Deuteronomy 33:22)

57 "And not in _____ speeches" (Numbers 12:8)
61 A. Levi
   B. Reuben
   C. Simeon
   D. Naphtali
64 "He planteth an _____, and the rain doth nourish it" (Isaiah 44:14)
65 Edmonton hockey player
66 "And of _____ oil a hin" (Exodus 30:24)
67 Follows *pi* in the Greek alphabet
68 "With _____ both the grayheaded and very aged men" (Job 15:10) (2 words)
69 "And _____ a right spirit within me" (Psalm 51:10)

DOWN

1 "All that her mother in law _____ her" (Ruth 3:6)
2 "And not _____ was left in it" (Nehemiah 6:1 NIV) (2 words)
3 "Any god, _____ unto the LORD only" (Exodus 22:20)
4 "Neither have two coats _____" (Luke 9:3)
5 "And be _____ forth with peace" (Isaiah 55:12)
6 _____ au lait
7 "There stood up a priest with _____ and Thummim" (Nehemiah 7:65)
8 NHL's Bobby
9 Capital of Lesotho, formerly part of South Africa
10 "They will set _____, under their standards" (Numbers 2:31 NIV) (2 words)
11 "It goes through _____ places" (Matthew 12:43 NIV)
12 "For with thee is the fountain of _____" (Psalm 36:9)
13 "But you have no _____ where I come from" (John 8:14 NIV)
18 "Then shall ye give me thirty _____" (Judges 14:13)

by David K. Shortess

19 "The fruit of the _____ his reward" (Psalm 127:3) (2 words)
24 Gyns. partners (abbr.)
25 Heat units
26 A son of Simeon (1 Chronicles 4:24)
27 Give the slip
28 Make a fast stop at the mini-mart (2 words)
29 "And the _____ defiled" (Leviticus 18:25) (2 words)
30 Dutch painter Jan
31 Pennsylvania sect
32 Scandinavian
33 Cheerless, to Wordsworth
38 Ode written by Horace for a Roman goddess
40 R & B pianist "Fats"
43 Large African stork
45 "Ye shall _____ surely die" (Genesis 3:4)
48 "A _____ as good as a mile"

49 Walk unsteadily, as a baby (2 words)
52 "There is not _____ left" (2 Kings 4:6 NIV)
53 "Be not _____ with thy mouth" (Ecclesiastes 5:2)
54 "Their calls will _____ through the windows" (Zephaniah 2:14 NIV)
55 "Her princes are like _____ that find no pasture" (Lamentations 1:6 NIV)
56 "As it were an half _____ of land" (1 Samuel 14:14)
58 "And there is _____ not unto death" (1 John 5:17) (2 words)
59 Peregrinate
60 "But they _____ not him" (Genesis 42:8)
62 Patty Hearst's former organization (abbr.)
63 "Thou, _____ thy son" (Exodus 20:10)

65

ACROSS

1 City of the priests (1 Samuel 22:19)
4 After eight
8 In this manner
12 A son of Benjamin (Genesis 46:21)
13 "Mountains shall reach unto
_____" (Zechariah 14:5)
14 Igdaliah's son (Jeremiah 35:4)
16 Adoniram's father (1 Kings 4:6)
17 "Of _____, the family"
(Numbers 26:17)
18 Similar
19 Eliasaph's father (Numbers 3:24)
20 "These are the families of the
_____" (Numbers 26:14)
22 "_____ whose fruit" (Jude 1:12)
24 Prophet for forty years (abbr.)
25 Her name means "star" (abbr.)
26 Jehoshua's father (1 Chronicles 7:27)
28 Snare
31 "He _____ Uriah unto a place"
(2 Samuel 11:16)
36 The butler's cellmate
(Genesis 40:2–3)
40 Capture tactic
41 "Dip the _____ of his finger in
water" (Luke 16:24)
43 Not dead
44 You do this to bread
45 "Which _____ the people of the
land" (2 Kings 25:19)
47 Dogs do this
50 Partook
51 Patriarch of a family of returned
exiles (Ezra 2:57)
54 Petroleum product
56 Increased
60 Force to do something (arch.)
64 "Day of _____ birth"
(Ecclesiastes 7:1)
66 "At _____" (1 Chronicles 4:29)
67 The beast and the false prophet will
be cast here
68 Jacob's brother
69 Trap
70 Great wickedness
71 "According to this _____"
(Galatians 6:16)
72 "Set it between Mizpeh and
_____" (1 Samuel 7:12)
73 Refuse to admit
74 To place

DOWN

1 Jeroboam's father
(1 Kings 11:26)
2 "Set in _____ the things that are
wanting" (Titus 1:5)
3 "People that were with him
from _____ of Judah"
(2 Samuel 6:2)
4 Salmon's father (Luke 3:32)
5 "Fourth to _____"
(1 Chronicles 25:11)
6 Ruth's mother-in-law
7 Firstborn
8 "Now the serpent was more subtil
_____ any beast" (Genesis 3:1)
9 "Helkath, and _____"
(Joshua 19:25)
10 Bring together
11 "They are beloved for the fathers'
_____" (Romans 11:28)
12 Girl (slang)
15 Bird home
21 Boat paddle
23 "Dwelt in strong holds at _____"
(1 Samuel 23:29)
27 Short name for the system link-
ing computers around the world
29 "Waters were _____ from off the
earth" (Genesis 8:11)
30 Little color
31 Pose a question
32 Transgression
33 "_____ that ye refuse"
(Hebrews 12:25)
34 Son of Nathan of Zobah
(2 Samuel 23:36)
35 Opposite of *bright*
37 The people of Syria shall go into
captivity here (Amos 1:5)

by N. Teri Grottke

38 "She would become the mother of all the living" (Genesis 3:20 NIV)
39 Color of blood
42 Issachar's son (Numbers 26:23)
46 "Satest upon a _____ bed" (Ezekiel 23:41)
48 One of Paul's four "prison epistles" (abbr.)
49 Slayed
51 Only NT history book
52 "Her new _____, and her sabbaths" (Hosea 2:11)
53 Micaiah's father (1 Kings 22:8)
55 "Intreat me not to _____ thee" (Ruth 1:16)
57 Accomplishers
58 "Let him seek peace, and _____ it" (1 Peter 3:11)
59 Doled out
61 Cut back

62 First garden
63 Epidermis
65 Take to court

66

ACROSS

1 "Which was the son of _____" (Luke 3:35)
5 "They _____ us with such things as were necessary" (Acts 28:10)
10 Reserve
12 Astonished
14 Emeritus
15 "_____ the word of the LORD came unto me" (Zechariah 4:8)
17 "Went out to the cities of mount _____" (Joshua 15:9)
19 Endeavor
20 Amusement
21 Spoil
23 Espy
24 "Judah went to the top of the rock _____" (Judges 15:11)
26 "Having understood that he was a _____" (Acts 23:27)
28 "That no man might buy or _____" (Revelation 13:17)
29 "Which is _____ in knowledge" (Colossians 3:10)
31 Dressing gown
33 "_____, she is broken" (Ezekiel 26:2)
34 Pekoe
35 Cord
37 "Fed them with bread and water?" (1 Kings 18:13)
39 "Southward were Kabzeel, and _____" (Joshua 15:21)
41 Jabal's mother (Genesis 4:20)
45 Opulent
47 Office
48 "Hariph, Anathoth, _____" (Nehemiah 10:19)
50 "There was war between _____ and Baasha" (1 Kings 15:16)
52 "If thy father at all _____ me" (1 Samuel 20:6)
54 Discover
55 "The Amorites would dwell in mount _____" (Judges 1:35)
57 Zoheth's father (1 Chronicles 4:20)
58 "Written in the story of the prophet _____" (2 Chronicles 13:22)
59 A son of Gad (Genesis 46:16)
60 Next
61 Eliasaph's father (Numbers 3:24)
62 "After they were come to _____" (Acts 16:7)
63 "Glean _____ of corn" (Ruth 2:2)
64 "So is thy praise unto the _____ of the earth" (Psalm 48:10)

DOWN

1 "Who shall _____ him up" (Numbers 24:9)
2 "Is not _____ the Levite thy brother?" (Exodus 4:14)
3 "Though ye have _____ among the pots" (Psalm 68:13)
4 Also
5 Flog
6 "Saying _____ hath conspired against thee" (Amos 7:10)
7 "To quench all the fiery _____" (Ephesians 6:16)
8 Son of the ruler of Mizpah (Nehemiah 3:19)
9 Concoct
10 Putative
11 "Zereth, and Jezoar, and _____" (1 Chronicles 4:7)
13 Grow
14 Point
16 "They _____ to and fro" (Psalm 107:27)
18 Gypsy
21 Pole
22 _____ and feather
25 "_____ that is beside the Sidonians" (Joshua 13:4)
26 "The plowman shall overtake the _____" (Amos 9:13)
27 Letter
28 "So shall the _____ be calm unto you" (Jonah 1:12)
30 "That he _____ loveth God love his brother" (1 John 4:21)

by Tonya Vilhauer

32 "Sent Jerubbaal, and _____"
(1 Samuel 12:11)

36 "Hadad the _____" (1 Kings 11:14)

37 "His flesh shall be _____ than a child's" (Job 33:25)

38 "Remembering mine affliction and my _____" (Lamentations 3:19)

40 "Elijah went with _____ from Gilgal" (2 Kings 2:1)

42 "He would not _____ himself" (Daniel 1:8)

43 Gideoni's son (Numbers 10:24)

44 "While he is weary and weak _____" (2 Samuel 17:2)

45 Shema's son (1 Chronicles 2:44)

46 "And _____ of this life" (Luke 21:34)

49 Graven images

51 "Stayed in _____ for a season" (Acts 19:22)

53 "For the remission of _____" (Acts 2:38)

56 "Samuel arose and went to _____" (1 Samuel 3:6)

67

ACROSS

1 Peaceful
5 A king of Midian (Numbers 31:8)
8 "Valley of _____" (Psalm 84:6)
12 "As he saith also in _____"
   (Romans 9:25)
13 "God hath numbered thy kingdom,
   and finished it" (Daniel 5:26)
15 Naum's son (Luke 3:25)
16 "For ye tithe _____ and rue and all
   manner of herbs" (Luke 11:42)
17 "To _____ all that call on thy
   name" (Acts 9:14)
18 "I travail in _____ again until Christ
   be formed in you" (Galatians 4:19)
20 Consume food
21 Cooking vessel
22 Happy (arch.)
24 Expert
25 Son of Nathan of Zobah
   (2 Samuel 23:36)
27 Arioch was king here (Genesis 14:1)
29 "The howling thereof unto _____"
   (Isaiah 15:8)
31 Lucre
32 "They _____ to and fro"
   (Psalm 107:27)
33 Gihon was this river coming out of
   Eden (Genesis 2:13)
36 Possessive pronoun
37 Children of aunts and uncles
39 "No man, having put his hand to the
   plow, and looking back, is _____
   for the kingdom of God"
   (Luke 9:62)
42 "Live delicately, are in kings'
   _____" (Luke 7:25)
43 Mud
44 "With a _____, with the voice of the
   archangel" (1 Thessalonians 4:16)
46 "The inhabitant of _____ came not
   forth" (Micah 1:11)
48 Bright red
50 Nagge's son (Luke 3:25)
51 Are (arch.)
52 Test

53 Where the mercy seat was
54 "And _____ lay at his feet until the
   morning" (Ruth 3:14)
57 A tenth
59 Thorny flower
61 Jezebel's husband
62 "Touched the _____" (Luke 7:14)
63 Gaal's father (Judges 9:26)
64 "And _____ destroyed of the
   destroyer" (1 Corinthians 10:10)
65 Type of trees
66 A son of Jether (1 Chronicles 7:38)
67 "Tower of _____" (Genesis 35:21)

DOWN

1 "_____ up before me" (Jonah 1:2)
2 Largest continent
3 "Then Jacob gave Esau bread and
   pottage of _____" (Genesis 25:34)
4 "The angels of God _____ him"
   (Genesis 32:1)
5 "Then Joseph directed the
   physicians in his service to _____
   his father Israel" (Genesis 50:2 NIV)
6 Blood vessel
7 Motel
8 "For then the king of _____ army
   besieged Jerusalem" (Jeremiah 32:2)
9 Patriarch of a family of returned
   exiles (Ezra 2:57)
10 Dead body
11 "Sheep going _____" (1 Peter 2:25)
14 Furthest part
19 "Ye shall point out for you mount
   _____" (Numbers 34:7)
21 "Name of his city was _____"
   (1 Chronicles 1:50)
23 "And _____ with her suburbs; four
   cities" (Joshua 21:18)
26 This equals four quarts (abbr.)
28 "Garments, _____ stood"
   (Zechariah 3:3)
29 A son of Gad (Genesis 46:16)
30 Acquire
33 A temple gate (2 Kings 11:6)
34 Mordecai's charge (abbr.)

by N. Teri Grottke

35 King Saul's father (Acts 13:21)
37 "For the _____, and for the forks" (1 Samuel 13:21)
38 "Cast ye the unprofitable servant into _____ darkness" (Matthew 25:30)
39 "When he had received the drink, Jesus said, 'It is _____'" (John 19:30 NIV)
40 "Helez the Paltite, _____" (2 Samuel 23:26)
41 "Hundred and _____ years old" (Joshua 24:29)
42 This book of First and Second addressed problems with immorality in the church (abbr.)
43 This prophet's name means "messenger of the Lord" (abbr.)
44 "Where is the wise? where is the _____?" (1 Corinthians 1:20)

45 "The children of Shephatiah, the children of _____" (Nehemiah 7:59)
46 Jeroboam the son of Nebat was from here (1 Kings 11:26)
47 Pose a question
48 "There came an angel of the LORD, and _____ under an oak which was in Ophrah" (Judges 6:11)
49 "And Herod was highly displeased with them of _____ and Sidon" (Acts 12:20)
53 Greek form of *Asher* (Revelation 7:6)
55 "Habor, and _____" (1 Chronicles 5:26)
56 Salah's son (Genesis 10:24)
58 Edge of a garment
60 This book was written to the Edomites and Judah's Jews, among others (abbr.)
61 Reverent fear

68 ▶

The First Woman

ACROSS

1 "Adam named his wife _____ "
 (Genesis 3:20 NIV)
4 During a storm, Jesus was asleep
 in the back, or _____, of the ship
 (Mark 4:38 NIV)
8 Rearrange letters of the name of the
 main heart artery
10 "Do you watch when the _____
 bears her fawn?" (Job 39:1 NIV)
11 Expression meaning "okay"
12 Precious stones
13 Child's plaything
14 "How often I have longed to gather
 your children together, as a _____
 gathers her chicks under her wings"
 (Luke 13:34 NIV)
15 "Prophesy to us, Christ. Who
 _____ you?" (Matthew 26:68 NIV)
18 "God _____ granted me another
 child in place of Abel"
 (Genesis 4:25 NIV)
19 While walking beside the _____ of
 Galilee, Jesus saw Peter and Andrew
 (Matthew 4:18 NIV)
21 "Whatever you do, whether in word
 or _____, do it all in the name
 of the Lord Jesus"
 (Colossians 3:17 NIV)
23 Bird (abbr.)
24 Natural gas organization (abbr.)
25 This is now bone of my _____ and
 flesh of my flesh (Genesis 2:23 NIV)
26 Eve became the _____ of all the
 living (Genesis 3:20 NIV)
27 To Cain, God said, "If you
 _____ what is right, will you not
 be accepted?" (Genesis 4:7 NIV)

DOWN

1 "God had planted a garden in the
 _____, in Eden" (Genesis 2:8 NIV)
2 The sound a vehicle's engine makes
3 Jesus said, "For my yoke is _____ ,
 and my burden is light"
 (Matthew 11:30)
4 During creation, God separated the
 water, "and it was _____ "
 (Genesis 1:7)
5 What God prepared for Adam and
 Eve
6 This book expounds on justification
 by faith alone (abbr.)
7 "Like a bird that strays from its
 _____ is a man who strays from his
 home" (Proverbs 27:8 NIV)
9 "It is not good for the man _____
 be alone" (Genesis 2:18 NIV)
12 "How long will you lie there, you
 sluggard? When will you _____ up
 from your sleep?" (Proverbs 6:9 NIV)
14 "God created man in _____ own
 image" (Genesis 1:27)
15 "God saw all that he had
 _____ made, and it was very
 good" (Genesis 1:31 NIV)
16 "So they _____ fig leaves
 together and made coverings"
 (Genesis 3:7 NIV)
17 "The first man _____ became a living being" (1 Corinthians 15:45 NIV)
18 The sun in the desert brings
 scorching _____
19 Cain was Eve's first _____
 (Genesis 4:1)
20 "He _____ made the stars"
 (Genesis 1:16 NIV)
22 Self-esteem

by John Hudson Tiner

23 The garden had "trees that were pleasing to the eye and good _____ food" (Genesis 2:9 NIV)

25 God said, "Let there _____ light" (Genesis 1:3)

69

ACROSS

1 Ground moisture
4 Darling
8 Before (arch.)
11 A king of Midian (Numbers 31:8)
12 "Sound of the _____" (Job 21:12)
14 Livestock feed
15 A son of Bani (Ezra 10:34)
16 Place of the dead
17 Common tree
18 Right hand (abbr.)
20 A daughter of Zelophehad (Joshua 17:3)
23 Foreigner
26 "Helez the Paltite, _____" (2 Samuel 23:26)
27 Roman emperor
30 "The Lord knoweth how to deliver the _____ out of temptations" (2 Peter 2:9)
32 Petroleum product
33 These First and Second books have an unknown author (abbr.)
34 Fight between countries
35 Cut
37 Elevate
39 "God _____ tempt Abraham" (Genesis 22:1)
40 "And _____ with her suburbs, and Rehob" (1 Chronicles 6:75)
42 A brother of Uz (Genesis 10:23)
43 Acquire
44 Conquered by Joshua (Joshua 8)
45 Hophni's father (1 Samuel 4:4)
46 Philistine idol (Judges 16:23)
48 Give (Psalm 116:12)
50 Exclamation of affirmation
51 "_____ of Judah" (2 Samuel 6:2)
53 "Until ye be _____ with power from on high" (Luke 24:49)
55 "Shall be astonished, and _____ his head" (Jeremiah 18:16)
58 Entrance
61 A city in Benjamin (Joshua 18:25)
64 Steal

66 Night flier
67 Idol
68 "_____ there yet the treasures" (Micah 6:10)
69 Color of blood
70 Show (arch.)
71 Zephaniah's son (Zechariah 6:14)

DOWN

1 This book is quoted more than 80 times in the NT (abbr.)
2 Always
3 "Knowing that thou _____ also do more than I say" (Philemon 1:21)
4 Canine
5 Make a mistake
6 A gem on the third row of the ephod (Exodus 28:19)
7 "Filled his holes with prey, and his dens with _____" (Nahum 2:12)
8 A son of Benjamin (Genesis 46:21)
9 "And _____ greedily after the error of Balaam" (Jude 1:11)
10 "But the _____ of their God was upon the elders of the Jews" (Ezra 5:5)
13 Saul's grandfather (1 Chronicles 8:33)
17 A son of Reuben (Genesis 46:9)
19 Possesses
21 "_____; nine cities" (Joshua 15:54)
22 Naaman's brother (Numbers 26:40)
24 The beast and the false prophet will be cast here
25 A son of Bela (1 Chronicles 7:7)
27 This book talks about giving and church discipline, among other topics (abbr.)
28 A son of Zibeon (1 Chronicles 1:40)
29 Achim's son (Matthew 1:14)
30 A son of Jacob (Genesis 30:11)
31 "Be ye not unequally _____ together with unbelievers" (2 Corinthians 6:14)

by N. Teri Grottke

34 "To _____, that God was in Christ, reconciling the world unto himself" (2 Corinthians 5:19)

36 "Upon a _____" (Numbers 21:8)

38 Killer (arch.)

39 "As a lion in his _____" (Psalm 10:9)

40 "_____ the Bethelite" (1 Kings 16:34)

41 The people of Syria shall go into captivity here (Amos 1:5)

43 Prod

44 A son of Jether (1 Chronicles 7:38)

47 Book of the patriarchs (abbr.)

49 Roosevelt had a _____ Deal during the 1930s

51 "Who layeth the _____ of his chambers" (Psalm 104:3)

52 "Shall I make thee as _____?" (Hosea 11:8)

54 "Shallum, and Telem, and _____" (Ezra 10:24)

56 A son of Ulla (1 Chronicles 7:39)

57 Pierce with horns

58 "Borders of _____" (Joshua 11:2)

59 Be indebted to

60 Elderly

62 Get older

63 Chop (arch.)

65 Zechariah, _____" (1 Chronicles 15:18)

70

An Agrarian Square

And Ruth the Moabitess said unto Naomi,
Let me now go to the field, and glean ears of corn.

RUTH 2:2

ACROSS

1 Ollie's friend
5 "And Zaavan, and _____"
(Genesis 36:27)
9 "_____ darkness lies in wait for his treasures" (Job 20:26 NIV)
14 Mercury or Saturn
15 Estee's rival
16 "According to the days _____ king" (Isaiah 23:15) (2 words)
17 "But grievous words _____ up anger" (Proverbs 15:1)
18 "But _____ was a tiller of the ground" (Genesis 4:2)
19 Bismarck and Preminger
20 "For we have treasures in _____" (Jeremiah 41:8) (4 words)
23 "'_____ ghost,' they said" (Matthew 14:26 NIV) (2 words)
24 "That we love _____ another" (2 John 1:5)
25 Whippets and greyhounds
28 "Why make ye this _____, and weep?" (Mark 5:39)
30 Follows *pro-* or *mo-*
34 "As _____ that is told" (Psalm 90:9) (2 words)
35 "Blessed ____ the meek" (Matthew 5:5)
36 _____ Rica
37 "My arms can _____ bow of bronze" (Psalm 18:34 NIV) (2 words)
38 "And cast him into the _____ of lions" (Daniel 6:16)
39 "Arise, cry _____ the night" (Lamentations 2:19) (2 words)
40 "To go _____ to lodge in Gibeah" (Judges 19:15) (2 words)
41 "If _____ man will come after me" (Matthew 16:24)
42 "He esteemeth iron as _____" (Job 41:27)
43 _____ *contendere* (Lat.)

44 A son of Jether (1 Chronicles 7:38)
45 "Whilst we are _____ in the body" (2 Corinthians 5:6) (2 words)
46 Boring routine
48 University employee (abbr.)
49 "As the ox licketh up the _____" (Numbers 22:4) (4 words)
57 Hindu queen
58 Attention getter
59 Ancient Greek colony in Italy
60 "He shall not _____ it" (Leviticus 27:10)
61 "More _____ desired are they than gold" (Psalm 19:10) (2 words)
62 "Neither shall I know the _____ of children" (Isaiah 47:8)
63 "Ye do the _____ of your father" (John 8:41)
64 Hard beef fat
65 "That dippeth with me in the _____" (Mark 14:20)

DOWN

1 "Saying, Proclaim a _____" (1 Kings 21:9)
2 Great-grandmother of David (Matthew 1:5–6)
3 Nobody won; it ended in _____ (2 words)
4 "Neither have we vineyard, _____" (Jeremiah 35:9) (4 words)
5 "By whom also we have _____ by faith" (Romans 5:2)
6 Teddy bear from down under
7 Sulfuric or nitric
8 "And your _____" (James 5:12 NIV) (2 words)
9 "The man. . .came _____ large flocks" (Genesis 30:43 NIV) 2 words)
10 "Prophesy against the forest _____" (Ezekiel 20:46) (4 words)
11 Lug

by David K. Shortess

12 Celebes buffalo
13 "Neither shall ye touch it, _____ ye die" (Genesis 3:3)
21 "And fastened to the cross. _____: JESUS" (John 19:19 NIV) (2 words)
22 Egg _____ yong
25 Israeli general and prime minister
26 "I _____ choice food" (Daniel 10:3 NIV) (2 words)
27 "I was beside the Ulai _____" (Daniel 8:2 NIV)
28 "To die in the _____" (1 Corinthians 4:9 NIV)
29 "Let him _____ himself" (Matthew 16:24)
31 Houston athlete
32 "And so become unclean through _____ the LORD" (Leviticus 22:8 NIV) (3 words)
33 "And how _____ know the way?" (John 14:5) (2 words)

35 Twelfth Jewish month (Esther 9:1)
36 "Who sinned at the _____ their lives" (Numbers 16:38 NIV) (2 words)
44 From _____ Z (2 words)
45 "Mercy and truth _____ together" (Psalm 85:10) (2 words)
47 Computer operators
48 "I commend unto you _____ our sister" (Romans 16:1)
49 New alum
50 Lung noise
51 Preceding (prefix)
52 Jazzman Domino
53 "_____ art worthy, O Lord" (Revelation 4:11)
54 "Jesus cried with a loud voice, saying, _____" (Mark 15:34)
55 "The _____ is blessed of the better" (Hebrews 7:7)
56 "Lest thou _____ thy foot against a stone" (Psalm 91:12)

71

ACROSS

1 Accomplish
3 Began prophesying "in the year that king Uzziah died" (abbr.)
6 "My speech distill as the _____" (Deuteronomy 32:2 NKJV)
9 Cut
10 "Now the serpent was more subtil _____ any beast" (Genesis 3:1)
12 In chemistry, a colorless liquid belonging to alkanes
14 Single
15 "The _____ after her kind" (Leviticus 11:19)
17 Incident
18 "And the herdmen of _____" (Genesis 26:20)
20 "Lod, and _____, the valley of craftsmen" (Nehemiah 11:35)
21 "I travail in _____ again until Christ be formed in you" (Galatians 4:19)
22 Solomon's great-grandson (1 Kings 15:8)
23 "Cuth made _____" (2 Kings 17:30)
25 Partook
26 Conquered by Joshua (Joshua 8)
27 Agreement
31 "To meet the Lord in the _____" (1 Thessalonians 4:17)
32 "Take unto thee sweet spices, _____, and onycha" (Exodus 30:34)
35 "Name of his city was _____" (1 Chronicles 1:50)
36 Tiger Woods: golf _____
37 "The name of the other _____" (1 Samuel 14:4)
38 Empty talk is _____ air
39 "Came to Joel the _____" (Joel 1:1)
40 "They shall _____ one against another" (Nahum 2:4)
41 This is attached to the shoulder
42 Response
44 Judah's firstborn (Numbers 26:19)

45 "Between Bethel and _____" (Genesis 13:3)
46 King of Damascus (2 Corinthians 11:32)
49 Obese
50 "No more _____" (Hosea 2:16)
53 "And a river went _____ of Eden to water the garden" (Genesis 2:10)
54 A son of David (1 Chronicles 3:5–6)
57 Bend
58 Bring together
60 A son of Caleb (1 Chronicles 4:15)
61 Moses' father-in-law (Exodus 2:18–21)
62 "And his _____ drew" (Revelation 12:4)
63 This is connected to the foot
64 Watch for this color of heifer near the end
65 Commanded militarily
66 An altar (Joshua 22:34)

DOWN

1 "For he hath _____ marvellous things" (Psalm 98:1)
2 "And there are diversities of _____" (1 Corinthians 12:6)
3 Amasa's father (2 Samuel 17:25)
4 "And _____ lay at his feet until the morning" (Ruth 3:14)
5 Priesthood
6 Demons
7 A son of Ram (1 Chronicles 2:27)
8 Desire
9 A measurement for oil (Leviticus 14:10)
11 Not any
12 "Didst _____ thyself even unto hell" (Isaiah 57:9)
13 "To the _____ degree" (common phrase)
16 "_____ was an hair of their head" (Daniel 3:27)
19 Greek form of *Asher* (Revelation 7:6)

by N. Teri Grottke

24 "All faces shall _____ blackness"
   (Joel 2:6)
25 Moses' brother
26 "And shall _____ our hearts before
   him" (1 John 3:19)
28 Elkanah was one (1 Samuel 1:1)
29 Ruth's mother-in-law
30 This biblical author took up the
   offering for Jerusalem's poor
   believers (abbr.)
33 Tiny insect
34 "The glory of the _____ is one"
   (1 Corinthians 15:40)
36 A biblical book of poetry (abbr.)
40 A son of Tola (1 Chronicles 7:2)
41 Jezebel's husband
43 The cities are great and _____ up
   to heaven" (Deuteronomy 1:28)
47 King of Hamath (1 Chronicles 18:9)
48 Sister of parent

49 "Shepherds abiding in the _____"
   (Luke 2:8)
50 Barrier
51 A brother of Eshcol (Genesis 14:13)
52 Fever
55 "Of _____, the family"
   (Numbers 26:17)
56 "For ye tithe mint and _____"
   (Luke 11:42)
59 Bind

72

Biblical Illumination

For these commands are a lamp, this teaching is a light

PROVERBS 6:23 NIV

ACROSS

1 Seth's father (Genesis 4:25)
5 "They _____ walls like soldiers" (Joel 2:7 NIV)
10 Swiss river
14 "The devil threw him down, and _____ him" (Luke 9:42)
15 Sugar stalks
16 Noah's oldest son (Genesis 5:32)
17 "As the camp _____ set forward" (Numbers 4:15) (2 words)
18 Playful prank
19 "It is a _____ offering" (Leviticus 2:6)
20 Start of **QUOTE** from Psalm 119:105, with 48 Across and 37 Across, in that order (5 words)
23 E.T.'s ship, for example
24 "The _____ of the scribes is in vain" (Jeremiah 8:8)
25 Gold purity units
29 "_____ is written" (Romans 3:10) (2 words)
31 RR stop
34 "The rest of all the acts _____" (1 Kings 15:23)
35 *Years* in Yucatan
36 Cornelia _____ Skinner
37 End of **QUOTE** (4 words)
40 "Either make the _____ good" (Matthew 12:33)
41 "And at _____, will I pray" (Psalm 55:17)
42 "The way of an _____ in the air" (Proverbs 30:19)
43 Socioeconomic status (abbr.)
44 "The Man" Musial
45 Jaw whalebone
46 _____ Lanka
47 _____ *Miniver* (WWII film)
48 Part 2 of **QUOTE** (5 words)
56 "This great thing _____ hath been heard like it?" (Deuteronomy 4:32) (2 words)
57 "Hide not thine _____ my breathing" (Lamentations 3:56) (2 words)
58 "And when the new _____ was come" (1 Samuel 20:24)
59 "There he _____ Jew named Aquila" (Acts 18:2 NIV) (2 words)
60 Argentine plain
61 "He goeth _____ meet the armed men" (Job 39:21) (2 words)
62 "And _____ of cedar beams" (1 Kings 6:36) (2 words)
63 "Of Nebat, who was _____ Egypt" (1 Kings 12:2) (2 words)
64 "The evidence of things not _____" (Hebrews 11:1)

DOWN

1 "And ye have snuffed _____" (Malachi 1:13) (2 words)
2 "Lest thou _____ thy foot against a stone" (Psalm 91:12)
3 Affectedly or showily artistic
4 Cat call
5 Buffet runners
6 "For without me ye _____ nothing" (John 15:5) (2 words)
7 Against (prefix)
8 Island souvenirs
9 Daydreaming, perhaps
10 "Or seest thou _____ seeth?" (Job 10:4) (2 words)
11 Attention getter
12 "They that sow in tears shall _____ in joy" (Psalm 126:5)
13 CPR provider (abbr.)
21 "And they went _____ noon" (1 Kings 20:16) (2 words)
22 "And God said, _____ there be light" (Genesis 1:3)
25 "Thirty milch camels with their _____" (Genesis 32:15)
26 "_____ goeth before him, and burneth" (Psalm 97:3) (2 words)

by David K. Shortess

27 "The fool _____ and scoffs, and there is no peace" (Proverbs 29:9 NIV)

28 "Simon the Leper, _____ sat at meat" (Mark 14:3) (2 words)

29 Composer and pianist Rubinstein

30 "Now as _____ as it was day" (Acts 12:18)

31 "And ran at flood _____ as before" (Joshua 4:18 NIV)

32 "And Pilate wrote a _____" (John 19:19)

33 Pale

35 Celebes buffalo

36 Lustrous gem

38 "Like the _____ birth of a woman" (Psalm 58:8)

39 "Eat nothing made with _____" (Exodus 12:20 NIV)

44 Sign of a success (abbr.)

45 Cape _____, Nova Scotia

46 "I will not give you _____" (Exodus 5:10)

47 "If you had known what these words _____ desire mercy" (Matthew 12:7 NIV) (2 words)

48 Computer operator

49 "It teaches us to say _____ ungodliness" (Titus 2:12 NIV)

50 Elihu's school

51 Greek organiation (abbr.)

52 Book after Joel

53 "Because it is _____ of his" (Job 18:15)

54 "And they shall _____" (Jeremiah 50:36)

55 "And _____ they tell him of her" (Mark 1:30)

56 "And _____ man with smooth skin" (Genesis 27:11 NIV) (2 words)

73

ACROSS

1 "Between Bethel and _____"
(Genesis 13:3)
4 "_____, Hadid, and Ono" (Ezra 2:33)
7 Opposite of *her*
10 "Restore all that was _____"
(2 Kings 8:6)
11 Seth's son (Genesis 4:26)
13 A son of Jahdai (1Chronicles 2:47)
15 Greek form of *Hagar* (Galatians 4:24)
16 Jesus' garden trial
18 A son of Raamah (Genesis 10:7)
20 Bed covering
21 Allow
22 Peter cut one off
24 A king of Midian (Numbers 31:8)
25 "_____, Bethzur, and Gedor"
(Joshua 15:58)
28 "Ointment and _____ rejoice the
heart" (Proverbs 27:9)
33 A son of Benjamin (Genesis 46:21)
34 Consume food
36 Beloved hymn: "_____, My God,
to Thee"
37 "Thee in this _____" (2 Kings 9:26)
38 Exclamation of affirmation
40 Exhaust
41 Rescue (arch.)
44 This book includes two censuses
(abbr.)
46 "_____ mouth is smoother than
oil" (Proverbs 5:3)
47 Azareel's son (Nehemiah 11:13)
49 "Aquila, born in Pontus, _____
come from Italy" (Acts 18:2)
51 To furnish with equipment, or a
body part
52 "Borders of _____" (Joshua 11:2)
53 "Against Jerusalem, _____"
(Ezekiel 26:2)
56 Snake poison
59 "Jozabad, and _____"
(2 Chronicles 31:13)
63 "He stood by the lake of _____"
(Luke 5:1)
66 Nagge's son (Luke 3:25)
67 A son of Zabad (1 Chronicles 7:21)
68 A son of Caanan (Genesis 10:15)
69 "And your feet _____ with the
preparation of the gospel of peace"
(Ephesians 6:15)
70 "O ye _____ bones, hear the word
of the LORD" (Ezekiel 37:4)
71 Buzzing stinger
72 Transgression

DOWN

1 The king's chamberlain (Esther 2:3)
2 "_____ the Canaanite"
(Numbers 21:1)
3 Jacob's descendants
4 Appendage
5 "Day of _____ birth"
(Ecclesiastes 7:1)
6 "What _____ the LORD require of
thee" (Micah 6:8)
7 Edge of a garment
8 Son of Nathan of Zobah
(2 Samuel 23:36)
9 "_____. God hath numbered thy
kingdom, and finished it"
(Daniel 5:26)
10 "He _____ horns" (Habakkuk 3:4)
12 Fleecy ruminant
13 Go to sleep
14 Became acquainted
17 Popular biblical number
19 Prophecy book only three chapters
long (abbr.)
23 "For ye tithe mint and _____"
(Luke 11:42)
25 David fought the Syrians here
(2 Samuel 10:17)
26 Ezra proclaimed a fast there
(Ezra 8:21)
27 Beat down
29 "To visit the _____ and widows"
(James 1:27)
30 Michaiah's father
(2 Chronicles 13:2)
31 Happy
32 Before (arch.)

by N. Teri Grottke

35 "Hundred and _____ years old" (Joshua 24:29)
37 This book was written between the times of Moses and Babylonian captivity (abbr.)
39 Another way to spell *awl*
42 Shorn
43 Weeds
45 Insane
48 Asher's firstborn (1 Chronicles 7:30)
50 This is connected to the foot
53 Get older
54 Gripped
55 A brother of Eshcol (Genesis 14:13)
57 "Brought the heads of _____" (Judges 7:25)
58 Measure (arch.)
60 Rephaiah's father (1 Chronicles 4:42)
61 Esau's father-in-law (Genesis 26:34)

62 "Bored a hole in the _____ of it" (2 Kings 12:9)
64 No (arch.)
65 "_____ word of the LORD was precious in those days" (1 Samuel 3:1)

74

What's His Line?

What was the occupation of each person named in all caps?

The labourer is worthy of his hire.

LUKE 10:7

ACROSS

1 Asner and Ames
4 "_____ in a poke" (2 words)
8 **ESAU** (Genesis 25:27)
14 "Fifteen in a _____" (1 Kings 7:3)
15 1947 biochemistry Nobel laureate
16 Gunsmoke actor James
17 Hophni's father (1 Samuel 1:3)
18 Shades
19 Fifth part of an act in a Roman play (2 words)
20 **ALEXANDER** (2 Timothy 4:14)
23 Pile driver head
24 "Nor on any _____" (Revelation 7:1)
25 School founded by Henry VI
26 Doctrinal ending (suffix)
28 "There is a _____ here" (John 6:9)
30 Winding in and out
34 "If you have _____ with men on foot" (Jeremiah 12:5 NIV)
37 Basic bread spread
39 Just barely got by
40 Good Judean king (1 Kings 15:9, 11)
41 **MALCHUS** (John 18:10)
44 "Sir, come down _____ my child die" (John 4:49)
45 "Neither shall they learn war any _____" (Isaiah 2:4)
47 "Waters to _____ in" (Ezekiel 47:5)
48 Island of western Scotland
50 "But a wise man will _____ it" (Proverbs 16:14 NIV)
52 "Blessed _____ . . ." (Matthew 5:3–11)
53 "Firm unto the _____" (Hebrews 3:6)
54 "And I saw when the _____ opened one of the seals" (Revelation 6:1)

57 "The open _____ between the side rooms" (Ezekiel 41:9 NIV)
61 "Then Gideon took _____ men of his servants" (Judges 6:27)
63 **DEMETRIUS** (Acts 19:24)
66 Choose (2 words)
68 _____ vera
69 "Was _____ unto him" (Matthew 18:34)
70 _____ Nevadas
71 "The _____ of the scornful" (Psalm 1:1)
72 Harem room
73 **EZRA** (Nehemiah 8:1)
74 Spreads hay
75 "I have _____ you with milk" (1 Corinthians 3:2)

DOWN

1 "And do not _____ a sacred stone" (Deuteronomy 16:22 NIV)
2 Sorrow
3 Filch
4 "Even in laughter the heart may _____" (Proverbs 14:13 NIV)
5 "His fury is _____ out like fire" (Nahum 1:6)
6 "I was not in safety, neither had _____" (Job 3:26) (2 words)
7 Gadget (var.)
8 "_____ thou eaten of the tree" (Genesis 3:11)
9 Street youngster
10 Compass point between N and NE
11 **AQUILA** (Acts 18:2–3)
12 "But _____ have I hated" (Romans 9:13)
13 Request for a formal answer (abbr.)
21 Soccer great
22 Pant leg length

by David K. Shortess

7 "And if any man will _____ thee at the law" (Matthew 5:40)

9 Classifieds

1 H+ or OH–

2 Trillion (prefix)

3 "On the east of _____" (Genesis 4:16)

4 "With the _____ third of a hin" (Numbers 28:14 NIV) (2 words)

5 "He it is, to whom I shall give _____" (John 13:26) (2 words)

6 **JESUS** (Mark 6:3–4)

7 *1984* author

8 CXII ÷ II

2 Follows *heir-* or *host-*

3 "Of stone, and _____ for mortar" (Genesis 11:3 NIV)

6 Follows *hallow-* or *eight-*

9 Enlarge a hole

1 Accumulate on a surface

52 "Now when this was noised _____" (Acts 2:6)

55 Nautical halt

56 Brawl

58 "Houses may be _____ the frogs" (Exodus 8:9 NIV) (2 words)

59 Piece for the piano

60 "My messenger _____ of you" (Mark 1:2 NIV)

61 "Waves thereof _____ themselves" (Jeremiah 5:22)

62 Heroic narrative

64 "*Dies* _____" (Latin hymn of mourning)

65 "So if the Son _____ you free" (John 8:36 NIV)

67 Day before Saturday (abbr.)

ACROSS

1 Melchi's father (Luke 3:28)
5 Uri's son (1 Kings 4:19)
10 "We _____ our bread" (Lamentations 5:9)
13 "Baalah, and _____" (Joshua 15:29)
14 Stayed in a place
15 Shammah's father (2 Samuel 23:11)
17 "Tappuah, and _____" (Joshua 15:34)
18 "This only would I _____ of you" (Galatians 3:2)
19 "_____ which is lent" (1 Samuel 2:20)
20 Sugar plant
21 Made a mistake
22 "_____ the waters" (Exodus 15:25)
23 "Who shall lay any thing to the _____ of God's elect?" (Romans 8:33)
25 Pass away
26 More or _____
27 Strange
29 "The wheat and the _____ were not smitten" (Exodus 9:32)
31 "An he _____ also" (Proverbs 30:31)
34 Strong wood
37 Gave a loan
40 "Take thy _____" (Luke 16:7)
41 "At his holy _____" (Psalm 99:9)
43 A son of Gad (Genesis 46:16)
45 Great wickedness
46 "Is not _____" (Isaiah 10:9)
48 City in Egypt (Hosea 10:8)
49 Book of ceremonial law (abbr.)
50 Jediael's brother (1 Chronicles 11:45)
51 "What _____ ye to weep" (Acts 21:13)
52 "The other _____" (Nehemiah 7:33)
54 King Hezekiah's mother (2 Kings 18:2)
56 "Wherefore _____ up the loins of your mind" (1 Peter 1:13)
57 Put it to good _____

59 "Shimei, and _____" (1 Kings 1:8)
61 A son of Lotan (1 Chronicles 1:39)
64 Solomon's great-grandson (Matthew 1:7)
67 One who stood at Ezra's right hand (Nehemiah 8:4)
72 A son of Joktan (Genesis 10:26–29)
73 "Jonah was gone down into the _____ of the ship" (Jonah 1:5)
75 Rephaiah's father (1 Chronicles 4:42)
76 Desire
77 Walked (arch.)
78 Precipitation

DOWN

2 Jacob and Leah's daughter (Genesis 30:16–21)
3 Pagan goddess of the Ephesians (Acts 19:35)
4 Pashur's father (Jeremiah 20:1)
5 What Jacob called Jegarsahadutha (Genesis 31:47)
6 Salah's son (Genesis 10:24)
7 "Under every _____ two sockets" (Exodus 36:30)
8 "Og the king of Bashan, which dwelt at Astaroth in _____" (Deuteronomy 1:4)
9 Give
10 "Nathanael of Cana in _____" (John 21:2)
11 "Three days _____ I fell sick" (1 Samuel 30:13)
12 "Lament for the _____" (Isaiah 32:12)
16 Seth's son (Genesis 4:26)
17 One of the books likely written by Solomon (abbr.)
24 Received
28 Accomplish
30 Sick
31 "Not _____ to filthy lucre" (Titus 1:)
32 Oily fruit
33 "Destroy _____ kings and people" (Ezra 6:12)

by N. Teri Grottke

35 Asher didn't drive out the inhabitants of this town (Judges 1:31)
36 Relatives
38 "For if ye do these things, ye shall _____ fall" (2 Peter 1:10)
39 Walk
40 A god of Babylon (Isaiah 46:1)
42 "For, _____, as soon as the voice of thy salutation" (Luke 1:44)
44 Motel
46 Rocky Mountain state (abbr.)
47 "Against Jerusalem, _____" (Ezekiel 26:2)
48 Patriarch of a family of returned exiles (Ezra 2:57)
50 Moses' successor (abbr.)
53 "And _____ great" (Ecclesiastes 9:14)
55 "Children of_____" (1 Chronicles 7:12)

56 "_____ is for him?" (Amos 3:5)
58 Direction of the rising sun
60 Comfort
61 "_____ shall we" (Hebrews 2:3)
62 Edom will be destroyed in its only chapter (abbr.)
63 "_____ greedily after the error of Balaam" (Jude 1:11)
65 Knight
66 Fuss
68 "To meet the Lord in the _____" (1 Thessalonians 4:17)
69 This prophet had a son named Shear-jashub (abbr.)
70 Abdiel's son (1 Chronicles 5:15)
71 A liquid measure (Leviticus 23:13)
74 An altar (Joshua 22:34)

76

Scriptural Snakes

And he laid hold on the dragon, that old serpent,
which is the Devil, and Satan, and bound him a thousand years.

REVELATION 20:2

ACROSS

1 "A _____ answer turneth away wrath"
   (Proverbs 15:1)
5 "Cometh to me I will in no wise
   _____ out" (John 6:37)
9 Danish physicist Niels and family
14 "Shammah the son of _____"
   (2 Samuel 23:11)
15 Quechuan
16 Nebraska cow town
17 "Now the coat was without _____"
   (John 19:23)
18 "Our end is _____"
   (Lamentations 4:18)
19 German city on the Moselle near
   Luxembourg
20 **IT SWEET-TALKED:** "And the
   woman said, The _____ me, and I
   did eat" (Genesis 3:13) (2 words)
23 _____ la-la
24 Entertainer Mineo
25 "When anyone went to a wine
   _____" (Haggai 2:16 NIV)
28 Singing brothers of yesteryear
31 Bay off the west coast of France
36 Islands in the Seine
38 Where Pearl Harbor is located
40 "Is he a homeborn _____?"
   (Jeremiah 2:14)
41 **IT HAD BEEN A ROD:** "And it
   became a _____ fled from before it"
   (Exodus 4:2–3) (3 words)
44 Halos
45 Countertenor
46 "I would thou _____ cold or hot"
   (Revelation 3:15)
47 Posture
49 "And led him out of the _____"
   (Mark 8:23)
51 Precedes -*king*, -*ring*, or -*wing*
52 "Stand in _____, and sin not"
   (Psalm 4:4)
54 "Thou shalt _____ kill" (Exodus 20:13)

56 **IT WAS ON A POLE:** "And Moses
   made _____" (Numbers 21:9) (4 words)
65 "Sent away Paul and Silas by night
   unto _____" (Acts 17:10)
66 "As _____ large number of God-
   fearing Greeks" (Acts 17:4 NIV)
   (2 words)
67 "That an _____ is nothing in the
   world" (1 Corinthians 8:4)
68 Cooped up
69 City on the Oka
70 "But the tongue can no man _____"
   (James 3:8)
71 "And Jacob _____ away unawares to
   Laban the Syrian" (Genesis 31:20)
72 "For my flesh is _____ food"
   (John 6:55 NIV)
73 "Leah was tender _____"
   (Genesis 29:17)

DOWN

1 Back talk
2 S-shaped curve
3 "And in thy _____ will I worship"
   (Psalm 5:7)
4 "Wherefore do ye _____ the LORD?"
   (Exodus 17:2)
5 "Calamus and _____"
   (Song of Solomon 4:14)
6 "For he is cast into _____ by his own
   feet" (Job 18:8) (2 words)
7 Sign of healing
8 "Then appeared the _____ also"
   (Matthew 13:26)
9 Food poisoning
10 "But _____ wrought evil in the eyes
   of the LORD" (1 Kings 16:25)
11 "And the _____ shall sweep away"
   (Isaiah 28:17)
12 Post-WWII Korean dictator Syngman
13 A semiprecious form of reddish
   chalcedony
21 Pitcher's stat (abbr.)

by David K. Shortess

22 Chatter

25 Passport add-ons

26 Alaskan native

27 Precedes *cotta* or *firma*

29 "That they may _____ whole month" (Numbers 11:21) (2 words)

30 "Thou _____ not kill" (Exodus 20:13)

32 "The LORD is _____ to anger" (Nahum 1:3)

33 "Is not under bondage in such _____" (1 Corinthians 7:15)

34 "Can consecrated meat _____ your punishment?" (Jeremiah 11:15 NIV)

35 "_____ your amazement he will show him" (John 5:20 NIV) (2 words)

37 "And children of a _____ long?" (Lamentations 2:20)

39 "And it shall be opened _____ you" (Matthew 7:7)

42 Foolhardy, reckless adventure

43 "Your sins have been your _____!" (Hosea 14:1 NIV)

48 "One _____ lamb of the first year without blemish" (Leviticus 14:10)

50 "And _____, the city of the priests" (1 Samuel 22:19)

53 "There is a woman that hath a familiar spirit at _____" (1 Samuel 28:7)

55 Hackneyed

56 Fundamentals

57 "I prepared my _____ in the street!" (Job 29:7)

58 Consequently

59 "The earth shall _____ to and fro" (Isaiah 24:20)

60 "Bind the _____ of thine head upon thee" (Ezekiel 24:17)

61 Greek theaters

62 "It is _____ of blowing the trumpets unto you" (Numbers 29:1) (2 words)

63 "The devil shall cast _____ of you into prison" (Revelation 2:10)

64 Winter coaster

77

ACROSS

1 "The fenced cities are Ziddim, _____, and Hammath" (Joshua 19:35)
4 Shiphi's son (1 Chronicles 4:37)
8 Interpreted by Daniel to mean "Thy kingdom is divided" (Daniel 5:28)
13 "Of Hena, and _____?" (2 Kings 19:13)
15 "_____, Hizkijah, Azzur" (Nehemiah 10:17)
16 A son of Elioenai (1 Chronicles 3:24)
17 "Gedaliah, and _____" (1 Chronicles 25:3)
18 "Whosoever shall say to his brother, _____, shall be in danger of the council" (Matthew 5:22)
19 A son of Eliphaz (Genesis 36:11)
20 A son of Eliab (Numbers 26:9)
22 "She waited on _____ wife" (2 Kings 5:2)
24 Verbalize
25 "Everything on _____ land that had the breath of life in its nostrils died" (Genesis 7:22 NIV)
26 Uzziah broke down this Philistine wall (2 Chronicles 26:6)
30 Largest continent
32 Barrier
35 "Myrrh and _____" (Song of Solomon 4:14)
36 "The LORD dwelleth in _____" (Joel 3:21)
37 Mighty man of David (2 Samuel 23:36)
38 Cook
39 Fuss
40 "_____ it, and smote the Philistine in his forehead" (1 Samuel 17:49)
41 Injured
42 "Though ye have _____" (Psalm 68:13)
43 A son of Ephraim (1 Chronicles 7:22–25)
44 Increase
45 Master
46 "Thou _____ up mine iniquity" (Job 14:17)
47 This book ends with Moses' death (abbr.)
48 Kona, Hawaii (airport code)
49 "From the _____ of the sea" (Isaiah 11:11)
53 Firstborn
57 Disburse
58 Load (arch.)
60 The city Lot fled to (Genesis 19:17–22)
62 Spear
63 A son of Shem (Genesis 10:22)
64 "According to this _____" (Galatians 6:16)
65 Come in
66 "The linen _____ at a price" (1 Kings 10:28)
67 Commanded militarily

DOWN

1 "Go ye down against them: behold, they come up by the cliff of _____ (2 Chronicles 20:16)
2 "_____ the death of the cross" (Philippians 2:8)
3 Not easily found
4 "At Enrimmon, and at _____, and at Jarmuth" (Nehemiah 11:29)
5 Country of Rome
6 Most apocalyptic and messianic book of all minor prophets (abbr.)
7 Uz's brother (1 Chronicles 1:42)
8 "Thence unto _____" (Acts 21:1)
9 Foe
10 "In _____ was there a voice" (Matthew 2:18)
11 Ahira's father (Numbers 1:15)
12 Iniquities
14 "They asked _____, 'Then who are you? Are you Elijah?' " (John 1:21 NIV)
21 Use (arch.)

by N. Teri Grottke

23 Patriarch of a family of returned exiles (Ezra 2:15)
26 Attai's father (1 Chronicles 2:35)
27 With the speaking voice
28 "Under every _____ two sockets" (Exodus 36:30)
29 Bird home
30 Helped
31 "Not _____ angry" (Titus 1:7)
32 "_____ of Judah" (2 Samuel 6:2)
33 "_____ and Caiaphas being the high priests" (Luke 3:2)
34 "If you do what is _____, will you not be accepted?" (Genesis 4:7 NIV)
36 Where Joram smote the Edomites (2 Kings 8:21)
37 What the wind did at the parting of the Red Sea
40 In place of (arch.)

42 "There will be _____ wailing throughout Egypt" (Exodus 11:6 NIV)
45 "The borrower is servant to the _____" (Proverbs 22:7)
46 "Call a _____ assembly" (Joel 2:15)
47 One way to praise the Lord
48 "The tents of _____!" (Psalm 120:5)
49 Island
50 Breadth
51 Gave a loan
52 Kill
54 This prophet's name means "help" (abbr.)
55 Human being
56 Story
59 Jether's son (1 Chronicles 7:38)
61 Color of blood

78

Follow the Leader!

*By this shall all men know that ye are my disciples,
if ye have love one to another.*

JOHN 13:35

ACROSS

1 Start of **VERSE** from John 15:12
5 "It is only _____ from the burn"
   (Leviticus 13:28 NIV) (2 words)
10 Israeli folk dance
14 "Be not _____ with thy mouth"
   (Ecclesiastes 5:2)
15 A silly one
16 "No, nor _____ shall be"
   (Matthew 24:21)
17 **VERSE**, cont'd from 1 Across
   (3 words)
20 Hot dog man Oscar
21 "Forbear, what am I _____?" (Job 16:6)
22 Nutritional intake guidelines (abbr.)
23 "The trees of the LORD are full of
   _____" (Psalm 104:16)
25 Lbs. or kgs. (abbr.)
27 **VERSE**, cont'd from 17 Across
   (3 words)
33 _____ Romeo
37 "And he shall smite the earth with the
   _____ of his mouth" (Isaiah 11:4)
38 "And when she had _____ it"
   (Exodus 2:6)
39 Durocher and Tolstoy
40 What most of the earth's people are
42 Prof's aides (abbr.)
43 "Let us _____ rebuilding"
   (Nehemiah 2:18 NIV)
44 "Six thousand shekels of gold and ten
   _____ of clothing" (2 Kings 5:5 NIV)
45 Cause to put on weight
47 "For God, said _____, hath
   appointed me" (Genesis 4:25)
48 "Wherein thou _____ been
   instructed" (Luke 1:4)
49 **VERSE**, cont'd from 27 Across
   (2 words)
51 "And all that handle the _____"
   (Ezekiel 27:29)
53 "Unto thee, O LORD, _____ lift up
   my soul" (Psalm 25:1) (2 words)
54 "The custom of the _____" (Luke 2:27)

57 "Tell me, art thou a _____?"
   (Acts 22:27)
61 Zoo favorite
65 End of **VERSE**, cont'd from 49
   Across (5 words)
68 "Sir, your _____ has earned five
   more" (Luke 19:18 NIV)
69 Rub out
70 Tight
71 "For my yoke is _____"
   (Matthew 11:30)
72 "And _____ between Nineveh and
   Calah" (Genesis 10:12)
73 "Come back _____ his own head"
   (Esther 9:25 NIV)

DOWN

1 "_____ her nails"
   (Deuteronomy 21:12 NIV)
2 "He _____ demon" (Luke 7:33 NIV)
   (2 words)
3 "What _____ strength, that I should
   hope?" (Job 6:11) (2 words)
4 Most bashful
5 "But also to be forward a year _____"
   (2 Corinthians 8:10)
6 "And _____ fell among thorns"
   (Mark 4:7)
7 Stupor
8 "The events of _____ reign"
   (2 Chronicles 16:11 NIV)
9 "And be _____ in the spirit of your
   mind" (Ephesians 4:23)
10 "Round about the _____ thereof"
   (Exodus 28:33)
11 "And passed _____, and came into
   his own city" (Matthew 9:1)
12 "And _____ your heart" (Joel 2:13)
13 "For thou _____ near kinsman"
   (Ruth 3:9) (2 words)
18 Colorful drawing implement
19 It was banned in the U.S. in 1972
24 Brio
26 "Eaten without _____?" (Job 6:6)

by David K. Shortess

27 Refuse
28 Book after Daniel
29 Mine openings
30 "Is pleased with me, _____ order be written" (Esther 8:5 NIV) (2 words)
31 First governor of New Mexico
32 The brightest asteroid
34 "Or put him on a _____ for your girls?" (Job 41:5 NIV)
35 "_____ was above all the people" (Nehemiah 8:5) (2 words)
36 Fall bloomer
41 "Had no leisure so much _____ eat" (Mark 6:31) (2 words)
43 Forty winks
45 "Been with me _____ a year" (1 Samuel 29:3 NIV) (2 words)
46 "There shall be no _____" (Luke 1:33)
50 "Are to be _____ the rings" (Exodus 28:28 NIV) (2 words)

52 One of the three sons of Jether (1 Chronicles 7:38)
54 "And the _____ walk" (Matthew 11:5)
55 "Which are in _____" (Revelation 1:4)
56 "He who _____ souls is wise" (Proverbs 11:30 NIV)
58 "A _____ man" (Romans 2:3 NIV)
59 "_____, my lord" (Numbers 12:11)
60 "The rings, and _____ jewels" (Isaiah 3:21)
62 "Confirmed it _____ oath" (Hebrews 6:17) (2 words)
63 "Shoot your arrows and _____ them" (Psalm 144:6 NIV)
64 Ford, for example
66 "Stones, wood, _____, stubble" (1 Corinthians 3:12)
67 Neighbor of Brazil (abbr.)

79

ACROSS

1 "_____ of truth shall be established for ever" (Proverbs 12:19)
4 Assist
8 "Zelah, _____, and Jebusi" (Joshua 18:28)
13 Thummim's partner (Exodus 28:30)
15 Cain's victim
16 A son of Ulla (1 Chronicles 7:39)
17 "For he hath _____ marvellous things" (Psalm 98:1)
18 "For in him we live, and _____, and have our being" (Acts 17:28)
19 "Go on your way _____ in the morning" (Genesis 19:2 NIV)
20 A son of Asaph (1 Chronicles 25:2)
23 "But the wheat and the _____ were not smitten" (Exodus 9:32)
24 No matter which
25 "On the east side of _____" (Numbers 34:11)
27 Belonging to Sarai's husband
31 Sunrise
33 "Bore his _____ through with a thorn?" (Job 41:2)
36 Elkanah's grandfather (1 Samuel 1:1)
37 People
38 Naomi wanted to be called this
39 Bellybutton
40 The people of one of the greatest empires (abbr.)
41 "Name of _____" (Judges 1:11)
42 Ancient Hebrew unit of dry capacity, 1/10 ephah
43 Hearing organs
44 Elevate
45 Saul's grandfather (1 Chronicles 8:33)
46 Weeks are made of these
47 "Now as _____ and Jambres withstood Moses" (2 Timothy 3:8)
48 Biblical spy turned leader (abbr.)
49 Plant seed
50 "Helez the Paltite, _____" (2 Samuel 23:26)
52 "Stones of _____" (Isaiah 34:11)
58 Hurt
60 A son of Dishan (Genesis 36:28)
61 Tubs
63 "Argob and _____" (2 Kings 15:25)
64 "In vain you rise early and stay up _____" (Psalm 127:2 NIV)
65 "_____ the Ahohite" (1 Chronicles 11:29)
66 "I would hasten my escape from the _____ storm and tempest" (Psalm 55:8)
67 Looked at
68 Are (arch.)

DOWN

1 A son of Shem (1 Chronicles 1:17)
2 Strong metal
3 Common tree
4 Belonging to Esther's enemy
5 "Ivory and _____" (Ezekiel 27:15)
6 Tribe of the priesthood
7 Guilty or not guilty
8 Before (arch.)
9 "This only would I _____ of you" (Galatians 3:2)
10 Chelub's son (1 Chronicles 27:26)
11 Heap
12 Livestock feed
14 Became acquainted
21 A son of Pharez (Genesis 46:12)
22 "Doth the _____ fly by thy wisdom" (Job 39:26)
26 Fort Wayne's state (abbr.)
27 Baptismal site of John the Baptist (John 3:23)
28 "Holy and without _____" (Ephesians 1:4)
29 The Jordan is the main one in Israel
30 "Sons of _____" (1 Chronicles 7:12)
31 Entances
32 Charity
33 "Until they had destroyed _____ king of Canaan" (Judges 4:24)
34 Get up

by N. Teri Grottke

35 Goods
37 "None shall _____ them away" (Jeremiah 7:33)
38 "What _____ ye to weep" (Acts 21:13)
41 "Drink of that which the young men have _____" (Ruth 2:9)
43 Comfort
46 Accomplish
47 "The whole body fitly _____ together" (Ephesians 4:16)
48 Maleleel's son (Luke 3:37)
49 "In whatsoever _____" (Philippians 4:11)
50 Zaccur's father (Nehemiah 3:2)
51 Precipitation
53 Not female
54 "_____ for the peace" (Psalm 122:6)
55 A king of Midian (Numbers 31:8)

56 Heber's father (Luke 3:35)
57 Night sky illuminator
58 Sharp-toothed tool
59 "So shall _____ seed be" (Romans 4:18)
62 "Turn aside, _____ down here" (Ruth 4:1)

80

The Lord's Compassions

Strength for today and bright hope for tomorrow—
blessings all mine and ten thousand beside!

THOMAS O. CHISHOLM

ACROSS

1 "And he was in his presence, as in times _____" (1 Samuel 19:7)
5 "Every man by his own _____" (Numbers 1:52)
9 "Behold, thou art but _____ man" (Genesis 20:3) (2 words)
14 "It is time for you to _____ LORD" (Psalm 119:126 NIV) (2 words)
15 "Which gendereth to bondage, which is _____" (Galatians 4:24)
16 Arbor _____ (Asian evergreen shrub)
17 Start of **VERSE**: Lamentations 3:23 (4 words)
20 "About the _____ of the robe to minister in" (Exodus 39:26)
21 "A tight _____ on his tongue" (James 1:26 NIV)
22 Rubs out
23 "To seek an _____" (Ezekiel 21:21 NIV)
24 "How much _____ man, that is a worm?" (Job 25:6)
25 **VERSE**, cont'd from 17 Across
28 Keats product
29 "The weasel, the _____" (Leviticus 11:29 NIV)
32 "Sort of error that _____ from a ruler" (Ecclesiastes 10:5 NIV)
33 Oriental sauce
34 "In _____ was there a voice" (Matthew 2:18)
35 "The choicest of its _____" (Isaiah 37:24 NIV)
36 "_____ ye here while I go and pray" (Matthew 26:36)
37 "Son of Ammiel in Lo _____" (2 Samuel 9:4 NIV)
38 "She had waited, and her hope was _____" (Ezekiel 19:5)
39 "Is he then his _____?" (Mark 12:37)

40 "Arose, and led him unto _____" (Luke 23:1)
41 Follows *ethyl-* or *methyl-*
42 Bad joke, often
43 **VERSE**, cont'd from 25 Across (2 words)
44 "So that the earth _____ again" (1 Samuel 4:5)
45 Rubicund
46 Toward the back of the boat
49 Small restaurant
50 Sheep-speak
53 End of **VERSE**, cont'd from 43 Across (2 words)
56 Recorded
57 "Whose faith is weak, _____ only vegetables" (Romans 14:2 NIV)
58 Beehive state
59 "How right they are to _____ you!" (Song of Songs 1:4 NIV)
60 Altar location
61 Back of the neck

DOWN

1 "They mar my _____" (Job 30:13)
2 "Even in laughter the heart may _____" (Proverbs 14:13 NIV)
3 "Out of the _____ of Jesse" (Isaiah 11:1)
4 Trifle
5 Drives recklessly
6 Getting old in Great Britain (var.)
7 Educator Horace
8 Prefix meaning "prior to"
9 "Securely as men _____ from war" (Micah 2:8)
10 Operatic prima donnas
11 Seine summers (Fr.)
12 Alpine river
13 Tunisian rulers

by David K. Shortess

18 "He sent for his _____, and destroyed" (Matthew 22:7)
19 Like an unkept garden
23 Beginning
24 "They have been made _____" (Isaiah 42:22 NIV)
25 Syrup source
26 "Or loose the bands of _____?" (Job 38:31)
27 Washer cycle
29 Capital of Morocco
30 He taught Stradivarius
31 "Then appeared the _____ also" (Matthew 13:26)
33 "The wilderness of _____" (Exodus 16:1)
34 Track event
36 "I was the _____ of the drunkards" (Psalm 69:12)
37 Type of engine
39 Branch of Islam

40 Copious
42 "They _____ their sin like Sodom" (Isaiah 3:9 NIV)
43 Nursery methods
44 "I _____ to those" (1 John 5:16 NIV)
46 "_____ boy!"
47 Roe source
48 Steno's error
49 Become raw
50 Follows *alpha*
51 Urgency letters
52 "Even _____ is pure" (1 John 3:3) (2 words)
54 It's in the bag, sometimes
55 Joshua's father (Exodus 33:11)

81

ACROSS

1 A son of Judah (1 Chronicles 2:3)
5 She met Peter at the door
10 "Go, wash in the _____ of Siloam" (John 9:7)
14 Rabbit
15 "_____, and Hara" (1 Chronicles 5:26)
16 This priest rebuilt the temple
17 "Alammelech, and _____" (Joshua 19:26)
18 "And _____ it, that the tent lay along" (Judges 7:13)
20 "David _____ of him how Joab did" (2 Samuel 11:7)
22 "Into my _____" (Lamentations 3:13)
23 "Ye have _____ rebellious against the LORD" (Deuteronomy 31:27)
24 Timothy's grandmother
26 A set of steps
29 A son of Shimei (1 Chronicles 23:10)
30 Take action
33 "Habor, and _____" (1 Chronicles 5:26)
34 "Shall be your _____" (Ezekiel 45:12)
35 The Assyrians' fall is predicted in this book (abbr.)
36 Elkanah's grandfather (1 Samuel 1:1)
38 Before (arch.)
39 Take an oath (biblical sp.)
41 Buzzing stinger
42 Ishmael and Hagar lived in this wilderness
44 "Day of _____ birth" (Ecclesiastes 7:1)
45 Type of tree (Isaiah 44:14)
46 "Ho, _____ a one!" (Ruth 4:1)
47 "Shall it break in pieces and _____" (Daniel 2:40)
49 "He shall grow as the _____" (Hosea 14:5)
50 Apostle to the Gentiles
51 Loaded (arch.)
54 "Every neighbour will walk with _____" (Jeremiah 9:4)
58 Jacob's descendants
61 King Hoshea's father (2 Kings 15:30)
62 A son of Zibeon (1 Chronicles 1:40)
63 Bathsheba's first husband (2 Samuel 11:3)
64 Very (arch.)
65 Worn-out clothing
66 "Chalcol, and _____" (1 Kings 4:31)
67 Bound

DOWN

1 "Jamin, and _____" (Genesis 46:10)
2 "That at the _____" (Philippians 2:10)
3 A son of Shem (Genesis 10:22)
4 A son of Jeconiah (1 Chronicles 3:17–18)
5 "Unto _____, and from thence unto Patara" (Acts 21:1)
6 Place of refuge
7 Ruth's son (Ruth 4:13–17)
8 "Borders of _____" (Joshua 11:2)
9 Are (arch.)
10 Part of the handwriting on the wall (Daniel 5:28)
11 A child of Gad (Numbers 26:16–18)
12 A son of Jerahmeel (1 Chronicles 2:25)
13 Boys
19 Belonging to Bathsheba's first husband
21 Saul's grandfather (1 Chronicles 8:33)
24 Flax cloth
25 Single
26 The visiting queen at Solomon's court was from here
27 Stories
28 "Argob and _____" (2 Kings 15:25)

by N. Teri Grottke

29 Pharez' twin brother
   (Genesis 38:27–30)
30 A son of Elioneai
   (1 Chronicles 3:24)
31 Concerns
32 "Thought on _____ things"
   (Matthew 1:20)
34 Undeserved favor
37 "These that have turned the world
   _____ down" (Acts 17:6)
40 "If thou _____ seek unto God"
   (Job 8:5)
43 Awl (biblical sp.)
47 Ahijah's son (2 Kings 9:9)
48 Sprint
49 Belonging to Jacob's first wife
50 Beg
51 "If we say that we have not sinned,
   we make him a _____"
   (1 John 1:10)

52 Largest continent
53 Pull
54 Mix
55 Jesus cried this on the cross
   (Mark 15:34)
56 Not easily found
57 Slough off
59 A child of Shem (1 Chronicles 1:17)
60 "The sixth captain for the sixth
   month was _____"
   (1 Chronicles 27:9)

82

ACROSS

1 "Straightway the spirit _____ him" (Mark 9:20)
5 City
9 "Jaresiah, and _____" (1 Chronicles 8:27)
14 "Duke Teman, duke _____" (Genesis 36:15)
15 Solomon's grandson (Matthew 1:7)
16 House
17 Zaccur's father (Nehemiah 3:2)
18 Menahem's father (2 Kings 15:17)
19 "Sons of Shemaiah; Hattush, and _____" (1 Chronicles 3:22)
20 "The whole world _____ in wickedness" (1 John 5:19)
22 Besides
24 "With a strong _____" (Jeremiah 21:5)
25 "Woe to them that are at _____ in Zion" (Amos 6:1)
28 "In that day shall this song be _____" (Isaiah 26:1)
30 "Thou shalt not _____ thyself" (Matthew 5:33)
34 Absalom's father (2 Samuel 3:3)
38 NT book after Galatians (abbr.)
39 "At the brook of _____" (Psalm 83:9)
41 "Whose name was _____ an Israelite" (2 Samuel 17:25)
42 Hushim's father (1 Chronicles 7:12)
44 "Whose soever sins ye _____, they are remitted unto them" (John 20:23)
46 "_____ stones and coals of fire" (Psalm 18:12)
47 "_____ between Nineveh and Calah" (Genesis 10:12)
49 "Offer a great sacrifice unto _____" (Judges 16:23)
51 A prophet son of Amoz (abbr.)
52 Servants
54 "Which was the son of _____" (Luke 3:27)
55 Hachaliah's son (Nehemiah 10:1) (abbr.)
56 "Out of the spoils _____ in battles" (1 Chronicles 26:27)

58 Lease
60 "They that followed, cried, saying, _____" (Mark 11:9)
64 "Which is neither _____ nor sown" (Deuteronomy 21:4)
68 Celeste
69 "My belly is as wine which hath no _____" (Job 32:19)
73 Beor's son (Genesis 36:32)
74 "He made narrowed _____ round about" (1 Kings 6:6)
75 "_____, lama sabachthani?" (Mark 15:34)
76 "Over the camels also was _____ the Ishmaelite" (1 Chronicles 27:30)
77 Awry
78 "Thy land shall be divided by _____" (Amos 7:17)
79 Level (arch.)

DOWN

1 Travail
2 "Say ye unto your brethren, _____" (Hosea 2:1)
3 Unique
4 "Of Eri, the family of the _____" (Numbers 26:16)
5 License plate
6 Minor prophet who wrote an OT book (abbr.)
7 Broad
8 "His _____ of brass" (Daniel 7:19)
9 And _____, and Zilthai, and Eliel" (1 Chronicles 8:20)
10 Timber
11 Thought
12 "This _____ is mount Sinai" (Galatians 4:25)
13 Wheel
21 Falcon
23 Addition total
26 "When thou wentest out of _____" (Judges 5:4)
27 "Though I forbear, what am I _____?" (Job 16:6)
29 "Fought against _____" (2 Kings 12:17)

by Tonya Vilhauer

30 "Delivered me from all my _____" (Psalm 34:4)
31 "The Nethinims dwelt in _____" (Nehemiah 3:26)
32 "Which was the son of _____" (Luke 3:27)
33 "Having understood that he was a _____" (Acts 23:27)
35 Shackles
36 "Her children _____ up" (Proverbs 31:28)
37 "Brought them unto _____" (1 Chronicles 5:26)
40 "Simeon that was called _____" (Acts 13:1)
43 Accelerate
45 Torus
48 Novelty
50 Adam lived _____ hundred and thirty years (Genesis 5:5)
53 Offspring

57 Belly button
59 "The coast reacheth to _____" (Joshua 19:22)
60 "Brought them unto Halah, and Habor, and _____" (1 Chronicles 5:26)
61 "Oren, and _____, and Ahijah" (1 Chronicles 2:25)
62 Gaddi's father (Numbers 13:11)
63 "Used curious _____ brought their books" (Acts 19:19)
65 "_____, which were dukes" (Joshua 13:21)
66 Asked for a double portion of Elijah's spirit (abbr.)
67 "Which is in the king's _____" (2 Samuel 18:18)
70 "Samuel arose and went to _____" (1 Samuel 3:6)
71 "_____ his son, Jehoshua his son" (1 Chronicles 7:27)
72 Bind

83

ACROSS

1 "His _____; on the eighth" (Exodus 22:30)
4 A king of Midian (Numbers 31:8)
7 Walk
12 Phares's brother (Matthew 1:3)
13 Before (arch.)
14 A son of Gad (Genesis 46:16)
15 Strong metal
16 "Will cause them to be _____ there" (1 Kings 5:9)
19 Strange
20 "To possess the land of the _____" (Amos 2:10)
21 "That _____ him up from the dead" (1 Peter 1:21)
24 Male sheep
25 "God created _____ heaven" (Genesis 1:1)
28 Astatine (sym.)
29 Possessive pronoun
30 "Shall be astonished, and _____ his head" (Jeremiah 18:16)
31 A son of David (1 Chronicles 3:5–6)
33 Snake sound
37 Refrain
39 "From the _____ of the sea" (Isaiah 11:11)
40 Palm Sunday praise
41 Metal pegs
42 Caleb's son (1 Chronicles 4:15)
43 This prophet's name means "festive" (abbr.)
45 Maine (abbr.)
46 Single
47 "God saw that it _____ good" (Genesis 1:21)
48 Not male
52 Joab's brother (2 Samuel 2:18)
55 A large salty body of water
56 Elkanah was one (1 Samuel 1:1)
59 "Nevertheless _____ heart" (1 Kings 15:14)
60 Adina's father (1 Chronicles 11:42)
61 Last book of the OT (abbr.)
62 Decomposing metal
63 Caused by or relating to tides
64 Increase
65 Are (arch.)

DOWN

1 "Chalcol, and _____" (1 Kings 4:31)
2 A son of Gad (Genesis 46:16)
3 Adam was the first
4 "As men go to _____" (Ezekiel 47:15)
5 Thummim's partner (Deuteronomy 33:8)
6 "And the people _____ unto him again" (Mark 10:1)
7 Specific one
8 Not easily found
9 Chicken product
10 Get older
11 "God _____ tempt Abraham" (Genesis 22:1)
12 "_____; nine cities" (Joshua 15:54)
17 "A great _____ from the hills" (Zephaniah 1:10)
18 "This time. . .the bird returned to _____ with a fresh olive leaf in its beak" (Genesis 8:11 NLT)
22 A son of Cush (1 Chronicles 1:9)
23 A son of Zerah (1 Chronicles 2:6)
25 Esau and Jacob were these
26 "The Lord is at _____" (Philippians 4:5)
27 These are sometimes painted for Easter
29 Tehinnah's son (1 Chronicles 4:12)
31 "An _____ of blood twelve years" (Mark 5:25)
32 Word preceding Psalm 119:121
34 He predicted the Messiah's birth to Ahaz (abbr.)
35 "Daubed it with _____ and with pitch" (Exodus 2:3)
36 "Melchisedec, king of _____" (Hebrews 7:1)
37 A son of Jehiel (1 Chronicles 9:35–37)

by N. Teri Grottke

38 "When he was _____"
(Hebrews 11:23)
44 An idol of Hamath (2 Kings 17:30)
47 "To _____, that God was in Christ,
reconciling the world unto himself"
(2 Corinthians 5:19)
48 "Shepherds abiding in the _____"
(Luke 2:8)
49 Esarhaddon was king here
(Ezra 4:2)
50 Smallest
51 "The LORD God stationed mighty
angelic beings to the _____ of
Eden" (Genesis 3:24 NLT)
52 Steward of Zimri's house in Tirzah
(1 Kings 16:9)
53 "Remnant of _____"
(Zephaniah 1:4)
54 Joseph mourned for Jacob at this
threshing floor (Genesis 50:11)

56 Jewish queen (abbr.)
57 Twenty-first letter of the Greek
alphabet
58 "Jacob _____ them under the oak
which was by Shechem"
(Genesis 35:4)
59 Jether's son (1 Chronicles 7:38)

84

Climbing the Walls

May there be peace within your walls and security within your citadels.

PSALM 122:7 NIV

ACROSS

1 "_____ a mocker" (Proverbs 19:25 NIV)
5 "A swelling, _____ or a bright spot" (Leviticus 14:56 NIV) (2 words)
10 "Rehob, toward _____ Hamath" (Numbers 13:21 NIV)
14 "The scarlet _____ in the window" (Joshua 2:21)
15 French river up north
16 "By_____ and living way" (Hebrews 10:20) (2 words)
17 Location of Rahab's house (Joshua 2:15) (4 words)
20 "Upon the great _____ of his right foot" (Leviticus 8:23)
21 "Have we not all _____ father?" (Malachi 2:10)
22 Formerly Shima Province, Japan, _____ prefecture
23 "And I _____ a vision" (Daniel 8:2) (2 words)
26 Follows *novel-* or *romantic-*
28 "_____ younger men as brothers" (1 Timothy 5:1 NIV)
30 What Ezekiel saw by the door of the court (Ezekiel 8:7) (5 words)
33 "Were cast into the _____ of fire" (Revelation 20:14)
34 "Behold, I will _____ new thing" (Isaiah 43:19) (2 words)
35 "To him that weareth the _____ clothing" (James 2:3)
36 Lincoln
37 Carnival workers
39 "I am like an _____ of the desert" (Psalm 102:6)
42 Sound from a massage recipient
43 Orthodontist's degree (abbr.)
44 "Am I _____, or a whale" (Job 7:12) (2 words)
45 Where they put the body of Saul (1 Samuel 31:10) (3 words)

49 Salsa base
50 Another northern French river
51 "Thou hast asked _____ thing" (2 Kings 2:10) (2 words)
52 Follows *switcher-* and *tab-*
53 G. H. W. Bush was once its director
55 Greek *h*
56 Where Ezekiel saw cherubims and palm trees (Ezekiel 41:20)
63 "The ants _____ people not strong" (Proverbs 30:25) (2 words)
64 "All of you be on the _____" (Joshua 8:4 NIV)
65 Relative of altitude (abbr.)
66 Hardy heroine
67 "From the tower of _____ shall they fall" (Ezekiel 30:6)
68 "And they shall _____" (Jeremiah 50:36)

DOWN

1 Winter bug
2 "They shoot out the _____" (Psalm 22:7)
3 "Beth Aven, lead _____ Benjamin" (Hosea 5:8 NIV) (2 words)
4 "And also of the _____" (Romans 2:9)
5 "_____ that setteth snares" (Jeremiah 5:26) (2 words)
6 "As light of foot as a wild _____" (2 Samuel 2:18)
7 Relative of quantity (abbr.)
8 "And I am a _____ man" (Genesis 27:11)
9 "Was _____ in stone" (Luke 23:53)
10 "Will not do the _____ of thy God" (Ezra 7:26)
11 Cloisonné covering
12 "The children of _____" (2 Chronicles 13:7)
13 Hooting chick
18 "Be with you now and change my _____" (Galatians 4:20 NIV)

by David K. Shortess

19 "With so many the _____ not torn" (John 21:11 NIV) (2 words)
23 "Which was the son of _____" (Luke 3:35)
24 Omri's son (1 Kings 16:28)
25 "Then I _____ up" (Genesis 41:21 NIV)
26 "Took thee _____ naked" (Matthew 25:38) (2 words)
27 "Which say, _____ thyself" (Isaiah 65:5) (2 words)
29 "Without a _____ of brightness?" (Amos 5:20 NIV)
31 Utah neighbor
32 Discharge
37 Multicolored cat
38 July 15, for one
39 Government safety group (abbr.)
40 "Thou wilt surely _____ away" (Exodus 18:18)
41 "Rowed hard to bring it to the _____" (Jonah 1:13)

42 "Hear, _____ ye people" (Micah 1:2)
44 Opposite of *proud*
45 "And said, _____ those with thee?" (Genesis 33:5) (2 words)
46 Bridal paths
47 Categorically
48 "For either he will _____ the one" (Matthew 6:24)
49 "Every _____ that which is before her" (Amos 4:3) (2 words)
54 "_____ one people speaking the same language" (Genesis 11:6 NIV) (2 words)
55 Suffix meaning "little one"
57 _____ Cruces, NM
58 Haw's TV partner
59 Directional suffix
60 Arafat's group
61 "_____ there be light" (Genesis 1:3)
62 Cain's mother (Genesis 4:1)

85

ACROSS

1 In this place
5 Pay scale
9 "Ye also, as lively stones, are built up a spiritual _____, an holy priesthood" (1 Peter 2:5)
14 David hid by this stone (1 Samuel 20:19)
15 Jacob gave Esau two hundred of these (Genesis 32:13–14)
16 "Believed the master and the _____ of the ship" (Acts 27:11)
17 "_____ the Canaanite" (Numbers 21:1)
18 "God hath given thee all them that _____ with thee" (Acts 27:24)
19 Below
20 Cut back
21 "And let him down through the _____ with his couch into the midst before Jesus" (Luke 5:19)
23 "Either good _____ bad" (Genesis 31:24)
24 "The same excess of _____" (1 Peter 4:4)
26 A son of Benjamin (Genesis 46:21)
28 A son of Korah (Exodus 6:24)
30 "Let not thy left hand know what thy _____ doeth" (Matthew 6:3) (2 words) (abbr.)
32 Lower often as a sign of respect
36 King Hezekiah's mother (2 Kings 18:2)
37 Chelub's son (1 Chronicles 4:11)
39 "Your brethren, _____" (Hosea 2:1)
40 "Melchizedek. . .was the priest of the most _____ God" (Genesis 14:18)
42 "The heathen _____" (Psalm 46:6)
44 Rabbit
45 "Of Harim, _____" (Nehemiah 12:15)
46 Belonging to them
48 Unhappy
49 First place
50 Haman was her archenemy (abbr.)

51 A pause or musical note used in the Psalms
53 "Her _____ was to light" (Ruth 2:3)
55 "_____ thee out of my mouth" (Revelations 3:16)
56 Arsenic (sym.)
58 A son of Reuben (Genesis 46:9)
61 "Dominion and power, _____ now and ever" (Jude 1:25)
65 Zattu's son (Ezra 10:27)
67 "Other _____ there" (John 6:22)
68 Asa's father (1 Chronicles 3:10)
69 Ephraim didn't drive out the Canaanites who lived here (Judges 1:29)
70 "_____ not the world" (1 John 2:15)
71 Salathiel's father (Luke 3:27)
72 Selected ones
73 A son of Ram (1 Chronicles 2:27)
74 Arad's brother (1 Chronicles 8:15)

DOWN

1 "For in so doing thou shalt _____ coals of fire on his head" (Romans 12:20)
2 This priest rebuilt the temple
3 "Thou shalt _____ up the tabernacle according to the fashion thereof" (Exodus 26:30)
4 "Ordain _____ in every city" (Titus 1:5)
5 "He shall be unto thee a _____ of thy life" (Ruth 4:15)
6 Expect
7 "Shall be eaten: as a _____ tree" (Isaiah 6:13)
8 Nagge's son (Luke 3:25)
9 "Thou shalt _____ their horses" (Joshua 11:6)
10 Possess
11 "I will _____ all that afflict thee" (Zephaniah 3:19)
12 Prophet (arch.)
13 Make a mistake

by N. Teri Grottke

22 Iranian wine tester (abbr.)
25 "And they departed from _____, and pitched in Dibongad" (Numbers 33:45)
27 "Of Hena, and _____?" (2 Kings 19:13)
28 Live with
29 Indicators
30 "Shall not the Judge of all the earth do _____?" (Genesis 18:25)
31 "Rest yourselves under the _____" (Genesis 18:4)
33 Absalom's captain (2 Samuel 17:25)
34 A son of Zophah (1 Chronicles 7:36)
35 Told an untruth
36 Jezebel's husband
38 Head covers
41 "That which _____ been" (Ecclesiastes 6:10)

43 "Where is the _____ of this world?" (1 Corinthians 1:20)
47 Peleg's son (Genesis 11:18)
50 Paul wrote this book about AD 62 (abbr.)
52 Patriarch of a family of exiles (Nehemiah 7:48)
54 Separate
55 Serf
56 "And _____ had six sons" (1 Chronicles 9:44)
57 Dimensions
59 Capable
60 See
62 Ruth's son (Ruth 4:13–17)
63 Exhaust
64 Delilah cut Samson's
65 Get older
66 Contemporary of the prophet Haggai (abbr.)

86

Who's the Greatest?

*In the world ye shall have tribulation:
but be of good cheer;
I have overcome the world.*

JOHN 16:33

ACROSS

1 *Olé* in the USA
4 Group of plotters
9 Like the sound of *m* or *n*
14 E.T.'s transport
15 "Man shall not live by bread _____"
(Matthew 4:4)
16 *Così fan tutte*, for example
17 2 and 3, for example (abbr.)
18 Lariat
19 Yea or nay
20 Start of **QUOTE** from 1 John 4:4
(4 words)
23 "Good comfort, when I know your
_____" (Philippians 2:19)
24 "On the head or on the _____"
(Leviticus 13:29 NIV)
25 Isle of exile
28 "And laid him in a _____" (Luke 2:7)
33 "There is a _____ here" (John 6:9)
36 "King of _____, which is, King of
peace" (Hebrews 7:2)
39 "No man can _____ two masters"
(Matthew 6:24)
40 **QUOTE**, cont'd from 20 Across
(2 words)
42 "And their words seemed to them as
idle _____" (Luke 24:11)
44 "Ye shall find a colt _____" (Mark 11:2)
45 Office notes
47 "But to _____ my right hand, and on
my left" (Matthew 20:23) (2 words)
49 For (prefix)
50 Hippodromes
52 Celebes buffalo
54 "Flew the _____" (on the lam)
57 "Who are _____ with thee?"
(Genesis 33:5)
61 **QUOTE**, cont'd from 40 Across
(5 words)
67 **QUOTE**, cont'd from 61 Across
(2 words)

68 Copland opus
69 "_____ calling Elijah"
(Matthew 27:47 NIV)
70 Skirt feature
71 Shaq of the court
72 "For Adam was first formed, then
_____" (1 Timothy 2:13)
73 Digestive and circulatory (abbr.)
74 End of **QUOTE**, cont'd from 67
Across
75 Actor Harrison

DOWN

1 Ladder parts
2 "And build _____ against it"
(Ezekiel 4:2) (2 words)
3 Book after Daniel
4 Consortia
5 "That they should believe _____"
(2 Thessalonians 2:11) (2 words)
6 "The _____ out of the wood doth
waste it" (Psalm 80:13)
7 Tomfoolery
8 "Or put him on a _____ for your
girls?" (Job 41:5 NIV)
9 Catholic nine-day prayer cycles
10 "He maketh the deep to boil like
_____" (Job 41:31) (2 words)
11 Cainan's grandfather
(Luke 3:37–38)
12 "The entire _____ will be holy"
(Ezekiel 45:1 NIV)
13 "So the _____ shall be first"
(Matthew 20:16)
21 "I _____ no pleasant bread"
(Daniel 10:3)
22 "What things ye have need of, before
ye ask _____" (Matthew 6:8)
26 "After her kind, and the lapwing, and
the _____" (Leviticus 11:19)
27 "_____ for the day! for the day of the
LORD is at hand" (Joel 1:15)

by David K. Shortess

29 "Yet was not the _____ broken"
(John 21:11)

30 "Days of suffering _____ me"
(Job 30:16 NIV)

31 "For his mercy endureth for _____"
(see Psalm 136)

32 Decorate again

33 South American capital

34 Anna's tribe (Luke 2:36)

35 FDR is on it

37 Samuel's mentor (1 Samuel 3:1)

38 "There he _____ Jew named Aquila"
(Acts 18:2 NIV) (2 words)

41 "_____ his son" (1 Chronicles 7:27)

43 "For I have born him a _____ in his
old age" (Genesis 21:7)

46 Clothes scenters

48 "For Zion's sake will I _____ my
peace" (Isaiah 62:1) (2 words)

51 "Iron sharpeneth iron; _____ man
sharpeneth" (Proverbs 27:17)
(2 words)

53 "_____, our eye hath seen it"
(Psalm 35:21)

55 "In Flanders fields the poppies blow,
between the crosses, row _____"
(McCrae)

56 Where platters used to spin, briefly

58 "Smite thee on thy right cheek, turn to
him the _____ also" (Matthew 5:39)

59 "Like as corn is sifted in a _____"
(Amos 9:9)

60 Suburb east of Baltimore

61 Puppy sounds

62 "And he said, Take now thy son, thine
_____ son Isaac" (Genesis 22:2)

63 Utah, Colorado, Arizona, and New
Mexico residents of yore

64 "And all _____ is within me"
(Psalm 103:1)

65 A son of Mushi (1 Chronicles 23:23)

66 Dark blue-green

87

ACROSS

1 "Go, wash in the _____ of Siloam" (John 9:7)
5 "And drew to the _____" (Mark 6:53)
10 "Mordecai for _____?" (Esther 6:3)
14 "_____, their brethren" (Nehemiah 12:9)
15 A baptismal site of John the Baptist (John 3:23)
16 "Who said, _____ it" (Psalm 137:7)
17 "Whosoever shall say to his brother, _____, shall be in danger of the council" (Matthew 5:22)
18 Achish's father (1 Samuel 27:2)
19 Haniel's father (1 Chronicles 7:39)
20 Green gem
22 A Levite upon the stairs (Nehemiah 9:4)
24 "_____ ye tribute" (Romans 13:6)
25 "He may _____ the tip of his finger" (Luke 16:24)
26 "He _____ in the valley" (Job 39:21)
30 "_____ of spices" (Song of Solomon 6:2)
32 "Helez the Paltite, _____" (2 Samuel 23:26)
35 Naum's son (Luke 3:25)
36 "The _____, were over the work" (1 Chronicles 9:19)
38 "Rend the _____ of their heart" (Hosea 13:8)
39 "The well of _____" (2 Samuel 3:26)
40 Opposite of *fat*
41 "God will _____ my darkness" (Psalm 18:28)
43 Jesus' first miracle was here
44 Unhappy
45 Told an untruth
46 King of Gath (1 Samuel 21:10)
48 Book after Zechariah (abbr.)
49 Fuss
50 "Thou _____ up mighty rivers" (Psalm 74:15)
54 "Lachish, and _____, and Eglon" (Joshua 15:39)

59 "Michmash, and _____" (Nehemiah 11:31)
60 Ishmael's mother (Genesis 16:16)
62 Rephaiah's father (1 Chronicles 4:42)
63 "_____ your lusts" (James 4:3)
64 Absalom's captain (2 Samuel 17:25)
65 King of the jungle
66 Not straight
67 "_____, and to Tobijah" (Zechariah 6:14)
68 "Praise the Lord, all ye Gentiles; and _____ him, all ye people" (Romans 15:11)

DOWN

1 "A _____ language" (Zepheniah 3:9)
2 A child of Shobal (Genesis 36:23)
3 The earth was destroyed by a flood this many times
4 "A _____ giveth ear to a naughty tongue" (Proverbs 17:4)
5 "And Hadad died, and _____ of Masrekah reigned" (Genesis 36:36)
6 "Traitors, _____, highminded, lovers of pleasures" (2 Timothy 3:4)
7 "Lod, and _____, the valley of craftsmen" (Nehemiah 11:35)
8 "That _____ was Christ" (1 Corinthians 10:4)
9 "And Remeth, and Engannim, and _____" (Joshua 19:21)
10 "In the twinkling of an eye, at the last _____" (1 Corinthians 15:52)
11 "Helkath, and _____" (Joshua 19:25)
12 Island
13 Closure
21 Capable
23 "That dippeth with me in the _____" (Mark 14:20)
26 "Had gone six _____, he sacrificed oxen and fatlings" (2 Samuel 6:13)
27 "Look from the top of _____" (Song of Solomon 4:8)
28 "They _____ no doubt have continued with us" (1 John 2:19)

by N. Teri Grottke

29 Nagge's son (Luke 3:25)
30 "The priest took a chest, and _____ a hole in the lid of it" (2 Kings 12:9)
31 "Shuthelah: of _____" (Numbers 26:36)
32 Ribai's son (1 Chronicles 11:31)
33 "He hath caused the arrows of his quiver to enter into my _____" (Lamentations 3:13)
34 "The children of _____" (Ezra 2:50)
36 "_____ after his kind" (Leviticus 11:14)
37 "And with the _____" (Deuteronomy 28:27)
39 A son of Zophah (1 Chronicles 7:36–37)
42 "Ye may be _____ also with exceeding joy" (1 Peter 4:13)

46 "And _____ was over" (2 Samuel 20:24)
47 Anub's father (1 Chronicles 4:8)
48 "But God _____ it" (Genesis 50:20)
49 To humble
50 "Say unto them which _____ it" (Ezekiel 13:11)
51 "Harvest is _____" (Joel 3:13)
52 "And smote _____, and Dan" (1 Kings 15:20)
53 Gentle
55 Slay
56 Largest continent
57 You (arch.)
58 Female red deer
61 Classical Austrian composer Bernhard

ACROSS

1 Vestige
5 Ahithophel's son (2 Samuel 23:34)
10 Crush
14 Ahira's father (Numbers 10:27)
15 A son of Hosah (1 Chronicles 26:10)
16 "Enter thou _____ the joy of thy lord" (Matthew 25:21)
17 Mellow
18 "Whom _____ bare unto Judah" (Ruth 4:12)
19 Fastener
20 "The sons of _____ his brother" (1 Chronicles 8:39)
22 "_____, which were dukes" (Joshua 13:21)
23 "As the camel, and the _____" (Deuteronomy 14:7)
24 "Ye are _____ unto the day of redemption" (Ephesians 4:30)
26 Shorelines
28 Agreement
30 Type of fruit
31 "_____ the people be ensnared" (Job 34:30)
35 "Now is our salvation _____" (Romans 13:11)
37 "_____ him out" (Genesis 39:12)
40 "By the river of _____" (Daniel 8:2)
41 Protected
42 "God shall _____ away all tears from their eyes" (Revelation 21:4)
43 Small underground animals
45 Covers
47 "The land is as the garden of _____" (Joel 2:3)
48 Crater
49 "The son of _____, keeper of the wardrobe" (2 Chronicles 34:22)
51 "He _____ him away to his house" (Mark 8:26)
52 "God formed _____ of the dust" (Genesis 2:7)
53 In time

54 "Their great _____ cut off" (Judges 1:7)
55 "He sold them into the hand of _____" (1 Samuel 12:9)
58 Selvage
59 Terminate
60 Ishbah's son (1 Chronicles 4:17)
62 Zaccur's father (Nehemiah 3:2)
64 Hint
65 Lodging
66 Cave
67 Care for
68 "Darius the _____" (Daniel 5:31)

DOWN

1 "Tarshish, _____, Marsena, and Memucan" (Esther 1:14)
2 Dill seed
3 "Nohah the fourth, and _____ the fifth" (1 Chronicles 8:2)
4 Genuflect
5 Estimate (abbr.)
6 One who is untruthful
7 Zadok's father (Nehemiah 3:29)
8 "_____, and Dumah, and Eshean" (Joshua 15:52)
9 Marvel
10 "The sons of Elpaal; Eber, and _____" (1 Chronicles 8:12)
11 "_____ and Caiaphas being the high priests" (Luke 3:2)
12 Inception
13 "For which _____ sake" (Acts 26:7)
21 Cay
25 "In _____ and caves of the earth" (Hebrews 11:38)
27 "_____ God is merciful" (Psalm 116:5)
29 Chairs
30 "That they may _____ a city" (Psalm 107:36)
31 "The same _____ to make one vessel" (Romans 9:21)
32 "_____, lama sabachthani?" (Mark 15:34)

by Tonya Vilhauer

33 Seasoning
34 Bind
36 "She is come _____" (Mark 14:8)
37 Abidan's father (Numbers 10:24)
38 Unlocked
39 "Abode we in _____ three days" (Ezra 8:15)
42 Occidental
44 To give a part of something
46 "Of _____, the family of the Shemidaites" (Numbers 26:32)
50 "Mizraim begat Ludim, and _____" (1 Chronicles 1:11)
52 "A nation _____ out and trodden down" (Isaiah 18:2)
55 "Which is the _____ of the Sadducees" (Acts 5:17)
56 "Ye inhabitants of the _____" (Isaiah 23:6)
57 Reject

61 "Thou believest that there is _____ God" (James 2:19)
63 "The young _____ from their musick" (Lamentations 5:14)

ACROSS

1 "Doth the _____ fly by thy wisdom" (Job 39:26)
5 Jesus' first miracle was here
9 A son of Ishmael (1 Chronicles 1:30–31)
14 Patriarch of a family of returned exiles (Ezra 2:15)
15 Salah's son (Genesis 10:24)
16 Audibly
17 Load (arch.)
18 Move quickly
19 A son of Jehaleleel (1 Chronicles 4:16)
20 "Being a servant, is the Lord's _____" (1 Corinthians 7:22)
22 "I am among you as he that _____" (Luke 22:27)
24 A son of Jether (1 Chronicles 7:38)
25 "_____ that ye refuse" (Hebrews 12:25)
26 Belonging to Esther's enemy
30 Opposite of *easy*
32 "Against Jerusalem, _____" (Ezekiel 26:2)
35 "Ivory and _____" (Ezekiel 27:15)
36 A brother of Shoham (1 Chronicles 24:27)
37 Ruth's son (Ruth 4:17)
38 Jesus turned water into it (John 2:1–11)
39 A son of Lotan (1 Chronicles 1:39)
40 "Thou, being a _____ olive tree, wert graffed in among them" (Romans 11:17)
41 "Mahli, and _____" (1 Chronicles 23:23)
42 A son of Ulla (1 Chronicles 7:39)
43 Serf
44 Opposite of *night*
45 A brother of David (1 Chronicles 2:15)
46 "All his bowels _____ out" (Acts 1:18)
47 Fuss
48 Bowling target
49 "Ye ought to _____ the weak" (Acts 20:35)
53 "Hammath, _____, and Chinnereth" (Joshua 19:35)
58 Elkanah's grandfather (1 Samuel 1:1)
59 A son of Jerahmeel (1 Chronicles 2:25)
61 Rephaiah's father (1 Chronicles 4:42)
62 "Nor _____ the thing" (Psalm 89:34)
63 "Ye shall not fulfil the _____ of the flesh" (Galatians 5:16)
64 Perished
65 Responsibilities
66 Opposite of *more*
67 Identical

DOWN

1 "Unto the _____ of my kingdom" (Mark 6:23)
2 Twelfth Hebrew month (Esther 9:1)
3 Opposite of *narrow*
4 "Every _____ should bow" (Philippians 2:10)
5 "His countenance is as Lebanon, excellent as the _____" (Song of Solomon 5:15)
6 A river of Damascus (2 Kings 5:12)
7 Saul's grandfather (1 Chronicles 8:33)
8 "Used curious _____" (Acts 19:19)
9 Mezahab's daughter (Genesis 36:39)
10 Not dead
11 Very (arch.)
12 Set of clothing
13 Jabal's mother (Genesis 4:20)
21 Multiple
23 Phares's son (Luke 3:33)
26 Chopped (arch.)
27 "Henoch, and _____, and Eldaah" (1 Chronicles 1:33)
28 Lucre
29 A brother of Eshcol (Genesis 14:13)
30 A child of Lotan (Genesis 36:22)
31 Zibeon's daughter (Genesis 36:2)
32 Hezron's wife (1 Chronicles 2:24)

by N. Teri Grottke

33 "Slippeth from the _____"
   (Deuteronomy 19:5)
34 Increased
36 Dig
37 "I am a brother to dragons,
   and a companion to _____"
   (Job 30:29)
39 Sisera was captain of this host
   (1 Samuel 12:9)
43 "He _____ down with sleep"
   (Acts 20:9)
45 Smells (var.)
46 Goliath and his brothers were these
47 There a wall fell upon 27,000 men
   (1 Kings 20:30)
48 "I _____ toward the mark for the
   prize" (Philippians 3:14)
49 Resting place
50 Haniel's father (1 Chronicles 7:39)
51 Deep holes

52 "It shall not be lawful to impose
   _____" (Ezra 7:24)
54 Baby goats
55 Largest continent
56 Others
57 Pelt
60 "For ye tithe mint and _____"
   (Luke 11:42)

ACROSS

1 "Thy word is a _____ unto my feet" (Psalm 119:105)
5 Mien
9 "Bind the chariot to the swift _____" (Micah 1:13)
14 "The burning _____" (Leviticus 26:16)
15 "Bare a son; and she called his name _____" (Genesis 38:4)
16 "_____ also, and Aphek, and Rehob" (Joshua 19:30)
17 "Lieth upon the top of a _____" (Proverbs 23:34)
18 "Ye _____ as sheep" (1 Peter 2:25)
19 "Blood, and fire, and pillars of _____" (Joel 2:30)
20 "Rams of the _____ of Bashan" (Deuteronomy 32:14)
22 Espy
24 "_____ with her suburbs" (1 Chronicles 6:73)
25 Costas
28 "They were _____ asunder" (Hebrews 11:37)
30 "Also I shook my _____" (Nehemiah 5:13)
33 Prod
35 "Thou hast _____ me" (Psalm 119:102)
39 Gaal's father (Judges 9:35)
41 Adam lived _____ hundred and thirty years (Genesis 5:5)
43 "Beriah, and _____ their sister" (Genesis 46:17)
44 Heart
45 "So is thy praise unto the _____ of the earth" (Psalm 48:10)
46 Bail
47 Azmaveth's father (1 Chronicles 27:25)
49 "Bunah, and _____, and Ozem" (1 Chronicles 2:25)
52 Short for tarpaulin
53 "The LORD _____ me" (Psalm 118:13)
55 Office
56 In time

57 "I _____, My strength and my hope is perished" (Lamentations 3:18)
59 Haze
61 "The name of his city was _____" (1 Chronicles 1:50)
64 Resemble
66 Turret
70 "The sons of Gershom; _____" (1 Chronicles 6:17)
72 Buss
75 "Take thee a _____" (Ezekiel 4:1)
76 "Is not _____ the Levite thy brother?" (Exodus 4:14)
77 Range
78 "_____ with joy receiveth it" (Matthew 13:20)
79 "No good _____ will he withhold from them" (Psalm 84:11)
80 "I _____ where I sowed not" (Matthew 25:26)
81 Imprest

DOWN

1 "The LORD will feed them as a _____" (Hosea 4:16)
2 "This _____ is mount Sinai" (Galatians 4:25)
3 Meditate
4 "Simon _____ having a sword drew it" (John 18:10)
5 Humble
6 "Thou believest that there is _____ God" (James 2:19)
7 Paddles
8 "He kneeled upon his _____" (Daniel 6:10)
9 Jitney
10 "They shall call his name _____" (Matthew 1:23)
11 Josiah's father (Jeremiah 1:2)
12 "I intreated for the children's _____" (Job 19:17)
13 "Have the preeminence among _____" (3 John 1:9)
21 Lade
23 Dine
26 "Neither shall ye break a _____" (Exodus 12:46)

by Tonya Vilhauer

27 Epidermis

29 "It _____ infinite" (Nahum 3:9)

30 "The sons of Shelah. . .were, Er the father of _____" (1 Chronicles 4:21)

31 "_____ there three days" (Ezra 8:32)

32 Danger

34 "The inhabitants of _____ and her towns" (Joshua 17:11)

36 Grind

37 "Achbor died, and _____ reigned in his stead" (Genesis 36:39)

38 Yonder

40 "All the _____ of the river" (Zechariah 10:11)

42 Aram's father (Matthew 1:3)

48 Renting

50 "Samuel arose and went to _____" (1 Samuel 3:6)

51 "Thou shouldest make thy _____ as high as the eagle" (Jeremiah 49:16)

54 "Neither shall ye touch it, lest ye _____" (Genesis 3:3)

58 "The son of _____, in Makaz" (1 Kings 4:9)

60 Aggregate

61 "Cast him into the _____ of ground" (2 Kings 9:26)

62 Rizpah's father (2 Samuel 21:8)

63 "Zaccur, and _____" (1 Chronicles 24:27)

65 Mud

67 Drink

68 "_____, and Thimnathah, and Ekron" (Joshua 19:43)

69 "They _____ every one his mantle" (Job 2:12)

71 "_____ his son, Jehoshua his son" (1 Chronicles 7:27)

73 "So shall the _____ be calm unto you" (Jonah 1:12)

74 "The trees of the LORD are full of _____" (Psalm 104:16)

ACROSS

1 Sack
4 A god of Babylon (Isaiah 46:1)
7 Mattathias's son (Luke 3:26)
12 A son of Judah (1 Chronicles 2:3)
14 Seth's son (Genesis 4:26)
16 Ribai's son (1 Chronicles 11:31)
17 Sea rhythm
18 "The joy of the_____ ceaseth" (Isaiah 24:8)
19 "This only would I _____ of you" (Galatians 3:2)
20 Show (arch.)
21 "Weeping may _____ for a night" (Psalm 30:5)
23 Sleeping place
24 Total
26 Resting place
27 Type of tree (Isaiah 44:14)
30 The giving of this revealed Jesus' betrayer (John 13:21–27)
32 "The woman took the child, and _____ it" (Exodus 2:9)
37 "Shall be proclaimed upon the _____" (Luke 12:3)
41 A son of Merari (Numbers 3:20)
42 Land measurement
43 Gomer's husband (Hosea 1:2–3)
45 "A little _____; and she waited on Naaman's wife" (2 Kings 5:2)
46 "Howbeit there came other _____ from Tiberias" (John 6:23)
48 "Some remove the _____" (Job 24:2)
50 "Haphraim, and _____, and Anaharath" (Joshua 19:19)
52 This is connected to the foot
53 Consume food
54 "A _____ of Jesse" (Isaiah 11:10)
57 Right hand (abbr.)
59 Diana was the goddess of this people (abbr.)
62 "He went forth with his disciples over the brook _____" (John 18:1)
64 "_____ for the day!" (Joel 1:15)
68 "_____ of Judah" (2 Samuel 6:2)
70 Comfort
71 Tibetan monk
72 Mistake
73 "There was a continual _____ given him of the king of Babylon" (Jeremiah 52:34)
74 Image
75 Prepared
76 This man served Artaxerxes (abbr.)
77 This man prophesied the destruction of Solomon's temple (abbr.)

DOWN

1 "And their _____ shall be broken" (Psalm 37:15)
2 Zibeon's daughter (Genesis 36:2)
3 "Abraham _____ the tenth of the spoils" (Hebrews 7:4)
4 "Behold now _____" (Job 40:15)
5 Ahira's father (Numbers 1:15)
6 "Made a supper to his _____" (Mark 6:21)
7 "Trophimus have I left at _____ sick" (2 Timothy 4:20)
8 Partook
9 Omri's son who reigned after his death (1 Kings 16:28)
10 Type of weed
11 Female red deer
13 Current events
15 "_____ thee out of my mouth" (Revelations 3:16)
22 "And _____ greedily after the error of Balaam" (Jude 1:11)
25 Make good _____ of something
27 "Letters in _____ name" (1 Kings 21:8)
28 "Shamir, and Jattir, and _____" (Joshua 15:48)
29 "_____ of the brooks of Gaash" (1 Chronicles 11:32)
31 "Go, wash in the _____ of Siloam" (John 9:7)
33 "In _____ was there a voice" (Matthew 2:18)
34 Allotment

by N. Teri Grottke

35 A Harodite guard of David
(2 Samuel 23:25)
36 Did (arch.)
38 Cain and Abel's brother
39 150 sections make up this book
(abbr.)
40 Caused to go to a destination
44 "As a bride _____ herself with her
jewels" (Isaiah 61:10)
47 "Which beforetime in the same city
used _____" (Acts 8:9)
49 Became acquainted
51 Greek form of *Noah* (Luke 17:27)
55 Azariah's father (2 Chronicles 15:1)
56 "_____ up a child"
(Proverbs 22:6)
58 "Helkath, and _____"
(Joshua 19:25)
59 Salah's son (Genesis 10:24)
60 Cut back

61 "Habor, and _____"
(1 Chronicles 5:26)
63 "As he saith also in _____"
(Romans 9:25)
65 Load (arch.)
66 Isaiah's father (Isaiah 1:1)
67 "_____ of his patrimony"
(Deuteronomy 18:8)
69 "_____, Hadid, and Ono"
(Ezra 2:33)

ACROSS

1 Mother of the Savior
4 "_____ will be great and will be called the Son of the Most High" (Luke 1:32 NIV)
6 Pleasant smell
8 Types of offerings are described in this OT book (abbr.)
9 Divide number of days Jesus fasted (Matthew 4:2) by the number of men who carried the man let down through the roof (Mark 2:3)
10 Christians have something to _____ about (happy expression)
12 Joseph was the husband _____ Mary
13 Mary's _____ would be called Immanuel, meaning "God with us" (Matthew 1:23 NIV)
14 Mary was pledged _____ be married
15 Calendar year (abbr.)
17 Informal expression for money; starts with the sound a cow makes
18 "_____ the holy one to be born will be called the Son of God" (Luke 1:35 NIV)
19 Better than okay
20 A close friend
21 "Mary treasured up _____ these things" (Luke 2:19 NIV)
22 Simeon told Mary, "This child is destined to cause the falling and rising of _____ in Israel" (Luke 2:34 NIV)
23 Mary's Son

DOWN

1 First day of the work week (abbr.)
2 Morning hours (abbr.)
3 Reckless
4 "Levi _____ a great banquet for Jesus" (Luke 5:29 NIV)
5 Mother of Abel and Seth (Genesis 4:1–2, 25 NIV)
6 Small particle that makes up matter
7 One who calls the shots (abbr.)
8 "I am a rose of Sharon, a _____ of the valleys" (Song of Songs 2:1 NIV)
11 A transparent, sheetlike mineral
13 One who prepares a meal
14 "Tubal-Cain, who forged all kinds of _____ out of bronze and iron" (Genesis 4:22 NIV)
16 Mary "was found to be with child through the _____ Spirit" (Matthew 1:18 NIV)
17 Gender of man
18 The foolish man built his house on _____ (Matthew 7:26)
20 Informal name for "Father"
21 _____ is to apple juice what OJ is to orange juice

by John Hudson Tiner

93

ACROSS

1 Possessive pronoun
4 Methuselah's father (Genesis 5:21)
9 "Stand in the _____" (Ezekiel 22:30)
12 "Cursed is every one that hangeth on a _____" (Galatians 3:13)
13 A son of Hodesh (1 Chronicles 8:9)
14 Anak's father (Joshua 15:13)
15 "Not in chambering and _____" (Romans 13:13)
17 Flesh food
18 Strange
19 "Jealous for his land, and _____ his people" (Joel 2:18)
20 "He shall _____ with his teeth" (Psalm 112:10)
21 Cain and Abel's brother
22 The other Simon of the twelve (Luke 6:15)
24 Serious lack of food
27 "At Lydda and _____" (Acts 9:35)
28 A son of Jehiel (1 Chronicles 9:37)
29 "See, here is _____; what doth hinder me to be baptized?" (Acts 8:36)
30 Take to court
33 Bread from heaven
35 Take action
36 Give up
38 A young prophet, he was twenty-five when the Babylonians arrived (abbr.)
39 Saruch's father (Luke 3:35)
41 Not female
42 "A _____ went out to sow his seed" (Luke 8:5)
43 "Tread the _____" (Nahum 3:14 NIV)
45 "Carry these ten _____ unto the captain" (1 Samuel 17:18)
48 A son of Zophah (1 Chronicles 7:36)
49 Haul
50 Arrived
51 A tree of Isaiah 44
54 Otherwise
55 "A living sacrifice, holy, acceptable unto God, which is your _____ service" (Romans 12:1)
58 Always
59 "Believed the master and the _____ of the ship" (Acts 27:11)
60 "Though ye have _____" (Psalm 68:13)
61 Scarlet
62 Tired
63 "Sin is the transgression of the _____" (1 John 3:4)

DOWN

1 Enoch's son (Genesis 4:18)
2 Take care of
3 To place
4 "The same was Adino the _____" (2 Samuel 23:8)
5 "In the _____ day" (Leviticus 23:32)
6 Carry out directions
7 King Saul's father (Acts 13:21)
8 Possesses
9 Large
10 To humble
11 Trails
12 "_____ wings of a great eagle" (Revelation 12:14)
14 David's incestous son (2 Samuel 13:1–14)
16 Opposite of *closed*
20 Honor and praise
21 "Come out of _____" (Romans 11:26)
22 Elioenai's father (Ezra 10:27)
23 Before (arch.)
24 Renown
25 "Jotham, _____" (Hosea 1:1)
26 Belonging to me
27 Ahiam's father (1 Chronicles 11:35)
29 Employment pay
30 Resting place
31 Haniel's father (1 Chronicles 7:39)
32 "The sons of Mushi; Mahli, and _____" (1 Chronicles 23:23)
34 Jesus did this at the resurrection
37 Zaccur's father (Nehemiah 3:2)
40 Reverent fear
42 Cut off

by N. Teri Grottke

43 What we remember with
44 A son of Jerahmeel
   (1 Chronicles 2:25)
45 "Then were they all of good _____"
   (Acts 27:36)
46 "Slippeth from the _____"
   (Deuteronomy 19:5)
47 Comforted
48 Lower
50 Jesus' first miracle was here
51 Asa's father (1 Chronicles 3:10)
52 Killed
53 Zephaniah's son (Zechariah 6:14)
55 "A _____ of cedar beams"
   (1 Kings 6:36)
56 Female sheep
57 "Destroy _____ kings and people"
   (Ezra 6:12)

94

A Plea from Jesus

*The promise is unto you, and to your children,
and to all that are afar off,
even as many as the Lord our God shall call.*

ACTS 2:39

ACROSS

1 "_____ know that my redeemer liveth" (Job 19:25) (2 words)
5 "The woodwork will _____ it" (Habakkuk 2:11 NIV)
9 "I will go out _____ other times before" (Judges 16:20) (2 words)
13 "That in the _____ to come he might show" (Ephesians 2:7)
14 "For they shall see eye _____" (Isaiah 52:8) (2 words)
16 "Shave her head, and _____ her nails" (Deuteronomy 21:12)
17 Ingrid's role in *Casablanca*
18 Intense feeling
19 Formerly Persia
20 Beginning of a **PLEA** from Jesus in John 14:1 (4 words)
23 One of the eleven dukes of Edom (Genesis 36:43)
24 Yearns
25 Jesus' **PLEA**, cont'd from 20 Across (3 words)
31 "Do you fix your _____ such a one?" (Job 14:3 NIV) (2 words)
32 Notable periods
33 "And a _____ of oil" (Leviticus 14:21)
36 A son of Dishan (1 Chronicles 1:42)
37 "And he shall be for an _____ of ships" (Genesis 49:13)
39 "I will arise and _____ my father" (Luke 15:18) (2 words)
40 *Pro* _____ (for the time being)
41 "More majestic than mountains rich with _____" (Psalm 76:4 NIV)
42 Slow in music
43 Jesus' **PLEA**, cont'd from 25 Across (3 words)
46 "I have been an _____ in a strange land" (Exodus 18:3)
49 "That _____ down and wept" (Nehemiah 1:4) (2 words)
50 End of Jesus' **PLEA**, cont'd from 43 Across (4 words)
57 "And the third beast had a face as _____" (Revelation 4:7) (2 words)
58 "A wholesome tongue is _____ of life" (Proverbs 15:4) (2 words)
59 "And a little child shall _____ them" (Isaiah 11:6)
60 "Than for a man to hear the _____ of fools" (Ecclesiastes 7:5)
61 "But such as is common _____" (1 Corinthians 10:13) (2 words)
62 Sea eagle
63 "And their words unto the _____ of the world" (Romans 10:18)
64 Relative of AMEX (abbr.)
65 "For it is _____ cut off" (Psalm 90:10)

DOWN

1 "He will not _____ thee" (Deuteronomy 31:6)
2 Stare amorously
3 "And I will give you _____" (Matthew 11:28)
4 "And thy neck _____ sinew" (Isaiah 48:4) (3 words)
5 HT (Greek equivalent)
6 Flat-topped flower cluster
7 "The works that I do shall _____ also" (John 14:12) (2 words)
8 "Lift up your heads, _____ gates" (Psalm 24:7 NIV) (2 words)
9 "Neither have two coats _____" (Luke 9:3)
10 "But _____ shall her name be" (Genesis 17:15)
11 "And it is _____ thing" (Daniel 2:11) (2 words)
12 "Dwelling in _____" (Genesis 25:27)
15 "Ye therefore do greatly _____" (Mark 12:27)
21 "_____ the holy day" (Nehemiah 10:31)

by David K. Shortess

22 Timothy and alfalfa
25 "And they shall _____ their swords into plowshares" (Isaiah 2:4)
26 Brontë's Jane
27 "A chariot with a _____ of horses" (Isaiah 21:9 NIV)
28 River dike
29 "How long will it be _____ thou be quiet?" (Jeremiah 47:6)
30 "From _____ even to Beersheba" (1 Kings 4:25)
33 "How _____, LORD?" (Psalm 79:5)
34 *Eight* in Milano (Ital.)
35 "Be of _____ cheer, Paul" (Acts 23:11)
37 Henry V nickname
38 "What _____ eased?" (Job 16:6) (2 words)
39 "For a light of the _____" (Isaiah 42:6)
41 Kelly or Autry
42 Chinese dynasty

43 "And slander celestial _____" (Jude 1:8 NIV)
44 "As _____ the thing they loved" (Hosea 9:10 NIV) (2 words)
45 Jewish ascetic
46 "Upon the ledges there was _____ above" (1 Kings 7:29) (2 words)
47 Detroit dud
48 "No man is an _____, intire" (Donne)
51 "When anyone went to a wine _____" (Haggai 2:16 NIV)
52 Harrow rival
53 "Terrible as an _____ with banners" (Song of Solomon 6:4)
54 Roman despot
55 "For I am a sinful _____ Lord" (Luke 5:8) (2 words)
56 "Forth from the garden of _____" (Genesis 3:23)

95

ACROSS

1 Book of destruction of Jerusalem, five chapters long (abbr.)
4 Make clean
8 No (arch.)
11 "Lod, and _____, the valley of craftsmen" (Nehemiah 11:35)
12 A son of Jacob (Genesis 35:26)
14 Get older
15 Paul greeted this man as "mine own son" (abbr.)
16 "The night is far _____, the day is at hand" (Romans 13:12)
17 "All the Chaldeans, Pekod, and _____, and Koa" (Ezekiel 23:23)
18 Became acquainted
20 Caleb's daughter (Judges 1:12)
23 Large sea mammal
26 "Neither shall ye _____ enchantment, nor observe times" (Leviticus 19:26)
27 "The pool of _____ by the king's garden" (Nehemiah 3:15)
30 "The Cretians are alway _____" (Titus 1:12)
32 This man prophesied to the Jews in Babylon (abbr.)
33 Titanium (sym.)
34 To place
35 "He may _____ the tip of his finger" (Luke 16:24)
37 Anger
39 A measurement for oil (Leviticus 14:10)
40 "_____, five cities" (1 Chronicles 4:32)
42 The oldest copy was found among the Dead Sea Scrolls (abbr.)
43 First book in the Pentateuch (abbr.)
44 King of Bashan (Deuteronomy 3:11)
45 Single
46 Walk
48 "Now there came a _____ over all the land" (Acts 7:11)
50 Unhappy

51 "Jonah was gone down into the _____ of the ship" (Jonah 1:5)
53 Belonging to Bathsheba's first husband (poss.)
55 Relatives
58 "Punish the men that are settled on their _____" (Zephaniah 1:12)
61 Er's son (1 Chronicles 4:21)
64 Oath
66 "Helez the Paltite, _____" (2 Samuel 23:26)
67 "Not to _____ thee" (Ruth 1:16)
68 Partook
69 Deep hole
70 "Now the serpent was more subtil _____ any beast" (Genesis 3:1)
71 This NT book was likely written after AD 70, but no one knows (abbr.)

DOWN

1 Abraham's nephew
2 "Eshtemoh, and _____," (Joshua 15:50)
3 "Beholdest thou the _____ that is in thy brother's eye" (Matthew 7:3)
4 "God saw that it _____ good" (Genesis 1:21)
5 "And the sucking child shall play on the hole of the _____" (Isaiah 11:8)
6 A son of Bani (Ezra 10:29)
7 "Come they not _____, even of your lusts" (James 4:1)
8 Book between Micah and Habakkuk (abbr.)
9 Time past
10 Exclamation of affirmation
13 Right hand (abbr.)
17 "Thou shalt break the _____ thereof" (Ezekiel 23:34)
19 "_____ wings of a great eagle" (Revelation 12:14)
21 Set of clothing
22 Solomon's great-grandson (1 Kings 15:8)

by N. Teri Grottke

24 "That which _____ been" (Ecclesiastes 6:10)
25 Son of Abdiel (1 Chronicles 5:15)
27 Stitch
28 "The fourth to _____" (1 Chronicles 25:11)
29 Smallest
30 Appendage
31 A river "before Egypt" (Joshua 13:3)
34 "Came to Joel the _____" (Joel 1:1)
36 "That _____ after the dust of the earth" (Amos 2:7)
38 Paul's hometown
39 Commanded militarily
40 Shammah's father (2 Samuel 23:11)
41 Leaders against him were Sanballat and Tobiah (abbr.)
43 Menahem's father (2 Kings 15:14)
44 Strange

47 "The barley was in the _____, and the flax was bolled" (Exodus 9:31)
49 Pose a question
51 Bed covering
52 Milcah's brother (Genesis 11:29)
54 "Destroy _____ kings and people" (Ezra 6:12)
56 "Of Hena, and _____?" (2 Kings 19:13)
57 "_____ that man, and have no company with him" (2 Thessalonians 3:14)
58 "The _____ of truth shall be established for ever" (Proverbs 12:19)
59 A son of Gad (Genesis 46:16)
60 Consume food
62 Area near Babylon (2 Kings 17:24)
63 Zephaniah's son (Zechariah 6:14)
65 Spider's art

96

Nations in the Promised Land

I will. . .destroy all the people to whom thou shalt come.

EXODUS 23:27

ACROSS

1 "Now the _____ shall live by faith" (Hebrews 10:38)
5 Book after Micah
10 "And there _____ certain man at Lystra" (Acts 14:8) (2 words)
14 "No _____ will pitch his tent there" (Isaiah 13:20 NIV)
15 Enraged
16 A tenth of an ephah (Exodus 16:36)
17 A **NATION** Israel encountered in the Promised Land (Exodus 23:23)
19 "That nothing be _____" (John 6:12)
20 "_____ woe is past" (Revelation 9:12)
21 _____ Moines, Iowa
22 "Which trieth our _____" (1 Thessalonians 2:4)
24 Wallet fillers
26 "Or if he shall ask an _____" (Luke 11:12)
29 Sprint rival
30 "He _____ to Moses" (Romans 9:15 NIV)
31 Growl
32 Bright tropical fish
35 Rocky hill
37 VIP transport
39 An age
40 "Come again?"
43 Another **NATION** from Exodus 23:23
45 "And Jacob _____ pottage" (Genesis 25:29)
46 "It _____; be not afraid" (Matthew 14:27) (2 words)
47 "As if he blessed an _____" (Isaiah 66:3)
48 "He planteth an _____" (Isaiah 44:14)
50 "The apostles and the elders _____ consider this" (Acts 15:6 NIV) (2 words)
52 "I have _____ him to the LORD" (1 Samuel 1:28)
54 Dog's comments

58 KLM rival, once
59 Boston _____ Party
60 "By _____ rebuke I dry up the sea" (Isaiah 50:2 NIV)
61 "Our houses to _____" (Lamentations 5:2)
64 Spread hay
66 "The wilderness of _____ (Exodus 16:1)
67 "Record this _____" (Ezekiel 24:2 NIV)
68 Another **NATION** from Exodus 23:23
72 Got an A
73 "Behold, _____ was opened" (Revelation 4:1) (2 words)
74 Unit of heredity
75 "A _____ of meat from the king" (2 Samuel 11:8)
76 "The fortified _____ ruin" (Isaiah 25:2 NIV) (2 words)
77 Not evens

DOWN

1 "Now _____ well was there" (John 4:6)
2 Muse of astronomy
3 With rationality
4 Schedule abbreviation
5 "And _____ parts to dwell" (Nehemiah 11:1)
6 "That wicked men have _____ among you" (Deuteronomy 13:13 NIV)
7 Pass the _____ (take a collection)
8 Colorado native
9 "And he wanders into its _____" (Job 18:8 NIV)
10 "Let us _____ ourselves with loves" (Proverbs 7:18)
11 Another **NATION** from Exodus 23:23
12 "But _____ the spirits to see" (1 John 4:1 NIV)
13 "Which used curious _____" (Acts 19:19)
18 Commercials

by David K. Shortess

23 Decorate in relief
25 WWII craft (abbr.)
27 "Departed into _____" (Matthew 4:12)
28 Clamp together tightly, as teeth
31 Network
33 "Is there any thing _____ hard for me?" (Jeremiah 32:27)
34 "_____ it came to pass" (Luke 2:1)
36 Akron resident
38 "And giveth _____ to her household" (Proverbs 31:15)
40 "For they all saw _____ (Mark 6:50)
41 "But when ye pray, _____ not vain repetitions" (Matthew 6:7)
42 Another **NATION** from Exodus 23:23
44 Unit of electrical potential
49 Canaan's father (Genesis 9:18)
51 Scotch fabrics
53 "O _____ not desired" (Zephaniah 2:1)

55 "And the land _____ from war" (Joshua 11:23)
56 "A _____ loveth at all times" (Proverbs 17:17)
57 "Have their _____ exercised to discern" (Hebrews 5:14)
60 Wood-cutting tool (var.)
61 Enos's grandfather (Luke 3:38)
62 "And thou shalt put it on a blue _____" (Exodus 28:37)
63 "He _____ on the ground" (John 9:6)
65 "And of _____ the priest, the scribe" (Nehemiah 12:26)
69 Former name of Tokyo
70 "And a _____ of new timber" (Ezra 6:4)
71 "Because _____ to the Father" (John 16:16) (2 words)

97

ACROSS

1 Child's favorite seat
4 Baby sheep
8 "Sharper than any twoedged _____" (Hebrews 4:12)
13 Zaccur's father (Nehemiah 3:2)
15 Carry out directions
16 Gomer's husband (Hosea 1:2–3)
17 Worry
18 Transgression
19 "Man named _____" (Acts 9:33)
20 "The mouth _____ meat" (Job 34:3)
22 This man convicted people for their non-Jewish wives (abbr.)
23 Paul founded their church, among others, and stayed three years (abbr.)
24 "What _____ ye to weep" (Acts 21:13)
25 Unload cargo (arch.)
28 To free
29 Petroleum product
30 Bird from the ark sent out three times
34 This OT book describes aspects of priesthood (abbr.)
36 "He bade them teach the children of Judah the _____ of the bow" (2 Samuel 1:18)
39 "Of Keros, the children of _____" (Nehemiah 7:47)
41 Color of blood
42 Before (arch.)
43 Sprint
44 Minor prophet who questioned God (abbr.)
45 Pass away
46 Possesses
47 Purim marks this queen's success (abbr.)
48 Abdiel's son (1 Chronicles 5:15)
49 Motel
50 "_____ the waters" (Exodus 15:25)
52 "Dip the _____ of his finger in water" (Luke 16:24)
54 "And _____ greedily after the error of Balaam" (Jude 1:11)

56 Opposite of *farther*
59 "Jotham, _____" (Hosea 1:1)
61 "Against Jerusalem, _____" (Ezekiel 26:2)
64 Untruth
65 "And also the name of the city shall be _____" (Ezekiel 39:16)
68 "Gather up the fragments that _____" (John 6:12)
70 Commanded militarily
71 Land measurement
72 "Shilshah, and Ithran, and _____" (1 Chronicles 7:37)
73 Gaddi's father (Numbers 13:11)
74 "_____, O Israel: The LORD our God is one LORD" (Deuteronomy 6:4)
75 Jehoshaphat's chief captain of Judah (2 Chronicles 17:14)
76 A child of Ezer (Genesis 36:27)
77 And _____ lay at his feet until the morning" (Ruth 3:14)

DOWN

1 "_____ up your eyes" (John 4:35)
2 Moses' father (Exodus 6:20)
3 "Thou _____ man and beast" (Psalm 36:6)
4 Opposite of *found*
5 A son of Aaron (Exodus 6:23)
6 "The sons of God saw the daughters of _____ that they were fair" (Genesis 6:2)
7 Near
8 "_____ to take fire" (Isaiah 30:14)
9 Opposite of *lost*
10 "As he saith also in _____" (Romans 9:25)
11 Harvest
12 Race
14 Ribai's son (2 Samuel 23:29)
19 Shaphan's father (2 Kings 22:3)
21 "For how can I _____ to see the evil that shall come unto my people?" (Esther 8:6)
22 Elijah's successor

by N. Teri Grottke

26 Nobelium (sym.)
27 An altar (Joshua 22:34)
31 "Are ye subject to _____"
(Colossians 2:20)
32 Blood vessel
33 First garden
34 Samson slew 1,000 Philistines here
(Judges 15:14–15)
35 "Shuthelah: of _____"
(Numbers 26:36)
37 "He shall _____ thee"
(Psalm 55:22)
38 Whole
40 Dathan's cohort in rebellion
(Numbers 16:1–3)
51 Suffix (inert gas)
53 Physical education (abbr.)
55 "And Abishua, and Naaman, and
_____" (1 Chronicles 8:4)
57 A son of Elam (Ezra 10:26)

58 Zorobabel's son (Luke 3:27)
60 Pharez's twin brother
(Genesis 38:27–30)
61 Anak's father (Joshua 15:13)
62 Pay attention to
63 So be it
66 Patriarch of a family of returned
exiles (Ezra 2:15)
67 In this place
69 A son of Jether (1 Chronicles 7:38)
70 Matthew, Mark, _____, John
(abbr.)
73 Its major cities are Cape Town and
Johannesburg (abbr.)

98

ACROSS

1 To move in any direction by turning over and over
5 "For the remission of _____" (Acts 2:38)
9 Pork
12 Joram's son (Matthew 1:8)
14 Genuine
15 "_____, which were dukes" (Joshua 13:21)
16 "Slew a lion in a pit in a _____ day" (1 Chronicles 11:22)
17 "Strangers of _____" (Acts 2:10)
18 Open
19 "Fourth part of an _____ of beaten oil" (Numbers 28:5)
20 Ahira's father (Numbers 10:27)
22 Simple
23 "I _____ that thou art a gracious God" (Jonah 4:2)
24 Actors play a _____
26 "_____ a right spirit within me" (Psalm 51:10)
28 "_____ said unto the king" (2 Samuel 13:35)
31 "Her mother in law _____ her" (Ruth 3:6)
32 "Mine eyes shall be _____ the faithful" (Psalm 101:6)
33 Youngster
35 Rim
36 "They _____ upon the camels" (Genesis 24:61)
38 "I am the _____ of Sharon" (Song of Solomon 2:1)
39 "Neither shall ye touch it, lest ye _____" (Genesis 3:3)
40 There was a marriage in _____ of Galilee" (John 2:1)
41 Type of fabric
42 Ratite
44 "He cast four _____" (Exodus 38:5)
45 Drink
46 "So that the earth _____ again" (1 Samuel 4:5)
47 "Nemuel, and Jamin, _____," (1 Chronicles 4:24)

50 "They _____ every one his mantle" (Job 2:12)
51 "Make thee an _____ of gopher wood" (Genesis 6:14)
54 King of the Amalekites (1 Samuel 15:8)
55 This man asked for a double portion of Elijah's spirit (abbr.)
57 "To the battle at _____" (Numbers 21:33)
59 "In _____ and caves of the earth" (Hebrews 11:38)
60 "God shall _____ away all tears from their eyes" (Revelation 21:4)
61 "Flee thou to _____" (Genesis 27:43)
62 Pose a question
63 "The land is as the garden of _____" (Joel 2:3)
64 Thirty-six inches

DOWN

1 "Naaman, Ehi, and _____" (Genesis 46:21)
2 "Of _____, the family of the Oznites" (Numbers 26:16)
3 "As a roaring _____" (1 Peter 5:8)
4 Statute
5 Dried grain stalks
6 Ferrum
7 Used in counting (abbr.)
8 Espy
9 "The gods of Sepharvaim, _____, and Ivah?" (2 Kings 18:34)
10 "Kish the son of _____" (2 Chronicles 29:12)
11 "The wilderness of _____" (1 Samuel 23:24)
13 "From the tower of _____" (Ezekiel 29:10)
15 "When the judges _____" (Ruth 1:1)
21 "A _____ commandment I give unto you" (John 13:34)
22 Scheme
23 "That at the name of Jesus every _____ should bow" (Philippians 2:10)
24 Cord

by Tonya Vilhauer

25 "Children of Lod, Hadid, and
_____" (Ezra 2:33)
26 Waves used in broadcasting
27 "The sharp sword with two _____"
(Revelation 2:12)
28 "_____ was comforted"
(Genesis 38:12)
29 Beside
30 "The two pillars, one sea, and the
_____" (2 Kings 25:16)
31 Resting place
34 Cave
36 "There is a sound of abundance of
_____" (1 Kings 18:41)
37 "He died unto sin _____"
(Romans 6:10)
38 "Sealed it with the king's _____"
(Esther 8:10)
40 Baby's bed
41 "The blood upon the _____"
(Exodus 12:23)

43 Small branches
44 "They _____ in the dry places like
a river" (Psalm 105:41)
46 "_____ between Nineveh and
Calah" (Genesis 10:12)
47 Shammai's brother
(1 Chronicles 2:32)
48 "Hath been hid from _____"
(Colossians 1:26)
49 Grade
50 Mellow
51 "They gave them the city of _____"
(Joshua 21:11)
52 Behind
53 "Be ye _____ one to another"
(Ephesians 4:32)
55 Sheep
56 Cover
58 "That I might rest in the _____ of
trouble" (Habakkuk 3:16)

ACROSS

1 City of the priests
   (1 Samuel 22:19)
4 A son of David (1 Chronicles 3:7)
9 Capable
12 Boat paddle
13 A river of Damascus (2 Kings 5:12)
14 Daniel had a vision by this river
   (Daniel 8:2)
15 "So they _____ it up" (Micah 7:3)
17 A grandson of Asher (Genesis 46:17)
18 Not any
19 "Then David put garrisons in
   _____" (1 Chronicles 18:6)
22 This is attached to the shoulder
23 Elderly
24 "The parts of _____" (Acts 2:10)
27 Her household reported contentions
   in the Corinthian church
30 "As he saith also in _____"
   (Romans 9:25)
31 A city of Judah (Joshua 15:52)
33 Twenty-first letter of the Greek
   alphabet
36 "Sons of _____" (1 Chronicles 7:12)
37 Saw
38 "Ye may be _____ also with
   exceeding joy" (1 Peter 4:13)
39 Type of tree
40 "Then they that _____ received his
   word were baptized" (Acts 2:41)
41 Revile
42 Bring together
43 Mineral potash (Proverbs 25:20)
44 A son of Jether (1 Chronicles 7:38)
45 A parson or Holy _____
46 "_____ the governor listeth"
   (James 3:4)
53 A king of Midian (Numbers 31:8)
54 "Plain from _____"
   (Deuteronomy 2:8)
55 "Tower of _____" (Genesis 35:21)
57 A son of Ulla (1 Chronicles 7:39)
58 A son of Seir the Horite
   (Genesis 36:20)
59 A son of Gad (Genesis 46:16)

60 "They fled before the _____ of Ai"
   (Joshua 7:4)
61 "Their _____ in wait on the west
   of the city" (Joshua 8:13)
62 Scarlet

DOWN

1 Currently
2 Hand-driven boat propellers
3 Donkey sound
4 Hodiah's brother
   (1 Chronicles 4:19)
5 Ruth's son (Ruth 4:13–17)
6 "Ramah and _____" (Ezra 2:26)
7 "Suburbs, and _____"
   (1 Chronicles 6:73)
8 "Habor, and _____"
   (1 Chronicles 5:26)
9 Audibly
10 "Baked it in _____" (Numbers 11:8)
11 Bind
14 Brother of a parent
16 "Watch unto _____" (1 Peter 4:7)
20 "Helez the Paltite, _____"
   (2 Samuel 23:26)
21 "Not _____ angry" (Titus 1:7)
24 "Than one _____" (Mark 8:14)
25 Rephaiah's father
   (1 Chronicles 4:42)
26 Name of the well that the Lord told
   Moses about (Numbers 21:16)
27 Scold
28 Back of foot
29 "The elect _____" (2 John 1:1)
31 Nagge's son (Luke 3:25)
32 Past tense of *spit*
33 "Thee in this _____"
   (2 Kings 9:26)
34 Delilah cut Samson's
35 Lazy
38 Mourn
40 Small flying insect
42 Bathsheba's first husband
   (2 Samuel 11:3)
43 Greek form of *Noah* (Luke 17:26)
44 A son of Abishur (1 Chronicles 2:29)

by N. Teri Grottke

45 "Some of _____ disciples"
   (John 3:25)
46 "And _____ destroyed of the
   destroyer" (1 Corinthians 10:10)
47 This will be cast into the lake of fire
48 Jesus cried this on the cross
   (Mark 15:34)
49 Charge
50 Night sky illuminator
51 "Mahli, and _____"
   (1 Chronicles 23:23)
52 Not easily found
53 Male sheep
56 To free

100

Biblical Brothers

A man of many companions may come to ruin,
but there is a friend who sticks closer than a brother.

PROVERBS 18:24 NIV

ACROSS

1 "Ourselves a _____ for you to follow" (2 Thessalonians 3:9 NIV)
6 "The wrath of the _____" (Revelation 6:16)
10 "And shall put it upon a _____" (Numbers 4:10)
13 Met offering
14 "To preach the word in _____" (Acts 16:6)
15 "_____ an Ithrite" (2 Samuel 23:38)
16 **BIBLICAL BROTHERS** found in Matthew 4 (3 words)
19 A grandson of Adam (Genesis 4:25–26)
20 "Commanded to _____ peoples" (Daniel 3:4 NIV)
21 "Wherefore _____ Sarah laugh" (Genesis 18:13)
22 Sun Yat-_____ (Chinese leader)
23 _____ Cruces, NM
24 Singer Martha
25 _____ Victor (abbr.)
28 **BIBLICAL BROTHERS** found in Matthew 17 (3 words)
31 British noblemen
34 Juan's aunt
35 "Suddenly _____ instant" (Isaiah 30:13) (2 words)
36 "Why _____ so fearful?" (Mark 4:40) (2 words)
37 "Followed the _____" (Genesis 24:61)
38 "How right they are to _____ you!" (Song of Songs 1:4 NIV)
39 Wonderful!
40 "And none _____ deliver" (Micah 5:8)
41 Bells and whistles
42 **BIBLICAL BROTHERS** found in Genesis 25 (3 words)
45 The start and end of a Wisconsin city
46 *Summer* in Paris (Fr.)
47 "And bored a hole in the _____ of it" (2 Kings 12:9)
48 "If a man _____, shall he live again?" (Job 14:14)

51 PC alternative
52 *Own* in Scotland (Scot.)
53 "And counteth the _____" (Luke 14:28)
54 **BIBLICAL BROTHERS** found in Genesis 5 (3 words)
58 "But the name of the wicked shall _____" (Proverbs 10:7)
59 "For I have _____ blameless life" (Psalm 26:1 NIV) (2 words)
60 Wood-shaping tool
61 "And _____ it up" (Revelation 10:10)
62 "From the _____ of the tongue" (Job 5:21 NIV)
63 "The men of the _____ Nebo, fifty and two" (Nehemiah 7:33)

DOWN

1 Jethro's son-in-law (Exodus 3:1)
2 "Wail, _____ tree" (Zechariah 11:2 NIV) (2 words)
3 "He has a _____" (Matthew 11:18 NIV)
4 Greek god of love
5 Ethernet, for example (abbr.)
6 Having woolly hairs
7 "The Gentiles to live _____ the Jews?" (Galatians 2:14) (2 words)
8 May be a POW
9 Head- or neckwear (var.)
10 "Like a _____, without cause" (Lamentations 3:52)
11 "Blessed _____ the meek" (Matthew 5:5)
12 "Or if the _____ flesh turn again" (Leviticus 13:16)
17 "The written account of _____ line" (Genesis 5:1 NIV)
18 "And Rachel _____, and was buried" (Genesis 35:19)
23 Freeway part
24 "Wind without _____" (Proverbs 25:14)
25 Helicopter part

by David K. Shortess

26 "_____ is deceptive, and beauty" (Proverbs 31:30 NIV)

27 Boleyn, et al.

28 "Shout with _____ God, all the earth!" (Psalm 66:1 NIV) (2 words)

29 "Behold, I _____ at the door, and knock" (Revelation 3:20)

30 Fifth son of Nebo (Ezra 10:43)

31 Guitar kin

32 "And towers in the wooded _____" (2 Chronicles 27:4 NIV)

33 "And his head _____ unto the clouds" (Job 20:6)

37 "His neck with a flowing _____?" (Job 39:19 NIV)

38 "There is _____ here" (John 6:9) (2 words)

40 Cry of disapproval

41 "Sin of Sodom, that was overthrown _____ moment" (Lamentations 4:6) (3 words)

43 "And, behold, a _____ is in thine own eye?" (Matthew 7:4)

44 Ravens fed him (1 Kings 17:1–6)

48 "Know what thy right hand _____" (Matthew 6:3)

49 "Now the parable is this: The seed _____ word of God" (Luke 8:11) (2 words)

50 Libnah, and _____, and Ashan" (Joshua 15:42)

51 "And with what measure ye _____, it shall be measured" (Matthew 7:2)

52 "If anyone _____ anything to them" (Revelation 22:18 NIV)

53 Chit's companion

54 Mrs. in Madrid (abbr.)

55 "My heart was _____ within me" (Psalm 39:3)

56 Teachers' organization (abbr.)

57 Arafat's organization (abbr.)

101

ACROSS

1 This is attached to the shoulder
4 A temple gate (2 Kings 11:6)
7 Patriarch of a family of returned exiles (Ezra 2:57)
10 "The sons of Carmi; _____" (1 Chronicles 2:7)
12 Very (arch.)
13 Goat baby
14 "Suddenly there _____ from heaven a great light" (Acts 22:6)
15 Furthest part
16 Beach surface
17 Kept from detection
18 Belteshazzar (Daniel 1:7)
20 "He had cast _____ the waters" (Exodus 15:25)
21 "Which before these days _____ an uproar" (Acts 21:38)
23 Naaman's brother (Numbers 26:40)
25 Exclamation of affirmation
26 A son of Pashur (Ezra 10:22)
31 Peace
34 David's eldest brother (1 Samuel 17:13)
35 Make a mistake
36 "Alammelech, and _____" (Joshua 19:26)
37 A duke of Edom (1 Chronicles 1:51)
38 A brother of Bethuel (Genesis 22:22)
39 "_____ of cedar beams" (1 Kings 6:36)
40 Esarhaddon was king here (Ezra 4:2)
41 A son of Ephraim (Numbers 26:35)
42 Agreed
44 Are (arch.)
45 Fuss
46 "Which come to you in _____ clothing" (Matthew 7:15)
49 Generations
52 "_____, that was about his head" (John 20:7)
55 Capable
57 Lease

58 A son of Merari (1 Chronicles 24:27)
59 Her household reported contentions in the Corinthian church
61 This book was likely written during Jehoram's reign in Judah (abbr.)
62 "Cain. . .dwelt in the land of Nod, on the east of _____" (Genesis 4:16)
63 "Country; upon _____" (Jeremiah 48:21)
64 A son of Jacob
65 Opposite of *night*
66 Sprint

DOWN

1 Eliud's father (Matthew 1:14)
2 She left Peter at the door (Acts 12:13–14)
3 Adam was the first
4 Gaddiel's father (Numbers 13:10)
5 "Pharisees began to _____ him vehemently" (Luke 11:53)
6 He came with Zerubbabel (Ezra 2:2)
7 A child of Ezer (Genesis 36:27)
8 "For ye tithe _____ and rue and all manner of herbs" (Luke 11:42)
9 Zechariah's father (Ezra 5:1)
10 Type of tree (Isaiah 44:14)
11 Rescue
12 Caused to go to a destination
16 Riverbank (Exodus 2:5)
19 Solomon's great-grandson (1 Kings 15:8)
22 Colored
24 Steal
26 Achim's son (Matthew 1:14)
27 "If we say that we have not sinned, we make him a _____" (1 John 1:10 NIV)
28 Border went to here from Remmonmethoar (Joshua 19:13)
29 Steward of Zimri's house in Tirzah (1 Kings 16)
30 Strong metal

by N. Teri Grottke

31 "Through faith also _____ herself received strength to conceive seed" (Hebrews 11:11)
32 Naum's son (Luke 3:25)
33 "I will put my _____ into their mind" (Hebrews 8:10)
34 Otherwise
37 Astonished (arch.)
38 Detest
40 "Garments, _____ stood" (Zechariah 3:3)
41 Ditch
43 Opposite of *west*
44 Abdiel's son (1 Chronicles 5:15)
46 Epidermis
47 A son of Reuben (Exodus 6:14)
48 Partner of fork and knife
49 "Of _____, the family of the Arodites" (Numbers 26:17)

50 A priestly city of Benjamin (Joshua 21:17)
51 Ahira's father (Numbers 1:15)
53 Adoniram's father (1 Kings 4:6)
54 "Will a lion roar in the forest, when he hath no _____?" (Amos 3:4)
56 "Hundred and _____ years old" (Joshua 24:29)
60 "Ye shall point out for you mount _____" (Numbers 34:7)

Answers

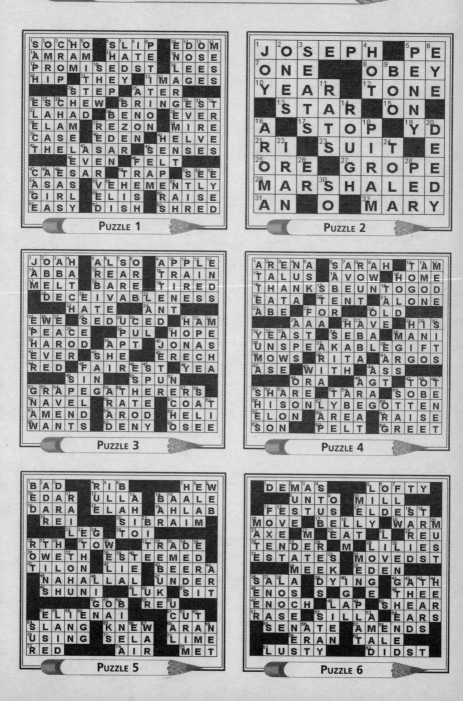

PUZZLE 1

S	O	C	H	O		S	L	I	P		E	D	O	M
A	M	R	A	M		H	A	T	E		N	O	S	E
P	R	O	M	I	S	E	D	S	T		L	E	E	S
H	I	P		T	H	E	Y		I	M	A	G	E	S
	S	T	E	P		A	T	E	R					
E	S	C	H	E	W		B	R	I	N	G	E	S	T
L	A	H	A	D		B	E	N	O		E	V	E	R
E	L	A	M		R	E	Z	O	N		M	I	R	E
C	A	S	E		E	D	E	N		H	E	L	V	E
T	H	E	L	A	S	A	R		S	E	N	S	E	S
	E	V	E	N		F	E	L	T					
C	A	E	S	A	R		T	R	A	P		S	E	E
A	S	A	S		V	E	H	E	M	E	N	T	L	Y
G	I	R	L		E	L	I	S		R	A	I	S	E
E	A	S	Y		D	I	S	H		S	H	R	E	D

PUZZLE 2

J	O	S	E	P	H		P	E
O	N	E			O	B	E	Y
Y	E	A	R		T	O	N	E
	S	T	A	R		O	N	
A		S	T	O	P		Y	D
R	I		S	U	I	T		E
O	R	E		G	R	O	P	E
M	A	R	S	H	A	L	E	D
A	N		O		M	A	R	Y

PUZZLE 3

J	O	A	H		A	L	S	O		A	P	P	L	E
A	B	B	A		R	E	A	R		T	R	A	I	N
M	E	L	T		B	A	R	E		T	I	R	E	D
	D	E	C	E	I	V	A	B	L	E	N	E	S	S
	H	A	T	E		A	N	T					
E	W	E		S	E	D	U	C	E	D		H	A	M
P	E	A	C	E		P	U	L		H	O	P	E	
H	A	R	O	D		A	P	T		J	O	N	A	S
E	V	E	R		S	H	E		E	R	E	C	H
R	E	D		F	A	I	R	E	S	T		Y	E	A
	S	I	N		S	P	U	N					
G	R	A	P	E	G	A	T	H	E	R	E	R	S
N	A	V	E	L		R	A	T	E		C	O	A	T
A	M	E	N	D		A	R	O	D		H	E	L	I
W	A	N	T	S		D	E	N	Y		O	S	E	E

PUZZLE 4

A	R	E	N	A		S	A	R	A	H		T	A	M
T	A	L	U	S		A	V	O	W		H	O	M	E
T	H	A	N	K	S	B	E	U	N	T	O	G	O	D
E	A	T	A		T	E	N	T		A	L	O	N	E
A	B	E		F	O	R		O	L	D				
	A	A	A		H	A	V	E		H	I	S	
Y	E	A	S	T		S	E	B	A		M	A	N	I
U	N	S	P	E	A	K	A	B	L	E	G	I	F	T
M	O	W	S		R	I	T	A		A	R	G	O	S
A	S	E		W	I	T	H		A	S	S			
	O	R	A		A	G	T		T	O	T	
S	H	A	R	E		T	A	R	A		S	O	B	E
H	I	S	O	N	L	Y	B	E	G	O	T	T	E	N
E	L	O	N		A	R	E	A		R	A	I	S	E
S	O	N		P	E	L	T		G	R	E	E	T

PUZZLE 5

B	A	D		R	I	B		H	E	W
E	D	A	R		U	L	L	A		B	A	A	L	E
D	A	R	A		E	L	A	H		A	H	L	A	B
R	E	I		S	I	B	R	A	I	M			
	L	E	G		T	O	I					
R	T	H		T	O	W		T	R	A	D	E
O	W	E	T	H		E	S	T	E	E	M	E	D
T	I	L	O	N		L	I	E		B	E	E	R	A
	N	A	H	A	L	L	A	L		U	N	D	E	R
	S	H	U	N	I		L	U	K		S	I	T
		G	O	B		R	E	U			
E	L	I	E	N	A	I		C	U	T
S	L	A	N	G		K	N	E	W		A	R	A	N
U	S	I	N	G		S	E	L	A		L	I	M	E
R	E	D			A	I	R		M	E	T

PUZZLE 6

D	E	M	A	S		L	O	F	T	Y
	U	N	T	O		M	I	L	L
	F	E	S	T	U	S		E	L	D	E	S	T
M	O	V	E		B	E	L	L	Y		W	A	R	M
A	X	E		M		E	A	T		L		R	E	U
T	E	N	D	E	R		M		L	I	L	I	E	S
E	S	T	A	T	E	S		M	O	V	E	D	S	T
	M	E	E	K		E	D	E	N	
S	A	L	A		D	Y	I	N	G		G	A	T	H
E	N	O	S		S		G		E		T	H	E	E
E	N	O	C	H		L	A	P		S	H	E	A	R
R	A	S	E		S	I	L	L	A		E	A	R	S
S	E	N	A	T	E		A	M	E	N	D	S
	E	R	A	N		T	A	L	E	
L	U	S	T	Y		D	I	D	S	T

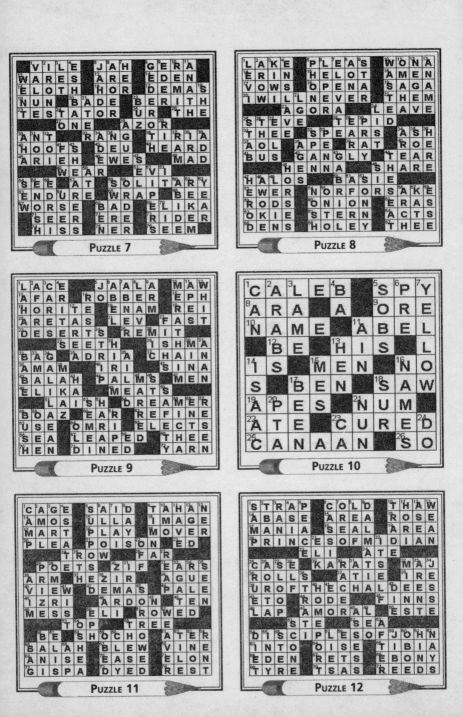

Puzzle 7

V	I	L	E			J	A	H			G	E	R	A
W	A	R	E	S		A	R	E			E	D	E	N
E	L	O	T	H		H	O	R			D	E	M	A	S
N	U	N		B	A	D	E		B	E	R	I	T	H
T	E	S	T	A	T	O	R		U	R		T	H	E
		O	N	E			A	Z	O	R				
A	N	T		R	A	N	G		T	I	R	I	A	
H	O	O	F	S		D	E	U		H	E	A	R	D
A	R	I	E	H		E	W	E	S		M	A	D	
	W	E	A	R			E	V	I					
S	E	E		A	T		S	O	L	I	T	A	R	Y
E	N	D	U	R	E		W	R	A	P		B	E	E
W	O	R	S	E		B	A	D		E	L	I	K	A
	S	E	E	R		E	R	E		R	I	D	E	R
	H	I	S	S		N	E	R			S	E	E	M

Puzzle 8

L	A	K	E			P	L	E	A	S		W	O	N	A
E	R	I	N			H	E	L	O	T		A	M	E	N
V	O	W	S			O	P	E	N	A		S	A	G	A
I	W	I	L	L	N	E	V	E	R		T	H	E	M	
	A	G	O	R	A				L	E	A	V	E		
S	T	E	V	E		T	E	P	I	D			A	S	H
T	H	E	E		S	P	E	A	R	S		A	S	H	
A	O	L		A	P	E		R	A	T		R	O	E	
B	U	S		G	A	N	G	L	Y		T	E	A	R	
			H	E	N	N	A			S	H	A	R	E	
H	A	L	O	S			B	A	S	I	E				
E	W	E	R		N	O	R	F	O	R	S	A	K	E	
R	O	D	S		O	N	I	O	N		E	R	A	S	
O	K	I	E		S	T	E	R	N		A	C	T	S	
D	E	N	S		H	O	L	E	Y		T	H	E	E	

Puzzle 9

L	A	C	E			J	A	A	L	A		M	A	W
A	F	A	R		R	O	B	B	E	R		E	P	H
H	O	R	I	T	E		E	N	A	M		R	E	I
A	R	E	T	A	S		L	E	V		F	A	S	T
D	E	S	E	R	T	S		R	E	M	I	T		
			S	E	E	T	H		I	S	H	M	A	
B	A	G		A	D	R	I	A		C	H	A	I	N
A	M	A	M		I	R	I		S	I	N	A		
B	A	L	A	H		P	A	L	M	S		M	E	N
E	L	I	K	A		M	E	A	T	S				
	L	A	I	S	H		D	R	E	A	M	E	R	
B	O	A	Z		E	A	R		R	E	F	I	N	E
U	S	E		O	M	R	I		E	L	E	C	T	S
S	E	A		L	E	A	P	E	D		T	H	E	E
H	E	N		D	I	N	E	D			Y	A	R	N

Puzzle 10

C	A	L	E	B			S	P	Y
A	R	A			A			O	R	E
N	A	M	E			A	B	E	L
		B	E			H	I	S		L
I	S		M	E	N			N	O
S		B	E	N			S	A	W
A	P	E	S			N	U	M	
A	T	E			C	U	R	E	D
C	A	N	A	A	N			S	O

Puzzle 11

C	A	G	E		S	A	I	D		T	A	H	A	N
A	M	O	S		U	L	L	A		I	M	A	G	E
M	A	R	T		P	L	A	Y		M	O	V	E	R
P	L	E	A		P	O	I	S	O	N		E	D	
			T	R	O	W			F	A	R			
P	O	E	T	S		Z	I	F		E	A	R	S	
A	R	M		H	E	Z	I	R		A	G	U	E	
V	I	E	W		D	E	M	A	S		P	A	L	E
I	Z	R	I		A	R	D	O	N		T	E	N	
M	E	S	S		E	L	I		R	O	W	E	D	
			T	O	P		T	R	E	E				
	B	E		S	H	O	C	H	O		A	T	E	R
B	A	L	A	H		B	L	E	W		V	I	N	E
A	N	I	S	E		E	A	S	E		E	L	O	N
G	I	S	P	A		D	Y	E	D		R	E	S	T

Puzzle 12

S	T	R	A	P		C	O	L	D		T	H	A	W
A	B	A	S	E		A	R	E	A		R	O	S	E
M	A	N	I	A		S	E	A	L		A	R	E	A
P	R	I	N	C	E	S	O	F	M	I	D	I	A	N
				E	L	I		A	T	E				
C	A	S	E		K	A	R	A	T	S		M	A	J
R	O	L	L	S		A	T	I	E		I	R	E	
U	R	O	F	T	H	E	C	H	A	L	D	E	E	S
E	T	O		R	O	D	E		F	I	N	N	S	
L	A	P		A	M	O	R	A	L		E	S	T	E
			S	T	E		S	E	A					
D	I	S	C	I	P	L	E	S	O	F	J	O	H	N
I	N	T	O		O	I	S	E		T	I	B	I	A
E	D	E	N		R	E	T	S		E	B	O	N	Y
T	Y	R	E		T	S	A	S		R	E	E	D	S

PUZZLE 13 · PUZZLE 14 · PUZZLE 15 · PUZZLE 16 · PUZZLE 17 · PUZZLE 18

Puzzle 19

Puzzle 20

Puzzle 21

Puzzle 22

Puzzle 23

Puzzle 24

Puzzle 25

```
BEST  BADE   HIS
UPHAZ AGES   TEMA
THEREABOUT   HARP
   TRUE  SERAH
ISRAEL  BASMATH
BOUND   BOSCATH
ROT   BAY   ERR
INHERIT  INTENTS
   MEN  ACT  AHI
  DISEASE  ALIEN
BENEATH  AMALEK
BETEN    GIRT
OREN  SEPARATETH
NEST  AZAL  MELEA
EAT   TEIL   RING
```

Puzzle 26

```
GUAM  SALEM  BARE
AGRA  OCALA  ENOS
THEREWEREGIANTS
   ABET   MORT
NET  BRIM  GALORE
ALOG   CEO   EREI
MEREST SHEA  ASO
 GOLIATHOFGATH
WAN  PROA  TENORS
ANTS   PCF   DREI
STOWED HULA  YDS
   AREA   LESS
THELANDOFGIANTS
HAVE  TENIA  NOWA
EYES  SNELL  DROP
```

Puzzle 27

```
HARE  DIED  UPHAZ
ASAS  UNDO  SHAGE
LIGHTENED  EMMOR
TASTE  ENOS  ONO
   OMER  USURER
HANNAH    ANER
ARE  NIGER  DINAH
RABBI  ARA  IMAGE
ABOUT  LIMIT  MAN
   ZEAL  SISERA
RESIST   MAON
EPH  ESLI  NAMED
SHARE  PALESTINA
TAKER  IMLA  CLAY
SIEVE  NEST  HEMS
```

Puzzle 28

```
NOAH     EDGE
END      ARK
SLAY     TREE
TYRE     HEWS
    AYE
SPAR     NETS
HAM      ARE
EVER     TSAR
MENE     MEME
```

Puzzle 29

```
TOMB  ALSO  CABUL
OBAL  BEAR  AMASA
BELA  DALE  LADED
 DECEIVABLENESS
    KNEE   OBA
WAR  OLDNESS  JOH
ISAAC  USE   HOME
NINTH  ART  VINES
EDGE   HIS  IMAGE
SEE  FORESTS  HAD
   SIR   THIS
 ADMINISTRATION
BEING  OREN  AZOR
DANCE  WEEK  HENA
ALTER  NETS  AMEN
```

Puzzle 30

```
PITY  PARTS  SETH
ELOI  ABIHU  HARA
SALE  WISER  ASAS
TILL   BEEN  MINT
   DAN   APIECE
EMERODS   MARRED
TRADED   OPEN
ART   TIE   HAS
GORE  PULL  SHEMA
RIGOUR  E  HOLON
 GULF  TRADING
DOEST    HERE
INN  ROAR  NAVEL
SOD  UNTO  DRAVE
H    NEED   HIT
```

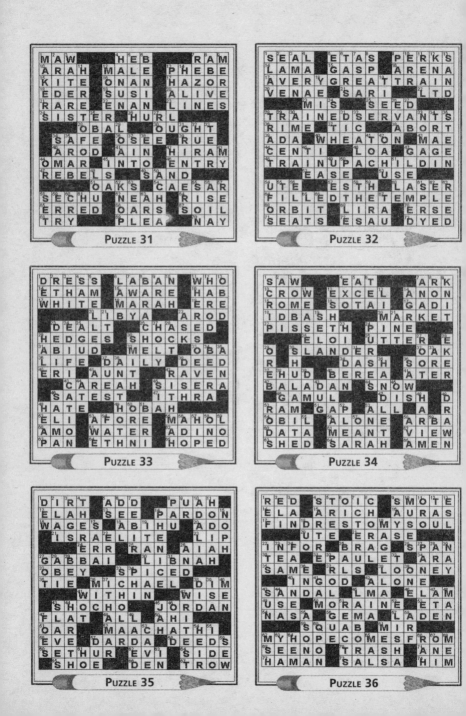

PUZZLE 31

M	A	W			H	E	B				R	A	M	
A	R	A	H		M	A	L	E		P	H	E	B	E
K	I	T	E		O	N	A	N		H	A	Z	O	R
E	D	E	R		S	U	S	I		A	L	I	V	E
R	A	R	E		E	N	A	N		L	I	N	E	S
	S	I	S	T	E	R		H	U	R	L			
			O	B	A	L		O	U	G	H	T		
	S	A	F	E		O	S	E	E		R	U	E	
	A	R	O	D		A	I	N		H	I	R	A	M
O	M	A	R		I	N	T	O		E	N	T	R	Y
	R	E	B	E	L	S		S	A	N	D			
			O	A	K	S		C	A	E	S	A	R	
S	E	C	H	U		N	E	A	H		R	I	S	E
E	R	R	E	D		O	A	R	S		S	O	I	L
T	R	Y			P	L	E	A			N	A	Y	

PUZZLE 32

S	E	A	L		E	T	A	S		P	E	R	K	S
L	A	M	A		G	A	S	P		A	R	E	N	A
A	V	E	R	Y	G	R	E	A	T	T	R	A	I	N
V	E	N	A	E		S	A	R	I		L	T	D	
			M	I	S		S	E	E	D				
T	R	A	I	N	E	D	S	E	R	V	A	N	T	S
R	I	M	E		T	I	C		A	B	O	R	T	
A	D	A		W	H	E	A	T	O	N		M	A	E
C	E	N	T	I		L	O	A		G	A	G	E	
T	R	A	I	N	U	P	A	C	H	I	L	D	I	N
	E	A	S	E				U	S	E				
U	T	E		E	S	T	H		L	A	S	E	R	
F	I	L	L	E	D	T	H	E	T	E	M	P	L	E
O	R	B	I	T		L	I	R	A		E	R	S	E
S	E	A	T	S		E	S	A	U		D	Y	E	D

PUZZLE 33

D	R	E	S	S		L	A	B	A	N		W	H	O
E	T	H	A	M		A	W	A	R	E		H	A	B
W	H	I	T	E		M	A	R	A	H		E	R	E
		L	I	B	Y	A		A	R	O	D			
D	E	A	L	T		C	H	A	S	E	D			
H	E	D	G	E	S		S	H	O	C	K	S		
A	B	I	U	D		M	E	L	T		O	B	A	
L	I	F	E		D	A	I	L	Y		D	E	E	D
E	R	I		A	U	N	T		R	A	V	E	N	
	C	A	R	E	A	H		S	I	S	E	R	A	
	S	A	T	E	S	T		I	T	H	R	A		
H	A	T	E		H	O	B	A	H					
E	L	I		A	F	O	R	E		M	A	H	O	L
A	M	O		W	A	T	E	R		A	D	I	N	O
P	A	N		E	T	H	N	I		H	O	P	E	D

PUZZLE 34

S	A	W			E	A	T				A	R	K	
C	R	O	W		E	X	C	E	L		A	N	O	N
R	O	M	E		S	O	T	A	I		G	A	D	I
	I	D	B	A	S	H		M	A	R	K	E	T	
P	I	S	S	E	T	H		P	I	N	E			
		E	L	O	I		U	T	T	E	R		E	
O		S	L	A	N	D	E	R			O	A	K	
R		H		I	D	A	S	H		S	O	R	E	
E	H	U	D		B	E	R	E	A		A	T	E	R
B	A	L	A	D	A	N		S	N	O	W			
	G	A	M	U	L		D	I	S	H		D		
R	A	M		G	A	P		A	L	L		A		R
O	B	I	L		A	L	O	N	E		A	R	B	A
D	A	T	A		M	E	A	N	T		V	I	E	W
S	H	E	D		S	A	R	A	H		A	M	E	N

PUZZLE 35

D	I	R	T		A	D	D		P	U	A	H		
E	L	A	H		S	E	E		P	A	R	D	O	N
W	A	G	E	S		A	B	I	H	U		A	D	O
	I	S	R	A	E	L	I	T	E		L	I	P	
		E	R	R		R	A	N		A	I	A	H	
G	A	B	B	A	I		L	I	B	N	A	H		
O	B	E	Y		S	P	I	C	E	D				
T	I	E		M	I	C	H	A	E	L		D	I	M
	W	I	T	H	I	N				W	I	S	E	
	S	H	O	C	H	O		J	O	R	D	A	N	
F	L	A	T		A	L	L		A	H	I			
O	A	R		M	A	A	C	H	A	T	H	I		
E	V	E		D	A	R	D	A		D	E	E	D	S
S	E	T	H	U	R		E	V	I		S	I	D	E
S	H	O	E		D	E	N		T	R	O	W		

PUZZLE 36

R	E	D		S	T	O	I	C		S	M	O	T	E
E	L	A		A	R	I	C	H		A	U	R	A	S
F	I	N	D	R	E	S	T	O	M	Y	S	O	U	L
			U	T	E		E	R	A	S	E			
I	N	F	O	R		B	R	A	G		S	P	A	N
T	E	A		E	P	A	U	L	E	T		A	R	A
S	A	M	E		R	L	S		L	O	O	N	E	Y
	I	N	G	O	D		A	L	O	N	E			
S	A	N	D	A	L		L	M	A		E	L	A	M
U	S	E		M	O	R	A	I	N	E		E	T	A
N	A	S	A		G	E	M	A		L	A	D	E	N
			S	Q	U	A	B		M	I	R			
M	Y	H	O	P	E	C	O	M	E	S	F	R	O	M
S	E	E	N	O		T	R	A	S	H		A	N	E
H	A	M	A	N		S	A	L	S	A		H	I	M

Puzzle 37

B	E	N			B	E	A	M	S		S	H	E
O	X	E	N		U	R	I	A	H		L	E	A	N
S	I	Z	E		D	I	A	N	A		E	L	S	E
O	L	I	V	E	S		H	E	R	E	W	I	T	H
R	E	B	E	L				H	O	R				
			R	I	T	E	S		N	E	S	T	S	
R	O	D		I	V	A	H			E	H	U	D	
T	R	A	P		T	I	R	A	S		T	A	R	E
H	E	R	S		L	O	V	E			N	E	W	
	B	A	A	R	A		N	E	E	D	S			
	A	R	A				E	I	G	H	T			
N	A	H	A	M	A	N	I		A	N	A	I	A	H
O	W	E	D		B	A	S	E	S		H	A	L	I
B	A	R	N		I	T	H	A	I		A	N	A	N
Y	E	A		A	H	I	R	A		T	H	E		

Puzzle 38

		R	E	B	A		A	R	T	S				
	R	O	L	L	S		R	E	H	U	M			
S	I	B	M	A	H		U	S	U	R	E	R		
R	A	N		S	C	R	I	B	E	S		T	H	E
A	U	N	T		K	I	S	O	N		T	H	E	Y
S	L	A	I	N		E	A	T		A	R	O	S	E
E	S	H	B	A	A	L		H	E	N	A	D	A	D
			H	I	P			H	A	I				
S	T	E	A	L	T	H		G	I	T	T	A	I	M
H	O	S	T	S		I	C	E		H	O	R	S	E
O	A	T	H		S	T	U	D	S		R	I	P	E
A	S	H		L	E	T	T	E	T	H		S	A	T
	T	E	M	A	N	I		R	A	A	M	A	H	
		R	E	M	I	T		A	T	T	A	I		
		T	A	R	E		H	E	E	D				

Puzzle 39

Z	O	A	R		A	F	A	R		P	I	T	C	H
A	L	S	O		B	O	L	T		I	T	H	R	A
H	I	N	D	E	R	E	T	H		S	H	E	E	T
A	V	A		L	O	S	E		S	I	N	E	W	S
M	E	H	I	D	A		R	H	O	D	A			
		J	A	D	A		E	M	I	N	E	N	T	
I	S	H	O	D		T	A	R	E	A		Y	E	A
L	E	A	N		T	W	O			W	E	B	S	
A	C	T		S	P	I	E	D		Z	A	D	O	K
I	T	H	A	M	A	R		S	T	I	R			
		P	E	L	E	T		H	O	N	O	U	R	
D	E	F	I	L	E		H	O	R	N		U	S	E
A	R	I	E	L		J	E	B	U	S	I	T	E	S
L	A	N	C	E		A	S	A	S		R	E	S	T
E	N	D	E	D		M	E	L	T		A	R	T	S

Puzzle 40

P	A	N	T	S		O	R	C		S	T	L	O
A	L	O	H	A		W	A	R		A	H	I	O
T	O	W	E	R	I	N	J	E	Z	R	E	E	L
S	E	A	T	A	S		A	P	O		C	O	I	N
			O	H	M	S		T	O	R	O	N	T	O
A	N	E	W		A	H	A		M	O	R	E	H	E
M	E	R	E		N	O	R			S	O	N		
P	A	I	R	S		W	A	S		M	E	T	E	D
	O	A	R		B	O	A		R	O	L	E		
S	T	A	F	F	I		S	A	T		T	W	I	N
C	O	N	S	E	N	T		R	E	D	O			
B	O	D	Y		S	O	W		N	E	W	A	G	E
T	H	E	T	O	W	E	R	O	F	E	D	A	R	
H	O	N	E		I	G	O			O	R	A	M	I
S	T	E	N		N	O	T		E	S	S	E	N	

Puzzle 41

	H	E		P	A	N				A	R	M
L	U	Z		A	N	I	M		A	G	A	I	N
E	R	I		L	Y	C	I	A		H	A	S	T	E
V	I	O	L	S		O	L	D		O	T	H	E	R
	N	A	Y		P	E	O	P	L	E				
A	G	E		N	O		L	A	S	T	E	D		
M	A	L		E	L	A	S	A	H		E	L	I	
H	A	B		K	I	S	H	I		L	E	G		
O	N	E		G	O	S	H	E	N		A	H	A	
W	A	R	N	E	D		A	S		G	A	D		
	A	S	A	H	E	L		S	U	R				
R	A	M	A	H		E	A	T		H	E	E	L	S
T	H	A	R	A		B	R	I	B	E		S	E	A
H	E	L	A	M		S	E	E	R		H	A	D	
R	E	I			L	E	D		A	H				

Puzzle 42

S	O	R	E		A	F	A	R		S	E	L	A
E	V	I	L		S	E	B	A		A	L	A	S
A	M	E	N	D		A	D	I	N		L	E	S	S
S	E	N	S	E		S	E	T		M	A	C	H	I
S	I	S	E	R	A		R	A	S	E		T	A	R
S			D		P	S	A	L	M	S				
				S	A	I	L		A	H	A	S	A	I
P	E	R	F	E	C	T		P	L	A	N	E	T	S
A	P	I	E	C	E		I	L	L		N	E	A	H
T	H	E	I	R		K	N	E	E		A	D	D	I
E			G	E	N		K	I	S	S				
H	U	N	T	E	R		A	T	E		A	W	E	
S	U	R	E		B	A	N	D		R	E	B	E	L
E	G	G	S		A	G	U	E		A	R	E	L	I
M	E	E	T		T	E	N	S		H	I	L	L	S

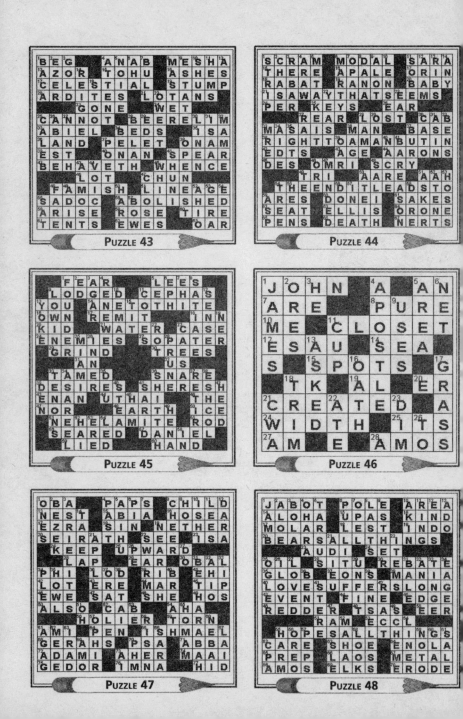

PUZZLE 43

PUZZLE 44

PUZZLE 45

PUZZLE 46

PUZZLE 47

PUZZLE 48

Puzzle 49

B	E	A	T		G	R	O	W		A	L	O	T	H
A	L	S	O		N	E	R	I		B	A	V	A	I
R	A	I	L		A	M	E	N		I	T	E	M	S
S	H	A	D	O	W	I	N	G		H	E	R	E	S
			W	E	T			B	U	L				
I	S	L	A	N	D		T	H	E		Y	A	R	N
S	H	A	R	E		B	E	A	N	S		R	I	E
P	E	T	E	R		O	A	R		C	H	I	D	E
A	B	I		S	H	A	R	P		H	E	S	E	D
H	A	N	G		I	T	S		T	O	W	E	R	S
			O	W	N			W	H	O				
H	A	S	T	E		B	E	H	O	L	D	E	T	H
A	G	A	T	E		E	D	E	R		I	L	A	I
R	U	L	E	D		L	E	A	N		S	O	L	E
M	E	A	N	S		A	N	T	S		H	I	L	L

Puzzle 50

Y	E	A	R		F	A	M	E		A	C	C	A	D
A	L	S	O		E	B	A	L		S	H	O	B	I
R	O	A	M		W	I	N	D		H	E	R	O	N
N	I	S	A	N		B	I	E	R		C	A	V	E
			N	O	N		F	R	E	C	K	L	E	D
P	U	R	S	U	E		E	S	A	U				
O	N	E		N	E	W	S		D	R	E	A	M	S
T	I	L	E		D	O	T	H		E	P	H	A	I
S	T	Y	L	E		N	E	A	R		H	E	A	D
			I	S	A		D	I	A	L		R	I	E
A	C	T		E	N	D		R	I	O	T			
F	L	O	C	K	S		E		L	A	A	D	A	H
T	A	K	E		W	O	V	E		T	H	O	S	E
E	V	E	N		E	B	E	R		H	A	D	S	T
R	E	N	T		R	A	R	E		E	N	O	S	H

Puzzle 51

K	O	R	E		A	D	E	R		H	I	S
O	M	E	R	S		L	I	V	E		C	A	M	E
R	E	Z	I	N		O	R	E	B		A	D	N	A
A	G	O		A	U	N	T		E	L	N	A	A	M
H	A	N	G	I	N	G		P	L	E	A	D		
			O	L	D		K	I	S	H		E	W	E
J	E	H	U		E	D	E	N		B	Z	A	N
O	V	E	R		R	A	Z	O	R		L	E	N	D
H	E	A	D	Y		V	I	N	E		A	R	T	S
A	N	D		A	B	I	A		G	O	D			
	S	E	R	E	D		R	E	V	E	R	S	E
L	O	T	A	N	S		S	O	M	E		A	P	T
A	M	O	S		T	A	L	L		N	O	H	A	H
M	A	N	Y		I	D	O	L		S	N	A	R	E
A	R	E		R	O	W	S		O	M	E	R

Puzzle 52

H	A	M	I	S		T	H	A	N		R	I	S	E
I	S	A	S	A		R	O	S	E		I	R	U	N
M	O	N	E	Y		U	R	I	S		S	E	N	D
			J	E	S	U	S	I	S	T	H	E		
A	G	O		O	T	T			U	N	D	E	R	
C	O	I	N		A	S	T	O	N		O	W	E	
T	I	N	E	D		P	E	A	G		G	E	D	
		R	E	A	S	O	N	F	O	R				
N	O	T		A	S	I	T		N	A	H	U	M	
A	R	E		R	A	N	S	O	M		M	Y	R	A
Y	E	A	S	T		N	E	O		M	I	X		
		T	H	I	S	S	E	A	S	O	N			
I	S	S	O		N	E	A	R		I	S	A	A	C
L	E	A	N		C	A	N	A		N	E	L	L	Y
L	A	T	E		A	M	E	N		G	A	S	P	S

Puzzle 53

A	S	A		A	N	E	M		I	D	D	O
A	R	T	S		M	E	T	E	D		D	E	E	D
G	A	A	L		I	T	H	A	I		L	E	N	D
E	D	R	E	I		A	N	S	W	E	R	S		
	G	E	S	H	E	M		T	I	N				
S	A	P	H	I	R		F	I	N	E	S	T		
C	O	Z		I	S	R	A	E	L		S	H	E	N
A	T	E	R		A	N	T		S	U	R	E		
B	A	R	E		O	N	Y	C	H	A		N	A	H
	I	S	L	A	N	D		H	O	G	L	A	H	
			E	L	I		S	T	R	E	A	M		
B	E	A	L	O	T	H		D	I	M	O	N		
L	A	D	S		N	O	A	H	S		D	I	N	E
O	S	E	E		S	E	M	E	I		S	T	A	R
T	E	N	D		S	E	B	A		T	E	N

Puzzle 54

	M	O	S	E	S		P	I	
B	E	N	O		A	L	A	S	
R	O	E		A	V	E	N		
I	N		S	A	I	N	T	S	
E		H	E	R	O	D		T	
F	L	A	V	O	R		P	A	
	O	V	E	N		P	O	M	
O	V	E	R		B	E	E	P	
H	E		E	G	Y	P	T		

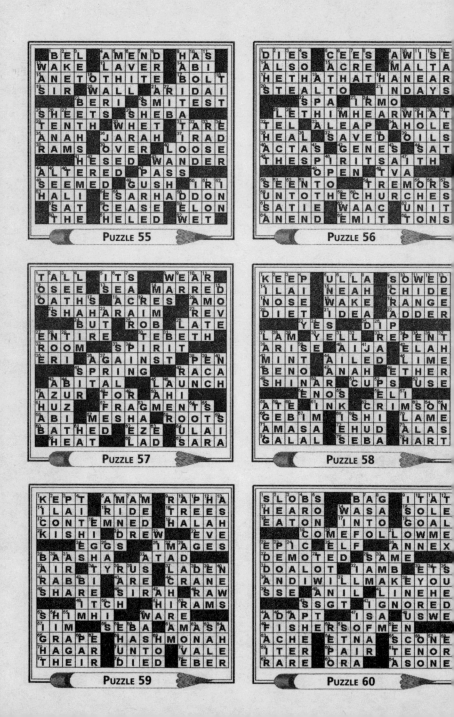

Puzzle 55

Puzzle 56

Puzzle 57

Puzzle 58

Puzzle 59

Puzzle 60

Puzzle 61

K	I	N	D	S		C	U	P	S		A	B	B	A
I	S	A	A	C		A	N	A	H		D	O	E	R
S	H	U	N	A	M	M	I	T	E		J	A	D	A
H	I	M		L	I	E	T	H		B	U	N	A	H
	B	E	L	L	Y		E	A	R	E	D			
C	H		U	S	E		U	T	T	E	R			
R	E	L	Y		C	A	L	A	H			G	A	T
A	R	A		R	A	H	A	M			E	R	R	
G	E	N		H	U	R	A	M		E	S	A	U	
	G	H	O	S	T		U	E	L		M	E		
B	U	I	L	T		B	E	S	A	I				
R	E	A	D	Y		F	E	V	E	R		S	A	W
U	R	G	E		M	A	G	I	S	T	R	A	T	E
L	E	E	S		A	M	A	L		H	O	R	E	B
E	A	S	T		N	E	T	S			Y	E	A	R	S

Puzzle 62

V	I	S	I	T						H	E	A	P	S
I	S	H	T	O	B		R		H	A	S	R	A	H
A	R	I	S	A	I		E		E	N	T	I	R	E
L	A	M		H	E	L	P	I	N	G		S	E	M
S	E	E	R		R	E	A	I	A		S	I	N	A
	L	A	E	L		D	I	M		R	E	N	T	
	S	H	A	U	L		R		R	I	N	G	S	
			S	C	U	M		R	A	G	S			
R	E	C	O	R	D		R		T	H	E	I	R	S
A	L	O	N	E		G	A	T		T		M	A	W
M	A	R		O	A	T	H	S			S	A	V	E
A	S	P	S		S	H	E	E	T		A	G	E	E
H	A	S	U	P	H	A		R	A	I	M	E	N	T
	H	E	A	R	E	R		E	R	R	O	R	S	
	S	H	O	A					E	A	S	Y		

Puzzle 63

M	A	R	T		S	H	E	E	P		A	B	E	L
E	L	A	H		P	A	L	L	U		M	E	N	E
L	I	V	E		A	V	O	I	D		A	N	O	N
E	K	E	R		N	E	T	H	E	R	M	O	S	T
A	E	N	O	N		H	U	N	T					
			F	O	E	S			S	H	O	B	A	B
U	S	E		S	C	A	B			U	R	G	E	
C	O	N	F	E	C	T	I	O	N	A	R	I	E	S
A	D	D	I			D	A	U	B		M	E	T	
L	I	S	T	E	N		K	N	I	T				
			S	A	L	A			B	A	T	H	E	
J	I	P	H	T	H	A	H	E	L		S	H	E	N
U	L	A	I		A	S	I	D	E		T	I	M	E
S	A	I	D		S	H	A	G	E		E	N	A	M
T	I	R	E		H	A	N	E	S		D	E	N	Y

Puzzle 64

B	A	S	A	L		C	U	O	M	O		A	L	I
A	G	A	P	E		A	R	R	A	U		R	I	D
D	A	V	I	D	S	F	I	R	S	T	W	I	F	E
E	P	E	E		H	E	M		E	L	O	D	E	A
			C	O	E		T	R	A	M				
J	E	Z	E	B	E	L	S	H	U	S	B	A	N	D
A	V	I		S	T	A	T	E		T	I	M	O	R
R	A	P	T		S	N	E	R	D		S	I	R	E
I	D	I	O	M		D	E	M	O	N		S	S	A
B	E	N	J	A	M	I	N	S	M	O	T	H	E	R
			U	R	I	S			I	T	O			
A	R	E	N	A	S		D	A	N		D	A	R	K
J	A	C	O	B	S	S	E	C	O	N	D	S	O	N
A	S	H		O	I	L	E	R		O	L	I	V	E
R	H	O		U	S	A	R	E		R	E	N	E	W

Puzzle 65

N	O	B		N	I	N	E		T	H	U	S
G	E	R	A		A	Z	A	L		H	A	N	A	N
A	B	D	A		A	R	O	D		A	L	I	K	E
L	A	E	L		S	I	M	E	O	N	I	T	E	S
	T	R	E	E	S		I	S	A		E	S	T	
			N	O	N		T	R	A	P				
A	S	S	I	G	N	E	D		B	A	K	E	R	
S	I	E	G	E		T	I	P		A	L	I	V	E
K	N	E	A	D		M	U	S	T	E	R	E	D	
	L	I	C	K		A	T	E						
A	M	I		O	I	L		A	D	D	E	D	
C	O	M	P	E	L	L	E	S	T		O	N	E	S
T	O	L	A	D		L	A	K	E		E	S	A	U
S	N	A	R	E		E	V	I	L		R	U	L	E
	S	H	E	N		D	E	N	Y		S	E	T	

Puzzle 66

		S	A	L	A		L	A	D	E	D
	R	E	T	A	I	N		A	M	A	Z	E	D
R	E	T	I	R	E	D		M	O	R	E	V	E	R
E	P	H	R	O	N		R		S	T	R	I	V	E
F	U	N		N		R	O	T		S		S	E	E
E	T	A	M		R	O	M	A	N		S	E	L	L
R	E	N	E	W	E	D		R	O	B	E		O	
	D		A	H	A			T	E	A		P		
		R	O	P	E		F	E	D					
	M		A		E	D	E	R		A	D	A	H
R	I	C	H		R	O	L	E		N	E	B	A	I
A	S	A		A		M	I	S	S		F	I	N	D
H	E	R	E	S		I	S	H	I		I	D	D	O
A	R	E	L	I		T	H	E	N		L	A	E	L
M	Y	S	I	A		E	A	R	S		E	N	D	S

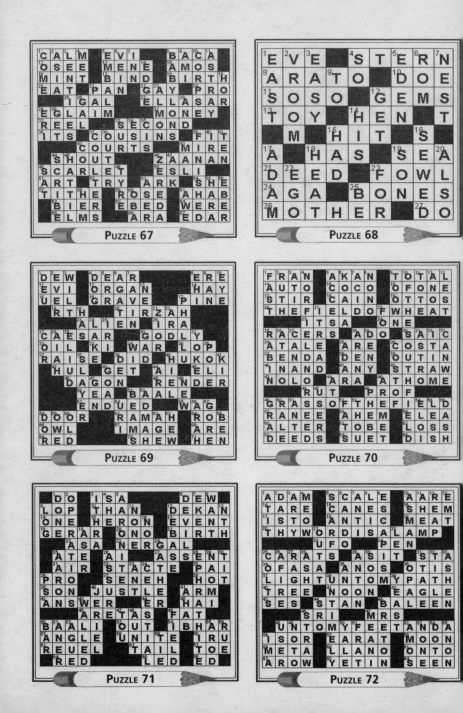

Puzzle 67

Puzzle 68

Puzzle 69

Puzzle 70

Puzzle 71

Puzzle 72

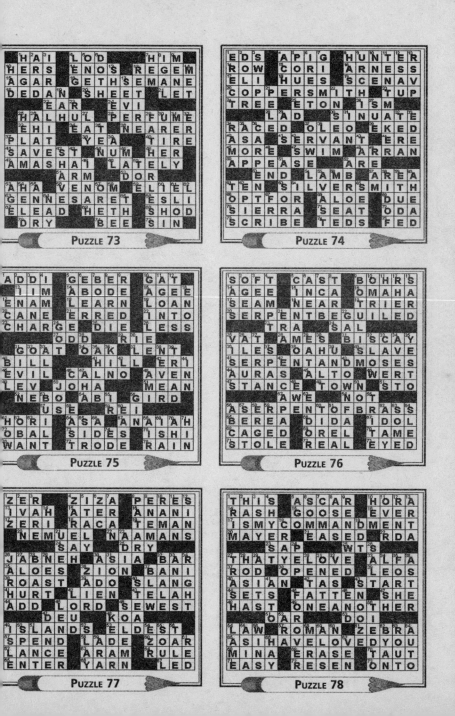

Puzzle 73

Puzzle 74

Puzzle 75

Puzzle 76

Puzzle 77

Puzzle 78

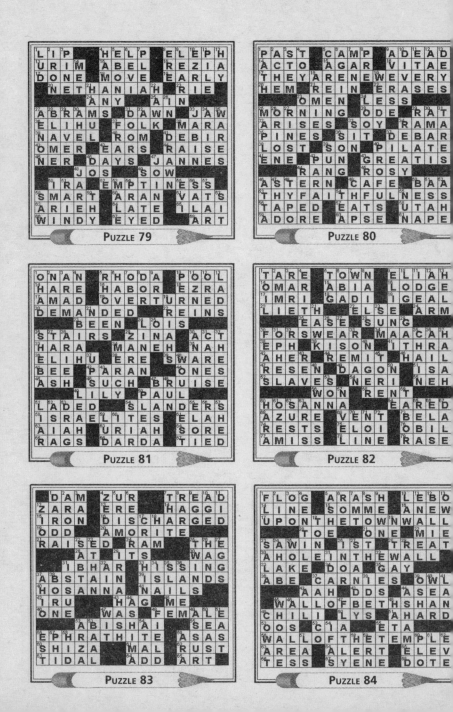

Puzzle 79

Puzzle 80

Puzzle 81

Puzzle 82

Puzzle 83

Puzzle 84

Puzzle 85

```
HERE  RATE  HOUSE
EZEL  EWES  OWNER
ARAD  SAIL  UNDER
PARE TILING   OR
    RIOT    EHI
 ASSIR  RTH  VAIL
ABI  MEHIR  AMMI
HIGH RAGED  HARE
ADNA  THEIR  SAD
BEST  EST  SELAH
    HAP  SPUE
AS PHALLU  BOTH
AZIZA  BOAT  ABIA
GEZER  LOVE  NERI
ELECT  EKER  ADER
```

Puzzle 86

```
RAH  CABAL  NASAL
UFO  ALONE  OPERA
NOS  RIATA  VOTES
GREATERISHETHAT
STATE      CHIN
    ELBA  MANGER
LAD  SALEM  SERVE
ISIN  TALES  TIED
MEMOS  SITON  PRO
ARENAS     ANOA
     COOP  THOSE
YOUTHANHETHATIS
INTHE  RODEO  HES
PLEAT  ONEAL  EVE
SYSTS  WORLD  REX
```

Puzzle 87

```
POOL  SHORE  THIS
UNNI  AENON  RASE
RACA  MAOCH  ULLA
EMERALD  KADMIEL
   PAY      DIP
PAWETH  BEDS  IRA
AMOS  KORAHITES
CAUL  SIRAH  THIN
ENLIGHTEN  CANA
SAD  LIED  ACHISH
    MAL   ADO
DRIEDST  BOZKATH
AIJA  HAGAR  ISHI
UPON  AMASA  LION
BENT  HELEM  LAUD
```

Puzzle 88

```
MARK  ELIAM  MASH
ENAN  SIMRI  INTO
RIPE  TAMAR  SNAP
ESHEK  REBA  HARE
SEALED  R  COASTS
    YES   PLUM
LEST  NEARER  GOT
ULAI  SAFE  WIPE
MOLES  TOPS  EDEN
PIT  HASRAH  SENT
    MAN  ERE  TOES
SISERA  HEM  END
ESHTEMOA  IMRI
CLUE  INN  DEN
TEND  MEDIAN
```

Puzzle 89

```
HAWK  CANA  MASSA
ADIN  EBER  ALOUD
LADE  DART  TIRIA
FREEMAN  SERVETH
    ARA    SEE
HAMANS  HARD  AHA
EBONY  BENO  OBED
WINE  HOMAM  WILD
EDER  ARAH  SLAVE
DAY  OZEM  GUSHED
    ADO   PIN
SUPPORT  RAKKATH
ELIHU  OREN  ISHI
ALTER  LUST  DIED
TASKS  LESS  SAME
```

Puzzle 90

```
LAMP  LOOK  BEAST
AGUE  ONAN  UMMAH
MAST  WERE  SMOKE
BREED  SEE  ANEM
    RIBS  SAWN
LAP  POKE  TAUGHT
EBED  NINE  SERAH
CORE  ENDS  LADE
ADIEL  OREN  TAR
HELPED  ROLE  ERE
    SAID  MIST
PAI  SEEM  TOWER
LIBNI  KISS  TILE
AARON  AREA  ANON
THING  REAP  LENT
```

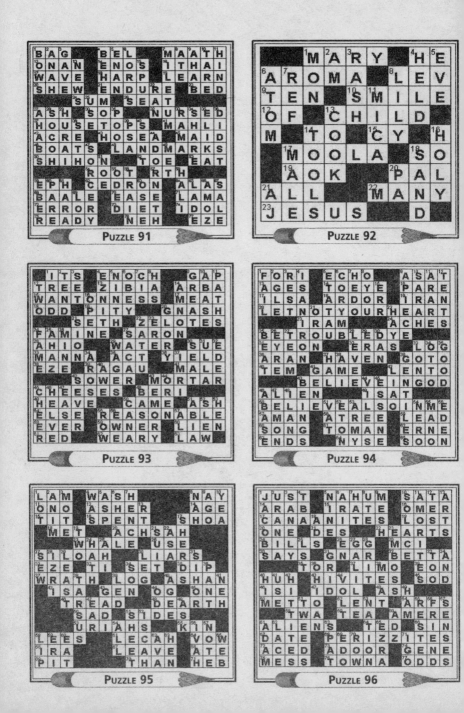

Puzzle 91

Puzzle 92

Puzzle 93

Puzzle 94

Puzzle 95

Puzzle 96

Puzzle 97

L	A	P		L	A	M	B		S	W	O	R	D
I	M	R	I		O	B	E	Y		H	O	S	E	A
F	R	E	T		S	I	N		A	E	N	E	A	S
T	A	S	T	E	T	H		E	Z	R		E	P	H
	M	E	A	N		U	N	L	A	D	E			
	R	I	D		O	I	L		D	O	V	E		
L	E	V		U	S	E		S	I	A		R	E	D
E	R	E		R	U	N		H	A	B		D	I	E
H	A	S		E	S	T		A	H	I		I	N	N
I	N	T	O		T	I	P		R	A	N			
			N	E	A	R	E	R		A	H	A	Z	
A	H	A		L	I	E		H	A	M	O	N	A	H
R	E	M	A	I	N		L	E	D		A	C	R	E
B	E	E	R	A		S	U	S	I		H	E	A	R
A	D	N	A	H		A	K	A	N			S	H	E

PUZZLE 97

Puzzle 98

R	O	L	L		S	I	N	S			H	A	M
O	Z	I	A	S		T	R	U	E		R	E	B	A
S	N	O	W	Y		R	O	M	E		U	N	D	O
H	I	N		E	N	A	N		P	L	A	I	N	
			K	N	E	W		R	O	L	E			
R	E	N	E	W		J	O	N	A	D	A	B		
B	A	D	E		U	P	O	N		L	A	D		
E	D	G	E		R	O	D	E		R	O	S	E	
D	I	E		C	A	N	A		L	I	N	E	N	
O	S	T	R	I	C	H		R	I	N	G	S		
			W	I	N	E		R	A	N	G			
J	A	R	I	B		R	E	N	T		A	R	K	
A	G	A	G		E	L	I	S		E	D	R	E	I
D	E	N	S		W	I	P	E		L	A	B	A	N
A	S	K			E	D	E	N			Y	A	R	D

PUZZLE 98

Puzzle 99

N	O	B		N	O	G	A	H		A	P	T	
O	A	R		A	B	A	N	A		U	L	A	I
W	R	A	P		H	E	B	E	R		N	O	N	E
	S	Y	R	I	A	D	A	M	A	S	C	U	S
			A	R	M				O	L	D			
L	I	B	Y	A		C	H	L	O	E				
O	S	E	E		E	S	H	E	A	N		P	H	I
A	H	E	R		S	P	I	E	D		G	L	A	D
F	I	R		G	L	A	D	L	Y		R	A	I	L
			U	N	I	T	E		N	I	T	R	E	
	A	R	A				J	O	E					
W	H	I	T	H	E	R	S	O	E	V	E	R		
R	E	B	A		E	L	A	T	H		E	D	A	R
A	R	A	H		L	O	T	A	N		E	R	I	
M	E	N		L	I	E	R	S		R	E	D		

PUZZLE 99

Puzzle 100

M	O	D	E	L		L	A	M	B		B	A	R
O	P	E	R	A		A	S	I	A		I	R	A
S	I	M	O	N	A	N	D	A	N	D	R	E	W
E	N	O	S		D	O	O		D	I	D		
S	E	N		L	A	S		R	A	E		R	C	A
		J	A	M	E	S	A	N	D	J	O	H	N	
B	A	R	O	N	S		T	I	A		A	T	A	N
A	R	E	Y	E		M	A	N		A	D	O	R	E
N	E	A	T		C	A	N		A	L	A	R	M	S
J	A	C	O	B	A	N	D	E	S	A	U			
O	S	H		E	T	E		L	I	D		D	I	E
		M	A	C		A	I	N		C	O	S	T	
S	H	E	M	A	N	D	J	A	P	H	E	T	H	
R	O	T		L	E	D	A		L	A	T	H	E	
A	T	E		L	A	S	H		O	T	H	E	R	

PUZZLE 100

Puzzle 101

A	R	M		S	U	R		A	M	I
A	C	H	A	R		S	O	R	E		K	I	D
S	H	O	N	E		E	D	G	E		S	A	N	D
H	I	D		D	A	N	I	E	L		I	N	T	O
	M	A	D	E	S	T		A	R	D				
		Y	E	A		E	L	I	O	E	N	A	I	
S	A	L	E	M		E	L	I	A	B		E	R	R
A	M	A	D		A	L	I	A	H		H	A	Z	O
R	O	W		A	S	S	U	R		T	A	H	A	N
A	S	S	E	N	T	E	D		A	R	T			
		A	D	O			S	H	E	E	P	S		
A	G	E	S		N	A	P	K	I	N		A	P	T
R	E	N	T		I	B	R	I		C	H	L	O	E
O	B	A		E	D	E	N		H	O	L	O	N	
D	A	N		D	A	Y		R	U	N				

PUZZLE 101